VC

VC

An American History

TOM NICHOLAS

Harvard University Press

Cambridge, Massachusetts
London, England
2019

First printing

Library of Congress Cataloging-in-Publication Data
Names: Nicholas, Tom (Professor), author.
Title: VC : an American history / Tom Nicholas.
Description: Cambridge, Massachusetts : Harvard University Press, 2019. |
Includes bibliographical references and index.
Identifiers: LCCN 2018037280 | ISBN 9780674988002 (alk. paper)
Subjects: LCSH: Venture capital—United States—History. | Entrepreneurship—
United States—History.
Classification: LCC HG4751 .N525 2019 | DDC 332/.041540973—dc23
LC record available at https://lccn.loc.gov/2018037280

Book design by Chrissy Kurpeski

Contents

6

Silicon Valley and the
Emergence of Investment Styles

7

High-Tech, an Evolving Ecosystem,
and Diversity during the 1980s

8

The Big Bubble

Epilogue: From the Past
to the Present and the Future

VC

Introduction

VENTURE CAPITAL (VC) IS LARGELY an American invention. It is a "hits" business where exceptional payoffs from a few investments in a large portfolio of startup companies compensate for the vast majority that yield mediocre returns or simply fail. This "long tail" distribution of payoffs has been embraced with more impact in the United States than anywhere else in the world. Today, Silicon Valley stands as the world's most important center of VC-based entrepreneurship, despite challenges to its leadership position. This book explains how America's advantage in VC finance was first created, why it has been so sustainable, and what history has to say about its future.

The origins of the venture capital industry in America are conventionally traced back to the founding of the Boston-based American Research and Development Corporation (ARD) in 1946. ARD was among the first investment firms to attempt to systematize long-tail investing in startups in a way that is analogous to the modern venture capital industry.[1] Yet, many of the characteristics defining modern venture finance can be clearly seen in much earlier historical contexts, such as New England whaling ventures and the early financing of industrialization provided by elites. History shows how some key financial institutions and precedents were developed early on, and offers valuable perspective on the industry's future. It also helps to reveal why venture capital is so prominently American.

Venture capital is concerned with the provision of finance to startup companies and it is heavily oriented toward the high-tech sector, where capital efficiency is at its highest and the potential upside is greatest.

Modern VC involves intermediation by general partners in VC firms, who channel risk capital into entrepreneurial ventures on behalf of limited partners—typically, pension funds, university endowments, and insurance companies which characteristically do not act as direct investors in startups. For their intermediation, VC firms receive remuneration in the forms of annual management fees (typically 2 percent of the capital committed by limited partners) and "carried interest" as a share of the profits generated by an investment fund (typically 20 percent). VC funds tend to last about seven to ten years, and the firms behind them often manage multiple funds simultaneously.

It is well known that the VC model of financing is characterized by a distinct approach to payoffs. Venture capital returns do not follow a normal, "bell-shaped" distribution like stock market returns, but rather tend to be highly skewed. A few exceptional investments in the long right-sided tail, such as Genentech or Google, generate the bulk of the aggregate return.[2] This book describes the attraction of these low-probability but high-payoff outcomes as the "allure of the long tail," and defines the pursuit of them as distinct, though not mutually exclusive from, the periodic behavior associated with manias and speculative bubbles, and the persistent behavior associated with long-shot betting events, such as lotteries, where expected value can be negative.[3] In the venture capital context, long-tail investing denotes a systematic approach to the deployment of risk capital into entrepreneurial ventures by intermediaries who attempt to use their domain expertise to generate large returns. In a world of perfect information and efficient markets, economic theory suggests, intermediaries should be absent.[4] The fact that venture capitalists do exist is arguably because they are able to maintain informational advantages in the selection and governance of startup investments. Another interpretation is that they function merely as capital conduits and organizers, but do not particularly add value in terms of startup outcomes.

Long-tail returns have always been difficult to generate, and the VC industry has sometimes been chaotic and subject to the destructive ebbs and flows of investment cycles. History shows, however, that the social benefits of venture capital have been immense. By facilitating the financing of radical new technologies, US venture capitalists have supported a large range of high-tech firms whose products, from semiconductors to recombinant insulin, telecommunications inventions, and search engines, have revolutionized the way we work, live, and produce. While technological change can often disrupt labor markets and increase wage inequality, in the long run, innovation is essential to productivity gains and economic growth. The venture capital industry has been a powerful driver of innovation, helping to sustain economic development and US competitiveness.

Given the importance of the United States to the history of venture capital, this book adopts a US-centric focus. Yet, the book's analysis could begin with a context more deeply historical and global. Early on, the need to divide financial payoffs from joint pursuits led mankind to establish rules and norms akin to those used in the modern venture capital industry. Some of the classical civilizations of the Mediterranean were characterized by stable, highly profitable, and well-developed systems of commercial enterprise. While markets were frequently rudimentary in both scale and scope, transactions could extend beyond familial ties to arm's-length exchanges between investors and traveling merchants. Medieval Venice was strikingly modern in terms of its contracting traditions, and it could be argued that the Venetians acted very much like venture capitalists in their operation of risky trading voyages.[5] A milieu of institutions and cultural norms facilitated the expansion of enterprise through commercial ventures.[6]

It was in the United States, however, that structure and contracting became embedded into capitalism through the provision of finance for entrepreneurship. As a way of organizing the narrative, this book identifies four main stages in the history of venture capital from the nineteenth century up to the early twenty-first century. These chronological stages are not always cleanly distinct from one another and the allure of long-tail investing is the theme that runs through them all. The stages reflect the development of some of the most important financial institutions and practices which were then carried forward. Over time, the VC function of providing capital to startups evolved from being conducted by collections of wealthy individuals to being the work of specialized firms. Enabled by the changing cultural and regulatory environment in the United States, the VC industry expanded to large scale and became increasingly impactful in the sphere of entrepreneurial finance.

The first stage saw early investors deploying risk capital into high-risk and potentially high-reward activities in ways that established historic precedents for VC-style investing. Chapter 1 focuses on risk capital deployment in the New England whaling industry, which has especially striking parallels with modern VC in terms of organization, payoffs, and more. Whaling was one of the largest and most important industries in America during the early nineteenth century.[7] In it, New England whaling agents looked a lot like modern venture capitalists.[8] There were wealthy individuals able to supply finance and there were captains and crew willing to initiate and manage voyages, and whaling agents intermediated between the two groups in much the same way that today's venture capitalists intermediate between entities like pension funds that supply risk capital and entrepreneurs capable of applying that capital to profit-making opportunities. Like venture capitalists, whaling agents charged fees and received a share of the profits in return for intermediation; they engaged in repeat business with the best captains; they sometimes syndicated to spread risk; and the most capable of them, along with the most capable captains, enjoyed returns that were persistent over time. Flexible partnership structures worked because of strong compensation incentives. And the reasoning behind profit splits on whaling voyages still persists today in the conventions regarding how equity should be allocated to the various roles in entrepreneurial startups. The allure of a successful multiyear whaling voyage was strong, but it carried significant downside risk. Chapter 1 provides extensive data on profits and incentives from this exceptional early industry to establish the strength of the correspondence between whaling ventures and modern VC.

Chapter 2 provides more insight into how risk capital was deployed in this first stage in the history of venture capital, focusing on the financing of leading-edge cotton textiles innovation in Lowell, Massachusetts—essentially the first Silicon Valley–type cluster in America. As New England financing elites redirected capital from merchant trading to industrial production, their need to access high-tech know-how compelled them to develop new heuristics to guide their contracting. Examining the structure of contracting, it is clear that tradeoffs between cash flow and control rights were being made in ways similar to the contracting strategies venture capitalists use today as they interact with entrepreneurs.[9] The intersection of entrepreneurship, technology, and finance was powerful. In 1820, Lowell had a population of only two hundred citizens. There was not much in that location but land and fast-moving water on the Merrimack River as a source of power. By 1836, however, Lowell's population had exploded to 17,633, and by 1845 it had topped 30,000.[10] The financing of new innovation hot spots further west gave rise to additional Silicon Valley–style clusters. Most notably, Cleveland and Pittsburgh became high-tech hubs between 1870 and 1914 in such areas as electric lighting, chemicals, oil, and steel.[11] The industrialist and politician Andrew Mellon became a pivotal venture capitalist as he devised ways to finance local enterprise in this region relying on syndicated lending, governance, and equity participation.[12]

Extending the analysis of the first stage in venture capital's history, Chapter 3 shows how the informal and formal markets for VC-style finance evolved over time in both the east and west coast regions. During the late nineteenth and early twentieth centuries, the kinds of affluent individuals who would today be called "angel" or "super angel" investors, and more formal (albeit small-scale) private capital entities, provided finance for new ventures. Investors captured upside in returns using convertible securities transferable into common stock later in the firm's life cycle, while simultaneously mitigating downside risk due to the seniority of these securities. Financing was often tied to board representation, managerial assistance, and other governance mechanisms. Looking at this first stage in the history of VC, the direct lineage from some early entities based on family wealth to various modern VC firms can also be traced. For example, Laurance Rockefeller, the grandchild of the oil baron John D. Rockefeller, was a prolific venture capitalist. Venrock Associates, founded in 1969, is an extension of his investing activities. Another well-known venture firm today, Bessemer Venture Partners, was founded in 1981 as a spinoff from a family office created by Henry Phipps, who had partnered with the famous steel magnate Andrew Carnegie. In 1946, John H. Whitney, the son of a wealthy industrialist, founded J. H. Whitney & Company, which also endures to this day. During the 1940s and 1950s, Whitney recognized the challenges associated with constructing a portfolio of early-stage investments to generate long-tail returns, as opposed to building a portfolio of more mature firms. This helps to explain why the firm shifted away from early-stage investing over time, and became increasingly oriented toward later-stage private equity.

The second stage in the history of venture capital roughly spans the 1940s to the 1960s. It involved the implementation by specialized firms of the VC model focusing on right-skewed returns, and the gradual shift toward adoption of the limited partnership structure. Chapter 4 covers the origins, organizational structure, strategy, and performance of the pivotal entity ARD, founded in Boston after the Second World War by local elites who felt a sense of civic duty to fund enterprise and regional growth in New England. From a modern-day perspective, ARD was unusual in that it was organized as a closed-end fund and did not employ the limited partnership structure that is the leading organizational form used in the venture capital industry today. Its highly successful 1957 investment in the computer startup Digital Equipment Corporation illustrated that the venture capital hits model could work. ARD was able to build a portfolio of investments in which the return from one big hit could offset many middling or loss-making investments. Furthermore, ARD was founded at a time when America was largely devoid of institutions to provide risk capital to startups, a problem that had prevailed since the Great Depression. Government efforts to close the "funding gap" culminated in the 1958 Small Business Investment Company program, which created private-sector investment companies to provide capital to small businesses. Given the sense that the gap was an instance of market failure, debate centered on the extent to which the government should intervene in the allocation of venture capital. ARD powerfully illustrated the potential effectiveness of a market-based approach to the intermediation of risk capital.

During this second stage, the venture capital industry came to be dominated by limited partnerships, an organizational form with a long history.[13] Chapter 5 shows that this structure made sense because it allowed venture capitalists to exploit tax advantages and avoid laws mandating the public disclosure of sensitive information regarding compensation and fund-level performance returns. It is no accident that the first limited partnerships emerged during the tax-shelter era from the mid-1950s to the mid-1970s. The choice of organizational form, however, also involved disadvantages. The limited partnership with a finite lifetime (typically less than a decade) worked against a more long-term investment focus. The first venture capital limited partnership in Silicon Valley, Draper, Gaither & Anderson, founded in 1959 in Palo Alto, California, generated poor returns, underscoring the difficulty of realizing payoffs from a portfolio of early-stage investments within the timeline of a limited partnership.[14] Other firms profiled in the chapter—east coast–based Greylock Partners, founded in 1965 by William Elfers after a long career at ARD, and Venrock Associates—did much better, however, providing impetus to expansion in the industry.[15] Crucially, this stage also saw government policy play a key role, with large, industrywide effects. In the late 1970s, the clarification of rules relating to the Employee Retirement Income Security Act of 1974 created a supply-side boost to venture capital and the limited-partnership model because it gave pension funds much more leeway to invest in risky asset classes.[16] Venture capitalists had helped to shape this aspect of the market framework through the National Venture Capital Association, founded in 1973, which lobbied heavily for legislative change. That trade group also expended considerable effort lobbying for the changes to capital gains tax policy that venture capitalists at the time considered necessary for the industry to flourish.

The third stage in the history of venture capital in America played out from the late 1960s through the 1980s, as the long-tail model of VC investing was repeatedly verified and the wider ecosystem to support early-stage investing developed. Chapter 6 explores against the backdrop of the history of startup finance in Silicon Valley how various factors came together, including human capital development facilitated by local educational institutions; government investment in military-based technologies; focal high-tech firms; and high-skilled immigrants. The combination of these meant that, by the mid-twentieth century, the area that became known as Silicon Valley was well poised to displace the east coast as a center of entrepreneurship and high-tech innovation. Three key figures in the history of venture capital—Arthur Rock (cofounder of Davis and Rock in 1961), Tom Perkins (cofounder of Kleiner Perkins in 1972), and Don Valentine (founder of Sequoia Capital in 1972)—responded to and helped compound that regional advantage. All were born and educated on the east coast but migrated to the opportunity-rich west coast. Rock, Perkins, and Valentine were responsible for some of the most important investments of the twentieth century, in companies such as Intel, Genentech, and Cisco Systems. Continually proving the VC model based on hits and long-tail investments, they generated staggering fund-level returns. They also personified the three oft-cited investment styles in the VC industry, since Rock tended to identify opportunities based on investing in people, Perkins emphasized investments in technology, and Valentine stressed the idea of investing in markets.

Chapter 7 examines a crucial decade in the third stage in the history of venture capital: the 1980s. For the first time, the industry experienced a pronounced high-tech boom-and-bust cycle, from about the time of

Apple Computer's 1980 initial public offering (IPO) through 1984. The industry grew in scale as a result of both the supply-side effects of the government policy changes discussed in Chapter 5 and the repeated verification of the VC hits model covered in Chapter 6. Scale created challenges associated with managing larger funds, and the decade was associated with more general industry-structure changes. The best venture capital firms were distinguished by their performance records, giving rise to the notion of a "top-tier" venture firm. The industry sorted itself into different varieties of venture capital formation, and segments formed according to firm size, geographic focus, and sector (that is, private venture capital, corporate venture capital, or government initiative). Mezzanine finance, specialized IPO intermediation, and venture debt all became instrumental to the industry's evolution. Leadership transitions in the marquee firms gave rise to a new generation of exceptional investors. Women's representation in venture capital became a discussion point, flagging issues that have yet to be resolved.

The fourth stage in the history of venture capital in America is defined by the widespread implementation of its investing model, culminating in the late 1990s stock market run-up and subsequent crash. Chapter 8 covers the 1990s and early 2000s as the most volatile period in US venture capital history. The high-tech revolution of the early 1990s witnessed a new era of hardware, software, and telecommunications innovations, mostly in response to the commercialization of the internet.[17] Importantly, this period witnessed a flurry of investments in software and online services, setting precedents for a trend in VC investing that continues to the present. Online retailing became a particularly "hot" area of investment because consumer buying was expected to shift rapidly from brick-and-mortar stores to online sellers.[18] As the IPO market became more active, opportunities for liquidity increased and expected payoffs rose steeply. Capital commitments in the venture capital industry peaked in 2000 at over one hundred billion dollars. In the immediate aftermath of the high-tech, dot-com, and telecommunications crash in 2001 to 2002—when trillions of dollars of stock market value were wiped out—attention focused on the destructive side of the venture industry and how its dynamics had created unproductive incentives. Yet, although venture capitalists were criticized for performance defects and a legitimacy crisis ensued, from today's vantage point this era looks considerably more productive than it did at the time. In retrospect, it can be seen as one of the most profoundly important epochs in the history of American business.

Given the impossibility of gaining useful historical perspective on events that have only recently unfolded, no attempt has been made to push the main analysis of this book beyond the early 2000s. A concluding Epilogue does, however, attempt to look forward by reflecting on points in history in light of the changed context and debates of recent years. In doing so, it builds on five main themes that are recurrent across the chapters. First, history shows that exceptional VC-style payoffs have been sporadic and infrequent, concentrated in specific firms and time periods. Indeed, the industry as a whole has reflected more of a cultural habituation to risk and a behavioral bias toward long-tail investing than an evolution toward any more systematic realization of outsized returns.

Second, if one asks how exactly VCs do what they do, it is not clear that the answer today is much different from half a century ago. The dominant form of organization is still the limited partnership with an ephemeral fund life, even though this places constraints on the time scale of investment returns. Although there have been some organizational structure and strategy innovations, these have been paradoxically rare in an industry that finances radical change.

Third, while it is often argued that Silicon Valley's special advantages can be challenged by competitive emulation, within America or globally, this misses the fact that the region's development as a center of VC-fueled entrepreneurship has been deeply historically contingent. It is largely because the US venture capital industry emerged in a specific cultural and regulatory context that replication efforts elsewhere have been largely unsuccessful. At the same time, the threat remains real as China and other countries seek their own pathways.

Fourth, and relatedly, it is important to note the often ignored fact that the venture capital industry became institutionalized partly as a consequence of government policy. Lawmakers shaped the enabling environment—kick-starting regional growth in what would become Silicon Valley—by crafting policies that allowed institutional investors to increase their risk tolerance in making investment choices, changed the taxation of investment gains, and promoted more high-skilled immigration. In many ways, the US government acted as America's VC writ large by funding the basic university research that would break open the development pathways to entrepreneurial businesses. Clearly, the future of the VC industry in the United States will depend on maintaining key aspects of that amenable, enabling environment.

Fifth, from a cultural standpoint, it is inescapable that the history of VC examined in this book centers on the activities and achievements of white males. This mirrors the composition of the American business and financial elite more generally.[19] Reversing the venture capital industry's poor record on diversity will be vital to its future, in terms of talent management, competitiveness, performance returns, and how the industry is publicly perceived.

As a final note, while the main objective of this book is to establish the major contours of venture capital's history in the United States from its early beginnings up to the recent past, the book is written with a broader context in mind. Through the lens of the history of the venture capital industry, the essence of American-style free markets is revealed, including the forcefulness of incessant competition in startup finance and the incentives that condition the inexorable pursuit of capital gain. The venture capital industry emerged in a cultural context where entrepreneurial risk, wealth accumulation, and financial payoffs were embraced in ways that have not been as palatable in other countries. The allure of the long tail can be seen as a manifestation of much deeper economic and cultural uniqueness, highlighting how capitalism in general has evolved and been embraced in the United States.

1

Whaling Ventures

THE INVESTMENT MODELS BEHIND WHALING expeditions and venture capital funds can be thought of as interchangeable. The payoff distributions in the two industries are strikingly similar. Whaling agents intermediated between the wealthy individuals who supplied funds and the captains and crew who undertook voyages, just as VCs intermediate between limited partners and entrepreneurial teams in portfolio companies. The rise of American inventiveness in whaling reflected a distinct culture of entrepreneurial exceptionalism, risk capital deployment, and the pursuit of outsized returns. Rates of return on capital could be high in whaling, but so was the downside risk associated with this unpredictable and hazardous industry. In the United States, whaling was one of the earliest kinds of enterprise to grapple with the complexities of risk capital intermediation, organizational form, ownership structure, incentives, team building, and principal-agent tradeoffs. The whaling business represents an important starting point for exploring the origins of American venture financing.[1]

Whaling first became a commercial industry in the sixteenth century as Icelandic and Biscayan whalers operated around sixty vessels in this business annually.[2] The Dutch became dominant later (and until about the 1770s), operating in the area east of Greenland, before competitive advantage shifted to Britain. Parliamentary bounties spurred "merchants to speculate in the trade" as annual voyages proliferated from coastal ports to the Arctic in search of bowhead whales.[3] By the nineteenth century, however, the United States had become the clear and unambiguous industry leader. By around 1850, almost 75 percent of the nine hundred whaling ships worldwide were American registered.[4] New England was the center of US whaling. Nantucket initially rose to be the most prominent location—in 1768 it possessed 125 whaling ships—and then New Bedford ascended, once larger ships struggled to navigate Nantucket's sandbar.[5] In their extensive study of the industry, Lance Davis, Robert Gallman, and Karin Gleiter suggest that the American advantage came from a mix of factors including entrepreneurship and management via the human capital of agents, captains, and crews, technological innovations such as vessel design, and the powerful "lay" system of incentive payments, which meant that whalemen essentially held equity in voyages.[6]

Despite these incentives, it was difficult to predict the likelihood of success. Consider the famous voyage of the *Essex,* which inspired Herman Melville's 1851 fictional masterpiece *Moby-Dick.* With a track record of success and a reputation as a "lucky ship," the *Essex* set sail from Nantucket Island in Massachusetts in August 1819 for the Pacific Ocean on what was expected to be a lucrative whale-hunting venture. In November 1820, on an otherwise uneventful day, an eighty-five-foot sperm whale rammed the ship's port side when the crew targeted a whale pod. The 238-ton whaleship capsized and sank, leaving the crew members scrambling into three whaleboats with provisions collected from the wreckage. In December 1820 the crew arrived at a deserted island. Some stayed while others headed for the coast of South America, almost three thousand miles away. Those who survived the ravages of the ocean were rescued two months later by whale-hunting ships operating off the coast of Chile.[7]

At first glance, it might be difficult to see that nineteenth-century whaling had any commonalities with modern-day venture capital. The decisions made by entrepreneurs in portfolio companies do not carry the mortal risks faced by the captain and crew of the *Essex.* Furthermore, while entrepreneurs can generate returns from new technologies using mechanisms like patents, the major challenge faced by the agent, captain, and crew associated with any whaling venture was to find new whale populations over which they held no property rights.

A detailed examination of the respective industries, however, shows how close the parallels are, especially regarding the distribution of payoffs. The vast majority of VC-backed companies fail, making for a pronounced long tail. The "hits" are expected to offset the investments that yield losses and mediocre returns. The recent performance of a top-tier venture capital firm shows that 52 percent of the gross return on its port-folio was generated by startups that accounted for just 6 percent of the total cost of the investment portfolio. Of the individual investment deci-sions made by this VC firm, 62 percent were loss-making while 5 percent generated multiples of more than ten on the original investments.[8] This distribution of returns reflects the fact that hit VC investments, just like successful whaling expeditions, are difficult to identify *ex ante*.

To illustrate the striking parallels between returns in modern VC and in whaling, I use the data on whaling voyages from Davis, Gallman, and Gleiter to describe the industry. They constructed their data from a va-riety of sources, including the voyages listed in Alexander Starbuck's mag-isterial 1878 *History of the American Whale Fishery* and the data set of 4,127 New Bedford whaling voyages from 1783 to 1906 compiled by Joseph Dias—who was likely himself a New Bedford whaling captain.[9]

With data on variables such as which agent organized the voyage, the length of time the ship was at sea, the cost of outfitting and provisioning, and the amount of sperm and whale oil and whalebone the ship brought back to port, Davis, Gallman, and Gleiter calculate the profitability of in-dividual voyages. They interpret the profit of a voyage as representing a mix of "payments for bearing uninsurable risks, rents on knowledge and managerial skill, disequilibrium profits (for example, profits arising out of a sudden increase in demand), and returns to innovation."[10] Although these estimates are prone to measurement error because of the limita-tions associated with historical data, they provide remarkable insights into the nature of whaling voyage returns.

Figure 1.1 plots the profitability of voyages in the Davis, Gallman, and Gleiter data set against the net internal rate of return (IRR) realized by all funds in the VC industry across vintage years 1981 to 2006 tracked by Preqin, one of the major vendors of venture capital data.[11] It is impor-tant to recognize that these are not like-for-like comparisons: the time periods, contexts, units of analysis, and metrics are all obviously dif-ferent.[12] Nevertheless, the distributions are extraordinarily similar in shape. Note in Figure 1.1 that 34.5 percent of whaling voyages ended up generating a return of zero or below, and that 32 percent of VC funds generated a zero or negative net IRR. Although 65.5 percent of whaling voyages were profitable, very few were exceptionally so, with just 1.7 percent of them achieving profit rates in excess of 100 percent. Simi-larly, only 2.9 percent of VC funds had net IRRs in excess of 100 percent.

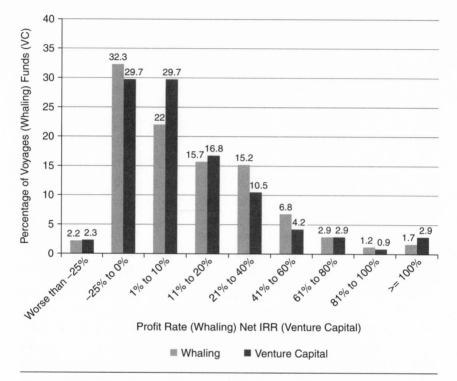

Profit Rate (Whaling) Net IRR (Venture Capital)

▨ Whaling ■ Venture Capital

Figure 1.1 The Distribution of Returns in Whaling and Venture Capital.
Based on data in Lance E. Davis, Robert E. Gallman, and Karin Gleiter, *In Pursuit of Leviathan: Technology, Institutions, Productivity, and Profits in American Whaling, 1816–1906* (Chicago: University of Chicago Press, 1997), 450. Venture capital estimates based on Preqin Venture Capital Database, accessed March 2016.

Similarity in the distributions shows up again in Figure 1.2 which focuses on the top twenty-nine whaling firms (a subset distinguished by Davis, Gallman, and Gleiter because these agents had organized at least forty voyages) and the top twenty-nine VC firms in Preqin. The returns for whaling voyages reflect Starbuck's contemporary observation that "while some vessels on their voyages have made but poor returns, even bringing . . . at times damaging loss to their owners, others have done extraordinarily well, and brought in fortunes to those investing in them."[13] When Peter Thiel writes of the heavily skewed distribution associated with modern VC that "a small handful of companies radically outperform all others" he might just as easily be describing the whaling industry two centuries earlier.[14]

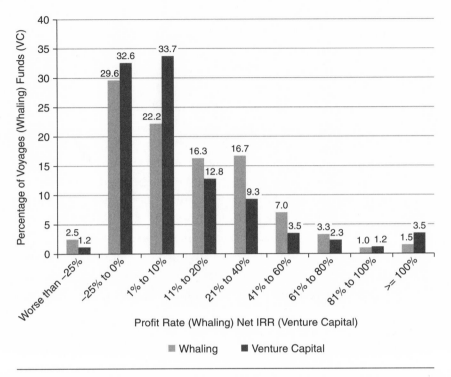

Profit Rate (Whaling) Net IRR (Venture Capital)

■ Whaling ■ Venture Capital

Figure 1.2 The Distribution of Returns in Whaling and Venture Capital (Top 29).
Based on data in Lance E. Davis, Robert E. Gallman, and Karin Gleiter, *In Pursuit of Leviathan: Technology, Institutions, Productivity, and Profits in American Whaling, 1816–1906* (Chicago: University of Chicago Press, 1997), 450. Venture capital estimates based on Pregin Venture Capital Database, accessed March 2016.

Success and Failure in Whaling

The distribution of returns in whaling was skewed for a variety of reasons. During the early years of the American whaling industry, proximate coastal waters could be exploited at low risk. But when local whale stocks were depleted, and whales began to be pursued further into the Atlantic, risk increased substantially. By the 1820s, the risks increased yet again as even more distant whale-hunting locations, especially in the North and South Pacific, became increasingly attractive.[15] Whales migrated thousands of miles between breeding areas and feeding grounds, and a location known as the "offshore ground" west of the Galapagos Islands became a popular destination for hunters. Generally, whale hunting spanned about fifteen regions within an enormous roughly triangular oceanic area defined by southerly points near Cape Horn and New Zealand, and extending as far north as the Arctic Ocean.[16]

On a typical voyage to the Pacific Ocean, a vessel would set sail from a port such as New Bedford in the early summer months to have time to navigate around Cape Horn and be able to pursue whales in the South Pacific in December and January. Then, it might sail north via the Marquesas Islands in French Polynesia and the Marshall Islands, loop around the North Pacific including the coast of Japan, the West coast of America, and Hawaii, and return to the South Pacific in November. Alternatively, it might sail directly to hunt in the North Pacific, using Hawaii as a stopping point before turning south again. If a vessel was late leaving New Bedford in the summer, it would instead cross the Atlantic and sail around the Cape of Good Hope to align with seasonal migration patterns, arriving in the South Pacific by March. About a quarter of voyages went this route instead of around Cape Horn.[17] Either way, the journey was long and treacherous. By the 1850s, the average American whaling voyage took 3.6 years.[18]

Whalers went in pursuit of lucrative sperm oil, whale oil, and whalebone. The product of a whale depended largely on the type of whale being hunted. Sperm oil came from the head, or case, of the sperm whale, and was the highest quality oil, used for both illumination and lubrication. It was taken in solid and liquid form. The solid form, *spermaceti,* was used for candles while the liquid form was used for lubricating fine machinery, particularly in the textile industry, and in applications that were exposed to a wide range of temperatures. Whale oil was rendered from the blubber of sperm, right, bowhead, and occasionally humpback whales. While it was widely viewed as inferior to sperm oil, whale oil was also sometimes used for lighting and lubricating heavy machinery. Whalebone (which is not actually bone but the baleen from the upper jaws of filter-feeding right, bowhead, and humpback whales) was used in applications that required plasticity. Once heated, it could be reshaped and after it cooled it would retain its new shape while also remaining somewhat flexible—a feature valued by makers of various consumer

value of a whale was large. The average sperm whale
ately twenty-five barrels of sperm oil (787.5 gallons) and
or bowhead, sixty barrels of whale oil (1,890 gallons).[20]
n whales, however, could contain eighty-five barrels of

sperm oil. The largest bowheads could yield 275 barrels of oil and 3,500 pounds of whalebone. In aggregate, the growing US whaling industry became financially significant, especially to the economy of New England. In 1845, US production reached a level of 525,000 barrels of whale and sperm oil. In 1854, whalers received net income of $10.8 million, the largest amount recorded in a single year—over $300 million in today's money. In each year from 1853 to 1857, the total whaling haul sold for about 50 percent of the capital value of the entire whaling fleet.[21] In other words, the return on assets in whaling ventures could be high.

For captains of voyages, tremendous income and wealth gains were possible. Although few voyages in the nineteenth century returned with more than $100,000 (about $3 million today) worth of product, accounts of the occasional outsized successes were used to motivate captains and crew. In 1830, the *Loper* completed what the *Nantucket Inquirer* hailed as the "greatest voyage ever made." Operated mostly by a black crew, the *Loper* returned to port with 2,280 barrels of sperm oil from a short fourteen and a half months at sea.[22] When the *Benjamin Tucker* returned to New Bedford in 1851 it held 73,707 gallons of whale oil, 5,348 gallons of sperm oil, and 30,012 pounds of whalebone, yielding a net profit of $45,320. The whaleship *Favorite* set sail from Fairhaven, Massachusetts, in 1850, returning three years later with a catch valued at $116,000. The New Bedford whaleship *Montreal* was acclaimed in 1853 for its $136,023 catch from a voyage also lasting close to three years.[23] Starbuck annotates the 1864 voyage of the *Pioneer*, captained by Ebenezer Morgan, with the words "made best voyage on record." Its cargo was worth $150,000.[24]

The long-tail distribution of payoffs meant accepting that a voyage could return full or empty, and that individual outcomes would be too difficult to determine in advance. Ships commonly returned to port without a sufficient load to compensate a captain and crew for their multiyear efforts.[25] According to Starbuck, the whaleship *Emeline* set sail in July 1841, bringing back just ten barrels of oil twenty-six months later. A year into that voyage, in July 1842, the *Emeline*'s captain had been killed by a whale. Of the sixty-eight whaleships returning to the ports of New Bedford and Fairhaven in 1858, Starbuck states that forty-four (or almost two-thirds) were unprofitable.[26] While a voyage that made a negligible profit was labeled as a "saving voyage," a loss-making voyage wa͟s a "broken voyage." Moral opprobrium was heaped on capt͟a returned with less than full cargos of oil, and the career con͟c reputational risks from doing so were substantial. Leonard Gifford, captain of the *Hope*, who set sail from New Bedford in April 1851, wrote to his fiancée in 1853: "If I live to reach home, no man shall be able to say by me, [there] goes a fellow that brought home a broken voyage."[27] A broken whaling voyage meant crews would be reluctant to sign on for a captain's next voyage, so it was tantamount to industry expulsion. Knowing this, Gifford extended his voyage another three and a half years in search of whale oil. The *Hope* returned to port in 1857 after hunting in the Pacific Ocean. Starbuck documents that it had 965 barrels of sperm oil at that time and 30 barrels of whale oil, and that the *Hope* had "sent home" 1,235 barrels of sperm oil on another ship during the voyage.[28] Gifford married his fiancée two weeks after his return to New Bedford.

A broken voyage as a whale captain brought all the stigma of modern-day entrepreneurial failure. To avoid this indignity, captains engaged in dynamic decision-making as they attempted to maximize profits. In pursuit of extraordinary returns, they might choose to jeopardize a middling return or even risk total loss. During voyages they sometimes decided, as Gifford did, to ship oil and bone back to New England ports from Hawaii or San Francisco, to prolong a voyage and, they hoped, raise its profitability. The exemplar case of this strategy succeeding was on a voyage of the whaleship *Nile,* which set sail from New London, Connecticut, in 1859 sending oil back regularly on surrogate ships, and not returning to its home port until eleven years later.[29] Because sperm oil and whale oil were kept separate, and commanded very different prices, it was not uncommon for a captain to throw barrels overboard of the cheaper commodity to make room for the more valuable sperm oil. In 1871, the captain of the *Myra* dumped one hundred barrels of whale oil overboard when he "fell in with some sperm whales."[30] Captains attempted to maximize the value of their haul throughout the period of the voyage.

Yet, given the nature of seafaring risk, the left-hand sides of the distributions in Figures 1.1 and 1.2 failure were an empirical reality. To give a sense of failure levels in the extreme, Davis, Gallman, and Gleiter note that 272 of the 787 whaleships (34.6 percent) in the New Bedford fleet were lost at sea.[31] Factoring in the multiple voyages undertaken by most ships, they estimate the probability that a voyage would not return to port *on any one voyage* at "more than 6 percent." Weather was a major risk. Also, hunting for whales was self-evidently dangerous, involving as it did the capture and processing of the largest creatures in the ocean. When a whale or whale pod was spotted, silence was demanded. The crew knew to avoid "gallying" or "spooking" their prey. Once the whaleboat was within striking distance of the whale, the boatsteerer, also known as the harpooner, would ship his oar, pick up the harpoon, set his knee in the notch cut into the forward thwart, and hurl the harpoon. Though in earlier times floats were attached to the lines, by the 1840s, the iron harpoon head was fastened to a sturdy line, and paid out from a tub in the bottom of the whaleboat. As the line passed around a post at the stern of the whaleboat and out over the bow, a crewman poured seawater over the line to keep it from catching fire due to the friction. Once the line had run out, the whale often pulled the whaleboat many miles. In the Arctic Ocean, right and bowhead whales had a tendency to head for icebergs, imperiling the whaleboat even before the whale returned to the surface. After the whale came back to the surface to breathe, the harpooner and boat-header would trade places. Once at the bow, the mate or captain would attempt to sever a vital artery or puncture the lungs or heart of the now-exhausted whale.

Whaling was a gruesome industry. Melville offers this account of a whale's end: "His tormented body rolled not in brine but in blood, which bubbled and seethed for furlongs in their wake."[32] When a whale was dead, the crew of the whaleboat set to the task of getting it back to the ship for processing. The whale may have pulled them many miles from the ship, making for a long row back. At the ship, the whale was secured to the starboard side, and a cutting-in platform was lowered in to the water. Regardless of the species of whale, the head was separated from the rest of the body. After the head had been removed, a strip of blubber was cut from the whale and a chain was passed through it. As the strip was winched up, the whale began to flip and the "blanket strip" was separated from the whale. When hauled onto the deck, the blanket strip was cut into smaller "horse pieces," which were then minced horizontally into "bible leaves" for storage. Large copper pots (the "try works"), designed to render blubber into oil, were set just aft of the foremast. At the whaling ground, the "try pots" would boil perpetually, the fire stoked by pieces ᵒᶠ ᵗʰᵉ ʷʰᵃˡᵉ'ˢ own skin. Once the oil had cooled, it was moved into the b
cooper (that is, a barrel maker) had assembled from the stave

brought from port and stowed below decks. After the baleen had dried out and been cleaned of its hair-like filters, it too was stowed.

This process of harpooning and handling a whale created significant risks for captains and crew, including death and life-threatening injury. In 1829, Captain Abner P. Norton of the *Victory* was killed by a whale when he became tangled in a towline and was pulled overboard. In 1844, Captain John Cunningham of the *Florida* drowned, and in 1856, Captain John Fisher of the *Bartholomew Gosnold* was "lost while fast to a whale." The risk of illness was high, and treatment at sea or port was quite rudimentary. In 1838, Captain Benjamin Durfee of the *Parachute* died from smallpox, and in 1852, Captain Joseph Bailey of the *Champion* died of intestinal bleeding.[33] Long-voyage whaling involved stops ashore at least every six months for provisioning and to replace injured crewmen, but interactions with native populations in these places could also be perilous. Supply towns in Hawaii were especially violent places. Elsewhere, one account of a Pacific voyage by the *Charles and Henry* has a deserter being beaten to death by natives in Tahiti.[34]

Adding to the downside risk, voyages could also lead to insanity, insubordination, crew desertion, or discharge. Thomas B. Peabody, captain of the *Morea* committed suicide by shooting himself in 1854. In 1857, Archibald Mellen, Jr., captain of the *Junior* lost his life on Christmas Day off the coast of New Zealand when between five and ten mutineers shot him and the third mate, beheaded both, and tossed them overboard.[35] Flogging was a legal punishment for sailors on American whaling ships until 1850 and captains were known to administer lashes for even minor infractions to maintain discipline. Yet, perhaps surprisingly, even in spite of such risks, the number of deaths was relatively small in comparison to crew desertions and discharges. Out of 489 crewmen originally setting sail on fifteen whaling voyages made by eight different vessels between 1843 and 1862, only 16 (3.3 percent) were killed compared to 143 (29.2 percent) who deserted and 166 (33.9 percent) who were discharged.[36] It is no accident that effective captains were at a premium; they knew who was more likely to desert or be discharged, and in turn, agents knew the captains better than the capital providers did. Value accrued to domain expertise. It could be argued that a good whaling agent was central to success because he could raise capital, organize a voyage, and alleviate informational gaps.

Organizational Model: Basic Structure and Ownership

Nineteenth-century whaling ventures were financed in ways broadly similar to modern venture capital, as shown in Figure 1.3. The basic model of VC fundraising revolves around the intermediation of risk capital. Investors, as limited partners, supply capital into funds that have fixed lifetimes, and VCs then deploy this capital to portfolio companies. Limited partners as capital providers often face difficulties when attempting to invest directly in entrepreneurial startups because they lack both the infrastructure to undertake effective due diligence and the domain expertise to help portfolio firms develop complex new technologies.[37] In whaling, capital was often provided by relatively wealthy individual investors such as doctors and lawyers. Like their modern counterparts in VC limited partnerships, capital providers in whaling ventures had little incentive to invest in voyages directly. They had neither the knowledge of the best whaling grounds nor the connections to hire captains and organize crews. Instead, they passed their capital on to whaling agents who acted as intermediaries. Most whaling ventures were organized as partnerships, and equity in the voyages was closely held by a small number of capital providers.[38]

The organizational structures in Figure 1.3 reflect a particular mode of governance. As in all principal-agent relationships, the challenge in the whaling industry was to create a system featuring sufficient incentives for whaling agents to maximize the gains of the principals (that is, the owners as capital providers). Operating through agents created opportunities for efficient intermediation and it also allowed for specialized human capital to develop. Like a general partner in a VC firm, the agent typically received a fee for his organizing services plus a share of the voyage's profits. He could also be an equity holder. Moreover, captains and crews held stakes in their voyages' successes under a fractional payout mechanism known as the "lay" system—just as entrepreneurs in portfolio companies hold equity stakes in VC-backed firms so they also have incentives to make sure they perform well. Their propensity for opportunistic behavior can be mitigated through *ex ante* due diligence on the part of VCs, by contract design such as staged financing, and by monitoring entrepreneurs post-investment. In theory, aligning the incentives of all parties in an organizational structure creates a collective incentive to maximize value. Similarly, a crew member on a whaling ship did not earn

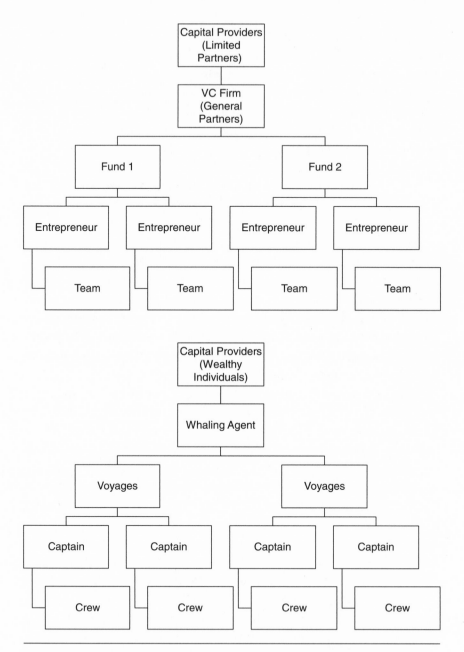

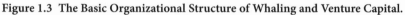

Figure 1.3 The Basic Organizational Structure of Whaling and Venture Capital.

wages in the normal sense, but rather received a share of the net value of the voyage. This increased commitment further down the organizational hierarchy. Thus, even when most of the ownership of a voyage was in the hands of outside capital providers, the principle of shared ownership helped to reduce agency conflicts. Due to their overarching significance, each of these elements in the organization of whaling ventures—voyage financing, the role and performance of the agent and crew selection, and the lay system of incentives—deserves exploration in more detail.

Voyage Financing

Financing needs for whaling ventures were extensive over the life cycle of a voyage. Ships had to be constructed or refitted and then provisioned for a multiyear journey. In the early years, whaleships and general merchant trading ships were substitutable, but as the industry developed, the need for specialized outfitting increased. Ships were designed with improved speed and stability to contest the maneuverability of sperm whales. Although the cost of a whaleship plus outfitting varied over time and by the type of ship, the industry became reliant on external financing for its capital needs. Davis, Gallman, and Gleiter report that "the typical New Bedford whaling venture of the 1850s called for an investment of $20,000 to $30,000." For comparison, the average US farm was worth $2,258 in 1850 and $3,251 in 1860, and the average capital stock of a manufacturing firm was valued at $4,335 in 1850 and $7,191 in 1860.[39] By the mid-1840s, the US industry as a whole consisted of 644 vessels displacing 200,484 tons and 17,594 crewmen, so the aggregate capital requirements were large.[40] An 1858 Consular Report on the US whaling system noted the intensity of financial requirements, stating that "there is no branch of trade or enterprise entered into in the United States in which so large a capital is invested."[41] It is a testament to the dynamics of capital markets at the time, and to the widespread taste for entrepreneurial risk-taking, that these ventures were ever financed.

Of particular interest with respect to financing is the role played by banks. Banks do not typically engage in VC-style investing today, and likewise banks were not the main conduit for the financing of whaling voyages. Banks can have multiple internal constituencies and revenue streams that distort how investments are selected. In a VC context, banks tend to prefer investing in startups that are likely to need standard loans in the future. That is, banks conditionally choose venture investments in early-stage firms that complement their existing business lines later on.[42] But pursuing greater margins in existing businesses may not be consistent with maximizing unconditional returns. Furthermore, following theoretical work by Michael C. Jensen and William H. Meckling, if a whaling venture were funded through bank debt, the agent might increase risk to undesirable levels, knowing he stood to gain upside if a risky voyage paid off, but that the debtholder would be left to bear the negative consequences if the voyage went wrong.[43] On the other hand, using equity financing would lead to dilution and induce wasteful expenditures by the agent, especially in a situation like a whaling voyage where monitoring was particularly costly. In theory, the optimal mix of debt and equity is at the point where the risk effect from debt financing and the disincentive effect from equity dilution are equal at the margin.[44] Nineteenth-century banks were not geared to deal with these types of complex incentive mechanisms.

In New England in the eighteenth and nineteenth centuries, the relationship between banking and whaling was more interpersonal than formal. While the direct financing of voyages was limited, the intersection of banking and whaling networks created a powerful web of overlapping interests. Naomi Lamoreaux shows that because capital markets were thin and information asymmetries between lenders and borrowers were significant during the early stages of industrialization, banks could effectively manage risk and mobilize funds to finance local economic development by engaging in business at an interpersonal and parochial level.[45] Interrelationships of this sort can be observed in whaling. In New Bedford, for example, it was common for presidents and directors of banks also to be whaling agents, or at least closely tied to whaling families. And the link was often made from whaling to banking, not the reverse. By the late 1850s, New Bedford was home to a cluster of banks and insurance companies, some of which had been financed because of wealth made in whaling. Most notably, when Merchants Bank received a state charter in 1825 its capital stock of $150,000 made it the largest bank in Massachusetts outside the Boston area. The bank's founders, stockholders, and directors were leading New Bedford whaling entrepreneurs who also established the closely affiliated Merchants Insurance Company. The whole New Bedford economy essentially revolved around kinship ties and intergroup monitoring. Although it was not uncommon for financing to be provided from more distant geographic areas of the United

States, including Pennsylvania, New Jersey, and even California, it was the local network structure of communities that generated financing systems favoring whaling.

In New Bedford, familial ties were especially dense due to the town's Quaker roots. Quakers dominated the city's politics and wealth until at least the 1830s. While there is something paradoxical about the association of this peaceful faith, known for its rejection of violent confrontation, with the brutality of whale hunting, in some ways the fit between Quakerism and whaling was ideal. The religious outgroup viewed trust-based transactions as a comparative advantage leading to "a high order of commercial probity and honor."[46] Violations of social and cultural norms in such communities could bring severe reputational punishment. This likely induced honesty and loyalty in the behavior of agents, and kept relationships from becoming contentious. Trust mattered because financing whaling ventures involved interacting with multiple constituencies. Since ordinary investors usually could not afford to supply all the capital required for voyages (and nor would they want to do so, from a portfolio perspective), a system of shared ownership of whaling voyages soon emerged. According to Davis, Gallman, and Gleiter, "it was common to divide the ownership of a vessel up into thirty-seconds, sixteenths, or sixty-fourths."[47] This meant that even "persons of moderate means" further down the social ladder might possess ownership stakes in a voyage ranging from perhaps 3 to 12.5 percent.[48]

While wealthy elites could frequently hold more equity in a voyage, financial diversification made sense given the variable distribution of voyage outcomes shown in Figures 1.1 and 1.2. Despite his substantial wealth, which would have permitted him to finance several fleets by himself, Jonathan Bourne, a successful New Bedford merchant who became a full-time whaling agent and owner, managed his risks by investing in forty-six separate whaleships.[49] In some cases, ownership structure was quite complex. Over the course of twelve voyages from New Bedford during a period of about twenty-five years, the *Amethyst* had shares owned by nine different groups, including the socially linked whaling-agent families the Howlands and the Wilcoxes.[50] In other words, the risks were syndicated, and this facilitated the origination of large pools of risk capital. A syndication partner could also verify the potential attractiveness of the investment. As vessels grew in size and voyages grew in duration, more extensive partnerships for financing and control arose.

Given the distributional characteristics of payoffs from voyages, some downside protection also became part of the financing structure. Venture capitalists use, among other things, financial instruments for this purpose. For example, preference shares financially subordinate entrepreneurs if a startup is liquidated by sale, merger, or acquisition. In the case of whaling, some level of downside protection could be gained through the insurance market. Both the vessel and the whale product were considered as insurable interests. Insurance underwriters, common in New Bedford and especially in Boston, charged about 2.5 percent per annum in normal times, since this allowed them to pay decent dividends to their investors. But the amount could go as high as 9 percent in riskier years, such as those affected by bad weather or war. Insurance costs also depended on factors such as the condition of the whaleship, the hunting area, and the length of the voyage. For a four-year voyage, the average cost of insurance could be about 10 percent of the total value of the vessel and cost of outfitting it, plus the premium on the catch.[51] A rigorous application of maritime law, including strict definitions of insurance upon "outfits" and "catch," meant that owners were able to enforce their maritime insurance contracts.

Approaches to insurance, however, tacitly admitted the risk-reward tradeoff associated with whaling's highly uneven returns. Despite the nontrivial chance that a ship would not return to its home port, some owners decided to forego insurance altogether because the premiums required would cut too sharply into their net returns. There is anecdotal evidence of how costly it could be to fail to insure against whaling catastrophes. In 1871, the Howland family suffered $300,000 in uninsured losses as its vessels were subjected to the ravages of an arctic ice storm. In 1876, the Howlands lost a further $817,000.[52] Partial coverage offered some mitigation. Charles W. Morgan and Samuel Rodman, Jr., the owners of the whaleship *Magnolia*, took out an insurance policy with a value of $11,000 on its voyage to the Pacific Ocean and other places—far short of the replacement cost of a vessel valued at $20,000 that had been outfitted at the additional cost of $17,000. Starbuck records that the *Magnolia* set sail from New Bedford on January 1, 1831 and returned June 15, 1834 with a healthy 3,400 barrels of sperm oil.[53] Insurance factored into the broader set of incentives used on whaling voyages. Because crew members were paid on the net value realized by a voyage (that is, minus the insurance cost), they basically subsidized the premium payment. Obviously, if a ship were lost at sea, only its owners back at the home port could collect on the insurance policy.

Agents as Intermediaries and Their Performance

Agents played a pivotal coordinating role in whaling ventures. They acted like venture capitalists as organizing and monitoring intermediaries. Not only were agents responsible for acquiring whaleships for expeditions, they also worked with captains to determine the necessary equipment and crew. They coordinated with owners to make decisions about insurance, and advised captains on the types of whale to target and the geographic scope of the hunting grounds. Good insight into agent practices can be gained from the records of Charles W. Morgan, who was born into a Quaker family in Philadelphia and first became prominent in New Bedford when he joined the mercantile firm of William Rotch, Sr. and Samuel Rodman, Sr. as a partner. He subsequently became an independent financier and organizer of whaling ventures. In 1834, he wrote to a captain that his whaleship "being now ready for sea, as agent I have to advise you that she is bound on a whaling voyage to the Pacific Ocean. That she is fitted for thirty months, and that we wish you to cruise for sperm whales for 20 to 24 months and if not then full, fill up with whale oil. We leave to your judgment the cruising ground on the Pacific, though we would recommend the neighborhood of New Zealand, where both right and sperm whales are to be taken, and it would be well, especially toward the end of the voyage to be where right whales could be taken."[54]

Agents used logbooks from prior voyages as a source of due diligence on hunting grounds. These were daily notes made by captains and first mates, providing detailed information on whale sightings, weather, locations, and crew morale. At a venture's end, the logbook became the property of the agent or owner, which acted as a repository of accumulated knowledge. Although whaling agents could entrust their captains with codebooks for confidential communication between captains sailing for similar, though not identical, partnerships, as a general rule, secrecy was of the utmost importance. "This book is given into your charge with the full understanding that all its contents will be kept by you in the strictest confidence," one captain was instructed, "and that you will make it a point of honor not to communicate any of its contents to any one whatever directly or indirectly or let anyone get them in any way, except the captains of our ships."[55]

The monitoring function of the agent was also crucial beyond the domestic port. Agents had to coordinate with captains during whaling ventures to stage investments and ensure that credit was available overseas for such things as provisions to feed crews and replace equipment. All this took place at a time when global communications were quite rudimentary. Letters sent to and from distant ports on ships could take months to arrive, if indeed they arrived at all. Agents sought information from families of crew members, who exchanged their own letters at distant ports. For example, the New Bedford whaling firm of Wilcox and Richmond wrote to Leonard Gifford's mother, sister, and fiancée when he was at the helm of the *Hope*. Messages were sometimes relayed from the most unusual places. Santa Maria, a small island in the Galapagos archipelago, became a mail hub because it was frequented by vessels hunting whales in the Pacific. Although the Post Office Act of 1792 had created a pathway to the growth of a geographically wide postal network, it was not until the middle of the nineteenth century that systematically arranged postal services existed between such distant places as New Bedford, San Francisco, and Honolulu.[56]

Whaling agents often had their own incentives to maximize the value of voyages because they held substantial ownership shares. Charles W. Morgan is recorded as having ownership stakes in at least forty-two voyages between December 1823 and September 1856.[57] For his eponymous whaleship the *Charles W. Morgan*, launched in 1841, Starbuck documents ten voyages between 1841 and 1877, mostly in the Pacific Ocean. Morgan is recorded as agent only for the first two voyages, after which the role passed to Edward M. Robinson in 1849, to the Howland family in 1853, and a few years after Morgan's death in 1861, to J. & W. R. Wing & Company in 1863.[58] Morgan derived great wealth from whaling. In 1855, he ranked number eight in the list of the wealthiest New Bedford taxpayers.[59]

General data on New Bedford wealth from tax records indicates that large fortunes could be systematically accumulated in whaling.[60] During the early-to-mid 1850s, the population of New Bedford was just over twenty thousand people. The taxable population (less than 3 percent of ~~~ulation) held wealth per capita at an extraordinary level of $1 million today. The average wealth of whaling agents ⟩le this amount ($63,725), and the most experienced ⟩ted substantially more. The average wealth of those New

Bedford agents who had organized twenty or more voyages by 1856 stood at $112,642.[61] Accordingly, the New Bedford Board of Trade commented in 1889 that "our wealth, our population, and our progress have been the fruits of this industry; and our position and fame among the cities of the world is due to its successful prosecution."[62] Investment returns generated from whaling were reinvested in further voyages, perpetuating a cycle of wealth accumulation. The effect on the local economy was substantial. In 1853, the *New York Times* confidently asserted that New Bedford was "probably the wealthiest place" in America.

Naturally, wealth accumulation for whaling agents was partly a function of the flow of returns from whaling voyages. Figure 1.4 plots the average profit rates across 1,566 voyages for the leading twenty-nine agents in the Davis, Gallman, and Gleiter data set. These top twenty-nine agents were responsible for organizing at least forty voyages each, so the returns were generated over lengthy time periods. Because agent fees are considered as costs in these calculations, the profit rates represent the average net-of-fee returns to voyages. For example, the figure shows that David R. Greene & Company generated a negative profit rate over thirty-three voyages, while Gideon Allen & Son achieved an astonishing profit rate of 59.2 percent from the sixty-four voyages it acted as agent for from 1830 to 1887. Gideon Allen & Son's profit rate was 4.4 times higher than the average seen by competing firms in the same year. One whaleship that Gideon Allen & Son agented, the *Milwood*, amassed a catch valued at $172,841 and realized a profit in excess of 3,000 percent in a single six-month voyage in 1864. This exceeded the catch value of 98.5 percent of the voyages included in the aggregated data in Figure 1.4. Of the 1.5 percent of voyages that bettered $172,841, the shortest voyage to do so took thirty months—five times longer. The longest voyage to exceed the *Milwood's* catch value took a staggering 8.6 years.[63] While Gideon Allen & Son generated a mean profit rate of 59.2 percent, the median profit rate was just 4.9 percent, showing the impact that an occasional huge hit could have on a long-tail portfolio's returns.

To put this return into perspective, New York Stock Exchange stocks, for which comprehensive data are available, returned a compound annual return of 7.6 percent between 1830 and 1887.[64] Gideon Allen & Son performed well under Gideon Allen's stewardship, when his son (Gilbert Allen) was active in the firm during the 1850s, and when Gilbert Allen took over the business fully after his father's death. One interpretation

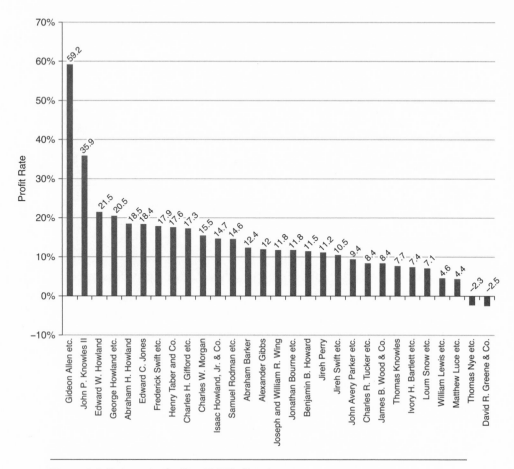

Figure 1.4 Returns to the Top 29 Whaling Agents.
Based on data in Lance E. Davis, Robert E. Gallman, and Karin Gleiter, *In Pursuit of Leviathan: Technology, Institutions, Productivity, and Profits in American Whaling, 1816–1906* (Chicago: University of Chicago Press, 1997), 448–449.

of this strong performance is serendipity. In fact, an 1851 listing of the *Rich Men of Massachusetts* describes Gideon Allen as being "very lucky in the whaling business."[65] This is analogous to the oft-cited modern VC refrain of "I'd rather be lucky than smart," and the skill-versus-luck debate concerning the determinants of VC performance.[66]

Several other key performance characteristics are worth highlighting in the context of analogies with modern-day VC. The performance of whaling agents exhibited a high degree of persistence over time.[67] Agents who outperformed one year were likely to outperform consistently.

Agents excelled when they were able to recruit the right captains and crew and effectively manage voyages. Because of persistence in the returns, the best whaling agents could command a fee premium for their services. Fee income came in two forms: fees for organizing the voyage, and fees for securing the sale of the whale product at the termination of the voyage. Davis, Gallman, and Gleiter report that for the *Culluo*'s voyage in the early 1870s, the agent Taber, Gordon & Company was paid a 2.5 percent fee for outfitting and a 15 percent commission on the value of products sold.[68] Gideon Allen & Son, unsurprisingly, charged a high fee compared to all other agents that had vessels returning to New Bedford in the same year.

Finally, whaling agents earned compensation in the form of performance-based equity. Agents were typically co-owners in the voyages. Just as VCs take a share of a fund's profits as carried interest, whaling agents did well when a voyage returned with a strong catch. Agents often took large ownership shares because the route to wealth accumulation required being an agent as well as an owner. For whaling ventures organized as partnerships (the most common and lucrative organizational form), the agent's ownership share was about 39 percent on average compared to 1 percent for voyages organized as corporations.[69] Such personal investments by agents in whaling partnerships meant that incentives were effectively aligned. Agents shared more in downside risk by putting large shares of their own personal wealth at stake.

Captain and Crew Selection, and the Lay System of Incentives

Once a vessel had been secured by the agent, a captain was selected to undertake the voyage. While some captains sailed only once or twice from New Bedford, many sailed recurrently for the same agent. Indeed, the Davis, Gallman, and Gleiter data set shows almost 750 agent-captain combinations lasting more than two voyages. In a handful of instances, captains sailed on fifteen or more voyages. Antone J. Mandley captained twenty voyages over his lifetime, logging a remarkable forty years at sea as a whaling vessel captain.[70] In whaling, past success had a sizeable impact on the probability of future success, as is also the case in entrepreneurial performance in modern VC-backed enterprises.[71]

Before assuming command of a first ship, a captain would typically have served on at least three voyages, perhaps first as a cabin boy, then as a third or second mate, then as a first mate. Having such experience, the captain was expected to contribute to decisions about outfitting the whaleship, selecting a promising whaling ground, and sometimes even specifying the whale species to be pursued. Agents performed governance functions, helping to professionalize the voyage, especially for captains with more limited experience.[72] They provided advice and encouragement. The well-respected agent Charles W. Morgan wrote to a young captain, George H. Dexter of the *Condor*, in 1834:

> As you have now taken the responsible station of Master of a Ship and are a young man you will permit me to offer some advice. The greatest difficulty I have observed with young Masters, is either too great indulgence or too great severity towards their crew. Discipline must be effectual, be administered with a steady hand especially among Sailors, and there is no station which requires more guard over the temper, than that of a master of a Ship. And on your first voyage depends in a great measure your future success in life. Let me then beg of you to keep a strict watch over the moral conduct of your crew, never permit your authority to be abused or set at naught, but at the same time never to use undue severity yourself or permit it in your officers. I have a real confidence in you and I trust you will not feel hurt at my giving advice which I feel it my duty to offer you.[73]

Much like a startup team, the agent and captain would recruit crew, filling approximately thirty positions on an average voyage, from first mate all the way down to cabin boy. Most whaling vessels carried three mates, although the number could be as low as one or as high as six. Each whaleboat needed a harpooner (or boatsteerer), and most voyages carried four. Other vital crew members included a cooper, who assembled the barrels in which oil would be brought home, a carpenter to make general repairs, a cook to prepare what passed for meals on the long voyages, and a steward to serve them. Sometimes a blacksmith or other specialized tradesman was also hired on. The rest of the crew were seamen, ranging from unskilled green hands to men who had spent decades at sea. Crammed into the forward section of the whaler, the green hands and other crew lived in separate accommodation from the teerers, cook, and stewards. The forecastle was dark and ated, likely contributing to the turnover in crews over the nths at sea.[74]

Incentive-based payments help to explain why captains and crew went through the pain and danger of these voyages. Fixed wages would have been ineffective in such settings because of information asymmetries between investors and crew and uncertainties of payoffs.[75] A captain without an equity stake in a voyage would be tempted to act in ways that served his own interests at the expense of capital providers.

In modern VC-backed startups, there are strong conventions regarding the equity allocation to people in key roles, such as founders and chief technology officers. Likewise, whaling captains and crew were compensated systematically using performance-based pay. For their services, they were paid out of the proceeds of the voyage. The share that a crew member received was called the "lay" and varied considerably by rank. Lays were fractional, and a "short lay" was better than a "long lay." Captains in New Bedford appear to have received between 1/20 (5 percent) and 1/8 (12.5 percent) of a voyage's catch, or profit.[76] First mates might sail on lays as short as 1/15 (6.7 percent) in rare circumstances, though lays between 1/30 (3.3 percent) and 1/20 (5 percent) were more common for them. A second mate could expect a lay of about 1/40 (2.5 percent) and a third mate, 1/60 (1.7 percent). Next in the hierarchy came the cook, cooper, and other skilled tradesman deemed essential to the voyage. Harpooners and boatsteerers were likely to receive 1/90 (1.1 percent) lays, while seamen were commonly paid between 1/250 (0.4 percent) and 1/100 (1 percent). In *Moby-Dick*, Melville famously describes Ishmael's bargaining for his lay, hoping for 1/200, finding the agent offering 1/777, and feeling some satisfaction when he ends up with 1/300 for his services on the *Pequod*. In some instances, cabin boys sailed for room, board, and clothes alone.[77]

Lays were agreed prior to the voyage but were paid net at the voyage's end. On the return of the whaleship to its home port, the catch was valued at prevailing market prices and the crew member paid an amount equal to the catch revenue (minus expenses such as insurance and costs of processing the catch at port) multiplied by the agreed lay, minus any personal expenses incurred during the voyage. Often, personal expenses were purchases from the "slop chest"—a store of clothing and provisions such as tobacco maintained by the captain. Cash advances could also be made to crew prior to or during a voyage and these had to be repaid with interest. Although idiosyncratic bonuses were sometimes awarded to individuals at the end of a voyage for such contributions as spotting whale pods, for the most part, the lay governed the payment to be received. Once these payments had been made and all other expenses had been netted out from the value of the catch, the remainder went to the owners.[78] By allowing captains and crew to participate in the upside of a voyage and discouraging them from engaging in too much risk-taking, the system dealt effectively with the threats of moral hazard and agency conflict.

When, as was frequently the case, a captain was also an ownership partner, responsible for contributing to the initial capital outlay, he received payment from both his ownership share and his lay. Often, the captain's ownership share was a simple acknowledgment of scarce talent, but in some instances the thinking behind it could be more nuanced. It was perceived, for example, that captains nearing the ends of their careers were more prone to shirking, and that the additional inducement of an ownership stake beyond the lay could effectively keep this selfish behavior in check. Overall, captains were reasonably well paid in whaling. According to an analysis of over a thousand voyages departing from New Bedford from 1840 to 1858, the average monthly wage of a captain was $98.31. In the merchant marine, by contrast, captains received an average monthly wage of $29.54.[79]

Captains received what could be considered reasonable (risk-adjusted) income for their services. Moving down the hierarchy of the ship, however, pay levels from whaling dropped sharply. Officers like first and second mates still did well in terms of earnings, presumably because their skills were also in high demand, but lower-order crewmen rarely made much. Consider the numbers compiled in 1858 by the US Consulate in Paita, Peru. Assuming a "liberal average" outcome for a sperm whaleship on a four-year voyage that it would bring home a 1,200-barrel take a green hand with a 1/180 lay would receive gross 210 gallons of oil. At the going market price that would fetch $262.25. But, after deducting the standard charge for oil shrinkage and leakage (10 percent), insurance costs (3 percent), cash paid out in advance of and during the voyage and associated interest charges, and some typical clothing and medical provisions, the crewman might be left with just $54.17. The compiler of these extraordinary numbers observes that, even if no deductions were made from the $262.25, the sum would be paltry. "It seems incredible that an intelligent, active young American should pass through four years of labor . . . separated from family and country," to make less than six dollars per month, he notes. "Yet such is the case."[80] In a similar vein, the limited payoffs to VC-backed entrepreneurs are sometimes difficult to comprehend, given that, as one study concludes, "the reward to the entrepreneurs who provide the ideas and long hours of hard work in these startups is remarkably small, once risk is taken into consideration."[81]

Unsurprisingly, due to the vagaries of whaling and the fact that risk-adjusted payoffs to the crew were quite small, one voyage was often enough to convince a man to try his luck in other occupational pursuits. There were some opportunities for upward mobility, however, so a few cabin boys and even some green hands were destined for command of a whaling voyage, if they could bear the costs of staying employed in the industry. For example, Charles Wood "began poor" but, by becoming a sea captain in New Bedford, ultimately amassed a fortune estimated at $100,000 in 1851 (about $3.2 million today). Jared Coffin, who started out as a cooper on a Nantucket whaleship, subsequently became a captain and owner, and was said to be worth $300,000. Joseph Starbuck, one of the most successful Nantucket whaling merchants, was initially a butcher. Career mobility was the only route to real prosperity because the lay system meant that financial returns accrued to the capital providers. Just as modern venture investing favors VCs and limited partners, contracts in whaling, while they provided effective incentive mechanisms, were mainly designed to maximize the share of total vessel profits going to capital providers.

Cyclicality, Bubbles, Risk, and Diversification

A few overarching similarities between whaling and the venture capital industry should also be noted, beginning with the cyclical nature that is an indelible characteristic of both.[82] Some of whaling's cyclicality was related to the seasonal nature of the industry, but even beyond that, whaling was characterized by recurrent boom and bust phases. Within particular whale-hunting grounds, returns were extremely volatile. Voyages, like venture capital portfolio companies, were high-variance investments with uncertain outcomes. They were extremely vulnerable to fluctuations in the price of whaling products at port, and to weather conditions at sea.

Perhaps surprisingly, for all their sophistication, agents active in the whaling industry did little to mitigate particular types of risk. In theory, the total risk of a whaling venture consisted of non-diversifiable and diversifiable components. For example, when the United States declared war on Britain in 1812, New Bedford's whaling fleets were exposed to the British Navy. No New Bedford whaleships set sail in 1812, 1813, or 1814. Later, during the Civil War (1861–1865), northern whaleships were attacked by Confederate privateers despite the presence of a strong Union maritime blockade. Not much could be done about these unexpected, non-diversifiable events. Other risks, however, could be diversified away. Even bad weather could be avoided given the range of available hunting grounds.

In a comprehensive empirical analysis, Eric Hilt argues that whale hunters' tendency to focus on common areas like the North Pacific, which accounted for about 50 percent of whaling voyages by the mid-1850s, meant they were foregoing the opportunity for efficient geographic diversification.[83] Although returns may have been lower in other hunting grounds, the risks from these voyages would have been uncorrelated with those of North Pacific–bound voyages. Thus, when the Bering Strait (a narrow passage of water connecting the North Pacific and Arctic Ocean) was jammed in late 1851 by severe ice floes, the season ended in failure. Because voyages were disproportionally clustered in this area, investors bore more risk than they needed to have done. Returns suffered because a shock that could have been diversified away instead had a large, industrywide impact. In that sense, voyages to the North Pacific were overfunded.

Cognitive biases and organizational choices help to explain this failure. With respect to cognition, it is well known that herding behavior arises to the extent that uncertainty exists about outcomes and signals about the future are imperfect. First movers provide information that affects the decisions of later movers, leading to copycat behavior as economic actors advance in lockstep, even when private information specific to late movers should encourage decisions in the opposite direction.[84] Captains in whaling simply followed what other whaling captains were doing, to the point that "ships almost without number" pursued whales in close proximity to one another.[85] Possibly, for a whaling captain anxious to protect his reputation, it made more sense to fail along with other voyages than to risk failure as a contrarian. The same herd-inducing cognitive biases tend to affect venture capitalists, causing concentrations of investments in specific time periods and sectors.

Meanwhile, whaling's prevailing organizational model also presented barriers to better diversification strategies. As noted already, the whaling industry was dominated by partnerships and not by corporations with more diffuse ownership. Because most whaling ventures were closely-held partnerships, shares were not typically traded in open markets, where they could have been priced to encourage geographic voyage diversification. If open-market transactions had been possible, then in a scenario where a voyage's risk was highly correlated with industry risk (as when the bulk of US vessels sailed to the same hunting grounds), the value of shares in that voyage would have been discounted. At the same time, equity in vessels sent to different places (making for a low correlation between industry risk and voyage risk) would have been offered at a relative premium.[86] In short, investments in whaling could have been more diversified had the industry's ventures been more widely held concerns.

There is a reason this opportunity to create diversification was missed, and it relates to the overwhelming advantages of concentrated ownership in partnerships discussed earlier. Outside investors needed the reassurance of joint-equity ownership with agents and captains, but this limited the amount of equity that could be placed externally. Partnerships were simply a better organizational form for managing moral hazard and the principal-agent dynamic. Thus, whaling involved maximizing expected value from portfolios of voyages subject to complex tradeoffs. On the one hand, closely-held concerns limited the deployment of certain risk management practices, including the geographic diversification of whaling voyages. On the other hand, whaling partnerships helped to align incentives between owners, agents, captains and crew in a world where multi-layered principal-agent concerns were present.

Three Complementary Factors

To briefly summarize, nineteenth-century whaling can be compared to modern venture capital in at least three major respects. First, whaling was the archetypal skewed-distribution business, sustained by highly lucrative but low-probability payoff events. Voyages often lasted several years and covered immense geographic areas in the search for the elusive whale pod. The long-tailed distribution of profits held the same allure for funders of whaling voyages as it does for a venture capital industry reliant on extreme returns from a very small subset of investments. Although other industries across history, such as gold exploration and oil wildcatting, have been characterized by long-tail outcomes, no industry gets quite as close as whaling does to matching the organization and distribution of returns associated with the VC sector.

Second, the organizational structure of whaling centered on agents acting as intermediaries. Like general partners in VC firms, they allocated the risk capital provided by limited partners on the supply side to portfolio companies on the demand side. Wealthy individuals keen to invest in whaling voyages did not have the knowledge or capabilities that would allow them to disintermediate these agents. To the contrary, the particular combination of activities that had to be coordinated for a whaling voyage to succeed demanded that a specialized role emerge, and agents having gained this domain expertise could capture substantial returns in the forms of both organizing fees and equity shares. As agents conducted *ex ante* due diligence, governed voyages, and built relationships with captains and crew across repeated dealings, they built advantages that tended to persist over time. The return on skilled human capital could be large.

Third, whaling was fraught with potential agency conflicts—between investors and agents, agents and captains, and captains and crew. Similarly, venture capitalists operate in a sector with a whole host of moral hazard concerns and information gaps, which they in their intermediary capacity help to alleviate. US whaling ventures exemplified a practical approach to managing this risk. The concentrated ownership ensured by the partnership structure discouraged free-riding behavior, and therefore avoided much of the cost incurred by corporations with dispersed ownership to monitor agents entrusted with day-to-day decision making in the owners' best interests. The lay system of payments also did its part to align the incentives of owners, captains, and crews, so that decision-making authority could be pushed lower down the hierarchy—an absolute necessity for distant whaling voyages requiring frequent judgment calls.

These three factors in whaling—the long-tail distribution of payoffs, the agent-centered organizational structure, and the system of incentives— were complementary in their impact. Productivity increased because of their interaction. They allowed American whaleships to dominate a global industry to a degree similar to American venture capital firms' domination of VC-based entrepreneurship today.

2

The Early Development of Risk Capital

WHALING WAS AN IMPORTANT but ultimately ephemeral business. As a consequence of extensive hunting, whale stocks were depleted and the rate of return on capital started to attenuate. In 1800, there were around 1.1 million sperm whales globally, but by 1880, due to the intensity of whaling, only about 780,000 remained. In 1853 alone, the US whaling fleet killed eight thousand whales.[1] While the mean rate of return on whaling ventures was somewhere in the region of 15 to 24 percent per annum during the golden age in the middle of the nineteenth century, by the 1870s annual rates of return were in the low single digits.[2] With the advent of alternative energy sources (specifically, crude oil) and higher costs of labor and foreign competition, the whaling industry declined and capital sought out new sources of return.

Some of the more forward-looking whaling elites began to diversify their investments in advance of the industry's decline. One study notes that of the twenty-two major whaling families in New Bedford, fifteen also had investments in cotton, fourteen were involved in banking, and eleven had interests in other industries like railroads.[3] Gideon Allen, whose outstanding career as a whaling agent was described in Chapter 1, was a Merchants Bank director. His son became president of the bank and also became involved in the New Bedford Copper Company, the New Bedford Gas Light Company, and other firms. George Howland, who headed one of the leading New Bedford whaling families, had always engaged in general merchant activities and land ownership in addition to whaling, but he was especially keen to diversify his portfolio during the 1840s. At about this time, New Bedford started to become a center for cotton textiles manufacturing. Indeed, the Howland family was part of an investment consortium responsible for establishing the Wamsutta Mill in 1846, New Bedford's first cotton manufacturing concern.

Financing entrepreneurship and technological development in the US economy depended on the intensive use of risk capital in high-risk and potentially high-return investments. It is well known that this venture financing function has contributed significantly to the development of high-tech innovation and entrepreneurial activity in recent time periods, but much less recognized is how entrenched it is in American history. This chapter focuses on the most pervasive VC-style risk capital arrangements, including the use of equity finance for early stage high-tech enterprises, intermediation, contracting to allocate cash flow and control rights, minority shareholding, and the provision of governance to startups.

Cotton textiles production is a good starting point because it involved the financing of high-tech innovation in an industry that was crucial to the development of capitalism.[4] Studies of modern VC show how venture capitalists deal with complex agency issues. The historical precedents for these types of contracting exchanges will be highlighted by this chapter's focus on negotiations between the Browns, a wealthy, Rhode Island–based merchant family who were keen to diversity into cotton textiles, and Samuel Slater, an immigrant entrepreneur with valuable technological knowledge to offer. Clauses in the agreement between the two parties essentially determined the allocation of cash flow and control rights, and the agreement is remarkably forward-looking when viewed from the vantage point of modern VC. More generally, capital providers helped to facilitate growth and scale in New England manufacturing. Risk capital deployment led to the creation of an ecosystem of entrepreneurial businesses.[5]

Beyond cotton manufacturing, the role of new venture finance was critical in creating other leading industries and industrial regions in America. In some cases this involved direct investments by capital providers, and in other cases funding flowed through intermediaries. For example, in financing railroads, intermediaries looked beyond their local markets for capital.[6] Financial requirements were immense given the scale of track construction needed. Between 1830 and 1860, over thirty thousand miles of railroad track were laid, extending the reach of markets and helping to integrate regional economies.[7] As the economy developed based on capital needs, finance increasingly divided into segments focusing on early-stage risk capital, later-stage private equity, and investment banking functions.

Sometimes the lines between these financing segments were blurred. Thomas Edison, pioneer of the incandescent light bulb, conducted early-stage experiments with capital from some of the leading financiers and investment bankers of the time, including J. P. Morgan, his partner Eggisto Fabbri, William H. Vanderbilt, Henry Villard, and others. Risk capital was a main driver of the Second Industrial Revolution, when high-tech businesses proliferated.[8] Cleveland and Pittsburgh became entrepreneurial hotspots. Andrew Mellon, a key banker and investor in the area, who later served as secretary of the treasury in the Harding, Coolidge, and Hoover administrations, often financed early-stage ventures through equity participation, exercising some managerial control through governance. Venture capital's emergence in America can be seen against the backdrop of a long-term historical trend toward more efficient allocation of risk capital in the most technologically dynamic sectors of the economy.

"High-Tech" Innovation in Cotton Manufacturing

To understand how venture finance became central to the emergence of a robust cotton manufacturing sector in the United States, it is first helpful to consider the broader development of technologies that began in Britain and diffused across the Atlantic. Cotton was arguably a "leading sector" in Britain's industrial development, to use W. W. Rostow's familiar phrase.[9] The vast scale of Britain's empire facilitated control of upstream and downstream activities. And in England's main manufacturing center of Lancashire—a geographic area stretching some thirty-five miles across the northwest—workers who learned by doing constituted a human capital advantage that drove world-leading productivity.[10] Britain dominated global production. By 1850, it produced half the world's output of cotton textiles, despite having just 1.8 percent of the world's population and 0.16 percent of the world's land mass.[11]

Explanations for Britain's advantage in cotton manufacturing are wide-ranging, with scholars pointing to its high labor costs, cheap energy, and low capital costs as drivers of innovation.[12] Another line of thought suggests Britain was able to advance the technical frontier because of its unique scientific mentality, which led to higher rates of invention and productivity growth.[13] Whichever argument holds true, it is certainly the case that a series of technical improvements on the spinning and weaving sides helped solidify Britain's preeminent global position in the industry. Highly competitive domestic and international markets rewarded innovation, spurring several breakthroughs in the mid-to-late 1700s. In particular, increasing the efficiency of the spinning process was considered a top priority for textile innovators. Exporters were beginning to see the supply of yarn as a constraint on growth and the labor intensity of the spinning step made it a bottleneck.

The "spinning jenny," invented by James Hargreaves, was therefore one of the most important innovations of the Industrial Revolution because it allowed spinners to multiply their labor, thereby deepening the use of capital in the economy. Instead of producing one spool of yarn at a time, using a traditional spinning wheel, the jenny allowed a single laborer to produce up to twelve spools at once. Incremental advances would further multiply the output of a single operator to eighty spools, and in some cases as many as one hundred and twenty.

Production technologies could be developed because finance was available formally and informally for innovation. Not all banks were averse to taking on risks that might yield negative returns, and the financing needs of inventors could also be met by relatively wealthy individuals acting as venture investors.[14] Hargreaves was an impoverished serial inventor and handloom weaver, needing everything from capital for research and development to somewhere to live. As Robert Allen points out, "at first, Hargreaves was supplied with accommodation in Ramsclough, a remote village in Lancashire, and support by Robert Peel, who was acting as his 'venture capitalist.'"[15] Although the jenny probably cost no more than £500 to develop (about £50,000 today), neither Hargreaves nor Peel generated significant financial returns from the innovation. The societal value, however, was immense. By the late 1780s, more than twenty thousand spinning jennies were in use in Britain.[16]

Although the spinning jenny represented a major step forward, yarn making still remained highly dependent on skilled labor. This changed with the introduction of a new spinning machine patented by Richard Arkwright in 1769. Arkwright's machine used rollers to draw out the fibers and produce a thread far stronger than that made by the spinning jenny. Moreover, Arkwright's innovation enabled the spinning process to be driven by an external power source. Called the "water frame" because it was typically powered by waterwheel, the new machinery could also be powered by horses—and later by steam engine, following the rotary-motion innovation developed by the firm of Boulton & Watt. Detaching yarn production from human labor was transformative. It enabled cotton spinning to move from individual households to purpose-built factories, dramatically lowering production costs. In 1780 there were twenty such factories operating in Britain, and by 1790 there were 150.[17] Arkwright's invention is important in its own right, not least because it earned him a knighthood and an enduring reputation as the "father of the factory system." It was also, however, a vital step toward the invention of the "spinning mule" by Samuel Crompton, who combined the technologies of the spinning jenny and water frame to create "the backbone of the British cotton industry."[18]

Following the initial development of his innovation, Arkwright teamed up in 1768 with two partners, John Smalley and David Thornley, to develop and commercialize the technology. Each partner had three one-ninth shares, and in any year in which each partner's share of the profits exceeded £500, Arkwright took 10 percent more on any surplus beyond that threshold. When the partnership struggled for capital during the patent registration process in 1769, Arkwright turned for help to financial intermediaries Ichabod and John Wright, who in turn connected him with Samuel Need and Jedediah Strutt, two wealthy Nottinghamshire hosiery manufacturers. They invested £500 for a one-fifth share each and joined Arkwright, Smalley, and Thornley as partners of Richard Arkwright & Company, opening up a cotton mill in 1771 in Cromford, Derbyshire. Arkwright and Thornley received annual salaries of £25 for managing operations. As in the initial partnership, Arkwright maintained his right to a 10 percent premium on surplus profits.[19] In 1774, Strutt estimated that approximately £13,000 (about £1.4 million today) in development costs had been incurred.[20] Arkwright and Strutt acquired Need's share for around £20,000 when he died in 1781.[21] When Arkwright died in 1792, his net worth was estimated at £500,000, or about £55 million in today's terms.[22]

Across the Atlantic, the Revolutionary War (1776–1783) had resulted in America's independence from its colonial master, but for a variety of important reasons it seemed unlikely that cotton manufacturing in America would produce goods of tradeable quality, let alone develop into an export-oriented industry. At the point of independence, the country was economically in a state of chaos with a large debt burden and a significant balance-of-payments deficit.[23] Despite steady population growth, domestic markets were still small. In 1790, New York—the largest city in the United States at the time—had a population of just over 33,000 people, whereas London's population topped 850,000 and Paris's was 500,000. Only four other US cities had populations greater than ten thousand. Crucially, America did not have access to key innovations that had been vital to industrialization in Britain. This situation would soon change, however, as risk capital formation intersected with technology diffusion.

Accessing Frontier Technology

In Britain, the government and individual firms attempted to limit the diffusion of innovations like the spinning jenny and water frame with formal and informal noncompete-style policies. As early as 1718, laws had been passed to restrict the outflow of artisans and their tools and protect the country's advantages in textile production. By 1749, anyone caught exporting textile manufacturing tools could be fined £200. Agents seeking to recruit technicians for emigration to America could also be imprisoned for twelve months and fined £500 per violation. Any skilled textile worker attempting to leave Britain could be arrested on sight. To thwart reverse-engineering, firms would close cotton mills to visitors, force employees to take secrecy oaths, design factories "with the defensive features of a medieval castle," and even embellish machinery with add-ons to make it appear more complex than it actually was.[24]

So valuable were Britain's leading innovations, however, that in America industrial espionage was not only sanctioned but actively encouraged.[25] Numerous efforts were made to import British technology into the United States, driven by a mix of commercial self-interest and civic duty to contribute to the vitality of the young nation. Yet, conducting effective due diligence was challenging in an environment with rudimentary communications and information gaps. Investors in the United States often found their hires to be incompetent or, worse still, rogues. John Bowler, for example, came to work as a machine maker for John Nicholson, a leading Pennsylvania merchant and entrepreneur seeking to establish a cotton manufacturing business there. First, Bowler secretly built equipment for Nicholson's competitors, then he fled to Ireland with

$10,000 of his sponsor's money.[26] There were many such stories of skilled textile makers taking advantage of their funders' trust, whether by mismanaging resources or simply stealing equipment.

Equally, the American sponsors could prove faithless. A number of reliable British inventors with technological knowledge attempting to relocate to the United States found, after leaving behind family and braving an arduous transatlantic voyage, that their investors were unable or unwilling to fulfill their obligations. Some sponsors simply had grandiose speculative visions. The above-mentioned John Nicholson had pledged to build an enormous, thousand-spindle mill, only to be bankrupted. In 1800, Nicholson died insolvent in a Philadelphia debtor's prison. Entrepreneurs also struggled to find financial partners who were truly focused on cotton manufacturing. Economic growth during the 1790s brought an explosion of interest in banks, turnpikes, and canals, and speculation in land as the "frontier" of the country moved west. These opportunities became attractive relative to a long and highly uncertain process of developing cotton technology.

The wealthy members of the Brown family in Providence, Rhode Island, believed they could overcome these challenges. They viewed cotton manufacturing as part of a diversification strategy, given that the mercantile activities they were heavily invested in were becoming riskier in a time of war and trade embargos. The Brown family had first entered the mercantile business in 1723, and by the end of the eighteenth century had amassed tremendous wealth. Their activities were extensive. Some Brown family members engaged in whaling. Obadiah Brown first organized a whaling voyage in 1754 and Nicholas Brown & Company hunted for whales on a regular basis between 1769 and 1777. Other members of the family, including the family patriarch James Brown, participated in the slave trade in a variety of capacities, including using their own vessels to transport slaves. Business activities in mercantile trade could be lucrative. In 1787, the family-controlled merchant firm Brown & Francis sent a ship with $26,000 worth of goods to trade in Asia, and when the vessel returned a year and a half later its hold was filled with goods worth $100,000. By moving cargoes of $200,000 to $400,000 in value, firms like those operated by the Browns could achieve net profits of $100,000 or more, or about $2.6 million in today's money.[27]

The Browns used capital generated in all of these activities to fund new entrepreneurial ventures. For example, prior to the Revolutionary

War, they had built the Hope Furnace into a successful pig-iron refinery and also became the colonies' largest producer of whale spermaceti candles. Both products were sold using their trading apparatus. When whale and iron products declined in importance after the war, the Browns applied their entrepreneurial talents to a host of other industries, including cod fishing and rum and gin distilling.

The Browns governed by a set of core principles in all of these businesses, starting with talent decisions. Rising generations were groomed for management roles, but younger family members were not forced to take specific roles, and if the requisite expertise could not be found within the family network, the elders would hire externally. Regarding strategic planning, a belief in moderation and caution prevailed. The Browns consciously reined in the rapid growth of their candle business to keep it from developing "out of proportion to the other branches." They practiced what management experts have since learned to call "data-driven decision making," maintaining exceptionally detailed business records and using this information to guide planning.[28]

Cotton manufacturing was a natural fit with the Browns' diversification strategy because it represented a new revenue stream that was largely uncorrelated with the vicissitudes of maritime trade. Furthermore, for Moses Brown—one of three brothers leading the family enterprise—it aligned with some public-spirited goals. He saw it as an industry that could help pull Rhode Island out of its economic malaise in the early years of the American republic, while avoiding the morally repugnant slave trade. Having begun his research into the cotton business in 1787, Moses Brown was ready by 1789 to launch a firm; he provided the capital for his son-in-law William Almy to enter a partnership with his cousin, Smith Brown. Brown & Almy, as the new firm was called, purchased a spinning jenny, a few crude, locally produced versions of Arkwright's water frame, and a building in Pawtucket situated alongside the Blackstone River—which would serve as its power supply.

Lacking a trained operator, however, or any knowledge of how to refine the technology, Brown & Almy could not get the machinery working properly. Discouraged, they mothballed the equipment—but did not sell it.[29] Despite this early failure, Moses Brown, William Almy, Smith Brown, and others in the family remained interested in textile manufacturing and believed a successful business enterprise could be built with the right technical knowledge and strategic approach. Moses Brown declared: "it is the machinery in the [cloth-making] business that will carry it to advantage."[30] They put out word through the family's broad network of commercial contacts that if a partner with the right technical skills could be found, they would be willing to experiment further and engage in a contract.

The Browns' call would be answered late in 1789 by Samuel Slater, a twenty-one-year-old Englishman highly experienced with water frame technology and keen to apply his knowledge in America. Slater had left Britain just weeks earlier, dressed as a farm laborer to avoid detection by British customs officials tasked with preventing skilled textile engineers from emigrating. Having joined a cotton manufacturing company in New York, he was growing frustrated by its limited machinery when he heard about the Browns' interest in cotton manufacturing from the captain of a Providence-based packet ship. He wrote to Moses Brown: "I can give the greatest satisfaction, in making machinery, making good yarn . . . as any that is made in England; as I have had opportunity and oversight, of Sir Richard Arkwright's works, and in Mr. Strutt's mill upwards of eight years." (See Appendix 1.) Slater was young but intelligent. His "pitch," to use modern VC terminology, is compelling in its signaling. The letter provides a brief account of Slater's merits, including his association with a pivotal innovator (Arkwright) and entrepreneur (Strutt); it outlines his current situation of employment; and it establishes a basis for taking subsequent steps toward a working relationship.

Slater was being truthful. He had worked for Strutt, serving as an apprentice at his mill under a six-year contract where he worked with the water frame spinner invented by Arkwright. That apprenticeship had developed his business acumen and technical expertise. He had also learned his way around employment contracts. When his father (a close friend of Strutt) died unexpectedly, Slater—who was just fourteen years old and still in the middle of his apprenticeship "trial period"—was forced to negotiate the terms of his indenture with the vastly more experienced Strutt. The contract stipulated Slater would serve his master and keep his secrets while complying with a number of restrictive covenants, including that he should "not commit fornication, nor contract matrimony." Strutt, in return, would provide food, lodging, and a small wage. Importantly, the contract stated that Slater would be "taught and instructed" in the "art of cotton spinning." Strutt was true to his word. (See Appendix 2 for the complete contract.)

As an apprentice, Slater devoted himself to learning all he possibly could about Strutt's factory, volunteering to spend even his Sundays at the mill. He so thoroughly mastered the mechanical operations that he was able to design an improvement to the equipment in use that would enable it to better distribute yarn onto spindles. Beyond technical skills, he also acquired commercial and management expertise and personal guidance from Strutt, who grew to become almost a second father. The law made breach of contract by employees a serious criminal offense, but Slater's obligation to Strutt was more interpersonal than legal. In fact, the depth and completeness of his commitment to Strutt was so strong that he honored the full length of his contract, even as other apprentices abrogated theirs.

Analogous to a modern sequence of contracting meetings between an entrepreneur and a venture capitalist, Moses Brown replied just eight days later on December 10, 1789. (See Appendix 1 for his complete letter.) He would not have been able to make due-diligence inquiries about Slater in that short time. His letter is clear and encouraging but also circumspect. It states that Almy & Brown (as the firm was now named) "want the assistance of a person skilled in the frame or water spinning" and honestly acknowledges that an "experiment has been made, which has failed." The letter goes on to outline a prospective partnership by which Slater would be entitled to a profit share. The letter states explicitly that the investment would be staged (as modern VC financings are), with an expected experimental period of six months, after which "if we find the business profitable, we can enlarge it." In that case, or perhaps even earlier "if sufficient truth be had on trial," Almy & Brown would negotiate an additional agreement to pursue the venture that would be "agreeable on all sides." The letter ends by emphasizing the goal of "perfecting the first water-mill in America" and stating that Almy & Brown would be "glad to engage" with Slater so long as the venture "can be made profitable to both, and we can agree." Overall, the letter is a fascinating response to Slater's original speculative correspondence. It provides a nonbinding framework for both parties to think about a longer-term financing and entrepreneurial relationship.

As a consequence of these written exchanges, Slater moved to Providence in January 1790 and within two months he had succeeded in assembling water-powered spinning machines according to Arkwright's principles. Both sides saw great potential in the combination of Almy &

Brown's risk capital and Slater's technical know-how. Yet, they had not agreed to formal terms to ensure the continuation of their business relationship. Writing to Brown in 1790, Almy recognized the crucial contribution that Slater could make, recommending that they invest capital in a joint enterprise with clear lines of operating responsibility and ownership. The letter notes that "in addition to contracting with Samuel to receive a part of the profits as a compensation for his services" the business should be structured so that "each one may know to which part his attention is to be particularly devoted."[31]

Contracting for Cash Flow and Control Rights

Almy, Brown, and Slater agreed to terms on April 5, 1790. (See Appendix 3.) The contract was predicated on a sophisticated deployment of risk capital. Slater was tantamount to a technical cofounder because he had the expertise in cotton machinery that Almy and Brown lacked. Complementing that, Almy and Brown performed functions akin to what modern VCs do for their portfolio companies; while they were not financial intermediaries, their role was to provide capital and governance. VC contracts are designed to allocate cash flows and control rights among investors and entrepreneurs in such a way that the value of the firm is maximized, incentives are provided for entrepreneurial effort, and capital providers are sufficiently protected against downside risk.[32] A close analysis of Almy & Brown's terms highlights that it was an effective agreement from the perspective of thinking about cash flow and control rights and contract design.

Almy and Brown recognized that although Slater lacked capital to contribute to the tie-up, he was "well-skilled" in the art of cotton manufacturing, and he could spend time managing the venture. In today's terms, he could provide sweat equity. A division of labor was specified that entrusted to one party the management of technology, to the other party the capital provision to "furnish materials" and governance. While untimely dissolution due to disagreement is an inherent risk in partnerships, an advantage is that this structure kept Almy and Brown close enough to the operations of the business to allow them to identify and respond to capital needs more quickly than would have been possible with a looser commercial relationship. The partnership model provided formality but also flexibility and enabled them to create a version of what we would call today a lean and nimble startup.

Instead of providing Slater, or the new partnership, with one initial, large, lump-sum infusion of capital, Almy & Brown's investment took the form of "payment bit by bit for the things needed in the construction and equipment of the mill," as well as raw materials and advances of cash for labor costs. In other words, they staged their commitments to reduce risk, just as modern venture capitalists do. Note also that Almy & Brown, prior to signing the agreement, had already experimented with Slater in the few months after he arrived in Providence. During that time, Slater had developed what the modern entrepreneurship literature would call a "minimum viable product" by replicating the Arkwright machine and making it operational. In a short period of time, Almy & Brown had managed potential problems arising from informational asymmetries, reduced the level of uncertainty associated with the new venture, and curbed any opportunistic behavior on the part of Slater. Hence, they could develop the relationship more formally.

In a remarkable demonstration of the value attributed to high-tech knowledge during the eighteenth century, Slater was considered "an owner and proprietor in one half of the machinery" and he was also entitled to "receive one half of the [net] profits." Almy & Brown willingly ceded a large amount of the equity and cash flow rights in the partnership to incentivize Slater, even though the commercialization of the product also depended on capital and business infrastructure (like a powerful distribution network). One explanation for Slater's favorable equity split might be that he learned how to increase his bargaining power from his interactions with Strutt. Another possibility is that Almy & Brown respected the value of Slater's human capital and knew his skills would be hard to replicate. Offering Slater less equity to develop the Arkwright technology might have invited competition from another capital provider, or made it likelier that Slater (despite his liquidity constraints) would build something on his own. As sophisticated investors, Almy & Brown appreciated the significance of the tradeoff between control and value. Studies of modern startups reveal that founders who are willing to cede equity to attract talented cofounders tend to realize greater value from their ventures.[33]

Expanding on this point further, the cash flow rights were well-defined and transparent. Slater would receive "full and adequate compensation for his whole time and services" but his profit share was net, calculated only "after every expense arising from the business is defrayed, including the usual commissions of two and a half per cent for the purchasing of the stock, and four per cent for disposing of the yarn." In effect, Almy & Brown created a "hurdle rate" by specifying the profit level that the partnership would need to exceed before Slater could collect any payoffs. Committed to objectivity in contracting, Almy & Brown did not inflate the stocking and sales commissions but rather specified them at the "usual" rates. While they had more leverage here, it is noteworthy that they opted for something reasonable and easily verifiable.

While the contracting framework was on the face of it favorable to Slater, Almy & Brown benefited from the use of restrictive covenants which limited downside risk by conditioning cash flow and control rights. Given that Slater was "accountable for one half of the expense" under the terms of the agreement, but did not possess sufficient capital resources, Almy & Brown agreed to advance amounts to enable Slater to "carry on his part of the business" provided that they would be repaid "with interest thereon." Moreover, assuming Slater did borrow from Almy & Brown, the agreement stipulated that his share of the profits from the partnership would be used to pay off the capital that had been advanced to him, "so that the business may go forward." Thus, Slater was tied to the partnership because his payoffs were subject to vesting. The strategy used by Almy & Brown achieved a number of complementary aims. It negated the threat of untimely dissolution or hold-up because Slater's payoffs were vested, only to be paid out much later in the life cycle of the venture, making it financially costly for him to leave the business in the short run. And it limited the amount of free cash flow available to Slater, which reduced expropriation risk.

Finally, Slater was required to "devote his whole time and service" to the venture, a clause that appears twice in the agreement. This implicit noncompete provision meant he could not under the conditions of the contract engage in another business, related or not. Also, he was prohibited from selling machinery he developed to any other entity unless he had already fulfilled his financial obligations to Almy & Brown, and even then, he was required to offer the machinery to Almy & Brown under a first-refusal provision "upon the lowest terms." At the same time, Almy & Brown could "put in apprentices to the business," presumably to facilitate the transfer of Slater's tacit knowledge. Overall, while the agreement provided Slater with strong cash flow incentives, Almy & Brown clearly focused on the need for control.

The partnership was ultimately successful, becoming technologically then commercially feasible as a yarn-spinning concern. Slater and his partners quickly understood that reaping the full benefits of water frame technology would require a change in where yarn spinning was located. Seeking to replicate the model of dedicated manufacturing facilities that Slater had experienced in England, they found a promising site adjacent to the Blackstone River a few miles from central Providence. After damming the river, constructing a waterwheel, and building the two-story factory facility, they opened the mill in 1793 in Pawtucket establishing what many historians believe to be the first factory in America. Consolidating manufacturing at a large, purpose-built facility saved on labor expenses, reduced transaction costs and waste, and facilitated economies of scale. Its significance was monumental for American capitalism. The model was replicated across the northeastern United States.

By 1812, there were thirty-three textile factories in Rhode Island with a collective capacity of 56,246 water-powered spindles—a dramatic increase from Slater's first 24-spindle machine just two decades earlier. Nearby towns in Massachusetts had an additional twenty mills with 45,438 spindles of capacity.[34] The partnership's pioneering efforts to link risk capital formation with the development of frontier innovation had given rise to a burgeoning ecosystem. Slater remained in partnership with Almy & Brown until 1798, after which he formed a partnership with his father-in-law. He died in 1835 with a fortune estimated at $1.2 million, or around $37 million in today's terms.

Risk Capital and Scaling in Cotton Manufacturing

Slater's anonymous arrival in America in 1789 turned out to be a pivotal, if unexpected, moment in American history. Likewise, a visit to Scotland and England two decades later by Francis Cabot Lowell would prove transformative. A Harvard College graduate and scion of a wealthy Boston merchant family, Lowell used business connections to gain access to Britain's large-scale mills. He returned to Boston shortly before the War of 1812 with enough trade secrets and proprietary machine drawings to launch an entirely new model for cotton manufacturing. This new approach, dubbed the Lowell System, was different from Slater's approach in terms of technology, organization, and financing, but it was still based on the mobilization of risk capital.

The Lowell System was based on the diffusion of another high-tech British innovation. The process of transforming raw cotton into finished cloth had several steps, chief among them the spinning of yarn and the weaving of cloth. Slater's model used water-powered machinery only for the spinning portion, and "outsourced" the weaving to a network of small, offsite facilities where laborers did the work by hand. The British designs Lowell brought back to Boston included blueprints for a power loom patented by Edmund Cartwright in 1785, which used water power to mechanize weaving, too. With this innovation, it made sense to accomplish both spinning and weaving inside the bounds of a single factory. Doing so could boost labor productivity, increase economies of scale, cut transportation costs, and achieve greater consistency of output.

Lowell also realized that, given the greater scale facilitated by the new technology, he would not have to locate mills in places with strong labor markets. Instead, large mills constructed where the water power was best could attract enough labor that new communities could develop around them. After Lowell's death, the Boott Mills—opened in 1835 alongside the fast-flowing Merrimack River—would provide the greatest proof of his vision. By 1860, over sixty-two thousand women, most of them single young women from Massachusetts and New Hampshire, were working at textile mills in New England.[35] Lowell had been interested in wealth accumulation but he also had a social conscience. Having witnessed deplorable working conditions in large textile mills during his time in England and Scotland, he wanted America's to provide quality housing and higher wages.

By integrating spinning and weaving, the Lowell system dramatically increased the range of activities a given firm would be expected to undertake, and with this new scope came a corresponding increase in the demand for capital. Almy & Brown had invested $1,560 incrementally over the first year of the Slater enterprise, yet Lowell aimed to raise $400,000 (about $11 million today) in start-up costs alone.[36] Raising funds was further complicated by the fact that the assets purchased—very large, tightly integrated, and customized spinning and weaving equipment— could not be easily divided among partners in the event of financial distress or untimely dissolution. To meet these challenges, Lowell adopted a novel approach to organizing risk capital for textile mills that marked a clear departure from the Slater model.

In contrast to the relatively informal partnership structure used by most textile manufacturers, Lowell created the Boston Manufacturing Company in 1813, in Waltham, Massachusetts, as a joint-stock company—even going so far as to petition the state legislature for incorporation. He offered family and close business acquaintances, together known colloquially as the Boston Associates, the opportunity to purchase a total of one hundred shares in the company. The share price was $4,000 each, with $1,000 payable to the company immediately upon closing. A total of twelve people, the "angel investors" of their day, bought up all the shares in Lowell's venture. This was a group small enough to manage as capital providers, but too large to be involved in daily operations. Management of the firm was therefore delegated to just Lowell and his brother-in-law Patrick Tracy Jackson, who was appointed as the company's first agent. In addition to relieving investors of the burden of day-to-day involvement, the joint-stock model provided liquidity: holdings could be sold as needed. This approach was effective. Lowell grew the pool of invested capital to $1,000,000.[37]

The combination of innovative technology, novel organizational design, and creative financing proved extremely successful in the cotton textiles industry. By 1828, five large-scale mills existed in Waltham and Lowell (formerly Chelmsford but renamed in Francis Cabot Lowell's honor in 1826). Although profits fluctuated widely, the fact that the industry was highly remunerative on average fueled a virtuous cycle of investment and expansion. By 1840, Lowell was the second-largest city in Massachusetts, with nine separate mills backed by $8 million in capital (about $225 million today).[38] In 1820, Lowell had had a population of a few hundred people, but by 1850, it was one of the most prominent industrial agglomerations in the United States. In 1853, Lowell had thirty-five cotton mills employing over ten thousand workers who operated 320,732 spindles, 9,954 looms, and produced in excess of two million yards of cotton cloth per week.[39] It had all begun with financial precedents and institutions that can still be found in the ecosystem of VC finance today.

Marking a difference between the Slater and Lowell financing scenarios was that, for the former, the capital provider was close to the operation of the venture through a partnership, and for the latter, financing was arranged through a corporate structure with outside shareholders. As Charles Calomiris and Carlos Ramirez point out, however, "virtually every financial transaction involves at least one intermediary [and therefore] the distinction between using intermediaries and using 'the market' is a false dichotomy."[40] One way to characterize the Lowell model of financing is to describe the Boston Manufacturing Company as an intermediary entity for capital pooling. Lowell and his associates were agents of this outside capital and also principals themselves through their own equity ownership, which aligned their interests with those of the more passive investors. These individuals bridged information gaps by specializing in the collection and communication of private information to facilitate efficient exchanges between contracting partners. Risk capital was ultimately deployed across numerous textile ventures. As equity rather than debt holders, investors shared in both the upside returns and the downside risks of these entrepreneurial concerns. This was fundamentally a long-tail investment. And, according to Robert Dalzel, it was "venture capital in its purest sense."[41]

Deploying Risk Capital through Financial Intermediation

Venture capital involves financial intermediation and this functional activity developed in America as a consequence of factors that predated New England's textile industry and even its organization of whaling ventures. While the colonial economy was virtually devoid of financial institutions, settlers developed creative ways to engage in activities that required capital amounts beyond what they could self-finance. For example, the New England fish trade was first supported by London merchants, who contracted with settlers to fill their ships with dried fish, which they then sent to southern Europe. By using personal relationships with settler communities to conduct due diligence, they could overcome the constraint of contracting at a distance.[42]

Merchant trading involved frequent interactions with third parties. Hence, financial intermediation became a natural progression. In Philadelphia in 1781, merchant trader Robert Morris established the Bank of North America. This was the first commercial bank in the country, helping to provide short-term credit to merchants and entrepreneurs by discounting notes and bills of exchange. By 1790, each of the main cities in America—New York, Boston, Philadelphia, and Baltimore—had a bank. By 1800, only four states—Vermont, Georgia, North Carolina, and New Jersey—had yet to charter one.[43] The first investment bank in the

United States—the Baltimore-based Alex. Brown & Sons—was founded in 1800 by an Irish immigrant with expertise in the linen trade. During the so-called "free-banking" period between 1837 and 1865, entry into banking was remarkably open, as most states sanctioned banks according to a common set of regulatory principles like demandable deposits. By the nineteenth century, an efficient system of financial intermediaries had begun to develop, aiding capital investment in entrepreneurial pursuits.[44]

But as the economy scaled during the mid-to-late nineteenth century, a significant change in the nature of intermediation occurred. While relational lending and equity-based financing had been well-suited to the needs of small-to-medium sized entrepreneurial ventures operating in localized environments, these mainstays of the New England textiles industry were less compatible with the funding of the very largest ventures associated with industrialization. Capital investment for canals, railroads, and other transportation infrastructure demanded new configurations. Although New England mostly persisted with equity-based financing in these sectors, bonds came to be more generally preferred by investors because they provided less risky and more regular income flows.

Railroads started to be built in the United States during the 1830s and competed directly with transportation ventures operating on navigable waterways. Thirteen miles of the pioneering Baltimore & Ohio railroad opened up for transit in 1830. From then, the growth in US railroad mileage and capital deployment was spectacular. By 1840, three thousand miles of tracks had been laid; by 1850, there were more than nine thousand miles; and by 1870, there were about fifty-three thousand miles. In 1897, the *Street Railway Journal* noted that 184,428 miles of track existed; the industry employed 823,476 men; the capital stock of railroad companies totaled $5.4 billion (about $161 billion today), consisting of $4.4 billion in common stock and $1 billion in preferred stock; and funded debt accounted for a further $5.3 billion. Financing on this scale required the services of intermediaries. According to Alfred D. Chandler "without such aid, American railroads would have had great difficulty in tapping outside capital."[45]

When railroad building was in its nascent stage, intermediaries in Philadelphia connected railroad builders with investors in London. The First Bank of the United States (1791–1811) and the Second Bank of the

United States (1816–1836) were established in Philadelphia, and the latter acted as a conduit for the placement of American securities on the London money market. During the 1840s, Boston took over as a center of railroad finance, and about a decade later, New York ascended to pre-eminence. Agents marketed bonds on a commission or fee basis and they also acted in an advisory capacity to railroad builders. The financial sector offered a fuller menu of instruments as it became increasingly institutionalized. A market for commercial paper emerged and investment banking syndicates began to develop.

Indeed, the nature of financial intermediation changed as a consequence of economic growth into areas that we would recognize today as the domains of venture capital, private equity, and investment banking. Smaller firms required entrepreneurial finance, but most of the new innovations in finance were available only to larger, later-stage enterprises. For example, financier John Pierpont Morgan famously acted as an intermediary for railroad and industrial investments and reorganizations during the late nineteenth and early twentieth century, during the rise of financial capitalism. Morgan used various mechanisms including basic financial engineering, voting trusts, and interlocking directorships to gain de facto control of the companies in which he was involved.[46] Networks were particularly important to this endeavor. When Charles H. Coster, a leading member of J. P. Morgan & Company, died in 1900, the *Railroad Gazette* reported he was probably "a director in more companies than any other man in the world." Coster held fifty-nine board positions, indicating an astonishing array of interlocking activities. Although potential conflicts of interest were widespread, this governance approach also created favorable returns, which may have swayed investors to hold securities in firms they knew very little about. In that sense, bankers acted as "delegated monitors" to keep a check on borrowers and fill information gaps.[47]

Furthermore, Morgan was more than just an investment banker because "he also played the role of venture capitalist."[48] The early development of electricity during this time period owed much to the provision of intermediated entrepreneurial finance. The work of Thomas Edison's labs was financed by a group of well-known investors including J. P. Morgan and some of his partners. Edison was connected to many of his investors by Grosvenor P. Lowry, a noted New York corporate lawyer with extensive experience as an intermediary. Under Lowry's guidance, the Edison Electric Light Company was formed in New York in 1878 to license and develop Edison's inventions with a $300,000 capitalization. This firm and other Edison enterprises later merged with the collection of firms that formed the General Electric Company in 1892. The merger was intermediated by J. P. Morgan, and both he and Coster joined the board governing the new entity.

More broadly, the Second Industrial Revolution, conventionally dated between 1870 and 1914, witnessed a wave of changes to the organization of production and the introduction and diffusion of breakthrough innovations in industries like electricity. Firms increased in size far beyond the largest textile enterprises in New England, facilitated by factors such as economies of scale and scope in manufacturing, an increase in market size due to the growth of transportation networks, and access to capital for expansion. Electricity typically stands out as the most significant innovation because it possessed what economists define as "general purpose" characteristics due to its "pervasive use in a wide range of sectors."[49] Electricity became the principal method of illumination for households and a source of power in factories. Its impact was analogous to that of the microprocessor and information and communication technology, which revolutionized enterprise management and much of daily life during the late twentieth century. Edison introduced the incandescent lamp in 1879 and, by 1900, a bulb was twice as efficient as it had been in 1880 and cost 80 percent less. Over time, electricity had a major impact on productivity and the nature of industrial production.[50]

Innovation Hotspots

Financial intermediation helped to shape the systematic provision of risk capital for entrepreneurship in America, and in consequence clear innovation hotspots began to develop. Venture capital tends to be clustered geographically, with Silicon Valley being the canonical modern-day example. As discussed in Chapter 1, innovative financing was crucial to the rise of New Bedford as a whaling center, and New England entrepreneurial finance produced clusters by providing a foundation for the introduction of frontier technologies in the textiles manufacturing sector.

The effect of venture-based financing was also quite pronounced in the development of other regions of the United States during the late nineteenth century. Pittsburgh grew entrepreneurially due to the impact of "new providers rather than established institutions of finance."[51] Naomi

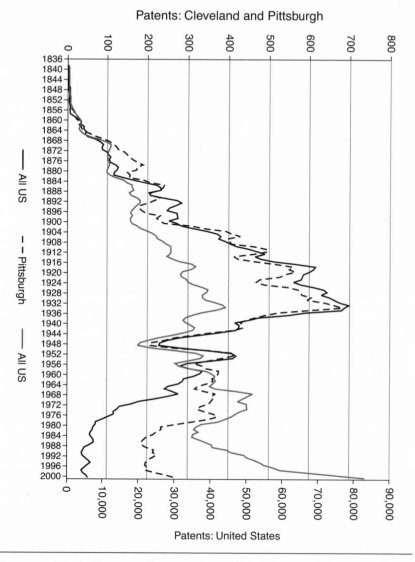

Patents: Cleveland and Pittsburgh

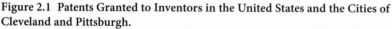

Patents: United States

Figure 2.1 Patents Granted to Inventors in the United States and the Cities of Cleveland and Pittsburgh.

Based on patent data from the United States Patent and Trademark Office.

Lamoreaux, Margaret Levenstein, and Kenneth Sokoloff show that Cleveland was a "hotbed of high-tech startups, much like Silicon Valley today."[52] The significance of these cities as hotspots of innovation is illustrated in Figure 2.1, which shows the number of patents granted by the United States Patent and Trademark Office to inventors located in Pittsburgh and Cleveland relative to patents granted in the country as a whole. During the 1860s and 1870s, both cities experienced strong upsurges in patenting activity, which continued until the late 1920s. Although it is clear that this patent-based advantage waned by the 1930s, and by around the 1970s both cities underperformed as heavy manufacturing declined in the American "Rust Belt," it is equally incontrovertible that, a century earlier, Pittsburgh and Cleveland were leading places for innovation.

Both cities were located in an area with a heavy emphasis on "new" industries like electricity. They witnessed the growth of startups, and they were vibrant entrepreneurially. George Westinghouse, a famous serial entrepreneur, got his start in Pittsburgh in the late 1860s in the railroad air-brake business with financial backing from friends and close associates. In 1881 Westinghouse founded the Union Switch and Signal Company to manufacture his railroad signaling and switching inventions. And in 1888 he acquired the patent rights of Nikola Tesla, who had been temporarily employed by Thomas Edison as a junior field engineer at his New York facility in 1884. Edison considered Tesla's alternating current power systems to be impracticable and the two had a respectful but also fractious relationship. Tesla left Edison's enterprise and his inventions were commercialized through the Westinghouse Electric Company, established in 1886 during the "war of the currents," characterized by an intense rivalry with Edison in the evolution of the US electricity industry.

Cleveland also played an important role in this sector. Lamoreaux, Levenstein, and Sokoloff point to the significance of the pivotal Brush Electric Company, established in 1880 through experimentation, high-tech innovation, and risk capital formation. The firm introduced an arc-lighting system invented by Charles F. Brush to illuminate buildings and streets. Brush had been unable to finance experiments by himself, so was permitted by a close friend, George Stockly, to use the facilities of the Telegraph Supply Company, where Stockly was vice president and general manager.

Following research and development efforts, Charles Brush acquired patents and the Telegraph Supply Company agreed to an exclusive license, paying royalties to him in return. Revenues from arc lighting soon surpassed those from the telegraph business, and the Brush Electric Company was organized with a substantial $3 million of authorized capital. Within a few years, Charles Brush was collecting more than

$200,000 in annual royalties (about $5.3 million today), as the firm was responsible for four-fifths of America's arc-lighting systems. In 1879, Brush had established America's first arc-lighting system in San Francisco. In 1889, Brush Electric was acquired by Thomson-Houston Electric Company.

These instances of entrepreneurship in Pittsburgh and Cleveland illustrate that personal connections between investors and entrepreneurs were of crucial importance. They continued to matter even as formal financial institutions developed and grew in scale. In 1906, for example, *Dun's Review* reported that Cleveland banks and trust companies held $233 million in deposits (about $5.9 billion today). Pittsburgh had a flourishing financial sector, as well. George Westinghouse was said to avoid bank-based financing because "he would not give up control to any man or group of men"—though he did rely on banks for short-term loans, and there is evidence he used banks for longer-term finance, too.[53] Furthermore, as firms scaled in size, formal finance did become complementary to early-stage risk capital. Well-functioning stock exchanges provide investors with opportunities to trade shares and gain liquidity beyond what can be achieved in private markets. The Pittsburgh Stock Exchange was established in 1864 and the Cleveland Stock Exchange in 1900.

The financing of new high-tech firms could also have much wider impacts on local economies, as dynamic clusters of entrepreneurs and capital providers grew up around "anchor" firms like Westinghouse Electric and Brush Electric. George Westinghouse founded multiple corporations in Pittsburgh, and he used internal capital markets to allocate funds across this network of ventures. Numerous new ventures were spawned in Cleveland as a result of Brush Electric's economic ascendency. Brush Electric both incubated new firms and attracted pools of skilled inventors and engineers to the area, promoting the further exchange and validation of technological ideas. Capital providers, in turn, were more likely to invest in inventors with track records.

During the 1880s, two Brush Electric employees, engineer Walter H. Knight and patent attorney Edward M. Bentley, invented and patented a new technology for delivering electric power below ground to power electric streetcars. The two men's positions at Brush "gave them sufficient visibility that they were able in 1884 to attract New York venture capital, organize their own firm, the Bentley-Knight Railway Company, and convince the East Cleveland Railway Company to lay a trial line."[54] Overall, strong externalities can be created in places where at least one large innovative firm exists alongside a mass of entrepreneurial startups.[55] Late nineteenth-century Cleveland and Pittsburgh typified this pattern of innovative development.

Capital and Governance

This geographic area of the United States also witnessed the powerful emergence of another feature that would become central in the provision of modern venture capital: the linkage between finance and governance. In some cases, governance was assured by contractual arrangements that spelled out cash flow and control rights, as in Samuel Slater's interactions with the Brown family. In other cases, it meant board representation. Understanding how monitoring and advisory roles developed is important in light of the longstanding debate in the venture capital literature over what drives VC returns more: the selection of good investments *ex ante* or the governance of ventures during their life cycles.

The influential Pittsburgh financier Andrew Mellon tied capital investments explicitly to governance. Richard Florida and Mark Samber argue that Mellon's activities "mirror those of contemporary venture capitalists in many respects, by providing both financial resources and management assistance."[56] Mellon got his start investing on behalf of T. Mellon & Sons Bank, established by his father in 1869. The bank focused principally on mortgages and real estate acquisitions. Mellon's father had helped to finance steel industry entrepreneur Andrew Carnegie, and during the 1870s the bank granted a series of loans to H. C. Frick Coal & Coke Company. Subsequently, Carnegie and Henry Clay Frick would become partners. As Frick also came to know Andrew Mellon personally, the two enjoyed a productive investing relationship and Frick became closely intertwined with the financial investments of the Mellon family.[57]

From the standpoint of parallels with modern venture capital, Mellon's approach to investing had several distinct elements. First, while Mellon engaged in debt financing, where the upside was capped by interest payments, he soon adapted his style to also include equity involvement and thereby long-tail returns. He engaged in equity participation across a portfolio of early stage ventures, often in new high-tech industries. For example, in 1889, Mellon received a request for a loan from the Pittsburgh Reduction Company, a startup founded in 1887 to exploit a novel patented technology to separate aluminum from its oxide. Over the next five years, he not only provided a loan, but also acquired an equity stake and became a director of the company. The fact that this startup grew into the corporate powerhouse the Aluminum Company of America speaks to Mellon's "extraordinary gift for spotting and nurturing outstanding individuals with promising ideas."[58] At the same time, his insistence on equity could be an obstacle for entrepreneurs who preferred to maintain strong control. In 1891, when George Westinghouse sought financing to expand his air brake enterprise, Mellon's equity-based approach, and his determination to decide managerial positions, caused negotiations to collapse.[59]

Second, Mellon was an intermediator of risk capital, creating an organizational structure to facilitate his investments. The Union Trust Company was established in 1889, with his brother (Richard Mellon), and Henry Clay Frick together holding a controlling interest. Organization as a trust was intentional. Trust companies were not subject to stricter bank-centered regulations. Following a lackluster performance during roughly its first decade of operation, Union Trust created a substantial capital base and pool of investment funds. It had capital of about $230,000 in 1889 ($6.2 million today), $7 million in 1900 ($206 million today), $20 million in 1901 ($583 million today), and $37 million in 1903 ($1 billion today). Its investment portfolio was valued at $103,625 in 1889 ($2.8 million today), at over $10 million in 1901 ($291 million today) and $14 million by 1903 ($394 million today).[60] Capital increased by a factor of about 161 in real terms between 1889 and 1903, and the investment portfolio by a factor of about 141. Union Trust evolved to incorporate a variety of Mellon family financial interests and it played a pivotal role in structuring their investments. Often, once Mellon had acquired sufficient equity in a concern, he would deploy a member of the Union Trust board into the firm and assign governance responsibilities to that person. Thus, he could manage multiple investments, syndicate with other capital providers, and diversify, all in the search of the rare hits in a long-tail distribution of returns. In that sense, Union Trust "was a type of venture capital firm."[61]

Third, Mellon appreciated how the capabilities of founders and professional managers came to the fore at different points in the life cycle of a firm. The skill set required to start a new venture is quite different than that required to manage it through its growth phases. When Mellon met Edward Goodrich Acheson, for example, Acheson was a star inventor, having gained experience at Thomas Edison's and George Westinghouse's research laboratories as an electro-chemist and engineer. Mellon invested in his efforts to manufacture carborundum (silicon carbide), an innovative abrasive for use in grinding and other industrial applications.

Mellon's initial investment in Acheson's Carborundum Company was during the mid-1890s and consisted of a $50,000 bond purchase. As part of the transaction, Mellon also received 6.25 percent of the firm's common stock and a board seat. When Acheson had the idea to meet growing demand by manufacturing carborundum using hydroelectric power at Niagara Falls, substantial new capital expenditures were required. Mellon provided more money—and received not only loan interest but more equity participation in return. Inevitably, after a series of such funding rounds, Acheson was diluted to the point where Mellon had de facto control. Although Acheson was widely celebrated for discovering one of the most significant inventions of the industrial age, Mellon and his brother, Richard, removed him from his role as chief operating officer in 1898 due to his managerial ineptitude. They installed a long-time associate of theirs, Frank W. Haskell, whom they knew to be a "good accountant and an efficient administrator."[62] Mellon frequently repeated this pattern of investment combined with governance, pursuing what the modern VC literature would describe as the "professionalization" of the startup firm.[63]

Mellon was also adept entrepreneurially and strategically. In 1891, he entered the oil business with his brother in western Pennsylvania, profiting when their pipelines and refineries were acquired by J. D. Rockefeller. Several years later, Mellon provided new venture finance to James Guffey and John Galey, who were attempting to find oil in Texas. Their efforts led them to found Gulf Refining Company in Port Arthur, which by the early 1920s was the largest refinery in the world.[64] Mellon was also instrumental in founding the Union Steel Company in 1899. When it was acquired by J. P. Morgan's US Steel Corporation in 1903, Mellon was paid at least forty times his original investment.[65]

Like J. P. Morgan, Mellon used interlocking directorships to exert control over companies and industries. In 1906, he sat on forty-one boards of Pittsburgh firms, where he was involved with a total of 250 different directors whose interests covered more than two hundred firms.[66] While Mellon tended to favor corporate growth through vertical integration—the model that became known as the "Mellon System"—he was also adaptable, conditioning his strategy on the types of technology, markets, and methods of production being pursued. Where he could pursue monopoly, he did—especially through patent rights. The Aluminum Company of America was once described as "the tightest metal monopoly known to history."[67]

Finally, Mellon was sensitive to the challenges of ownership structure. He chose a mix of minority and majority shareholdings as determined by circumstances. An example was his investment in an innovative coke-oven company founded by Heinrich Koppers, a German industrialist. When that company became subject to sale under the 1917 Alien Property Act, Koppers's shares were acquired at a substantial discount by a Mellon-controlled syndicate. Mellon proceeded from minority to majority ownership, not haphazardly but because it made economic sense to do so.

Although for most of his career he was quite secretive, by virtue of the disclosures required by his political career, much is known about Mellon's investing activities. When he was preparing for the position of Secretary of the Treasury in the Harding administration, he resigned from at least fifty-one directorships, and left his brother Richard to exercise control over his investments.[68]

Figures 2.2 and 2.3 illustrate the culmination of Mellon's activities. Together with his brother, he amassed a wide portfolio of investments in Pittsburgh and in other parts of the country. Gulf Oil stands out, accounting for about one-third of the value of all corporate assets he owned. Mellon's activities led to an extraordinary level of wealth accumulation. By 1931, when Mellon was Secretary of the Treasury in the Hoover administration, these investments alone summed to over $1.9 billion (around $30 billion today).

Importantly, these data indicate that, while Mellon is often considered to be an early example of a venture capitalist, it could be argued he was really a mixture of early-stage investor, later-stage private equity financier, and banker. Whereas VCs typically take minority equity interests in a company in order to spread risk across a portfolio of investments, Mellon often took majority stakes. Mellon's approach, however, was consistently VC-like in its application. He combined

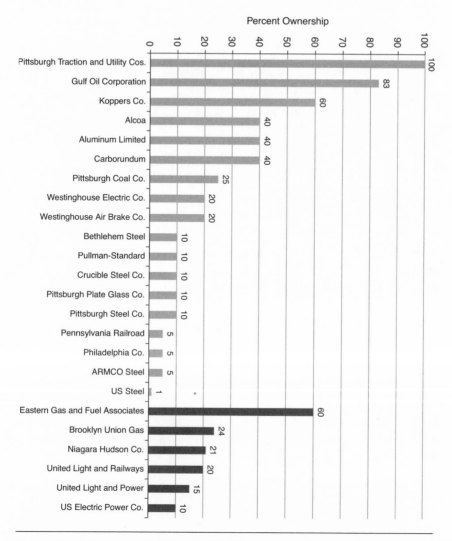

Figure 2.2 Mellon Industrial Financial Holdings in 1931: Percent of Corporate Assets Owned.

Based on data in Mark Samber, "Networks of Capital: Creating and Maintaining a Regional Industrial Economy in Pittsburgh, 1865–1919" (PhD diss., Carnegie Mellon University, 1995), 188.

equity interests with governance practices in order to realize high returns from a right-skewed distribution. The array of Mellon's approaches also powerfully illustrates how early-stage investing in the United States emerged alongside later-stage arrangements for business finance.

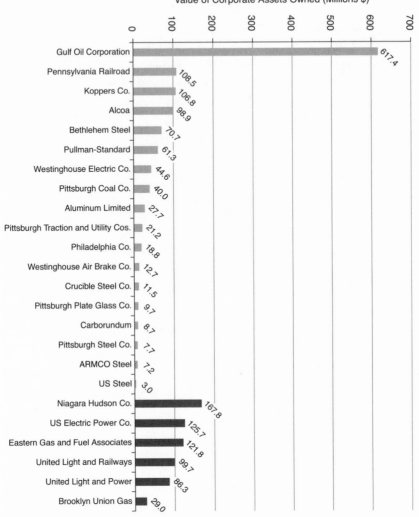

Figure 2.3 Mellon Industrial Financial Holdings in 1931: Value of Corporate Assets Owned.

Based on data in Mark Samber, "Networks of Capital: Creating and Maintaining a Regional Industrial Economy in Pittsburgh, 1865–1919" (PhD diss., Carnegie Mellon University, 1995), 188.

The Roots of Entrepreneurial Finance

This chapter has shown that from very early on in its history, mechanisms for the provision of startup finance existed in America, and in many cases the strategies used by capital providers were remarkably sophisticated when viewed through the lens of the modern VC industry. The contractual relationship between Samuel Slater and the Brown family defined how cash flow and control rights were allocated. The emergence of specialized intermediaries showed that there could be large returns to domain expertise, and that efficiencies could be gained by the allocation of capital to growth areas of the economy. Early-stage equity investing and the governance of startups by intermediaries further accentuated the impact of American entrepreneurship.

Furthermore, the process of organizing risk capital had a much wider effect. It led to significant wealth accumulation in American society during the late nineteenth and early twentieth centuries. The Mellon fortune was one of the outstanding examples, but there were many others, too. The top 0.1 percent wealth share peaked at around 25 percent during the early twentieth century.[69] As Chapter 3 will argue, private capital entities like family offices emerged as conduits for coordinating and investing wealth, often with productive consequences for the economy at large. The availability of increasing pools of risk capital set in motion developments that had profound implications for the organization of entrepreneurial finance in America, and for the rise of the modern VC industry.

APPENDIX 1

Initial Correspondence between Samuel Slater and Moses Brown

To Moses Brown on December 2, 1789

Sir,

A few days ago I was informed that you wanted a manager of *cotton spinning, &c.* in which business I flatter myself that I can give the greatest satisfaction, in making machinery, making good yarn, either for *stockings or twist*, as any that is made in England; as I have had opportunity, and an oversight, of Sir Richard Arkwright's works, and in Mr. Strutt's mill upwards of eight years.

If you are not provided for, should be glad to serve you; though I am in the New York manufactory, and have been for three weeks since I arrived from England. But we have but *one card, two machines,* two spinning jennies, which I think are not worth using. My encouragement is pretty good, but should much rather have the care of the perpetual carding and spinning. *My intention* is to erect a *perpetual card and spinning.* (Meaning the Arkwright patents.)

If you please to drop a line respecting the amount of encouragement you wish to give, by favour of Captain Brown, you will much oblige, sir, your most obedient humble servant,

Samuel Slater

To Samuel Slater on December 10, 1789

Friend,

I received thine of 2nd inst. and observe its contents. I, or rather Almy & Brown, who has the business in the cotton line, which I began, one being my son-in-law, and the other a kinsman, want the assistance of a person skilled in the frame or water spinning. An experiment has been made, which has failed, no person being acquainted with the business, and the frames imperfect.

We are destitute of a person acquainted with water-frame spinning; thy being already engaged in a factory with many able proprietors, we can hardly suppose we can give the encouragement adequate to leaving thy present employ. As the frame we have is the first attempt of the kind that has been made in America, it is too imperfect to afford much encouragement; we hardly know what to say to thee, but if thou thought thou couldst perfect and conduct them to profit, if thou wilt come and do it, thou shalt have all the profits made of them over and above the interest of the money they cost, and the wear and tear of them. We will find stock and be repaid in yarn as we may agree, for six months. And this we do for the information thou can give, if fully acquainted with the business.

After this, if we find the business profitable, we can enlarge it, or before if sufficient proof of it be had on trial, and can make any further agreement that may appear best or agreeable on all sides. We have secured only a temporary water convenience, but if we find the business profitable, can perpetuate one that is convenient.

If thy prospects should be better, and thou should know of any other person unengaged, should be obliged to thee to mention us to him. In the mean time, shall be glad to be informed whether thou come or not. If thy present situation does not come up to what thou wishest, and, from thy knowledge of the business, can be ascertained of the advantages of the mills, so as to induce thee to come and work ours, and have the *credit* as well as advantage of perfecting the first water-mill in America, we should be glad to engage thy care so long as they can be made profitable to both, and we can agree.

I am, for myself and Almy & Brown, thy friend,

Moses Brown

Source: E. H. Cameron, *Samuel Slater, Father of American Manufactures* (Portland, ME: Bond Wheelwright Co., 1960), 37–39.

Agreement between
Samuel Slater and Jedediah Strutt, 1783

This Indenture Witnesseth that Samuel Slater of Belper in the County of Derby, doth put himself Apprentice to Jedediah Strutt of New Mills in the Parish of Duffield in the said County of Derby Cotton Spinner, to learn his Art and with him (after the Manner of an Apprentice) to serve from the day of the date of these presents unto the full End and Term of Six Years and an half from thence next following to be fully compleat and ended.

During which Term the said Apprentice his Master faithfully shall serve his Secrets keep his lawful commands every where gladly do he shall do no Damage to his said Master nor see to be done of others; but to his Power shall let or forthwith give Warning to his said Master of the same he shall not waste the Goods of his said Master nor lend them unlawfully to any, he shall not commit fornication nor contract Matrimony within the said Term he shall not play at Cards Dice Tables or any other unlawfull Games whereby his said Master may have any loss With his own goods or others during the said Term without License of his said Master he shall neither buy nor sell he shall not haunt Taverns or Play Houses nor absent himself from his said Master's Service day or Night unlawfully. But in all things as a faithfull Apprentice shall behave himself towards his said Master and all his during the said Term.

And the said Jedediah Strutt in consideration of the true and faithful Service of the said Samuel Slater his said Apprentice in the Art of Cotton Spinning which he useth by the best Means that he can, shall teach and instruct or cause to be taught and instructed, Finding unto said Apprentice Sufficient Meat Drink Washing and Lodging during the said Term.

And for the true Performances of all and every the said Covenants and Agreements, either of the said Parties bindeth himself unto the other by these Presents In Witness whereof the Parties above named to these Indentures interchangeably have put their Hands and Seals the Eighth Day of January and in the Twenty Third Year of the Reign of our Sovereign Lord George the Third by the Grace of God of Great Britain France and Ireland King Defender of the faith &c. and in the Year of our Lord One Thousand Seven Hundred and Eighty Three

Samuel Slater
Jed Strutt

Sealed and delivered being first duly Stamped in the presence of
J. Leeper and Geo. Williams

Source: Archives of the National Museum of American History, Smithsonian Institution, Washington, DC.

APPENDIX 3

Final Agreement between
Samuel Slater, William Almy, and Smith Brown

The following agreement, made between William Almy and Smith Brown of the one part, and Samuel Slater of the other part,—Witnesseth that the said parties have mutually agreed to be concerned together in, and carry on, the spinning of cotton by water, (of which the said Samuel professes himself a workman, well skilled in all its branches;) upon the following terms, viz :—that the said Almy and Brown, on their part, are to turn in the machinery, which they have already purchased, at the price they cost them, and to furnish materials for the building of two carding machines, viz :—a breaker and a finisher; a drawing and roving frame; and to extend the spinning mills, or frames, to one hundred spindles.

And the said Samuel, on his part, covenants and engages, to devote his whole time and service, and to exert his skill according to the best of his abilities, and have the same effected in a workmanlike manner, similar to those used in England, for the like purposes.

And it is mutually agreed between the said parties, that the said Samuel shall be considered an owner and proprietor in one half of the machinery aforesaid, and accountable for one half of the expense that hath arisen, or shall arise, from the building, purchasing, or repairing, of the same, but not to sell, or in any manner dispose of any part, or parcel thereof, to any other person or persons, excepting the said Almy and Brown; neither shall any others be entitled to hold any right, interest, or claim, in any part of the said machinery, by virtue of any right which the said Slater shall or may derive from these presents, unless by an agreement, expressed in writing from the said Almy and Brown, first had and obtained— unless the said Slater has punctually paid one half of the cost of the said machinery with interest thereon; nor then, until he has offered the same to the said Almy and Brown in writing upon the lowest terms; that he will sell or dispose of his part of the said machinery to any other person, and instructed the said Almy and Brown, or some others by them appointed, in the full and perfect knowledge of the use of the machinery, and the art of water spinning.

And it is further agreed, that the said Samuel, as a full and adequate compensation for his whole time and services, both whilst in constructing and making the machinery, and in conducting and executing the spinning, and preparing to spin upon the same, after every expense arising from the business is defrayed, including the usual commissions of two and a half per cent for purchasing of the stock, and four per cent for disposing of the yarn, shall receive one half of the profits, which shall be ascertained by settlement from time to time, as occasion may require; and the said Almy and Brown the other half—the said Almy and Brown to be employed in the purchasing of stock, and disposing of the yarn.

And it is further covenanted, that this indenture shall make void and supersede the former articles of agreement, made between the said Almy and Brown and the said Slater, and that it shall be considered to commence, and the conditions mentioned in it be binding upon the parties, from the beginning of the business; the said Samuel to be at the expense of his own time and board from thenceforward.

And it is also agreed that if the said Almy and Brown choose to put in apprentices to the business, that they have liberty so to do. The expense arising from the maintenance of whom, and the advantages derived from their services during the time the said Almy and Brown may think proper to continue them in the business, shall equally be borne and received as is above provided for in the expenses and profits of the business.

It is also to be understood, that, whatever is advanced by the said Almy and Brown, either for the said Slater, or to carry on his part of the business, is to be repaid them with interest thereon, for which purpose they are to receive all the yarn that may be made, the one half of which on their own account, and the other half they are to receive and dispose of, on account of the said Slater, the net proceeds of which they are to credit him, towards their advance, and stocking his part of the works, so that the business may go forward.

In witness whereof the parties to these presents have interchangeably set their hands, this fifth day of the fourth month, seventeen hundred and ninety.

Wm. Almy
Smith Brown
Samuel Slater

Witnesses:
Oziel Wilkinson, Abraham Wilkinson

Source: George S. White, *Memoir of Samuel Slater, the Father of American Manufactures* (Philadelphia: No. 46 Carpenter Street, 1836), 74–75.

3

The Rise of Private Capital Entities

INFORMAL NETWORKS CONSISTING of wealthy individuals represented a key source of finance for early-stage entrepreneurial ventures as the US economy expanded. Investment banking intermediaries organized capital for later-stage ventures, including railroad and industrial concerns, which were more heavily dependent on external finance. This growing specialization in capital allocation did not mean that entrepreneurs no longer faced liquidity constraints. They often struggled to access capital, and bank-based financing was quite limited. A multilayered system of financing did begin to emerge over time, however, by which "firms progressed up the financial 'pecking order' as they matured."[1] If an entrepreneur could finance startup costs through accumulated savings or an informal financing network, then the venture could migrate to bank-based finance later in its lifecycle.

The initial stage of the institutionalization of US venture capital saw the range of investment entities for allocating funds into startup enterprises begin to expand within this pecking order. Figure 3.1 provides a simple overview of early-stage finance entities established in the 1940s and early 1950s. Although the boundaries between these entities were not always distinct, the taxonomy helps to illustrate the evolution toward the investing structure associated with the modern VC industry. Given the breadth and importance of the changes these entities brought, two chapters are devoted to their analysis. Chapter 4 examines corporations with public sales of stock, and highlights the particular significance of the American Research and Development Corporation, established in 1946. It also explores government efforts to supply venture capital to

Figure 3.1 A Basic Taxonomy of Early-Stage Investing Entities.

small businesses through investment companies established under the Small Business Investment Act of 1958. The focus of this chapter is on the informal provision of venture finance through individual investors and the roles of three organizational forms: family offices, private partnerships, and corporations with restricted sales of stock.

Individual investors were the equivalents of today's "angel" and "super angel" investors, a group considered distinct from VC. Angel investors tend to use their own money for early-stage investing rather than intermediating capital supplied by limited partners. Super angels typically go beyond investing their own capital and also pool capital from members of their networks. In the mid-twentieth century, this same kind of financing took place on a highly localized and often syndicated basis. Failure in a prior venture did not preclude access to capital, and financing was regularly tied to governance in the form of mentoring and managerial assistance.

More formalized organizational structures started to emerge as a consequence of family office formation, akin to the structures that modern billionaires use to manage their wealth. The scale of wealth accumulation associated with US economic growth from the late nineteenth century onward, and the desire for intergenerational planning, often called for a formalized and disciplined structure. While family offices tended to manage capital conservatively, some made investments that contributed to the development of new high-tech industries. Furthermore, modern venture capital firms can be directly traced to the lineage of wealthy families. Venrock (of which more will be said in Chapter 5) was founded in 1969 by Laurance Rockefeller, the grandchild of oil magnate J. D. Rockefeller. Another prominent modern example is the VC firm Bessemer Venture Partners. Founded in 1981, it was spun off from a family office created by steel magnate Henry Phipps, who generated enormous wealth through his association with the industrial titan Andrew Carnegie.

Corporations and partnerships were also influential in the period just after the Second World War in deploying risk capital across a wide range of nascent enterprises and industries. Notably, J. H. Whitney & Company, founded in 1946 by a scion of multiple wealthy families, is closely linked with the beginnings of American venture capital. These private-capital entities have much in common with modern venture capital firms, including their emphasis on due diligence in investment selection, governance of portfolio companies, and aim to generate substantial payoffs from long-tail investment portfolios. Collectively these early-stage investing entities constitute a key step in the rise of the US venture capital industry.

The Informal Market: Financing High-Tech Startups

Throughout the history of American entrepreneurship, founders of new firms have sought capital from informal sources. Chapter 2 documented the significance of this risk-capital channel during the early phases of industrialization in places like New England and the areas around Cleveland

and Pittsburgh during the Second Industrial Revolution. While it is difficult to assess the quantitative magnitude of this channel, an exposition of anecdotal evidence shows how critically important it was in the evolution of several US high-technology enterprises.

Some of America's leading entrepreneurs and technologists owed their start to wealthy individuals providing finance for investment and expansion. George Eastman, the transformational photo industry pioneer, was twenty-six years old in 1881 when he left his job as a clerk at the Rochester Savings Bank, where he was earning around $1,500 per year ($36,000 today). A practical tinkerer and hobbyist with an interest in photography, he had devised a way to produce photographs superior to the traditional wet-plate photography method. To develop his innovation, he formed a partnership with Henry Strong from Rochester, New York, who had made his fortune, in the days of horse-drawn carriages, manufacturing buggy whips. Strong committed to an initial investment of $1,000 to be followed by an additional $5,000.[2] A few years later, when their Eastman Dry Plate Company was incorporated as a joint stock concern with $200,000 in capital at $100 par value per share, Strong received 750 shares in the new concern, to reflect the capital he provided to start the original enterprise, and Eastman received 650 shares.[3] This company was a precursor to the Eastman Kodak company whose revolutionary low-cost camera, priced at $25 in 1888, kick-started the amateur picture-taking industry.[4] Although later in the life cycle of the business Eastman exercised a greater degree of ownership and control than did Strong, it is clear that Strong's capital was an essential factor in Eastman's experimentation and commercialization efforts.

Henry Ford also owed his start as an automobile manufacturer to wealthy individuals, and American society benefited immensely from his ingenuity in production-line innovation. Around the turn of the twentieth century, the car industry was a crowded space with about five hundred startups in the Detroit area alone. Ford's first enterprise, the Detroit Automobile Company, was financed by the efforts of William Murphy, "a wealthy Detroit businessman who acted as a proto-venture capitalist" arranging startup finance.[5] Prior to the foundation of this business, Ford had been a salaried chief engineer at the Edison Illuminating Company in Detroit, so he was not in a position to invest on his own account. Instead, he took a minority share in the Detroit Automobile Company in return for his sweat equity and design blueprints. As the majority shareholders demanded control, however, and instigated close supervision of him, Ford soon balked and the company was dissolved in 1901. His next venture, the Henry Ford Company, was established the same year. Ford received a 17 percent equity interest, but again reacted negatively to being monitored by his shareholders. Ford agreed to leave the firm (or was fired) with a $1,000 payoff for his equity interest ($29,000 today). In 1902, the company was reorganized and renamed the Cadillac Automobile Company.[6]

Despite these failures, both involving contentious interactions with investors, Ford does not appear to have suffered much in terms of the market's expectations of his abilities. In 1903, Alexander Malcomson, one of Detroit's wealthiest and best-connected coal merchants, approached Ford to start a new business. Malcomson devised the business plan and the two agreed they would build an automobile prototype, then seek investors and incorporate. After outsourcing the manufacturing of the prototype (which became the Model A) to entities such as the Dodge Brothers of Detroit, who received equity participation in place of fees, Malcomson became "Ford's new venture capitalist," arranging finance from local investors.[7]

The Ford Motor Company (FMC) was established in 1903 with authorized capital of $100,000 and paid-in capital of $28,000. Ford and Malcomson each held 25.5 percent of the equity, but Malcomson retained de facto control through his affinity with the other shareholders. Malcomson also "professionalized" the firm by recruiting individuals such as John Gray, his uncle and a respected financier, as president of the company, and James Couzens, with whom he had a long-standing working relationship, who ran much of the business. Furthermore, both Gray and Couzens were stakeholders. Gray invested $10,500 for 105 shares and Couzens invested $2,500 for 25 shares. Although the new company was profitable within a year, the relationship between Ford and Malcomson soon deteriorated. In 1906, Malcomson sold his shares for $175,000 to Ford. The latter, continuing to consolidate his position, owned 59 percent of the equity in FMC by 1908.[8] That year, the Model T was launched and the firm's capital was increased to $2 million. In 1913, Ford introduced assembly-line manufacturing, allowing the price of the Model T to drop substantially—from $950 in 1908 to $269 in 1923.[9] As an indication of the returns possible from early-stage, long-tail financial investment, in 1919 Couzens sold his 11 percent equity interest in FMC for a staggering $29.3 million, or approximately $406 million today.[10]

George Eastman's Rochester, New York, and Henry Ford's Detroit, Michigan, became well-established centers in the manufacturing belt by the late nineteenth and early twentieth centuries, just as Cleveland and Pittsburgh had by the 1870s. Informal investing relationships also existed elsewhere—for example, in the rapidly developing parts of the west coast region. In 1860, ten years after California was admitted to the union, San Francisco had had a population of only fifty thousand people, but by 1900 its population of 342,782 made it the ninth largest city in the United States. Opportunities for new firm foundation went hand in hand with rapid urbanization, and increased market access came with the diffusion of railroads. Meanwhile, the proliferation of education did much to develop the nation's human capital. In 1891, Senator Leland Stanford, one of the "big four" who (with Mark Hopkins, Collis Huntington, and Charles Crocker) built the Central Pacific Railroad as the eastern section of the transcontinental railroad, gifted eight thousand acres of his Palo Alto, California, stock farm to establish Stanford University. His vision was to produce "useful" and "cultured" graduates with intellectual but practical mindsets, thus contributing to an environment favorable to invention and entrepreneurship.[11]

Important enterprises in this geographic area developed through interactions among wealthy angel investors, educators, and entrepreneurs. In 1909, Cyril Elwell, a recent Stanford graduate in electrical engineering who had been working on telegraph systems, founded the Poulsen Wireless Telephone and Telegraph Company with private capital from a group including three Stanford leaders: President David Jordan (who contributed $500), Civil Engineering Department Chairman Charles D. Marx, and John Casper Branner, Professor and Chair of the Department of Geology and father of a local ham-radio enthusiast. The firm's name came from the inventor of its core technology. In 1902, Danish engineer Valdemar Poulsen had invented an arc converter to generate continuous-wave radio signals, which dramatically improved on the prevailing Marconi spark system because it enabled voice rather than just Morse code transmission. Elwell travelled to Denmark and arranged for a license to use the technology, for which he agreed to pay $450,000 ($13 million today). Soon, the company reorganized into a holding company and an operating arm—the Poulsen Wireless Company and the Federal Telegraph Company, respectively. With a serendipitous boost from government contracts—thanks to the US Navy's strong belief in the benefits of wireless transmission—and with its financial backing from a group of San

Francisco investors, the Federal Telegraph Company built a network of stations to support the new technology.[12]

The financing of this entrepreneurial venture was significant for a few reasons. The Federal Telegraph Company became an archetypal firm in much the same way that the Brush Electric Company (discussed in Chapter 2) did in 1880s and 1890s Cleveland, or that Fairchild Semiconductor (discussed in Chapter 6) would half a century later in Silicon Valley. It attracted talent; led to spinoffs, including Magnavox (consumer electronics), Fisher Research Laboratories (metal detectors), and Litton Industries (defense contracting); and created productively linked finance, technology, and entrepreneurship. The great inventor Lee De Forest, whose invention of the triode vacuum tube for amplifying electrical signals was described as "the most important single step in the whole development of radio communication," worked from 1911 to 1913 as a director in the Federal Telegraph Company's research lab.[13] The much-celebrated Stanford University academic and administrator Frederick Terman interned at the Federal Telegraph Company during his youth. He would later become a pivotal figure at Stanford, known for building links between the university's scholars and people in industry, and encouraging technology transfer and financial intermediation between the two groups.[14]

The story of the Federal Telegraph Company reflects the triumph of localized west coast risk capital and its networks of early- and later-stage investors. Elwell had initially sought funding from Wall Street financiers to commercialize Poulsen's invention, and was turned down. Indeed, it was a lucky break that the inventor, Poulsen, agreed to accept staggered payments for the rights he granted Elwell. Later, in 1910, a Stanford alumnus and local investor named Beach Thompson acquired Elwell's interest in the firm and replaced him as company president, moving Elwell to the position of chief engineer. Thompson brought the company under the financial management of William H. Crocker, a well-respected San Francisco financier and son of Charles Crocker (one of the aforementioned "big four" railroad entrepreneurs). Although he maintained a wide portfolio of investments, from real estate to oil, Crocker has been described as "Silicon Valley's first true venture capitalist" because of his involvement in financing the Federal Telegraph Company and other high-tech startups.[15]

During the 1920s, William H. Crocker and his own son, William W. Crocker, would also provide venture finance and governance to Philo

Farnsworth, the "forgotten father of television" who developed a system for the electronic transmission of images.[16] At nineteen years of age, while working for a philanthropic organization in Utah, Farnsworth connected with two California-based consultants, George Everson and Leslie Gorrell, who provided seed capital of $6,000 under an equal partnership structure to develop the idea. They also introduced Farnsworth to Crocker and his associates, and he relocated to San Francisco in 1926, after spending a little time in Los Angeles with Everson and Gorrell drawing on expertise at the California Institute of Technology. In return for capital of $25,000 ($340,000 today) the San Francisco investors received 60 percent of the equity in the partnership.[17]

Using practices similar to Andrew Mellon's, discussed in Chapter 2, Farnsworth's backers tied capital to governance in an effort to discipline the process of research and development and the commercialization of innovation. They provided capital for a research laboratory, set a deadline of a year for completion of a prototype, and arranged for a patent attorney in San Francisco to secure intellectual property rights on the invention. Two years later, on September 3, 1928, the *San Francisco Chronicle* reported: "The inventor is Philo T. Farnsworth and local capitalists headed by William W. Crocker and Roy N. Bishop [an engineer] are financing the experiments and have aided him in obtaining basic patents." Development and patent expenses amounted to $139,759 between 1926 and March 1929, about $2 million today.[18]

By the early 1930s, Farnsworth was prepared for commercialization and his investors were ready to exit from the investment. While the investors wanted a complete buyout, they ultimately maintained an interest in a contractual arrangement with Philco, a major Philadelphia-based manufacturer of radio sets. Philco was eager to diversify into television. In return for a nonexclusive right to develop Farnsworth's patented inventions, Philco provided working capital and laboratory space. The early insistence by William W. Crocker and his associates on obtaining patents turned out to be critical, given the acrimonious lawsuits that soon developed between Farnsworth and RCA, the owner of Vladimir Zworky's patents for a similar television technology. The two sides' infringement claims were finally resolved in 1939 when Farnsworth agreed to license his patented technology to RCA. Farnsworth was among the greatest inventors of his generation, but turning his ingenious ideas into commercial realities depended on access to startup capital and on governance. In the hierarchy of twentieth-century inventions, the television stands out for its profound effect on consumers and the diffusion of information.[19]

Admittedly these are extreme stories, yet general insights can still be gained from them. First, the investors who allocated capital to these early-stage high-tech ventures had to accept a risk-return tradeoff that meant mediocre returns, or large losses, were more likely than the substantial payoffs they sought. Couzens's investment in Ford yielded an extraordinary nominal compound annual return of 79.8 percent, excluding dividends. Yet, his overall investment portfolio also reflected the long-tail distribution of payoffs associated with the many early automobile enterprises in Detroit. Their failure rate stood at about 60 percent.[20] Couzens would later recall how, as Ford's business manager, he had struggled to raise investment for the Ford Motor Company in 1903 Detroit— to the point that one day on the street he sat down on a curb and burst into tears.[21] Despite the immense social value created by the invention of television, neither Farnsworth nor his San Francisco investors generated much of a private return.[22]

Second, the investing relationships epitomized by these examples of breakthrough innovation featured efforts to provide robust incentives to founders. Eastman, Ford, Elwell, and Farnsworth invested little, or none, of their own capital due to financial constraints, but given the importance of their technological knowledge, each held an equity share. There was a clear division of labor between inventors and investors in terms of who developed the technology and who controlled operational expertise, and it was the same as the division between Samuel Slater and the Brown family in Chapter 2. Thus, the relationships addressed some of the "real world" incentive problems faced by modern-day VC contracting. Entrepreneurs took equity in return for their noncash contributions, with the expectation of realizing sizable long-term payoffs.

Third, investors were closely connected to entrepreneurs geographically, which facilitated syndication (in that multiple investors were frequently involved) and post-investment monitoring. Venture capitalists syndicate to diversify risk and leverage expertise across networks. Although Eastman relied only on Strong for backing at the startup stage, Ford accessed finance from multiple capital providers in Detroit, and Elwell and Farnsworth were financed by a group of west coast investors. Physical proximity made monitoring much easier. Strong, as a local investor, became a professional manager in Eastman Kodak; Ford was monitored extensively early on; Elwell's firm was located in the Bay Area, close to investors and advisors connected to Stanford University; and Farnsworth was pulled out of Utah to settle into San Francisco laboratory space, where his investors could observe his progress and assert influence. While information about potential entrepreneurial opportunities tends to be localized in nature, the venture capital literature underscores that geographic proximity between investors and entrepreneurs is also strategic, because it facilitates monitoring and professionalizing new ventures.[23] Overall, these historical examples of new firm foundation show the deft use by investors of a variety of control mechanisms to manage risk and govern their investments. This was not formal venture capital, but it was highly analogous.

Family Wealth and Family Offices

The demand for formal structures to manage capital increased as firm founders and financiers generated increasingly sizable payoffs. The pace of wealth accumulation at the top of American society was staggeringly fast as entrepreneurs exploited large and growing markets. By the late 1920s, the top 1 percent of families in the United States earned almost a quarter of national income and held over half of national wealth.[24] It is true that "many of the super-rich spent lavishly on consumption and philanthropy and thus dissipated much of their fortune before death."[25] Wealthy families also started to establish investment vehicles, however, for the purposes of long-term asset management and securing intergenerational transfers. As Chapter 2 notes, the Mellon family had done this successfully since the beginning. The aforementioned Crocker family offers another example; it managed a bank which became the Crocker National Bank and First National Bank of San Francisco in 1906, and also maintained a series of separate investment companies.

The Phipps family was also an early mover in this regard. Henry Phipps generated considerable wealth in the steel industry through his connection with Andrew Carnegie. The two became partners, with several others, in a mid-nineteenth-century iron foundry venture in Pittsburgh which was an early adopter of the Bessemer process—Carnegie having negotiated licensing rights from the English inventor, Henry Bessemer. The Bessemer process involved blowing air through molten pig iron to remove impurities. Because this could be done at scale, it offered greater efficiency than the traditional use of puddling furnaces. The prominent Edgar Thomson Steel Works plant that Carnegie and his partners built in Braddock, Pennsylvania, began producing Bessemer steel in 1875. Many other plants soon followed. In 1886, Carnegie, Phipps & Company was formed as an organizing entity, and its interests were folded into the Carnegie Steel Company in 1892.

In an era when steel became common in railroad construction, framing buildings, and more, the Carnegie Steel Company generated substantial returns. By 1900, its profits stood at $40 million annually ($1.2 billion today). J. P. Morgan believed that, to avoid ruinous competition, the steel industry would have to consolidate, and to that end he acquired the Carnegie Steel Company at Carnegie's asking price of $480 million. The transaction involved merging it in 1901 with several other enterprises to create the United States Steel Corporation—the first company to have a capitalization in excess of a billion dollars ($1.4 billion, to be precise). Carnegie's share was about $225 million, while Phipps received shares and bonds worth more than $67 million, or approximately $1.5 billion today.[26]

Carnegie and Phipps held opposite views on the disposition of wealth. Carnegie's viewpoint was outlined in *The Gospel of Wealth,* an essay he wrote in 1889. In short, he favored philanthropy. Phipps was also a philanthropist, but chose to consolidate most of his assets into the Bessemer Investment Company, which held around $17.5 million in real estate and stocks and around $23 million in bonds. The organization of his wealth and the pathway leading to venture capital is illustrated in Figure 3.2.

In 1907, Phipps organized Bessemer Trust Company to administer trusts for his five children. In 1911, he wrote letters to them noting that each would receive $2 million in bonds and $2 million in stock (totaling $104 million today), which they should invest in "a prudent and conservative" way.[27] Bessemer Securities Corporation became the primary institution where Phipps' family capital was located and invested. Within his lifetime, Phipps made inter vivos transfers of $45 million to his children and $28 million to his wife, whose capital also ultimately went to the children. By the time of his death in 1930, Phipps himself held only around $3 million in assets ($43 million today).[28]

Over the course of the twentieth century, Bessemer Securities invested conservatively in staple American companies such as International Paper Company, Ingersoll Rand Corporation, and W. R. Grace & Company, but

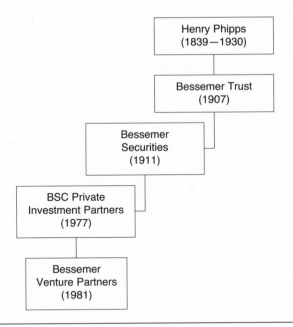

Figure 3.2 The Evolution of a Modern Venture Capital Partnership from a Family Office.

it also diversified into riskier areas including real-estate operations and shipping ventures. By the 1960s, it was committing over $6 million per year to a venture finance practice managed within Bessemer Securities. This arm was formalized in 1977 as BSC Private Investment Partners; later, in 1981, Bessemer Venture Partners was formed with limited partner support from its parent organization. From 1967 through the 1980s, Bessemer Securities averaged a 17 percent annual return on its private investments, substantially outperforming the S&P Composite, which experienced an annualized return, including dividends, of 11 percent over the same time period.[29]

A number of other families with great accumulated wealth created similar means for engaging in risk capital investing, many having migrated toward venture capital even earlier than the Phipps family. Like the Mellons and the Crockers, the Vanderbilt family played a role. William A. M. Burden was the great-grandson of Commodore Cornelius Vanderbilt, who made his fortune as a shipping and railroad entrepreneur. In 1949, he established the limited partnership of William A. M.

Burden & Company in New York, setting up the family's "venture capital investments" to be handled by Burden's Investors Services, Inc.[30] In 1946, *Businessweek* reported on a "new trend in managing hereditary fortunes" whereby wealth was being shifted from family holding company structures (used for tax purposes) to private capital entities.[31] These entities, though few in number, would have a large effect on the recycling of capital over generations and on the formation of the American venture capital industry.

The Role of Laurance Rockefeller

The Rockefeller family was especially influential in this regard. John D. Rockefeller's path to wealth is widely recognized, so a brief sketch should suffice. To be in Cleveland, where Rockefeller had moved with his family as a teenager, was fortuitous in the late nineteenth century, as its access to the Great Lakes and to railroads made it a transfer hub for heavy industry. As a base for many of the new industries of the Second Industrial Revolution, it was also a key center for entrepreneurship and venture finance.

John D. Rockefeller was just twenty-three years old when, in 1863, he formed the partnership of Andrews, Clark & Company to participate in the newly emerging oil-refining industry. By 1865 he had acquired Clark's share for $72,000. In 1867, Stephen Harkness, a wealthy Cleveland investor, contributed $100,000 ($1.7 million today) for a share of the equity on the condition that Henry Flagler, a relative of his, must be made a partner and professional manager to monitor the investment. In 1869, various Rockefeller partnerships were combined, and 1870 brought the formation of the corporation Standard Oil. Rockefeller proceeded relentlessly to monopolize the business of refining the crude production from oil fields in Pennsylvania and West Virginia. By 1872, Standard Oil controlled over 25 percent of total US daily refining capacity. Just six years later, it controlled over 90 percent. By integrating such disparate activities as transport, production, exploitation, wholesale, and retail under one structure, Rockefeller was able to dominate the industry.[32]

The upshot of Rockefeller's activities was significant wealth accumulation. His estimated $1.4 billion net worth in 1937 ($23.5 billion today) was equivalent to an astonishing 1.5 percent of US GDP. In 1882, Rockefeller established a family office to organize his wealth. His investment holdings included a number of later-stage enterprises which he attempted to consolidate, such as American Linseed Oil Company, of which his son, John D. Rockefeller, Jr., was a director. Rockefeller was also actively engaged in philanthropy, distributing several hundred million dollars over his lifetime to institutions from the University of Chicago to the Rockefeller Sanitary Commission for the Eradication of Hookworm Disease—which succeeded dramatically in containing what had been a pervasive public health problem in the South.[33]

The connection to venture capital came through one of Rockefeller's grandchildren, Laurance Rockefeller, the son of Rockefeller, Jr. While his siblings tended to focus principally on links with philanthropy or established businesses, Laurance chose to invest in early-stage high-tech ventures, as well. He invested on his own account and through entities that evolved from the original Rockefeller family office. As an avid science and technology enthusiast, Laurance was keen to address the financing constraints of startups. He once stated about his investment philosophy: "what we want to do is the opposite of the old system of holding back capital until a field or an idea is proved completely safe. We are undertaking pioneering projects that with proper backing will encourage sound scientific and economic progress in new fields—fields that hold the promise of tremendous future development."[34]

In this spirit, Laurance helped to transform the early development of the aviation industry. Following the Wright Brothers' influential involvement in making manned flight possible through technological development in the early 1900s, the aviation industry became a fertile area for startups by the 1920s. For example, National Air Transport (which became part of United Air Lines) was founded in 1925, with $10 million in venture finance, as a New York-to-Chicago express mail service. Colonial Air Transport was established in 1926 by a group of individual venture investors to transfer mail among New York, Hartford, and Boston. Just as automobile manufacturers had proliferated in Henry Ford's early days in Detroit, by 1929 there were 286 aircraft manufacturers in the United States.[35]

Laurance made a range of aviation investments. His connection to Eddie Rickenbacker, a flamboyant First World War fighter pilot, has been documented extensively.[36] In 1938, he invested in Rickenbacker's attempt to turn around Eastern Air Lines, which had been founded in 1926 as an airmail carrier between New York and Atlanta. By the time of Laurance's investment, it was a struggling passenger-airline subsidiary of General

Motors. As well as directly providing capital and advice, Laurance's involvement facilitated much wider access to capital than would otherwise have been the case. Rickenbacker was able to raise $3.5 million ($60 million today) for the buyout, allowing Eastern to reach profitability and grow into one of America's largest airlines.[37] By the 1950s, Laurance held about a 3 percent interest in the company.

Strictly speaking, Laurance's investment in Eastern Air Lines was closer to what is today called a later-stage private equity transaction. More in the startup-funding vein, Laurance invested in 1939 in the McDonnell Aircraft Corporation that James McDonnell, Jr. founded near St. Louis, Missouri. Although McDonnell had failed in a prior venture in 1929, reportedly it took only a short pitch meeting for him to persuade Laurance to advance the capital. Impressed with McDonnell's plan to build an advanced fighter aircraft and with his opinions on jet propulsion, Laurance supplied $10,000 of the founding capital, adding to McDonnell's investment of $30,000 of his own savings, and the $125,000 raised from St. Louis financiers (for a total of $165,000 or $2.9 million today).[38] Although the planned aircraft was never produced, McDonnell Aircraft went on to become a major contractor to the Pentagon during the Second World War. In 1943, McDonnell was awarded a contract by the US Navy to develop the first jet-engine plane for an aircraft carrier. In 1967, the company merged with the Douglas Aircraft Company to solidify its position as a leading defense supplier and aviation manufacturer.

During the Second World War, Laurance became counsel on matters of aviation to Assistant Secretary of the Navy James Forrestal, and after the cessation of hostilities he continued investing in this sector. In 1946, he syndicated with Felix du Pont, Jr. and Douglas Dillon to invest $500,000 ($6.1 million today) for a share of the equity in the Piasecki Helicopter Corporation founded by engineer and pilot Frank Piasecki. Additional investments included Reaction Motors, Inc., a pioneer in the nascent field of liquid propellant engines, which led to a successful payoff in 1958 when the firm was acquired by Thiokol Chemical Corporation. Laurance's 1950 aviation investment in Marquardt Aircraft Corporation, a formative ramjet propulsion enterprise, yielded a more mediocre return.

Although he focused on long-tail investing, and the payoffs from these investments were generally favorable, Laurance's primary objective was not financial return. In 1959, the magazine *Time* described Laurance as a "space-age risk capitalist" because, by easing the financing constraints for startups and later-stage companies, he was extending the frontier of technological development.[39] By virtue of his public standing as a member of the exceptionally wealthy Rockefeller family, Laurance viewed his contribution to society as paramount.

Laurance's investment style revolved around a belief in the disciplinary function of venture finance and the principle of good governance. Sometimes his commitments were staged, consistent with the idea that staging helps to mitigate problems associated with information asymmetries. For example, by 1941, he had upped his stake in McDonnell to $475,000 for 20 percent of the equity.[40] In several instances, Laurance replaced founder-CEOs with professional managers, a common control tactic in modern VC-backed ventures. He became a director of Eastern Air Lines in 1938 and replaced Rickenbacker in 1963 when the company began to falter under his stewardship. From the beginning of his investment in the Piasecki Helicopter Corporation, he recognized the inventive genius of Frank Piasecki but also noted Piasecki's lack of business acumen. Consequently, Piasecki was moved away from managerial operations.

But perhaps the most distinguishing characteristic of Laurance's approach to venture finance was that his post–Second World War investments proceeded in a much more structured way than was typical in the informal market for venture capital covered earlier in this chapter. Laurance evolved from an individual investor at the time of the Eastern Air Lines and McDonnell investments to deploy capital in a systematized manner—much as some wealthy entrepreneur investors do today. Peter Thiel, for example, invests through a range of complex vehicles, including Thiel Capital, a private investment office he founded in San Francisco in 2011.

In 1946, Laurance and his siblings established a private-capital arm of the family office called Rockefeller Brothers, Inc., to pool their capital with a focus on venture investments. The small group they assembled at the RCA building in New York (30 Rockefeller Plaza) to screen business plans and undertake due diligence included a specialist in finance from Chase Manhattan (which, having been acquired by John D. Rockefeller, Jr. in 1930, was fast becoming the largest bank lender to the aircraft industry), a procurement expert in wartime technology, and a Massachusetts Institute of Technology engineer with expertise in aeronautics.

Within a few weeks of this new investing entity's announcement that it was open to the submission of business plans, four hundred had been received. By 1951, Rockefeller Brothers had invested approximately $5 million ($46 million today) and held a portfolio of about twenty-five companies. Although this represented risk-capital deployment on a small scale by the standards of modern VC limited partnerships, the investment method was similar in its sophistication. In 1947, Laurance wrote down an "aviation investment policy" to codify its approach.[41] Its aviation investments would generally be confined to projects meeting certain criteria:

- Capacity for continued growth if successfully developed.
- An existing or going concern or business which does not require the formation of a new business entity and whose aggregate requirements for new capital investment are not less than $300,000.
- A competent management group; preferably one that has demonstrated its competence through actual management of the particular business concerned; in any event no investment commitment should be made until adequate management is assured and any new personnel required have been selected.
- Aircraft manufacturing enterprises should have reasonable prospects for government contracts, particularly in research and development work.

Each of these bulleted items is revealing about the investment strategy. First, Laurance's objective was to address a new and growing market: aviation. The modern literature on entrepreneurial business plans suggests acquiring a share of a growing market is typically more favorable than competing with an incumbent in a more mature market space.[42] Second, it is interesting to note from that Laurance targeted firms that already had some kind of track record—ideas that did "not require the formation of a new business entity." He was avoiding the seed-stage investments that present highest risk. Third, by stipulating the need for a "competent management group," he acknowledged that "people problems" are a significant source of performance defects in new ventures. Finally, context was all-important. By specifying that R&D plans should consider government contracting, he was addressing the big picture of what to sell and to whom.

In practice, Laurance came close to defining modern VC. Consider, for example, a 1957 investment in Itek Corporation, an innovator in satellite camera reconnaissance. Itek famously produced cameras for the U-2 spy plane used during the Cold War. Its founder, Richard Leghorn, at the time an executive in Eastman Kodak's European division, initially asked Laurance for $2 million in startup funds ($71.1 million today) to develop an information processing company, in exchange for 49 percent of the equity. Leghorn projected that Itek would capture a 30 percent share of a billion-dollar industry.

Laurance offered to contract with Leghorn for about one-third of the requested $2 million, believing a sufficient amount of progress could be achieved with a more modest amount of startup capital. Moreover, he conditioned his offer on staged financing. He proposed a first stage of financing totaling $100,000 in stocks, bonds, and warrants, to be followed six months later by a second stage of $550,000 split roughly equally between stock and convertible bonds. To manage his downside risk, Laurance could also exit the investment without a loss prior to the completion of the second stage. At that point, the agreement stated, Leghorn had the option to buy Laurance out of the investment at the original cost. Leghorn agreed to these terms subject to some minor contractual adjustments.[43]

Laurance's staff at 30 Rockefeller Plaza monitored the investment closely, writing regular reports as updates. Furthermore, Laurance frequently traveled to Itek's facilities on his private plane. Between 1958 and 1959, Itek reported a more than sevenfold increase in revenues, from $3.5 million to over $25 million ($206 million today). Between 1957 and 1973, Laurance invested a total of $3 million in Itek. On exit, the total value of his investment was almost $14 million, making for an investment multiple of 3.6.[44] As a contemporaneous benchmark, the S&P Composite would have returned a multiple of 2.1.

Despite the success of some individual investments, however, especially in aviation, Laurance's total investment portfolio did not generate VC-style returns. Between 1938 and 1969 he made fifty-nine investments. Around 44 percent of his investments failed to produce positive returns, and those investments accounted for over a quarter of the total amount invested. Only 7 percent of investments produced a realized sale-value multiple of more than ten times the investment cost and these rare "hits" did not fully compensate for the loss-makers.

Overall, Laurance's portfolio returned an investment multiple of 3.2, but the stock market returned a multiple of 8.6 over the same time period. Furthermore, given that the timing of the investments and distributions can be observed, it is possible to conduct a more refined "public market equivalent" (PME) analysis which involves estimating how well the portfolio would have done in the counterfactual circumstance that the investments had been made in public equities.[45] Laurance's portfolio generated a PME or "market-adjusted multiple" of 0.86, indicating a return that was only 86 percent of what a hypothetical investment in the stock market index would have achieved. While he had done much to formalize VC-style investing, Laurance had also highlighted the fortitude required for long-tail distributions of returns. He aptly remarked: "Venture capital endeavors are not for the impatient, the faint of heart, [or] the poor loser. Nor are they for widows and orphans or people who cannot afford to lose."[46]

Investment Corporations and Partnerships

The efforts of Laurance Rockefeller to deploy risk capital into entrepreneurial ventures should be seen in the context of a broader set of private capital entities developing in the United States in the aftermath of the Second World War, especially in the east and west coast regions. In a 1951 survey of this emerging sector in the *Journal of Finance*, two finance Professors, Carl Dauten and Merle Welshans, remarked on "the recent appearance of a new form of financial organization" which they described as "privately established profit-seeking organizations whose primary function is that of providing venture capital not otherwise available to new and growing business ventures."[47] They describe these entities as "investment development companies." Table 3.1 lists the entities active in this sector, based on that study and related sources.

Most of these entities operated on a small-scale basis. Between 1945 and 1954, only about a dozen venture capital companies were established. Even by the mid-1960s there were only about ten VC firms "of real consequence," typically holding five to ten firms in their portfolio.[48] To put this into perspective, 225 venture capital partnerships were formed in 1979 when the industry was still at a nascent stage of development, and by 1989 that number had risen to 674.[49] In 2000, a peak year, 861 VC firms existed. Moreover, the size of the capital deployed by the early private capital entities was small relative to modern standards. Laurance

TABLE 3-1

Some of the Main Private Capital Entities Established after the Second World War

Name	Established	Location	Size of Original Capital	Structure
American Research and Development Corporation	1946	Boston	$5 million	Corporation—Public Securities
J. H. Whitney & Company	1946	New York	$10 million	Limited Partnership
Rockefeller Brothers, Inc.	1946	New York	$5 million	Limited Partnership
New Enterprises, Inc.	1946	Boston	$300,000	Corporation—Restricted Securities
T. Mellon & Sons	1946	Pittsburgh	—	Association
Industrial Capital Corporation	1946	San Francisco	$2 million	Corporation—Restricted Securities
Pacific Coast Enterprises Corporation	1946	San Francisco	$1 million	Corporation—Restricted Securities
Payson and Trask	1947	New York	$5 million	Limited Partnership
Henry Sears & Company	1949	New York	—	Partnership
William A. M. Burden & Company	1949	New York	—	Limited Partnership
"Fox, Wells and Company"	1951	New York	—	Partnership

Compiled from information in Carl A. Dauten and Merle T. Welshans, "Investment Development Companies," *Journal of Finance* 6, no. 3 (1951): 276–290; Martin Kenney and Richard Florida, "Venture Capital in Silicon Valley: Fueling New Firm Formation," in *Understanding Silicon Valley: The Anatomy of an Entrepreneurial Region*, ed. Martin Kenney (Stanford, CA: Stanford University Press, 2000), 104–105; and "Capital That Takes a Chance," *Business Week*, no. 1134, April 14, 1951.

Rockefeller's investment by the late 1960s of a total of $21.6 million (about $180 million today) in fifty-nine companies would, in the modern era, be equivalent to a fund of below-average size.[50] The VC industry was minuscule relative to the size of the corporate debt and equity market.[51]

Many of the private capital entities in Table 3.1 were concentrated in the east and west coast areas, a geographic pattern in the provision of venture finance that persists to the present. One explanation for this spatial concentration would be that finance develops where the supply of new venture opportunities is available and vice versa. Equally, since venture financing was frequently tied to the governance of portfolio companies, the east-west coast bifurcation may have reflected the constraint of traveling distance to portfolio companies. While Laurance Rockefeller had the means to traverse the country using a private plane, his circumstances were unique. A flight between New York and San Francisco in the mid-1940s took eleven hours, and planes carried at most sixty passengers. Larger planes, such as the DC-7C, would not be used on this route until the late 1950s.[52]

The private capital entities adopted a mix of legal arrangements. Although the VC industry ended up being dominated by the limited partnership structure, early entities did not always take this organizational form. For example, T. Mellon & Sons adopted a hybrid approach. Its structure was considered an "association," or coordinating device for family members to think about investments, as opposed to a corporation or partnership. Several entities were organized as corporations with restricted sales of securities. These fell outside the regulatory scope of the Securities and Exchange Commission. With a small group of private investors as shareholders, they could adopt a flexible policy toward venture investments. Although the limited partnership structure had substantial advantages as a pass-through entity (with income from investments going untaxed at the entity level and passing through to the underlying investors), tax liability could also be managed under the corporate form. Specifically, investors would hold direct investments in portfolio companies rather than indirect holdings through the intermediary entity. This avoided the double taxation problem where the investor and the intermediary would be taxed on the same investment as separate legal entities.

Because of the variable organizational structures shown in Table 3.1, the notion of a venture capital "fund," with investors subject to management fees and profit-sharing rules, was not clearly defined. In modern venture capital limited partnerships, fund lives are typically projected to be between seven and ten years, but historically, investing horizons could be much shorter or longer. Some of the entities listed in Table 3.1, such as New Enterprises Inc., had revolving capital and no particular duration appears to have been specified. In the case of entities based on family wealth, such as Rockefeller Brothers, Inc., or William A. M. Burden & Company, pools of investment funds were more like permanent capital— quite unlike modern VC funds with their specified lifetimes. Historical information on fees and incentive payments is limited, but it appears outside investors did pay for intermediation. For example, New Enterprises, Inc., retained around 10 percent of its portfolio companies' equity to cover its management costs.[53]

Despite the variety of organizational forms of the entities shown in Table 3.1, Dauten and Welshans argue that, in terms of the underlying approach to venture finance, the "investment activities and general objectives are approximately the same."[54] From the text of their article, some main features of investing activity can be identified, as presented in the list below.

- Focus on a particular sector of investment, mostly in a "special field of interest"
- Extensive due diligence through "rigorous examination" of venture proposals, with a "very high percentage" of proposals rejected
- "Equity positions" in financed ventures (limited use of loan capital)
- Use of "bonds and preferred stocks" in financing
- Mostly minority ownership, involving "interests of 1 per cent to 50 per cent"
- Follow-on financing, with "continued financial assistance" available to the ventures financed until they can "secure needed funds from other sources"
- Syndication of investments, as "more than one" entity participated in the "financing of the same project"
- Governance through representation "on the board of directors of the new enterprise" and through "management counsel and guidance"

- "Mutual confidence and respect" between investors and
  founders as "an absolute requisite"

These aspects of investing equate to a strikingly modern and formal
approach to venture capital deployment. The points cover due diligence,
investment selection, preferred stock financing, minority ownership, syndication, and governance—all of which are textbook features of modern
VC. Finally, it is worth underscoring the list's final point, emphasizing
the mutually respectful interactions expected between founders and investors. This implies a holistic approach to venture capital as a method
of investing that is not only formalized but also relational.

J. H. Whitney & Company and Other East Coast and West Coast Entities

The approach to venture finance encapsulated by this list can be further
evidenced by a more detailed analysis of entities in Table 3.1. In particular, J. H. Whitney & Company is considered to be pivotal in the history
of the venture capital, not least because the entry of the term "venture
capital" into the modern vernacular has been ascribed to its founder,
John Hay Whitney.[55] By the time Whitney was founded in 1946, however, the term was already in widespread use. In 1938 the *Wall Street
Journal* noted "venture capital" being deployed by Lammot du Pont, head
of E. I. du Pont de Nemours and Company, as a form of "investment
without definite assurance." The term "venture capital" was used twenty-
four times in a 1940 Congressional report, *Investment Trusts and Investment Companies*. In his 1945 book *Small Business and Venture Capital*,
Rudolph L. Weissman of the Securities and Exchange Commission describes venture capital as an identifiable class of investment. Jules I. Bogen,
a finance professor at New York University, uses the term repeatedly in
his 1946 book *The Market for Risk Capital*.

John Hay Whitney's pathway into venture finance was quite similar
to that of Laurance Rockefeller. His father, William Payne Whitney, was
born into a distinguished and wealthy family which had built up a fortune
in a wide range of heavy industries including oil, railroads, and mining.
By his death in 1927, William Payne Whitney held over $50 million in
tobacco company stocks and had a net worth in the region of $200 million
($2.7 billion today). By inheriting most of it, John Hay Whitney became
one of America's wealthiest men. Like Laurance, he started off as an

individual investor before formalizing an investment entity. In 1932, he and his cousin, Cornelius Vanderbilt Whitney, invested $180,000 to acquire a 15 percent equity interest in the Technicolor Corporation, helping to finance innovation and expansion in the emerging high-tech area of color films. In 1934, he helped to form Pioneer Pictures, which contracted with Technicolor to produce motion pictures in Hollywood.

Whitney was established with six partners after John Hay Whitney provided the $10 million in investment capital ($123 million today). Its first investment, in the Kansas-based fertilizer producer Spencer Chemical Company, was highly successful. This investment involved $1.25 million in preferred stock and $250,000 for 33 percent of the common stock. Within a year, the common stock investment had multiplied in value to over $10 million.[56] This represented an archetypal VC investment because a single portfolio company returned the entire value of the fund. Another early success involved an investment in the Minute Maid Corporation, the frozen orange juice producer originally known as the Florida Foods Corporation. It was founded by Richard Morse, a Massachusetts Institute of Technology and University of Munich physicist, under the umbrella of the 1940 National Research Corporation, a Cambridge, Massachusetts, incubator-type entity specializing in R&D and innovation. Between 1947 and 1949, several investments were made in Minute Maid's common and preferred stock totaling more than $1.5 million. A loan for $500,000 was also granted to the company in 1950. Minute Maid's investors enjoyed a successful exit when it was acquired by The Coca-Cola Company in 1960.[57]

As a private capital entity, Whitney did not need to disclose extensive details about its performance or methods of operation. A remarkable insight into Whitney can be gained, however, through testimony that one of its partners, Charles Wrede Petersmeyer, gave to a Congressional briefing session on the Small Business Investment Act of 1958.[58] Petersmeyer stated that by 1958 Whitney had thirteen partners whose expertise spanned business, law, finance, and academia, and twenty additional support staff to help with investment due diligence. Whitney's investment policy was succinctly stated by Petersmeyer. It invested in ventures that were "worthwhile and [had] a profit potential commensurate with their risk." It would deploy between $500,000 and $1 million into each investment for a sizable equity stake with an expectation of a multiple between three and five, realizable within five to ten years. Exits for investors were expected through mergers and acquisitions, or initial public offerings, with the proceeds recycled through Whitney so that additional investments could be made. Whitney did not invest in listed companies.

In what was surely one of the first references to the challenging economics of running a venture capital partnership, Petersmeyer emphasized the need for perpetual fundraising to generate "adequate capital" to make portfolio investments and to compensate a support staff to exercise due diligence on submitted proposals. He also emphasized problems stemming from illiquidity, given the timescale associated with a five-to-ten-year investing horizon, noting that "you are in a business where there is no substantial continuing income that you can rely on to support the operations of the firm." Petersmeyer was essentially advocating the collection of a management fee in intermediated investing to offset costs.

Reinforcing the idea that venture finance revolves around investment selection, Petersmeyer noted that between 1946 and 1958 over seven thousand proposals for investment had been screened. Just fifty of them (less than 1 percent) were financed. Investment decisions were made by the "pooled" judgments of partners. Whitney engaged in significant amounts of post-investment governance. In 1958, the thirteen partners held forty directorships in portfolio companies. Petersmeyer estimated that 95 percent of partner time was spent in interactions (often daily) with the management team. He reported that two Whitney partners once spent three months searching for a president for one of their portfolio companies. Whitney aimed to establish a bond of trust between investors and founders by being respectful toward existing management. Petersmeyer stated, however, that Whitney's equity interest enabled a "strong voice" in their portfolio companies "in order to effect changes if necessary."

As an indication of Whitney's investing focus, Petersmeyer noted that "we are not interested in propositions that are still in the experimental or inventive stage . . . we like to see and feel and touch the products intended to be marketed and on which the business is to be based." For Whitney this was a position adopted after some hard experience with earlier-stage investments. As another Whitney partner told *Businessweek* in June 1958, "the whole concept of venture capital has changed for us. We're no longer interested in the brand new company, but we're looking first for a growth industry and then picking a vehicle within that area."[59]

Although Whitney continued to survey early-stage investment opportunities, its primary focus changed to providing growth equity to later-stage businesses. In terms of target sectors, Whitney was quite broad. It held investments in frozen foods, electronics, oil and gas, nuclear, uranium, new tool products, and television broadcasting.

Petersmeyer made an astonishingly frank and revealing statement to the briefing session with respect to Whitney's overall investment performance. But while estimating that the original capital contributed by John Hay Whitney had almost quadrupled in value over the twelve years, he also put those gains in perspective: "I am quick to point out that if in 1946, when J. H. Whitney & Co. was started, one had taken the same capital and put it into a diversified portfolio of listed securities—even those that do not have unusual growth possibilities—that capital would have tripled. We have not batted much better than we would have if we had put the capital in listed securities, with far less trouble and far less risk." Petersmeyer's public equity benchmarking relates to the longstanding discussion in the literature of the extent to which intermediated early- and later-stage investments can outperform a passive investing strategy.[60]

From this benchmarking perspective, Whitney's early-stage investments were particularly troublesome. Of the thirty-eight investments Whitney made in this category (each under $500,000), Petersmeyer noted that 39 percent lost everything, 6 percent broke even, 11 percent had low-to-middling returns, and 34 percent were successful over a period of five to six years. Petersmeyer estimated the annualized return on this portfolio to be "something less than 2 percent a year." He also stated that even the return on the successful investments, at between 9 and 10 percent on an annualized basis, was not even sufficient to "cover the overhead of J. H. Whitney & Co."

Trying to explain why Whitney had persisted with its investment strategy when a passively managed portfolio of public equities may have been preferable, Petersmeyer acknowledged the role of serendipity and path dependency, as can also be observed in the VC industry today.[61] "Timing was on our side. If it had not been for one of these early successes," he said, referring to Spencer Chemical, "J. H. Whitney & Co. may not have been nearly so venturesome, nor able to make the later major investments." As Laurance Rockefeller had found, long-tail investing was alluring but hard to operationalize in practice.

Of the investments and methods of the remaining entities in Table 3.1, much less is known. Nevertheless, important insights can still be gained from the available evidence. One factor relating to the earlier discussion of the significance of family wealth is how networked the east coast entities were. For example, Payson & Trask was established with family money through John Hay Whitney's sister, Joan Whitney Payson. Henry Sears & Company was established by Henry Sears, who originated from a long line of east coast elites. It is no accident that most of the east coast entities were located in New York, where family wealth grew in strongly fused finance and social networks. As *Businessweek* reported in June 1958, wealthy families "out to chalk up capital gains" were "still the backbone of the risk capital business."

The direct or indirect connectedness of venture investing to family wealth at this time is striking. Spencer Chemical Company, one of Whitney's major investments, was acquired by Gulf Oil for $130 million in 1963 ($1 billion today). Gulf Oil, as noted in the last chapter, had been one of Andrew Mellon's major investments. Interrelationships promoted trust and syndication. Whitney and Payson & Trask co-invested on four occasions.[62] In another instance, Whitney joined Fox, Wells & Company in backing the development of cable television during the 1950s through an investment in Jerrold Electronics founded by Milton J. Shapp. Whitney took 50 percent of the equity, Fox Wells 10 percent, and Jerrold the remaining 40 percent. Like Whitney, Fox Wells selected from a large pool of investment opportunities. One of its founders estimated that about two percent of proposals submitted were ultimately financed.[63]

While many of the entities followed Whitney in shifting toward later-stage investments, Boston-based New Enterprises, Inc., focused on early-stage ventures. New Enterprises aimed to make "venture capital more readily available for the development of untried business enterprises of a scientific nature" so inventors could experiment, found firms, and commercialize their ideas. New Enterprises would provide capital for research and development facilities, or contract externally with a local university, taking advantage of Boston's intellectual advantage in this area. Its founder, William A. Coolidge, had helped to facilitate financing through the American Research and Development Corporation for Tracerlab, Inc., an MIT spinoff in radiation-detection instruments. Highlighting further the connectedness of venture investing, Coolidge also invested in the National Research Corporation, which spawned several new startups—including Minute Maid, one of Whitney's main portfolio companies. The pivotal Georges Doriot, discussed in the next chapter as president of American Research and Development, was a director of New Enterprises. Like Whitney, New Enterprises struggled to achieve success from long-tail investing. It made five investments by 1949, but appears not to have continued its existence after 1950. Henry Etzkowitz describes New Enterprises as just "a group of rich people who had formed an investment club."[64]

The two San Francisco-based entities, Industrial Capital Corporation and Pacific Coast Enterprises Corporation, are crucially important because they represent "precursors to West Coast venture capital."[65] Industrial Capital had links to east coast elites through its president and director S. Marshall Kempner, who was a prominent New York banker before he relocated to San Francisco after the Second World War. Pacific Coast Enterprises was an outgrowth of a group of individual investors, mostly local to the region, who decided to pool their investment capital. Both entities were designed to exploit a perceived gap in the funding of startups, although Pacific Coast Enterprises was more focused in this area. Industrial Capital adopted a more generalist approach, providing financing for entrepreneurs and intermediary services such as merger advice to small and medium-sized businesses.[66]

Ultimately, however, both of these entities were too small to have meaningful impact given the substantial capital requirements of local entrepreneurs. A 1946 report entitled *The Availability of Capital to Small Business in California* estimated the startup capital requirements of new enterprises at the time to be between $100 million and $200 million ($1.2 to $2.4 billion today).[67] Yet, together, Industrial Capital and Pacific Coast Enterprises held only $3 million. The venture capital industry on the west coast was small-scale and largely limited to a few well-heeled local capitalists with surplus funds to invest. For this reason, the 1946 report concluded that "the market for equity capital for the small enterprise . . . is predominately local and informal."[68] Over the next several decades, however, that would change. As Chapter 6, will describe, a group of individuals, some from the San Francisco area and others who migrated there, began to connect entrepreneurs with startup finance through VC firms in ways that would radically fuel high-tech innovation and economic growth.

Promising Beginnings

This chapter began by outlining the vital role of individual investors in the informal market for new venture finance. In an environment where bank-based early-stage capital was in short supply, individual investors could meet the needs of entrepreneurs, leading to the financing of some of America's most influential firms and industries. Alongside this informal network, a formal market for venture finance began to emerge—especially following the Second World War, when several important VC-like private capital entities were established. These frequently acted as sophisticated intermediaries by pooling capital across investors, developing due diligence skills for vetting and selecting portfolio firms, staging investments to mitigate risk, and governing portfolio companies to generate higher returns from long-tailed distributions of payoffs. Some even operated as limited partnerships to channel capital from wealthy individuals to entrepreneurs.

The pathway to a well-developed VC industry was still incomplete, however, for at least two interrelated reasons. First, the supply of capital in each entity was limited to either a single wealthy family or a group of wealthy individual investors. The scale of intermediation would need to become significantly larger to have real impact on the startup sector. Second, and perhaps more important, none of these entities reached a level of investment performance in line with what is expected in modern venture capital—helping to explain why the scale of investing continued to be small. Although individuals like Laurance Rockefeller and John Hay Whitney "were not in venture capital primarily for the financial reward" they were still attempting to generate outsized payoffs from long-tail investing.[69] To raise funds on a larger scale, it was necessary to show that a portfolio could be constructed in a systematic fashion whereby the hits would substantially offset the losses and mediocre investments. None of the entities in Table 3.1 achieved this on a recurring basis. Chapter 4 shows how the American Research and Development Corporation attempted to solve this problem, in a context of a wider debate over whether the market could effectively channel capital into entrepreneurial businesses.

4

The Market versus the Government

THE PERIOD AFTER THE SECOND WORLD WAR marked an inflection point in the evolution of the American venture capital industry. Although private capital entities had begun to provide startup finance for entrepreneurship, the industry as a whole was still at an embryonic stage of development. The limited partnership structure had not yet become the consensus approach to VC; a variety of organizational arrangements existed, including both corporate and partnership forms. Furthermore, the industry had yet to scale. One observer noted that "venture capital companies today number less than ten, and their total resources probably do not exceed $25 million by very much."[1] The long-tail investing model remained largely unproven.

During the immediate post–Second World War years, entrepreneurs faced many opportunities to exploit the science-based technologies developed in preceding decades and especially as part of the war effort. Policy makers were concerned, however, as the sphere of startup finance showed signs of market failure. Commercial banks were not able to deploy risk capital systematically or offer managerial guidance to new high-tech firms in a substantive way. They simply lacked domain expertise. While life insurance companies, investment trusts, and other institutional investors held substantial pools of funds, they were unable to allocate their capital into risky asset classes because of regulatory constraints, their conservative investment styles, and the lack of facilitating intermediaries. Capital market imperfections represented major obstacles to the development of entrepreneurship and the commercialization of new innovations.

It was in this context that a group of New England academic, political, and business elites established the American Research and Development Corporation (ARD) in 1946. Located in Boston's financial district, ARD was designed to channel institutional investment funds into venture capital to boost regional development. ARD is widely recognized as a key entity in the evolution of the modern venture capital industry.[2] It was the first VC firm to access the resources of institutional investors, and its 1957 investment in Digital Equipment Company, a pioneer in the minicomputer era, created the proof of concept for the long-tail investing model. It showed that a venture capital entity could build a portfolio of high-tech investments fully expecting that most of those investments would generate little or no return, but that a small fraction—perhaps only one—of them would be successful enough to offset those other challenging investments. Although ARD was organized as a closed-end fund with tradeable shares, under the regulations of the Investment Company Act of 1940, its ongoing experimentation with this organizational form revealed its advantages and disadvantages.[3] From here, the structure of a modern VC limited partnership began to emerge.

Yet, it was still not clear that venture capital could be supplied through market mechanisms alone. Another contemporaneous attempt to stimulate the startup sector originated from a controversial source—the US government. Debate over public efforts to stimulate new business formation through the financing channel became prominent in political discussions from the 1930s onward, and culminated in the 1958 Small Business Investment Company (SBIC) program. This allowed for the formation of investment companies which could back small businesses using not only private capital but also capital borrowed from the government at favorable rates. SBICs also received special tax privileges. Given this leverage, SBICs could achieve scale where private venture capital firms could not. Over seven hundred of these were in operation in the 1960s, serving a critical function as "helping hands" as the private VC industry developed its own independent capabilities.[4]

SBICs are important to analyze in terms of their structure, performance, and investment approach. Although they tended to underperform by way of returns, their very existence strongly influenced the evolution of US venture capital. The SBIC program was an early commitment by government to create an auspicious environment for startup finance. Among its many beneficial spillovers was the rich network of supporting businesses it cultivated, including the specialized law firms on which private VC would later depend.[5] In many cases, too, SBICs created points of entry into small-business finance for individuals who would later found influential VC firms. Government efforts to spur VC finance in the 1950s and 1960s helped to shape the context in which a market-based approach became institutionalized.

The Funding Gap for Startups

Anecdotal evidence often implies that entrepreneurs with creative ideas were able to access capital even at the most challenging times in American history. During the Great Depression, for example, Edwin H. Land was able in 1932 to cofound his Land-Wheelwright Laboratories in a barn in Wellesley Hills, Massachusetts, to develop and manufacture synthetic sheet polarizers. That invention would later be commercialized in 1937, with $750,000 ($12.5 million today) in backing from a group of Wall Street financiers, by Land's founding of the Polaroid Corporation. By 1950, Polaroid had 429 employees and net sales of $6.5 million ($64.8 million today). In 1958, it had 2,500 employees and net sales of about $90 million ($760 million today).[6] More evidence that a successful high-tech enterprise could be created with a financially lean approach to entrepreneurship came from two Stanford University graduates, William Hewlett and David Packard. In 1939, with just $538 ($9,300 today) in startup funds, they established from a garage in California an enterprise that proved to be an innovation powerhouse: the Hewlett-Packard Company.[7]

Other examples, however, speak to the difficulties of financing new ventures. Chester Carlson, inventor of the photocopier, struggled to raise capital between 1938 and 1946 to turn his xerography machine prototype into commercial reality.[8] (He eventually secured funds from the Haloid Company, which became known as Haloid Xerox in 1958 and the Xerox Corporation in 1961.) Private capital was more readily available for later-stage enterprises, where a track record of earnings could be observed, but there was little early-stage capital for entrepreneurs to fund experimentation and commercialization of promising ideas—and a growing consensus that capital market imperfections were undermining entrepreneurship in America.[9]

While large companies had less trouble obtaining risk capital because they financed research investments through retained earnings, small companies tended to have greater needs for externally sourced risk capital to facilitate technological development, expansion, and growth. The crux of the matter was that entrepreneurs could not systematically obtain startup capital or long-term financing because of the high-risk nature of the activity and the likelihood of poor returns. With the passage of time, moreover, these constraints seemed to be worsening. A prominent Chicago banker put it this way in a 1939 Congressional hearing on capital formation: "In my opinion, it has always been difficult for small business to get risk capital. I think the difficulties today, for a variety of causes, are greater in getting proprietary risk capital for small and moderate-size businesses than was the case in former years."[10]

One reason for the capital shortage was the changing tax environment. Whereas, during the 1920s, Secretary of the Treasury Andrew Mellon had lowered taxes for the rich, the 1930s brought more progressive taxation. It was frequently argued that this diminished the supply of entrepreneurial finance. As part of the New Deal reforms, President Roosevelt implemented "soak-the-rich" policies in a series of Revenue Acts that increased the tax burden. In 1936, the top federal tax rate on regular income was 79 percent and the rate on capital gains reached 39 percent. Even when a reversal of these policies toward the end of the 1930s reduced the burden on the capital gains side, the top personal income tax rate was increased. In 1939, the president of the Investment Bankers Association of America lamented this situation, stating: "No one in the high income tax brackets is going to provide the venture capital and take the risk which new enterprises and expansion require, and thereby help create new jobs, if heavy taxes take most of the profit when the transaction is successful."[11] According to many observers, the situation was even worse during the 1940s when top personal tax rates were unusually high.

Furthermore, it was argued that the specific operation of the tax code acted as a strong disincentive to formal organization of venture capital. Capital gains accrued under an investment company structure were taxed more heavily than gains from individual investing, given that individuals could use losses to offset capital gains in a more straightforward way. At the same time, entrepreneurs faced large tax hurdles when their ventures expanded, because tax withdrawals put a dent in working capital. Entrepreneurs had few opportunities to smooth out their cash flows or make capital purchases. Access to the money market was limited, and what would be termed "venture debt" today did not yet exist.

Paradoxically, this was precisely the time when VC-style capital could have been most impactful because opportunities for innovation and entrepreneurship increased in the US economy. Even during the Great Depression, innovation and entrepreneurship did not stop. R&D employment increased by a factor of almost three between 1933 and 1940 as large firms advanced basic and applied science through in-house laboratory research. As they developed and commercialized new discoveries, some of this innovation proved transformative. Between 1931 and 1934, DuPont invested over $1 million in the R&D that brought synthetic fibers to market. By 1937, 40 percent of DuPont's sales came from products that did not exist prior to 1929. Naturally, these developments created spillovers into the wider economy. In one economist's phrase, the 1930s was "the most technologically progressive decade of the twentieth century."[12]

During the Second World War, the US government added to the pool of knowledge by assuming the significant financing risk required to develop new weapons—most notably, the atomic bomb—and the advanced electronics demanded by radar-based navigation systems and new communications technologies. Universities and corporate R&D facilities were enlisted in the war effort, creating a strong interconnected system for harnessing innovative talent. A new federal agency established in 1941, the US Office of Scientific Research and Development, spent a total of $450 million (about $4.9 billion today) on technology contracts before it was phased out in 1947. It was headed by MIT's Vannevar Bush, whose influential 1945 report *Science: The Endless Frontier* would lay out the fundamental framework for federal funding of US science institutions in the postwar era.

With advances in "big science" creating abundant opportunities for commercial exploitation, the US government also attended to human capital formation in the economy. State support for education took the form of the 1944 Servicemen's Readjustment Act (also known as the GI Bill) which sent a huge cohort of returning soldiers to college, adding to their intellectual development and to the supply of potential entrepreneurs. America benefitted enormously from this growing talent pool and its useful technical knowledge. In terms of firm-level profitability, small firms that were able to access capital tended to perform better than successful large firms.[13] In aggregate, however, startup capital was scarce, and for the US economy's further development, that threatened to be a major impediment.

Founding the American Research
and Development Corporation

ARD was founded in June 1946 against this backdrop of growing concern with the pace of small-business creation. Incorporated in Boston, it was an attempt to avert the expected shortage of venture capital in the postwar period, and also the culmination of a long-standing debate among members of the New England Council, a prominent regional development association, over how best to supply entrepreneurial finance. The council had been established in 1925, and by the mid-1940s was governed by eminent individuals from academia, industry, and finance who all shared a common sense of civic duty and a desire to stimulate regional growth through entrepreneurship and innovation.

Most accounts of ARD's history emphasize the pivotal role of Georges Doriot, a well-to-do French émigré and business school professor who is often called the father of US venture capital.[14] Doriot came to America to study at Harvard Business School beginning in 1921, joined the faculty as an assistant dean and associate professor in 1926, and became a full professor in 1929. During the Second World War, he joined the Quartermaster Corps, the US Army's logistical arm, where he rose to the rank of brigadier general and was decorated with the Distinguished Service Medal. He continued to work for the military in various capacities until 1959. His military service was renowned among his students who affectionately nicknamed him "the General."

Yet, while much of the history of ARD is described as the work of Doriot, it is important to note that he was not actually its founder. Despite the fact that Doriot participated in early discussions at the New England Council of an ARD-type entity, it was only in December 1946 that he was appointed to serve as president of the new entity and run its operations. While Doriot is often seen as a visionary in some ways— mainly in his focus on the role of personal interactions between investors and firm founders—he could be overly cautious as an early-stage investor, and was often reluctant to discard underperforming assets from ARD's portfolio, to the detriment of its overall returns.[15]

Furthermore, he was prone to act in ways that would be distantly unpalatable by modern-day standards. He could be parochial and downright bigoted. His management style was autocratic to the point of being dismissive to his peers and subordinates.[16] Although he nurtured the career of his administrative assistant Dorothy Rowe, who became a senior vice president at ARD, he generally exhibited a strong gender bias. Even when Harvard Business School began admitting women MBA candidates in 1963, Doriot largely succeeded in denying them access to his influential second-year Manufacturing course—and defended his refusal of them as something he was "damn proud of."[17] His patronizing affect toward women's role in society is evidenced by his January 1967 speech to the Harvard Business School Club of Buffalo. "I did have one girl take Manufacturing," he told the group. "I let her in because she told me that she would work and not marry for several years. Two months later she was engaged to the student sitting next to her in Manufacturing. So there is a Manufacturing couple living happily in California. They both work. Last week I received a letter from her boss telling me that she was doing extraordinarily well. We can all be proud of our one and only Manufacturing girl."[18] Given that Doriot educated and influenced a generation of individuals at Harvard Business School who would play prominent roles in the formation of leading venture capital entities in the United States and elsewhere, his strong biases, even for the time period, seeded a narrowmindedness on gender issues that the industry still grapples with today.

While some disagreement lingers as to who originally raised the idea of ARD, in Doriot's mind the source was clear. In 1967, giving testimony before Congress on the status and future of small business, he said in his opening remarks: "The job I was given twenty years ago was to create new companies and help small ones. The idea came from Senator Flanders."[19] Ralph Flanders could not have been more different from Doriot. He had been elected president of the New England Council in 1940 and elected senator for Vermont in 1946. Just a few months earlier, ARD had been established with him as its first president. He was born in Barnet, Vermont, into a humble household (his father was a woodworker) and did not receive much by way of formal education. He was the ideal self-starter. He trained as an engineer, served a full apprenticeship, and eventually acquired over twenty United States patents for technological developments related to machine tools. In 1944, Flanders was awarded the prestigious Hoover Medal in engineering for his corporate and industry association work, and his contributions to public policy. The citation for the award states: "Few men combine as he does, actual experience in engineering, administration and finance with broad knowledge of economic and social conditions."[20]

Aside from Flanders, the members of the New England Council most influential in ARD's formation were Karl Compton, president of the Massachusetts Institute of Technology (MIT), Donald David, dean of Harvard Business School, Bradley Dewey, president of Dewey & Almy Chemical Company, Frederick Blackall, Jr., president of Taft-Peirce Manufacturing Company, and Merrill Griswold, chairman of the board of trustees of the Massachusetts Investors Trust. This was an auspicious group. Compton in particular had great influence. He played key roles in national innovation policy-making during the interwar years and in discussions about how best to promote innovation in New England. Although his main emphasis was on the creation of an ecosystem of science-based enterprise to exploit the unique capabilities of MIT, he recognized the vital need for organized venture capital. Compton believed the most pressing problem associated with startup finance was the need for a valid framework by which investment opportunities could be systematically evaluated.[21]

Like Compton, Donald David, as the third dean of Harvard Business School, was well connected to government and industry. He held directorships in several of America's largest corporations. Bradley Dewey, a graduate of MIT, had founded a leading chemical company (which would subsequently become a division of W. R. Grace & Company) focused on producing latex sealants and synthetic rubber. Frederick Blackall, son of a wealthy machine-tool industrialist, became president of the New England Council in 1946. Under the guidance of Merrill Griswold, Massachusetts Investors Trust (the largest investors trust in New England and oft-cited as the first modern-day mutual fund) became a pioneer in terms of governance; the firm performed extensive due diligence on its investments and maintained an advisory board to assure oversight. Collectively, this group, with its mix of academic, political, industrial, and financial influence, epitomized the power of New England networks.

A key moment in the genesis of ARD occurred in 1939 when Compton was asked to chair the influential "New Products Committee" of the New England Council. Recognizing that some traditional sectors like textiles were in decline, its wide-ranging remit considered how new comparative advantages could be gained through the development of innovative industrial products. Given New England's favorable science and educational infrastructure, the committee focused on the capabilities required for newly formed businesses to exploit commercial opportunities. Its final report to the council underscored the difficulty of mobilizing capital and reallocating resources to new areas of innovation. The report lamented that "much of New England capital took the form of trust capital funds not properly available for use as venture capital."[22]

The committee had highlighted a crucial fact. It was estimated that about 45 percent of New England wealth was held by institutions like trust and insurance companies. Flanders estimated that institutions held in excess of $25 billion ($250 billion today).[23] Because of their traditional investment philosophy and the need for regulatory compliance, fiduciaries engaged in very conservative management of assets. Also, even if these institutional investors could overcome their conservatism, direct investments in entrepreneurial startups would be implausible. "We would under no circumstances directly make investments in risky new undertakings for the reason that we are not staffed for that purpose," Griswold would later comment. "We do not know anything about the technique of the thing, and we would probably end up making fools of ourselves if we tried."[24]

Unlocking this pool of institutional capital on the supply side of investment finance would be critical to ARD, and more generally to the development of the venture capital industry. Griswold articulated the need for an entity like ARD in terms of the long tail. "It is very risky to put money into a brand new project. Some of them are bound to fail," he cautioned. "But if you secure diversification, by buying fifteen or twenty of those indirectly through a special company, it does not matter that four or five of them may fail because the others, the hope is, will more than make up for it."[25] Although the committee headed by Compton was short on action steps to increase the supply of venture capital in New England, it had crucially planted a key idea in the minds of individuals who had the networks and ability to turn it into reality.

Still, the pathway to ARD's establishment was uncertain. During the early 1940s, two VC-like institutions were established, as the debate deepened over precisely how an entity to supply entrepreneurial finance should be organized. First, the New England Industrial Development Corporation was established. Its model, however, involved charging the selected ventures for the cost of further due diligence to screen potential investments prior to the decision of whether it would take an equity stake. Second, the New England Industrial Research Foundation, which Compton was instrumental in forming, was designed as a fee-based intelligence service to carry out due diligence on potential investments.[26] These early experiments illustrate the tentative and sometimes muddled thinking that preceded the formation of ARD. Neither institution created anything long-lasting.

Ralph Flanders, meanwhile, having failed in his first run at a US Senate seat in 1940, had joined the Federal Reserve Bank of Boston in 1941. There he gained more in-depth knowledge about the macroeconomic environment and local financing dynamics. He became president of that institution in 1944. Within a few more years, a consensus had emerged that a venture capital entity (initially to be called the Development Capital Corporation) could be established on the basis of institutional capital to simultaneously select the most promising entrepreneurial ventures for investment, generate a return on capital, and encourage regional and national economic development. In 1946, Flanders articulated the main impetus behind the strategy and the grand vision:

> As president of the Federal Reserve Bank of Boston, I became seriously concerned with the increasing degree to which the liquid wealth of the Nation is tending to concentrate in fiduciary hands. This in itself is a natural process, but it does make it more and more difficult as time goes on to finance new undertakings. The postwar prosperity of America depends in a large measure on finding financial support for that comparatively small percentage of new ideas and developments which give promise of expanded production and employment, and an increased standard of living for the American people. We cannot float along indefinitely on the enterprise and vision of preceding generations. To be confident that we are in an expanding instead of a static or frozen economy, we must have a reasonably high birth rate of new undertakings. There are in particular two large-scale repositories of wealth which have a stake in the Nation's future and who should be concerned with a healthy basis for the prosperity of these postwar years. These two groups are the life-insurance companies and investment trusts. A project on which we have been making excellent progress in the last few months is for a development corporation financed in a large measure by these two groups of institutions, under the directorship and management of the most capable men available in the fields of business and technology.[27]

By using institutional capital and a systematic approach to the intermediation of venture finance, Flanders was envisioning a setup completely different from existing private capital entities, most of which deployed family wealth. The approach was forward-looking and innovative. Yet, despite that—or perhaps because of it—not everyone shared Flanders's enthusiasm and confidence of success. Flanders solicited the opinions of others, including General Motors' vice president in charge of research and development Charles Kettering, one of the most respected inventors in motor vehicle engineering. "I can make one forecast that will come true," Kettering responded pessimistically. "If you do it, in five years, [ARD] will be dead, busted, and forgotten."[28]

ARD's Organizational Structure

ARD was incorporated in June 1946 by Flanders (as president), Dewey, Blackall, and Horace Ford—the latter being MIT's treasurer, who would serve as ARD's treasurer, as well. At this stage, ARD was just an amalgam of individuals who had been influential in discussions at the New England Council about the need for a new entity to provide venture finance. Compton also served in an advisory role. But Flanders's participation would be short-lived. Appointed to the United States Senate in November 1946, he handed the ARD presidency over to Doriot.

Figure 4.1 shows ARD's organizational structure. It was created as an intermediary to link outside capital with portfolio investments. It was quite distinct from the modern VC limited partnership form, however, in that it was organized as a closed-end fund under Section 12(d)(1) of the 1940 Investment Company Act. ARD had a permanent pool of capital, as opposed to operating funds with specified lifetimes as is conventional in venture capital today. In addition to an executive committee, ARD provided for general oversight by a board of directors, some of whom were stockholders, and also assembled an eminent technology advisory board to weigh in with specific expertise. As a testament to the intent behind the advisory board, Vannevar Bush was even invited to join, though he ultimately declined. Despite its strong New England heritage, ARD intended to be "national in its scope," with regional advisory boards planned across the country to generate deal flow and provide assistance to portfolio companies.

A particularly salient issue is the structuring of ARD as a closed-end fund. The choice was rational. The limited partnership structure had not yet become the norm for organized venture capital, and in any case would have been an unsuitable structure given ARD's particular circumstances. The mission statement Flanders outlined for ARD included a remit to use institutional capital and encourage broad participation from private

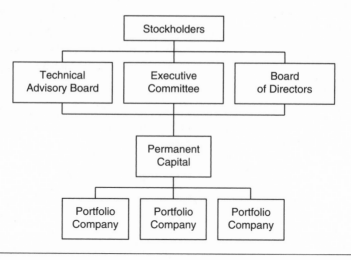

Figure 4.1 The Organizational Structure of ARD.

investors. ARD treated its stockholders as "partners of this business in the most inclusive sense of the word."[29] A limited partnership, by contrast, vests control in the hands of the general partners. Conservative institutional investors at the time would not have agreed to delegate governance to a risky investment entity. Additionally, because ARD was open to individual investors as well as institutions, the size of its stockholder base—numbering 484 by 1949—obviated a limited partnership structure with all the opaqueness that form entailed. A closed-end fund was more appropriate and it also gave ARD a greater sense of legitimacy.

The closed-end form meant ARD could issue a fixed number of shares to be traded on the secondary market. It had no obligation to buy its shares back from investors upon their request. This differed from an open-end fund where new investors have redemption rights and shares can be created and continuously offered for sale to meet demands for liquidity or to increase the fund's size. Given this difference, it made sense for ARD to opt for the closed-end structure. "As a matter of fact," the chief counsel of the Securities and Exchange Commission (SEC) explained in 1940, "if one has an open-end company he cannot go into that type of activity—venture capital. Why? Because if he is going to make capital available to a small business and get an equity position, he does not have a listed security; he does not have a marketable security; but he has an illiquid block of stock." He spelled out the implication: "if there are re-demptions, the company cannot liquidate the illiquid block of stock to raise cash to meet the redemptions. If an investment company is going to perform the function of supplying a small industry with capital, the investment company cannot be an open-end company; that is clear."[30]

Even with the choice of a closed-end structure, however, ARD faced significant barriers associated with regulatory compliance. Because it had a large group of shareholders, ARD was subjected to more rigorous legal standards than the private-capital entities discussed in Chapter 3. In fact, ARD needed special dispensation from the SEC to be formed, given the prevailing rules in America at the time. The general aversion to both speculation and the pyramiding of investment companies during the in-terwar years meant that entities like ARD faced tight regulatory stan-dards. The 1940 Investment Company Act was a significant piece of legislation in this area.

The upshot of this regulatory situation was that an investment com-pany could not own more than 3 percent of the voting stock of another investment company, which would undermine ARD's capacity to raise institutional capital from entities like Massachusetts Investors Trust. For-tuitously, the Act contained an exemption—Section 12(e)—which ARD could exploit. It allowed the SEC to make a precedent-setting decision approving ARD's registration in the "public interest." ARD was permitted to have institutional investors who could each acquire up to 9.9 percent of its stock, so long as ARD was able to raise $3 million ($36.8 million today) in a first round of subscriptions, of which $1.5 million needed to come from institutional investors.[31]

Despite this SEC exemption, it would still be problematic for ARD to raise capital from life insurance companies, a group of institutional in-vestors it intended to attract. In Massachusetts, life insurance companies could invest up to 25 percent of their reserve, and their entire surplus, in alternative asset classes—but they could not purchase more than 10 percent of the capital stock of a company. Other states were even more restrictive. Of the fifteen states holding the vast bulk of life insurance assets when ARD was founded, two-thirds (most notably including New York) did not permit life insurance companies to place capital into entities like ARD at all. Consequently, ARD's founders spent much of their time in its early years lobbying local officials and the federal government to relax these regulatory constraints.

Finally, ARD faced an additional hurdle to raising capital because it was not considered to be a pass-through entity for tax purposes. Although it could technically acquire any amount of equity in a portfolio company, if this amount exceeded 10 percent of the voting stock of the portfolio company, ARD would lose its entitlement to tax treatment as a conduit. As such, any capital gains accruing to ARD from a portfolio investment would be taxed at the capital gains rate, and the investor would be "double-taxed" on distributions. Griswold noted the negative effect on fund-raising: "We have had wealthy individuals who are properly advised make exhaustive inquiries into this subject and not invest in the company when they found out."[32]

It is no accident, therefore, that ARD initially struggled to raise capital from both institutional and individual investors. It offered 200,000 shares at $25 each ($300 today) in minimum lots: one thousand shares for institutional investors, including investment companies, and two hundred shares for others, including individual investors. Later, it would place maximums on the number of shares that could be purchased, a restriction designed to limit holdings to experienced investors who could tolerate the risk.[33]

Due to the SEC's tough requirements for institutional subscribers, ARD "came close to scratching before it ever got off the ground."[34] Yet it did ultimately succeed in raising the necessary capital. The amounts ARD pooled in 1947 from institutions (investment companies, insurance firms, and educational endowments), brokers, and companies accounted for 57 percent of the total. Individual investors accounted for the remaining 43 percent. Rather presciently, given the role that pension funds would play in the 1970s and 1980s as capital providers of VC funds, ARD's treasurer noted in 1949 that there was "one more aggregation of capital coming into the picture which so far has been regarded as more or less sacred as far as venture capital is concerned, and that is the pension funds."[35] With its pool of permanent capital secure, ARD's challenge was to define and execute its investment strategy.

ARD's Investment Approach and Method

Although ARD's approach to deploying risk capital established precedents for modern venture capital investing, at the outset it was unclear if it would engage with entrepreneurial ventures at all. ARD's SEC prospectus implied that a conservative strategy would be followed, with little mention of the creative approach to entrepreneurial finance for which ARD would become noted. It stated that ARD would not make investments unless "in the judgment of the Company's Board of Directors, research or development work, which has already been carried on, indicates that the product or process to which the new enterprise relates, is commercially practicable and embraces prospects of ultimate profit."[36] While this phrasing may have been designed to placate institutional investors who were worried about ARD's taking on too much risk, it is also true that its early investments did reflect a cautious approach.

ARD's first investment was in Circo Products, a Cleveland-based automobile fluids company, to which it provided a $150,000 ($1.8 million today) loan, at 5 percent interest, convertible into preferred stock. Circo required the funds to develop a method for degreasing an auto transmission by delivering a vaporized solvent into the housing.[37] But Circo was not a new company. It had been filing for US patents in this broad domain since the 1930s.[38] Furthermore, ARD invested in or acquired the assets of several existing firms in 1947 that were creating what might be described as incremental innovations, including Snyder Chemical Corporation, a Connecticut firm developing a wood adhesive; a New Jersey company called Jet-Heet Inc., applying jet propulsion technology to furnace manufacturing; and Colter Corporation, a Texas food producer holding a patent on a machine for deveining shrimp.[39]

Three other early investments, however, did involve more radical technologies. All were made locally, and through trusted connections. First, ARD invested $150,000 in Tracerlab Inc., founded in March 1946 by a group led by MIT graduate William Barbour to manufacture and sell equipment for measuring radiation. Tracerlab had grown through bootstrapping, but then struggled to raise capital for development of the technology. Having been turned down by local investors in Boston, and having rejected Wall Street investors who were willing to invest only for 51 percent of the equity, Barbour was introduced through the MIT network to ARD, which did its due diligence and provided financing on more reasonable terms.[40]

Second, in 1946, on the advice of Karl Compton, ARD invested $200,000 ($2.5 million today) in convertible debentures for an 80 percent stake in High Voltage Engineering, an innovative manufacturer of particle accelerators.[41] Doriot would later offer this insight into ARD deal flow: "One day Karl Compton called me and said Dr. Van de Graaff at

MIT has developed a machine which will be useful for certain types of cancer treatment. And I said, but, Karl, I will be competing with two *small* American companies if I start a company to make the Van de Graaff machine, one of them called General Electric and the other one called Allis-Chalmers. And Karl Compton said, look, it's going to be useful. Do it."[42]

ARD made a third local investment in Ionics, Inc., founded in December 1948, of $100,000 ($1 million today) for a 75 percent equity stake.[43] Ionics was originally located in a basement on the MIT campus, with the university covering infrastructure expenses and ARD financing wages, working capital, and some R&D expenditure.[44] The company was engaged in the development of science related to ion exchange, based on the discovery of a membrane for saline water conversion by Walter Juda, who held a PhD in physical chemistry from the University of Lyon and became a research chemist at Harvard. Ionics pursued patents on the invention and would become a leader in water-purification technology.

Taking the portfolio as a whole, ARD's investments were biased toward later-stage concerns during its first decade, with the relative importance of early-stage investments increasing over time. This made sense because it limited ARD's risk exposure while it was trying to prove its venture investing model. Furthermore, it took time to develop the capabilities to assess and govern truly entrepreneurial projects. ARD was aware of the need to diversify its portfolio of interests across these stages. "A company like American Research has to have one or two things that are not three months, six months, two years away in the offing," its treasurer noted. "You have to have a little knitting, as it were, to go on."[45]

ARD developed an investment style that in many respects mirrored that of the private-capital entities discussed in Chapter 3. It selected investments from a large pool of proposals using rigorous due diligence. It used its technical advisory board, professional investment staff, and external contacts to assess projects. Between 1946 and 1950, it evaluated 1,869 proposals and made just twenty-six investments (1.4 percent). Indeed, during its entire history, ARD's investment rate never exceeded 4 percent.[46] A firm would make it into ARD's portfolio of investments only after a demanding selection process. Projects would initially be screened by ARD's staff and the most promising would be shown to its technical advisory group and board of directors. ARD's staff would then conduct more due diligence by meeting with founders and writing up "operational sheets" to describe their business plans and funding needs over the next eighteen months. If an operational sheet provided to the board of directors for further scrutiny won its approval, the project was passed by ARD's legal counsel and its executive committee for final review.

Although it is difficult to be definitive about the origins of ARD's deal flow, many of its investments, at least in the early period, were sourced from contacts like Karl Compton. ARD would co-invest with other financial groups if more capital were required or if another financing partner could provide specialized expertise to the portfolio company. Tellingly, given that governance was easier locally, over three-quarters of ARD's investments from 1946 to 1950 were in firms based in Massachusetts or other areas of the east coast. Over time, however, ARD became more diverse geographically to the point that about a quarter of its investments from 1966 to 1973 were in west coast firms.[47] ARD generated its deal flow from the networks of its own investment professionals (it employed between four and seven during the 1950s) in addition to investment banks and brokerages. Interestingly, ARD also approached the research laboratories of large firms in search of inventions emerging from these facilities that might be peripheral to their firms' product lines, and therefore candidates to spin off into new entities. This suggests that ARD was active in developing the market for ideas.

ARD's investment approach was technology-driven and team-oriented. Many of its investments involved ventures that had secured patent protection, and ARD was willing to engage in the commercialization of academic science. Figure 4.2 shows that, during its early years, ARD focused on chemicals and industrial equipment companies, but during its later years its investments also included newer sectors such as electronics. The people behind the ventures were crucial. As Doriot put it, ARD's remit was "to find men and to find ideas." ARD documentation stated its intent "to invest only in situations and companies where able management by men of competence and integrity seems assured."[48]

ARD also placed a heavy emphasis on governance. Doriot asserted that, for all of ARD's investments, "in practically no case have we had what I would call a technical failure. It has been human failures."[49] To mitigate people-based problems, ARD implemented stringent monitoring while also granting founders some degree of autonomy. It sent its investment professionals to assist with the management of portfolio companies and make personnel changes when necessary. Doriot's view was

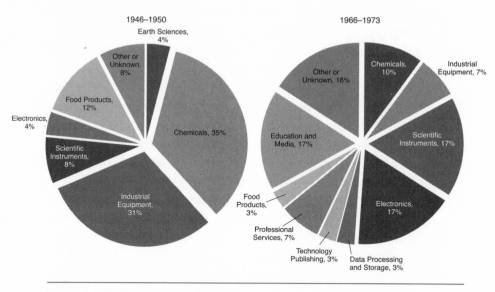

Figure 4.2 ARD Investments by Sector.

Based on data in David H. Hsu and Martin Kenney, "Organizing Venture Capital: The Rise and Demise of American Research & Development Corporation, 1946–1973," *Industrial and Corporate Change* 14, no. 4 (2005): 579–616, 593.

that "men who are most capable of starting the company seldom become good operators."[50] Although ARD did not typically take a controlling interest in a firm, it did require board representation so that it could exert influence on the direction management was taking, and identify and correct for any brewing agency issues. ARD usually required two board seats. Both Karl Compton and Merrill Griswold were elected to the Board of Tracerlab, while Doriot served on the boards of High Voltage Engineering and Ionics.

Beyond oversight, Doriot recognized the need for post-investment guidance to instill excellent management practices. He had learned that "research and development, new technical ideas, and young small businesses are not in themselves the certain keys to great success. They must be supplemented by sound management, adequate financing, competent production methods, and aggressive merchandising."[51] He also thought globally as well as locally. Hoping to create an infrastructure to connect his portfolio firms to overseas markets, Doriot established the European Enterprises Development Company and the Canadian Enterprise Development Corporation in the early 1960s as ARD-type entities.[52] Both had distinguished stockholders to facilitate "human help" and the "exchange of technical ideas" across countries. For Doriot, successful venture investing involved an amalgamation of entrepreneurial finance, people, ideas, and networking.

By virtue of its organizational structure as a closed-end fund with permanent capital, ARD could take a somewhat patient approach to venture investing, allowing its governance approach to work and its portfolio companies to mature over time. Archival evidence shows that for 120 investments made between 1946 and 1973, the average investment horizon was 6.5 years—and a small but important share of investments took a decade or longer to play out. At the same time, ARD was subject to shareholder pressures to deliver results. It had to invest for the long run and simultaneously create liquidity to finance its operations. ARD tackled this challenge differently from most venture capital entities in that, from the outset, it charged management fees to portfolio companies as part of its business model. In 1948, fees covered about 12 percent of ARD's staff salary costs.[53] This, of course, required a tradeoff: although management fees would satisfy ARD's need for interim liquidity, they would draw on the working capital that portfolio companies needed to achieve long-run growth.

The demand for liquidity affected how ARD financed its portfolio companies. It used convertible debt and convertible preferred stock to generate cash flow. The $500,000 it had collectively invested in Circo Products, Tracerlab, and High Voltage Engineering yielded 5 percent in interest or preferred dividends, which was more than double the rate of interest on government securities at the time.[54] Note that while convertible notes today also generally carry high-interest rates, the investor does not typically expect an actual cash payment; rather, conversion occurs at a future point in time when the debt converts at face value and the accrued interest gets translated into additional equity ownership.

ARD maintained a sophisticated approach to financial contracting. In addition to using board representation as leverage, it would write restrictive covenants into agreements to compel portfolio companies to comply with ARD's objectives under certain conditions. Restrictive covenants were used to gain control at Circo Products in 1950 as the company underwent a financial recapitalization. ARD was less likely to use debt-only financing for R&D-intensive investments, which is consistent with theories of optimal capital. Because R&D is highly intangible and tends to be specific to the firm in which it is being used, it has limited liquidation value. As a general rule, the use of debt tends to decrease with asset intangibility.[55]

From a contracting perspective, ARD also believed in founder incentives. In Doriot's words, "participation by the management in the ownership of the company is considered to be of great importance to its growth."[56] He also cautioned that "there are many reasons why it is advisable for the new company to have a limited amount of capital at the very start." Chief among these was that "in the hands of an inexperienced person commitments of all types are often made quite recklessly and capital has a way of disappearing at a remarkable high rate of speed."[57] Hence, ARD staged investments. For example, Tracerlab received infusions in 1946 and 1948, and then raised $1.3 million in a public offering in 1949.

Yet, despite the fact that ARD adopted a sophisticated approach to investment selection, governance, and financing, it initially suffered from the same fundamental problem associated with the private-capital entities discussed in Chapter 3. In its first decade of operation, ARD did not generate VC-style returns, which severely constrained its ability to raise and invest more funds. Doriot adopted a policy that, whenever ARD reached a threshold of $1 million in liquid assets, it would go to the market for more—which he did in 1949 and 1951. But ARD's shares often traded at a heavy discount, which made this form of fundraising unattractive. In 1955, ARD's shares traded at just 65 percent of their net asset value.[58]

Another option for generating liquidity was to sell successful portfolio companies earlier, which ARD did start to do with more frequency. At the same time, however, the flow of new projects also slowed, from a mean of 382 proposals annually from 1947 to 1951 to only 127 in 1954. In 1954, no new investments were made. Clearly, it was a struggle to manage the dynamics of the venture capital cycle of fundraising, deploying capital into portfolio companies, and exiting investments in a timely manner. The perverse effect on ARD's strategy was that it focused more on minimizing risk and less on maximizing expected returns.[59] Some of ARD's investments generated decent payoffs in a short time span, but others took longer for returns to materialize, or ended in losses. Competing with a buoyant stock market, Doriot seemed to lose some enthusiasm for the effort. "It is interesting to see how the great interest that existed seven or eight years ago in venture capital has disappeared and how the daring and courage which were prevalent at that time have now waned," he reflected. "Venture capital is not fashionable anymore. A good climbing stock market seemingly has killed the great hope of the after-war period. . . . Bankers, investors, brokers, etc. generally speaking and contrary to manufacturers, have come to the conclusion that creative venture capital was a fanciful idea of the past which should be mostly discarded on account of the fact that it cannot be made to pay very quickly."[60]

Doriot's pessimism was justified based on an assessment of ARD's financials. Having deployed $10 million ($92.4 million today) in risk capital across portfolio investments between 1946 and 1956, ARD achieved a compound annual growth rate of 5.2 percent in net asset value per share, including the dividends ARD paid to investors between 1954 and 1956. This translated to -1.3 percent based on the market value per share, again including dividends.[61] Over the same time period, the S&P Composite returned a compound annual growth rate of 8.9 percent from the index alone, or 15.2 percent with dividends included. By the mid-1950s, ARD's ability to sustain itself as a VC entity was limited by its performance results. Its goal had been to generate capital gains from long-tail investing in entrepreneurial firms, but it had underperformed relative to equities.

Verifying the Long Tail: Digital Equipment Corporation

A 1957 investment in a nascent Massachusetts-based firm originally called Digital Computer Corporation changed the course of ARD's portfolio performance. The high-tech startup that would become known as Digital Equipment Corporation (DEC) also assured ARD's place in the history of American venture capital. DEC was the brainchild of Kenneth Olsen and Harlan Anderson, two MIT graduates who worked at MIT's Lincoln Laboratory, a federally funded research and development center. During the mid-1950s, Olsen was seconded to IBM to work on SAGE, a computerized aircraft monitoring and defense system. Returning to Lincoln Labs, he helped to design the TX-0, a room-sized computer that used transistors to store and process information. The TX-0 had 64K of eighteen-bit words of magnetic core memory, which although trivial by today's standards was enormous at the time. While physically large, the TX-0 was significantly more space efficient than the first generation of similarly capable computers built with vacuum tubes. Like the SAGE system, it was also interactive with a cathode-ray-tube display, which allowed the user some real-time functionality. IBM, with its vacuum tube–based 709 (to be replaced by a transistorized version, the 7090, in 1959) was the leading provider of scientific, business, and administrative computing technology in the late 1950s, but the powerful data processing machines it offered could cost several million dollars to purchase.

In August 1957, Olsen and Anderson left Lincoln Laboratory to form DEC. Their idea was to make circuit board modules for research institutions and businesses that needed cheaper but still high-powered computing solutions. They started out in a former textile mill in the town of Maynard, Massachusetts. In a 1967 Congressional testimony on small business finance, Doriot recalled how ARD became connected with DEC:

> About ten years ago, a young man came to see me from the Lincoln Laboratory in Bedford, Mass. He told me that he wanted to start a company to make modules. Modules are components of computers. And he said, "If we do fairly well, later on we might make computers." Now, Senator, think back ten years—a young man comes and says he wants to do what—he wants to compete with a *tiny* American company called IBM. Well, we started the company. And you would be interested in the figures. Ten years later, that company is selling $30 million worth of computers, competing successfully with IBM. And we gave the man $70,000 to start the company and today we value that investment at $52 million.[62]

Three aspects of Doriot's comments are noteworthy in the context of other known facts about ARD's relationship with DEC. First, the investment in ARD reflected an *ex ante* selection subject to *ex post* uncertainties about the future direction of the technology and the potential for market gains. The threat of incumbent advantages—in this case, IBM's—was pertinent, and this appears to have been a constant theme in ARD's investment strategy going back to the financing of High Voltage Engineering, which competed with General Electric. Doriot could be both concerned and attracted by competition from strong incumbents. By investing in startups like DEC, he felt he was creating value by encouraging business dynamism. Even if the investment did not pay off *ex post,* ARD was contributing to a process of experimentation by financing new technical innovations. If it did pay off, ARD would maximize its financial return for a tolerable level of risk.

Second, because of this uncertainty around technologies and markets, the founders' cost of capital was high. ARD typically made investments of $50,000 to $1 million. The $70,000 ($600,000 today) that ARD provided to Olsen and Anderson was at the lower end of this range. In addition to the threat from incumbents, DEC faced competition from other startups, such as the pioneering mainframe computer maker Control Data Corporation. For its $70,000 investment in DEC, ARD received 78 percent of the ownership.[63] This was consistent with ARD's approach of taking a majority stake in especially risky projects where "the men need a great deal of help." It also reflected Doriot's belief that venture investing required an understanding that the value created by an innovative idea was fundamentally separate from the value created by skillful execution. He recognized that Olsen and Anderson "were very good engineers" but "they had no experience in management."[64] In line with ARD's approach, Doriot played an active role in DEC's governance and also provided DEC with loans to enable growth and development. At the same time, Doriot respected the founders. Olsen would later recall that ARD "gave us freedom. They didn't interfere, either when things were going poorly, or when things were going well."[65]

Third, the payoff to ARD validated the long-tail investment approach, proving something possible that no other venture capital entity had yet managed to achieve. In fact, DEC was the epitome of a long-tail portfolio investment. Buoyed by its revolutionary series of programmed data processor (PDP) computers, DEC combined low price with impressive functionality and high-end performance. In 1960, the PDP-1 sold for $120,000 ($1 million today), but by 1965, the PDP-8 dropped to an $18,000 price point ($140,000 today), making it the first mass-produced minicomputer.[66] Motivated by its success, DEC issued its initial public offering in 1966 and subsequently experienced strong growth in market capitalization. While Doriot put the market value of ARD's investment in DEC at $52 million in March 1967, *Dunn's Review* estimated it to be worth $230.2 million in November 1968, and by the end of 1971, DEC was worth an extraordinary $355 million to ARD in unrealized gains.[67] Beyond that, it confirmed the vision of ARD's founders that investing in innovative firms would accelerate regional growth. DEC became the largest employer in Massachusetts, and America's second largest computer manufacturer behind IBM.

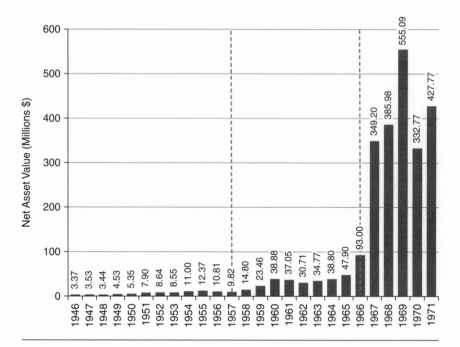

Figure 4.3 ARD's Net Asset Value.

Based on data in annual reports. Georges F. Doriot papers, 1921–1984, Baker Library Business Historical Collections, Business Manuscripts Mss 784 1921–1984 D698, Harvard Business School. The dashed lines represent the year ARD invested in DEC (1957) and the year of DEC's IPO (1966).

The importance of DEC was not lost on ARD, which called it "possibly the most successful venture capital investment in modern times." Later, another venture investor would underscore the precedent, noting that "what the true venture capitalists aspire to, at least dream of, is to duplicate something like the Digital Equipment experience."[68] It should be noted, moreover, that ARD lost money on only 11.3 percent of the funds it invested from 1946 to 1971.[69] Therefore the significance of the DEC investment was that it compensated not for outright losses but for the middling returns ARD generated from the great majority of its portfolio firms.

Figure 4.3 makes clear the importance of DEC to ARD's portfolio, showing the significant spike in ARD's net asset value following DEC's IPO. This was a key signaling moment for investors. Figure 4.4 shows ARD's financial returns. Based on the net asset value growth of its shares and dividends, ARD generated a compound annual growth rate of

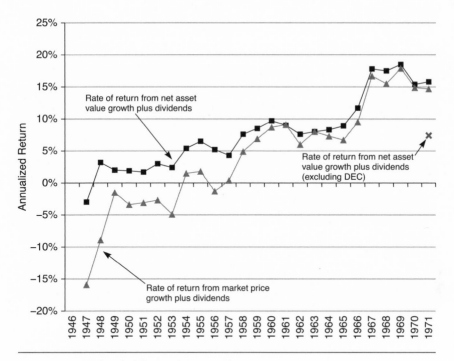

Figure 4.4 ARD's Portfolio Performance from 1946 to 1971.

Based on data in Patrick R. Liles, *Sustaining the Venture Capital Firm* (Cambridge, MA: Management Analysis Center, 1977), 83.

15.8 percent between 1946 and 1971, or 14.7 percent based on the market value of its shares and dividends. Exclude DEC from the portfolio, however, and the return is about half of that. Given that the S&P Composite index returned 6.9 percent (11.6 percent with dividends) over the same time period, ARD outperformed equities with DEC included in its portfolio, but would have underperformed equities without it. DEC made all the difference to ARD's overall portfolio performance.

Ironically, however, the more successful that ARD became, the more its business model was undermined. Because it was a closed-end fund, regulations stipulated that ARD's employees could not hold equity or options in its stock or the stock of its portfolio companies. They could receive only wages and bonuses. That meant, in the event of a successful exit, the founder of a portfolio company could make millions, whereas an ARD investment professional might take home a few thousand dollars in bonus payments. In one instance during the 1960s, a founder of a portfolio company ended up being worth $10 million, while the ARD investment professional who had governed the investment received a bonus of just $2,000.[70]

ARD lost some of its best professionals to other companies with more favorable compensation practices, and others left to found their own competing venture capital entities. William Elfers, a senior vice president, left ARD in 1965 to start Greylock & Company; Henry Hoagland, who had succeeded Elfers, left in 1969 to establish Fidelity Ventures; and William Congleton left in 1971 to start Palmer Partners. All three established limited partnerships to overcome some of the problems that the closed-end fund structure had exposed with respect to compensation and regulation. Accordingly, by the late 1960s, ARD did not look anything like a VC firm. Publicly-traded stocks made up 98 percent of its portfolio.[71] To ensure continuity, ARD merged with a Providence-based corporate conglomerate, Textron Inc., in 1972. Under the terms of the agreement, DEC was to be distributed to ARD shareholders. Doriot finally retired in 1974.

Competition from Quasi-Government Entities: An Ideological Debate

Just over a decade after it was established, ARD found itself not only competing with new venture capital limited partnerships. Another trend in the venture capital industry was also posing challenges. In 1958, the Small Business Investment Company Act had been passed, giving rise to a wave of new investment entities with the potential to compete with ARD. Doriot was well aware of the implications of the new legislation. During his 1967 Congressional testimony on the topic, the presiding senator asked him a question: "General, are there other companies in this country now engaged in the work that your American Research undertakes?" Doriot offered a wry response: "Oh, yes, sir. Thanks to what the Congress has done, I have 750 competitors in the form of SBICs. You were very kind to me, sir!"[72]

SBICs were the culmination of a long effort by the US government to engage in the development of entrepreneurship. This ambition was rooted in the banking crisis of the Great Depression, when the capitalist system was on the brink of collapse and government stepped in to ease credit conditions. In 1931, the National Credit Corporation, a private centralized lending institution supported by the treasury secretary, Andrew

Mellon, planned to raise $500 million from banks and prominent finan-
ciers.[73] When the crisis extended beyond the resources available to the
National Credit Corporation, Eugene Meyer, who was governor of the
Federal Reserve Board at the time, argued that a government program
should be established to address the problems facing the nation.

With Meyer as chairman, the Reconstruction Finance Corporation
was established in 1932. Initially it was designed with a ten-year lifespan,
but it operated until the early 1950s under legislative extensions. The
Reconstruction Finance Corporation was capitalized with $500 million
($8.8 billion today) from the US Treasury and was permitted to raise a
further $1.5 billion ($26 billion today) by issuing debentures. Its borrowing capacity was soon increased to $3.3 billion. Between 1933 and
1935, it acquired over $1 billion in preferred stock in individual banks
to help them rebuild their capital. Its activities also expanded beyond the
capital structure of banks, into areas like public works programs and
loans to small businesses.[74]

With respect to entrepreneurial finance, however, the Reconstruction
Finance Corporation was criticized on a number of levels. A general perception that it was unfavorable to startup businesses was supported by
the statistics. As of February 1940, less than one-third of the loans
disbursed were in amounts of $100,000 or less.[75] Loans went mostly to
existing businesses hoping to stave off bankruptcy rather than to new
entrepreneurial ventures. Additionally, almost a quarter of the Reconstruction Finance Corporation's industrial loans ended up in default,
raising the question of whether a government agency could screen investments properly. This debate connected to a much broader one
taking place in America concerning the appropriate role for government
in the development of the entrepreneurial sector.[76]

Financial industry constituent groups believed that small business
finance should stay largely in the domain of the market. Commercial
banks worried that government involvement would negatively impact
their short-term lending business, while investment bankers were against
any source of startup or growth finance that might undermine their
lucrative business of financial intermediation. Protecting these interests
came at an increasing cost, however, as a number of studies conducted
by government agencies, research groups, and academics showed that
small businesses needed better access to equity and long-term sources
of finance. The language of the debate had far-reaching implications. One

study cautioned that if privately controlled capital failed to fill this institutional void, "socially controlled capital will do the job."[77]

Unsurprisingly, the political divide was between proponents of free-market enterprise on one side and advocates of government action on the other. The lending authority of the Reconstruction Finance Corporation, which had been heralded by Democrats as a handmaiden of small business development, was revoked by a Republican administration in 1953. As a concession to Democrats (for most of the 1950s, the Democratic and Republican parties were quite evenly balanced in both houses of Congress), the Small Business Administration was founded that same year. Its remit was to interact with banks to ensure there was an adequate supply of finance to smaller-sized firms, and to also make collateralized loans. The problem, from the perspective of market needs, was that the agency itself did not provide equity capital. Although venture capital entities existed at this time, there was no organized institutional source to provide such financing at scale. One estimate put the gap in equity finance at around $500 million per year.[78] To put this gap into economic perspective, consider that ARD raised a total of $19.5 million in external capital over its entire history between 1946 and 1971.[79]

During the late 1950s, efforts to encourage financing for new ventures took on a greater urgency in the United States. Although two reports—one by the Hoover Commission and the other by the Council of Economic advisors—did not find any need to boost capital availability to small business, an influential study by the Federal Reserve advocated for "a new type of private investment institution to specialize in small business financing."[80] The prevailing climate also changed in response to stepped-up Soviet investments in high-tech industry, culminating in the launch of the satellite Sputnik. During the Cold War era, new priority was placed on increasing the returns to talent and capital. In 1958, President Eisenhower signed into law the National Defense Education Act, an attempt to enhance technical and scientific education. NASA was established in the same year to administer US space exploration policy. This was the context in which Congress considered the problem of small business finance, and the Small Business Investment Act was signed into law in August 1958. Its statement of policy summed up the intent: "It is declared to be the policy of the Congress and the purpose of this Act to improve and stimulate the national economy in general and the small-business segment thereof in particular by establishing a program to stimulate and supplement the flow of private equity capital and long-term loan funds which small-business concerns need for the sound financing of their business operations and for their growth, expansion, and modernization, and which are not available in adequate supply."

Not everyone received this legislation with enthusiasm. One Chicago economist, in a paper published in the *Journal of Finance*, noted the "strength and economic soundness" in the small business sector and a lack of need for any corrective government policy.[81] Debate centered on the types of financing activities in which government should engage. In an editorial in November 1958, *Barron's* made this forceful argument: "If Congress truly wants to be helpful, the way is plain. Let it seek to foster, through fiscal prudence and sensible government policies, the kind of economic climate in which all enterprise can flourish. Small business needs no federal crutch. All it needs—and all it has a legitimate claim on—is opportunity."[82] In *Barron's* view, the Small Business Investment Act meant an undue extension in the reach of government beyond regulatory oversight. The tenor of the editorial was that governmental action was unnecessary in the area of new venture finance. The focus, it argued, should be the same as with tax policy: creating the enabling environment to allow the free market to prosper.

The Small Business Investment Company Program

Under the Small Business Investment Act, privately owned small-business investment companies (SBICs) were established and licensed by a division of the Small Business Administration and chartered by US states. The financing mechanism worked as follows. For a new SBIC to form, it had to have a minimum private capital investment of $150,000. The Small Business Administration would then acquire subordinated debentures in that SBIC to match the private paid-in capital, allowing it to reach a statutory capital threshold of $300,000. The agency could then further lend up to 50 percent of the statutory capital, so that, at a minimum the SBIC had a total pool of $450,000 (about $3.7 million today) in available investment funds. In addition to their ability to borrow from the government at nominal rates, SBICs received quite favorable tax treatment. Any losses from portfolio investments could be deducted from regular income, and 100 percent of dividend income could be deducted before calculation of their income tax, in contrast to the normal 85 percent rate.

Furthermore, stockholders could deduct any incurred losses from regular income instead of from capital gains.

In return for these benefits, SBICs had to comply with a number of regulations. Any investment had to be for a minimum term of five years (unless the small business involved did not survive that long). A "small business" was defined as one that had, in the two years prior to the investment, an after-tax income not exceeding $250,000, a net worth no more than $2.5 million, and less than $5 million in assets (meaning it had no more than a few hundred employees). SBICs were to be minority investors; to take a controlling interest required special approval by the agency. No more than 20 percent of an SBIC's funds could be allocated to a single investment. Initially, investments had to take the form of debentures (convertibles were permitted), but this limitation was soon lifted so that SBICs could make equity investments. The objective was for SBICs to act as venture capitalists for enterprises with high growth potential. In principle, it was an attractive setup. Borrowing the language of modern VC profit-sharing rules, one journalist explains it this way: "the US government was a limited partner that didn't need 80 percent of a firm's carry: It just wanted its money back."[83]

Despite the opportunities that the SBIC program afforded, the initial uptake was slow, as shown in Figure 4.5. ARD was offered the very first SBIC license, but declined.[84] Some of the first movers, however, were highly influential entities. One of significance, called Continental Capital Corporation, was started in San Francisco by Frank Chambers, a Harvard Business School graduate who was aware of Doriot's teachings. Chambers became a focal high-tech investor in the Bay Area venture community. In 1959, he and an associate established Continental Capital with an original net capital of $5.5 million, raising an additional $3 million in 1960 and $2.5 million in 1969 (totaling about $86 million today). In two decades of operation, Continental Capital made over a hundred investments, almost half of which were in startups, distributing cash and securities of about $90 million ($590 million today).[85] One of Chambers's most prominent investments was in American Microsystems, Inc., a technologically innovative semiconductor firm founded in Santa Clara in 1966. His 1969 investment of $48,000 ($314,000 today) grew by a factor of thirty in under two years.

Boston Capital Corporation was another early mover—on a scale that significantly surpassed Continental Capital. It was established in 1960 by

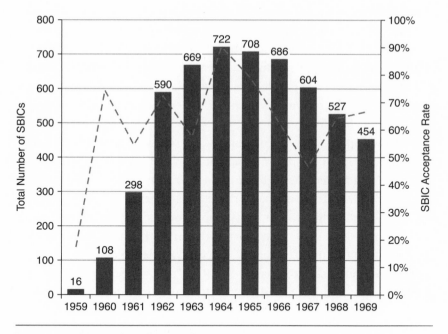

Figure 4.5 The Number of SBICs, from 1959 to 1969.
Based on data in Charles M. Noone and Stanley M. Rubel, *SBICs: Pioneers in Organized Venture Capital* (Chicago: Capital, 1970), 90. The dashed line is the acceptance rate, which reflects the percentage of applications approved.

a group of well-respected investors with the help of Wendell B. Barnes, who had just left his post as the first administrator of the Small Business Administration. It was Barnes who had offered ARD that first SBIC license. Continuing the link with ARD, Joseph Powell, Jr. was recruited to be the firm's president. Powell had been a vice president at ARD in the early 1950s before leaving for better compensation at an information processing corporation located in Cleveland, Ohio. Boston Capital raised $20.6 million in equity funds, which it could leverage to generate an investment pool of about $100 million ($810 million today)—making it easily the largest SBIC in existence at the time. In its first eighteen months of operation, Boston Capital invested over $10 million of its funds, an enormous amount compared to ARD.[86]

Like ARD, Boston Capital could be selective about its investments. In its first year of investing, it received more than 250 proposals from small businesses seeking financing, of which it invested in just seven (2.8 percent), all of which were in high-tech areas. In line with ARD's investment approach, Boston Capital also stated that it would "provide advisory and management counseling services for small business concerns" with at least one representative from Boston Capital placed on the board of each of its portfolio firms.[87] Furthermore, it built a portfolio with the expectation of a long-tailed distribution of payoffs. The strategy succeeded as the value of its investment in Berkey Photo, Inc., increased fivefold in its first five years.[88]

Boston Capital was not alone in making some favorable investments. Electronics Capital Corporation had been launched as an SBIC in 1959, also in Massachusetts, with 1.8 million shares sold to the public at $10 per share. In May 1961, its shares traded at 440 percent over the offering price. Greater Washington Industrial Investments, Inc., was organized as an SBIC in 1960 to focus on opportunities in the DC area. Inside of nine months, its $900,000 ($7.3 million today) convertible debenture investment in computer services firm C-E-I-R (formerly the nonprofit Council for Economic and Industrial Research) was worth over $7 million in market value ($56.7 million today).[89] Consequently, SBICs soon began to proliferate. In 1961, twenty-nine SBICs were publicly traded, representing about 10 percent of all SBICs active that year. Just as a closed-end structure had served ARD, public listing gave individual investors a way to participate in this realm of investing. In a sense, the SBIC program democratized access to venture capital activity.

Soon, however, SBIC returns showed themselves to be for the most part unfavorable and the rush of new entrants slowed down. Larger SBICs tended to be more profitable than smaller SBICs, but even the best performers (those with capital over $5 million) generated returns (measured by net income as a percentage of assets) averaging about 8 percent, not much different from the S&P Composite.[90] Examining SBIC performance from another angle, Figure 4.6 compares the compound annual returns of ARD and Boston Capital Corporation across their lifetimes. In both cases, the math of long-tailed returns is obvious. Each fund, if its single most successful investment is included in the calculation of total return, outperforms the S&P Composite—and if that investment is excluded, underperforms it. The implication is that, whether venture financing comes through a purely market-based system or a government- subsidized one, it is difficult to profit systematically from a long-tail investing approach. Facing growing pressure on its business model, Boston Capital ceased investing in 1970.

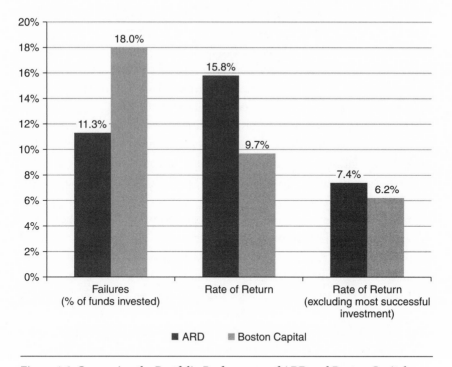

Figure 4.6 Comparing the Portfolio Performance of ARD and Boston Capital.
Based on data in Patrick R. Liles, *Sustaining the Venture Capital Firm* (Cambridge, MA: Management Analysis Center, 1977), 150.

The early experience of the SBICs exposed several core problems at the program level seriously militating against the achievement of outsized returns. By the mid-1960s, over seven hundred SBICs operated, but most were small and undercapitalized, having paid-in capital of just a few hundred thousand dollars. This constrained the abilities of most SBICs to hire talented investment professionals and to finance diversified portfolios of venture investments. Moreover, few SBICs were actually engaged in entrepreneurial or small-business growth investments due to the risks, and it was estimated that 90 percent of SBICs violated the rules under which they were established, including false filings and late filings of financial reports. Borrowing at privileged rates from the government led to adverse selection. Fraud and malpractice were commonplace.[91]

Naturally, Congress reacted by imposing more oversight, but this added to existing burdens. SEC registration rules for portfolio companies were particularly constraining and, despite tax breaks, SBICs and their shareholders were still exposed to double taxation. In light of Continental Capital's experience, Chambers was unequivocal in stating that "regulations have had a major role in bringing about the end of the majority of public SBICs in the twenty years since the act was passed." Interestingly, he went on to say that "the principals of Continental intend to go into partnership form using institutional money and our own funds. We will have a substantial stake in the limited partnership." Chambers was aware of the broader implications of this shift. The new structure avoided regulation but, he noted, "the individual investor will not be able to participate in our new venture."[92] He knew that limited partnerships would be exclusionary.

Yet, despite these fundamental defects in program design, the SBICs' experience helped to shape the development of the US venture capital industry in some important ways. Even Chambers, a vocal critic of the Small Business Administration, described the 1958 act as "a highly perceptive piece of legislation." It established a framework for thinking about the design of risk capital deployment in a context in which market-based venture capital was in limited supply. Laws originally crafted were subject to modification as unintended consequences occurred and the context changed. In that way, the legislation had long-lasting consequences. Regulatory boundaries were shifted and exemptions were made, helping to create the environment in which the modern venture capital industry operates. In 1974, for example, venture capital investments in portfolio companies were exempted from time-consuming SEC registration laws, thereby removing undue delays in capital allocation decisions.[93]

By offering finance and management guidance, SBICs also created competition for venture capital entities. As a general rule, competition is unambiguously good for innovation. Doriot noted a pecking order in venture finance with advantageous competitive dynamics: "If a man comes to us and we tell him that we are willing to finance him, it's fairly easy for him to go to an SBIC and say, 'American Research is willing to finance me.' And usually the SBICs will try hard to do it."[94] SBICs provided crucial capital to high-tech companies at the startup and growth stages. For example, in 1969, Intel (founded in 1968) received $299,390 ($2 million today) from an SBIC, Wells Fargo Investment Company. One study (albeit one that was commissioned by the National Association of Small Business Investment Companies) found that firms receiving SBIC finance outperformed equivalent firms in average employment, sales, pretax profit and asset growth, and federal taxes paid. It went on to calculate that SBIC-induced employment growth cost about a quarter of the amount the government typically spent on programs to create jobs. The study concluded that the SBIC program was welfare-efficient.[95]

SBICs created indirect benefits in the form of positive externalities that supported the development of entrepreneurial clusters. Given the scale of the SBIC program—involving about $3 billion in investment funds during its first decade—demand increased for intermediary services, such as specialized lawyers to address venture contracting issues. Clusters tend to form when there are strong and beneficial linkages among economic actors, and those clusters in turn attract new entrants as their communities develop. Law firms in Silicon Valley played a key role in the region from the late 1960s onward as they developed specialized capabilities to facilitate interactions among venture capitalists and entrepreneurs.[96]

Finally, SBICs created an entry point for talented startup investors who would later engage in the venture capital industry. One example is Sutter Hill Ventures, a Palo Alto VC firm created by William Draper III and Paul Wythes in 1964 out of two SBICs: the Draper & Johnson Investment Company and the Sutter Hill Land Company.[97] Commenting on the difficulties associated with raising investment funds, Draper would later claim that, if it weren't for the SBIC, "I never would have gotten into venture capital." It made all the difference between having the ability to invest and "not being able to do it, not having the money."[98] Sutter Hill Ventures went on to generate annualized returns of 37 percent from 1970 to 2000.[99] Draper's partner, Franklin "Pitch" Johnson, agreed that the SBIC program had "formed the seed" of the VC industry and created a "cadre of people like us." As he saw it, "inexperienced guys like us couldn't have raised money without the SBICs."[100] Another prominent example is George Quist, who in 1968 left an SBIC to cofound San Francisco–based Hambrecht & Quist, an entity used extensively by VC firms as an IPO intermediary.

Through all of these mechanisms, government influence was firmly tied to the rise of the modern venture capital industry. While governments can distort markets, leading to suboptimal outcomes, it is important to remember that markets work effectively because they are underpinned by a system of governance determined by a political authority.[101] In other words, markets typically need "rules of the game" to function. It is

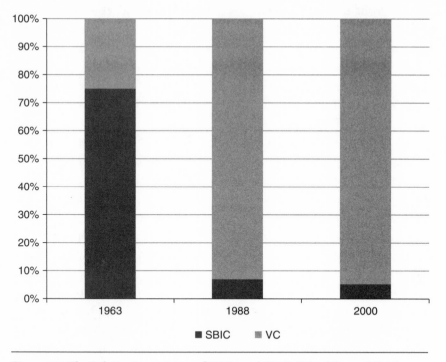

Figure 4.7 The Relative Importance of SBICs and VC Entities (Share of Total Investment).

Based on data in National Venture Capital Association yearbooks and Paul Gompers, "The Rise and Fall of Venture Capital," *Business and Economic History* 23, no. 2 (1994): 1–24, 8.

true that, as Figure 4.7 shows, VC firms accounted for a minority of the total value of investments relative to SBICs in 1963 but, within a few decades, the market-based approach to venture investing began to dominate. It is not true, however, that the government was a passive actor in this development. The SBIC program yielded deeper understanding of government policy and how the right kinds of legal and financial institutions could allow entrepreneurship and venture finance to flourish.

Moving toward the Limited Partnership

By the mid-1960s, aspects of the modern VC investment model had started to be established. The idea of governance to link capital with managerial expertise was carried over from the private capital entities examined in Chapter 3, as was the notion of conducting rigorous due diligence to select investments from a large pool of proposals. Furthermore, the industry now had proof of concept. ARD's investment in DEC had shown that the long-tailed venture finance model had the potential to generate substantial payoffs. ARD took managed risks with institutional capital which materialized as outsized returns, and this primed other investors to take similar risks in a broader engagement with early-stage investing. New Enterprise Associates, a leading venture capital firm founded in 1977, noted how the "fantastic record of ARD's . . . investment in Digital Equipment" caused more investment dollars to flow into the VC industry.[102]

Yet venture capital was still a small-scale industry at this time. While ARD had been successful in mobilizing institutional investors and generating returns from a long-tailed portfolio, the closed-end fund approach was profoundly unworkable. Over the next two decades, thanks to a mixture of government efforts to shape the enabling environment and human agency on the part of venture capitalists, the VC industry did begin to scale. This happened through a system of incentives and capabilities, operating through the organizational form of the limited partnership.

5

The Limited Partnership Structure

THE VENTURE CAPITAL INDUSTRY is closely associated with the limited partnership structure. By the late twentieth century, this organizational form accounted for over four-fifths of the total pool of VC money in the United States.[1] Although limited partnerships existed among the private capital entities discussed in Chapter 3, with J. H. Whitney & Company and Rockefeller Brothers, Inc., being prime examples, this structure was not generally used in the provision of entrepreneurial finance. The scope of this form was mostly restricted to situations in which wealthy families used it to channel their fortunes into early and later-stage investment opportunities.

American Research and Development Corporation (ARD), with its closed-end fund structure, had been a first mover in leveraging the supply of capital beyond families to institutional investors, and had shown the power of the long-tail investing model in generating outsized returns. But as discussed in the last chapter, the organizational model was ineffective. Relative to the closed-end fund, the limited partnership offered key benefits in terms of tax liability and the possibility of high-powered compensation incentives, with an emphasis on generating payoffs in a short period of time. It also created an effective regulatory workaround. Paul "Pete" Bancroft, a general partner in Draper, Gaither & Anderson (a firm discussed later in this chapter) emphasized that the idea behind the limited partnership was "to get the money in and report on it as little as possible."[2]

Yet, the limited partnership in venture capital was not especially innovative. One can even question why it took so long for the VC industry to settle on this organizational model. From a legal standpoint, the origins of the limited partnership date back to medieval times. In 1882, the English jurist Sir Frederick Pollock remarked in his *Essays in Jurisprudence and Ethics* that "this form of partnership has been known on the continent for many centuries. The Mediterranean trade of the middle ages was carried on principally by its means."[3] In America, the limited partnership form of business organization first existed in New York in the early 1800s, where it "facilitated investments that would not have occurred in the absence of the form."[4] By the early 1900s, the law had evolved to clarify the distinction between managing "general partners" who were subject to unlimited liability and outside investors with limited liability.

This chapter documents the origins of the limited partnership, then examines the structure in practice in the VC industry by focusing on three examples of early adoption. The first Silicon Valley venture capital limited partnership—Draper, Gaither & Anderson (DGA)—was established in Palo Alto in 1959. Although DGA was a short-lived limited partnership, it provides an important insight into how intermediation worked and management fee and profit-sharing rules were first established.[5] Moreover, DGA struggled to profit by early-stage portfolio investing, highlighting that the limited partnership form was not a cure-all for managing risk. The second firm profiled—Greylock Partners—was founded in Massachusetts in 1965 by William Elfers after a long career at ARD. Greylock was a much more successful limited partnership. Finally, the career of Laurance Rockefeller (introduced in Chapter 3) is revisited through an examination of the formation and performance of Venrock Associates, the VC entity associated with the Rockefeller family, established as a limited partnership in New York in 1969.

Finally, this chapter shows that the spread of VC limited partnerships did not take place in isolation. A VC limited partnership is organized so that venture capitalists intermediate between the supply side of entrepreneurial finance, largely pension funds and other institutional investors, and the demand side of entrepreneurial startups. Government policy had powerful supply- and demand-side effects. The liberalization of rules in the late 1970s pertaining to the Employee Retirement Income Security Act of 1974 created a large supply-side boost to the venture capital industry because it freed pension funds to invest in high-risk asset classes.[6] Furthermore, venture capitalists often argue strongly that reductions in the capital gains taxation burden around this time created incentives that promoted innovation and startup growth. The capital gains tax policy debate highlights how venture capitalists became powerful advocates for tax reform.[7]

Ultimately, the limited partnership structure began to powerfully interact with the historical context in the evolution of the US venture capital industry. While ARD had struggled to generate sufficient incentives to hold on to the most talented investors within its organizational boundaries, the small business investment companies (SBICs, as discussed in Chapter 4) were constrained by excessive regulatory oversight. Limited partnerships offered an antidote to both of these problems in an environment where mitigating tax liability was a first-order concern. Long-tail VC investing became successfully applied in practice in limited partnerships, and government policy acted as a spur to the growing importance and persistence of this organizational form.

Early Limited Partnerships
and the Changing Legal Framework

To understand the significance of the limited partnership in the venture capital industry, it is necessary to take a step back in time. The limited partnership form of business organization was introduced in the State of New York in 1822. It was closely modeled on the French *société en commandite,* which operated in medieval times and subsequently developed into the French Commercial Code to facilitate capital deployment and the partial separation of ownership from management.[8] New York's promulgation of the limited partnership according to French standards was historically important because it represented the first time that the statute law of any country other than Great Britain had been followed in the United States.[9] The idea soon spread geographically. Connecticut adopted the law in 1824 and Pennsylvania in 1836. By the late nineteenth century, limited partnership statutes existed across most states with little material difference in the content of the legal provisions.

Prior to the introduction of limited partnership laws, business owners were constrained in their ability to raise capital from passive sources other than through incorporation. Smaller businesses that were organized as partnerships faced customary contracting rules, meaning the outside investor would be held personally liable for the unsatisfied obligations of the partnership. Such risks were difficult to manage in a world of imperfect information. An important advantage of the limited partnership was its potential to unlock passive investment capital through "the bringing into co-operation for mutual and public benefit men having capital and willing to risk a limited amount of it" alongside "men without capital but with enterprise skill and capacity."[10]

Limited partnerships provided a conduit for wealthy investors to place their capital in what they hoped would be productive ventures—without the risk of subsuming the debt or tort liabilities of the business (beyond their capital contribution) in the event that things went wrong. This restriction on liability opened up the investor pool relative to ordinary partnerships, which were structured more around kinship ties, presumably to alleviate asymmetric information concerns. For this reason, most outside investors in limited partnerships were also themselves active as general partners in ordinary partnerships, and it was not uncommon for these individuals to make investments across multiple limited-partnership businesses.

Of course, allowing outside investors to hold limited liability posed moral-hazard concerns, because it created incentives to shift the burden of risky activities to creditors. Consequently, limited partnerships became a controversial form of business organization.[11] To mitigate the potential downside risk associated with granting limited liability, New York's 1822 law included stringent registration requirements for limited partnerships, and penalties for noncompliance. Courts interpreted the rules diligently. Passive investors could lose their limited-liability status if they interfered in the running of a business. As part of the registration process, limited partnerships had to be publicly announced in a newspaper. In one instance, because of a printer's error, the contribution of capital by a limited partner was mistakenly published as $5,000 instead of the true amount of $2,000. The limited partner was subsequently held liable in a dispute as a general partner.[12]

Important insights can be gained into the limited-partnership structure from a thorough empirical study of New York businesses conducted by Eric Hilt and Katharine O'Banion. They show that the initial take-up of the model was slow but, over time, the new organizational form gathered momentum, especially during economic boom periods when more risk capital was available to invest. Between 1822 and 1858, 1,098 limited partnerships were formed. While limited partnerships accounted for only about 4 percent of all partnerships by the middle of the nineteenth century, they tended to be larger than ordinary partnerships on a total-capital basis. General partners were not required to contribute capital, but many clearly did. On average, limited partners contributed about 53 percent of the total capital in the average venture in New York, and the average net worth of each limited partner at the time was $190,000, or about $6 million today.[13] The contribution of capital by limited partners had to be clearly delineated in the registration certificate because it was "an essential part of the terms of the partnership."[14] Withdrawal of capital was largely prohibited during the lifetime of the limited partnership.

According to Hilt and O'Banion's data, limited partnerships were quite distinctive. Members of ordinary partnerships tended to live in close proximity to one another. By contrast, while general partners in limited partnerships tended to reside in New York or Brooklyn, passive investors tended to be more geographically spread across the east coast. In terms of sector, the limited partnership was overwhelmingly associated with mercantile activities. As with the whaling industry described in Chapter 1, it made sense for passive investors to seek returns on their capital through intermediaries. This concentration also resulted from restrictions imposed by statutes in the areas where the organizational form could be chosen. Typically, a limited partnership could be formed only in mercantile, mechanical, and manufacturing sectors, with banking and insurance almost always excluded. Like modern VC funds, limited partnerships in nineteenth century New York operated for finite durations. Average *expected* duration was 3.6 years with a slightly shorter *actual* duration of 3.2 years. Some limited partnerships were especially long-lived, and new certificates were required for renewal. The maximum duration of a limited partnership in Hilt and O'Banion's data is just over twenty years.

Two contrasting aspects of historical limited partnerships are worth emphasizing in the context of modern venture capital. First, unlike in the VC industry, where it is common to observe standard fees and profit-sharing payoffs (notably, the "two and twenty" rule, denoting a 2 percent annual management fee on committed capital and a 20 percent profit share to the VC firm), no such standardization existed in limited partnerships that operated during the nineteenth century. Instead, it was generally accepted that a limited partner "contributes a certain sum to the capital stock *in cash,* which he is to receive back at the termination of the partnership with interest" and that "he is also entitled to a share of the profits."[15] Limited partners received interest, usually annually, and a profit share in line with the capital they had committed. Importantly, this meant income could be contracted on *ex ante,* whereas income from a corporation, as an alternative organizational form, was conditional on the *ex post* approval of the board of directors to make a distribution.

Second, as in the modern venture capital industry, there was value associated with a division of labor between passive limited partners and active investors. According to the *New York Supplement,* the expectation was "that persons having capital would be encouraged to become partners with those having skill."[16] Or, as Leone Levi's *Mercantile Law* also argued, "a limited partnership is essentially a union of labor and capital."[17] Most importantly, this division of labor entailed performance gains. Hilt and O'Banion's analysis shows that limited partnerships outperformed otherwise equivalent ordinary partnerships. One interpretation of this finding is that the structure was useful because general partners had the talent to deploy capital from passive investors, and to manage ventures more effectively. Through intermediation, the limited partnership form could help to allocate capital to where it could be most efficiently used.

Despite the positive performance of limited partnerships that the Hilt-O'Banion analysis highlights, the threat of being subjected to personal liability for the obligations and liabilities incurred by the general partners of a venture stymied the diffusion of this business form. Interpretation of the law by the courts varied geographically in ways that increased this threat, especially where the law was strictly applied in the interests of creditors. It was not until the early twentieth century that legislation was introduced to address this tension. The 1916 Uniform Limited Partnership Act was part of a broad initiative to assimilate the laws of the different US states and specifically to balance the needs to increase the supply of limited partners on the one hand and to protect the rights of creditors on the other. The act is significant because it formed the basis of limited partnership law for six decades.

Many of the changes introduced through the Uniform Limited Partnership Act were designed to both standardize and reinforce the rigorous registration requirements for limited partnerships. Under the new law, a more detailed certificate of registration was required, including information on specific financial contributions and payouts to limited partners. At the same time, other legal requirements were relaxed. To expand participation, the new law allowed limited partners to contribute assets such as property, as opposed to requiring contributions in cash. They could also transact with the business as a third party and withdraw their capital at any point if such a clause was written into the certificate. Crucially, limited partners were not held to such strict standards of accountability as they had been under the old law, as long as they refrained from being active in the business. This was a key development because of the division of labor in a venture it implied. As the *Columbia Law Review* put it in 1922, "the position of the [limited] partner has been changed from that of a general partner with certain immunities to that of an investor."[18]

Within that context, specific standards for the governance of limited partnerships and the distribution of payoffs began to emerge. In a fascinating study, Stanley Howard documents that some limited partnerships were formed in the securities brokerage business during the 1920s under the statutes prevailing in New York, New Jersey, and Philadelphia.[19] Although Howard was writing in a period before institutionalized venture capital existed, the payoff parallels are apposite. The distinction he found between payments to general partners in terms of "salaries" and their claims to "profits" speaks to the venture capital distinction between a management fee and a share of the profits of an investment fund. Furthermore, the limited partnerships he studied operated according to what the VC industry would call a "hurdle rate," whereby limited partners were guaranteed a specified rate of return before general partners received their profit shares on a "residual claimant" basis. Typically, limited partners observed by Howard received a return between 6 and 10 percent prior to general partner profit distributions, but they could receive even higher percentages to the extent the business performed better. In one instance, limited partners received 12 percent on their capital if net income in the business was less than $250,000—but 18 percent if net income exceeded $500,000. Within a group of limited partners, some were granted what Howard describes as "first-preferred" status. His analysis suggests that limited partners held an advantageous negotiation position. Passive capital, it would seem, was the scarce resource.

Yet, although these important examples illustrate how the limited partnership form operated, even Howard concludes that the limited partnership did not "secure a strong foothold" in important areas of enterprise. One explanation he offers for the lackluster take-up is that "it was hardly to be expected that active entrepreneurs would continue long to regard as an attractive form of enterprise organization one in which they must be denied the limited-liability privilege accorded to their passive associates."[20] This would have added to the burden of potential restrictions on the financial upside general partners may receive, as illustrated by the payoffs in the examples above.

More generally, although limited partners appear to have been able to secure highly favorable terms, some observers were more circumspect about the benefits of the form. A 1938 *Yale Law Review* commentary, for example, argued that "to the investor who desires merely a share of the profits and a limited liability, the limited partnership today offers no advantages that are not otherwise obtainable. For it is now possible in almost every jurisdiction for an investor to obtain a share of the profits of an enterprise, and yet limit his liability to the amount which he wishes to invest."[21] Surveying newspaper articles and trade journals, one finds no evidence of any significant increase in the use of this organizational form in the early twentieth century.

Oil and Gas Limited Partnerships and Tax Implications in VC

Adoption of the limited partnership structure in the venture capital industry was spurred by tax law changes and by its successful use in an unusual but ostensibly similar industry: oil and gas exploration.[22] During the tax-shelter era, from the mid-1950s to the mid-1970s, limited partnerships became prevalent.[23] A limited partnership combined the limited liability aspect of an investment in corporate stock with the tax benefits of a partnership. Whereas corporations paid a separate tax on their incomes, pursuant to section 701 of the 1954 Internal Revenue Code, partnerships did not. Instead, partners reported their proportional share of gains as their own income as those gains passed through the partnership. While the basic link between venture capital and oil and gas exploration has previously been noted in the literature, the importance of the effects of tax law on how these industries functioned has not been explored.

It is important to note how similar the industries were in terms of their structure and payoffs. In a typical oil or gas exploration venture of that time, a company (or promoter) established itself as a general partner and solicited outside capital from limited partners to facilitate the process of exploratory drilling. Many investment arrangements were possible, but in one configuration, limited partners would purchase an interest in the venture agreeing to "carry" the general partners by paying a large share of the interim exploration costs. General partners, in return for their expertise in running oil and gas operations, were entitled to a share of the profits or "carried interest."[24] The principle of carried interest is fundamental to modern venture capital—indeed, it dominates how the industry is structured.[25] Limited partners contribute capital to a fund, and general partners are compensated through the management fee and carried interest according to their ability to invest in portfolio companies.

With respect to payoffs, extracting oil or gas from the ground could require heavy upfront capital expenditure, just as, in entrepreneurial startups, the tendency is to incur losses in the early years and make gains later on (assuming the venture develops successfully). Exploration could produce substantial returns, but the discovery of oil and gas was a low-probability event. For example, only one in nineteen wells (5.3 percent) drilled for exploratory purposes during the 1960s produced oil or gas of commercial quality. In oil and gas exploration, these dynamics meant that "the most important consideration is the experience, business reputation, financial resources, and track record of the general partner."[26] The same holds true in the VC industry.

Financing oil and gas investments through limited partnerships in the mid-to-late twentieth century had distinct tax advantages for limited and general partners. Passive investors in high federal income tax brackets benefited in three main ways. First, they could deduct all intangible drilling costs, such as survey work, from their income—and these often amounted to about two-thirds of total costs. Second, a depletion allowance on production, introduced in the early twentieth century as an incentive for risky exploration, permitted a depreciation-like charge to enable the recovery of capital investment in wells.[27] Third, because the interest of a limited partner was considered by tax laws to be "real property used in the trade or business," any financial gain made through the sale or exchange of this interest was treated for tax purposes in the same way as the transfer of a capital asset. Thus, the limited partnership enabled the conversion of ordinary income from exploration into long-term capital gains.

General partners benefited because, although their entitlement to receive carried interest was established in the limited partnership's registration certificate, it was not paid out until later in the life cycle of the enterprise. Such proceeds, according to interpretation of the 1954 tax code pertaining to partnerships (including the limited form), could be assessed as long-term capital gains because they reflected a return on capital rather than a performance-based payment for labor services. A 1963 report, *Choosing a Form of Business Organization*, noted that "Any increase in value of a partner's interest in the partnership from the time it is acquired to the time it is disposed of will, generally speaking, be taxed as capital gain. Often the increase in value will result from . . . the partner's efforts over the years. This means that the partner realizes a portion of the reward for his efforts at capital gain tax rates."[28]

In effect, the law allowed for a tax privilege and deferral. This provided a clear incentive in risky businesses like oil and gas exploration and venture capital, marked by early losses and potential gains arriving later on, to organize as limited partnerships.[29] Moreover, the law essentially permitted a situation in which general partners could invest a fraction of the amount of capital coming from limited partners and yet be allowed to treat their share of the profits as capital gains rather than be taxed on them at ordinary income tax rates. The preferential treatment of this carried interest continues to be a contentious issue in public policy debates.

Such was the significance of the tax advantage that one publication— the 1963 *Encyclopedia of Tax Shelter Practices*—advised entrepreneurs "raising venture capital" to organize their own ventures as limited partnerships because "operating losses during the early years can be offset against the partner's other income." The *Encyclopedia* noted that "after the business starts making money, the investors can sell their partnership interests. Or they can incorporate the business, and then sell their stock. Either way, they get their profits out at capital gain rates."[30] Although entrepreneurs did not typically use the limited partnership form, venture capitalists did.

Finally, it is important to recognize that the choice of a limited partnership structure had broader implications for financial contracting. Notably, the 1963 *Encyclopedia* implied a complementarity between the limited partnership form and the arrangement of financing through the use of an instrument that dominates the modern venture capital industry: convertible preferred stock. It noted that giving an investor an "option to convert his shares" into common stock "gets him out at capital gain rates."[31] Convertible preferred stock is advantageous to venture capitalists because it has priority over common stock in the event of liquidation. It also permits VCs to convert their preferred equity into common stock at a specified ratio, so their share in the enterprise's upside value is essentially uncapped (as opposed to being capped by the fixed preferred dividend payout). When participation rights are attached to these securities, VCs can gain added protection over their investment. This is tantamount to a risk-management tool.[32] One study of VC contracts between 1986 and 1999 shows that convertible preferred stock was used in 204 of 213 financing rounds (96 percent), with participating preferred stock being used extensively, as well.[33] A large and influential literature in financial economics links convertible preferred stock to novel contracting efficiencies and incentive alignment between venture capitalists and entrepreneurs. While these factors are important, they can also be observed in the early history of corporate finance, when "convertibles" were used to provide investors with an ideal combination of "safety of income" and "possibilities for a substantial appreciation in principal."[34] During the 1960s and 1970s, the limited partnership structure and tax reasoning further facilitated the adoption of this form of securities for financing entrepreneurship.[35]

Draper, Gaither & Anderson

Amidst this historical context, DGA was established in 1959 in Palo Alto, California. DGA is commonly recognized as the first venture capital limited partnership in the United States.[36] Although some of the private capital entities discussed in Chapter 3 had already adopted this organizational structure, DGA was unquestionably the prototypical venture capital limited partnership in Silicon Valley.[37] DGA pooled capital from sources that were distinct from the individuals who ran the firm. It was an intermediary entity: general partners directed passive capital from limited partners into portfolio investments.

DGA was organized by an eminent group of general partners: William H. Draper, Jr., H. Rowan Gaither, Frederick L. Anderson, and Laurence G. Duerig. Collectively, they brought military, political, legal, and financial backgrounds to bear. Draper had worked for the New York investment banking firm of Dillion Reed and Company before serving in the US Army during the Second World War, becoming a major general. He became the Army's undersecretary during peacetime and then the United States' ambassador to NATO, formed in 1949. Gaither was a San Francisco–based lawyer who became assistant director of the

Radiation Laboratory at MIT between 1942 and 1944. He held high-level positions at the Rand Corporation and the Ford Foundation, and acted as an influential national security advisor in the Eisenhower administration. He was described as having a "powerful intellect, extensive experience, and unimpeachable character."[38] Anderson became a major general in the US Army and worked alongside Draper in the administration of the Marshall Plan to aid Europe's postwar reconstruction. As an investor—notably in Raychem, founded in 1957 in Menlo Park, California, which became an industrial electronics giant—Anderson was the key impetus behind the formation of DGA. Finally, Duerig served DGA in more of an administrative capacity. Yet, *Businessweek* also described him as "an outstanding security analyst and investment counselor."[39]

Under these four general partners, a small group of four or five associates, mostly in their thirties, were tasked with screening investments and exercising due diligence. These individuals were often well connected to the founders. For example, William H. Draper III was the son of Draper, Jr., and A. Crawford Cooley was the son of Gaither's law firm partner Arthur Cooley. Pete Bancroft, who joined DGA in 1962 as a junior associate, knew a senior partner at Dillion Reed & Company by virtue of a friendship he had made at Yale, thus connecting him to the firm where Draper, Jr. had worked prior to the Second World War. Beyond this, DGA was connected to the investment community and specifically to ARD. Draper, Jr. knew Doriot well, and Gaither had worked with MITs Karl Compton. DGA was essentially a networked VC limited partnership.

The decision to organize DGA as a limited partnership is not documented in detail, but it is generally agreed that "it was Ed Huddleson, the law partner of Rowan Gaither . . . who suggested the limited partnership form."[40] Furthermore, Frederick Anderson had made a number of oil and gas investments, where the limited partnership was used, so he would have been aware of this structure and its advantage.[41] The limited partnership agreement was invoked in 1959 and set to run until the end of 1964.[42] Given the time period context described above, this structure offered tax advantages. As one contemporary observer argued, it made "more sense to finance high-risk ventures with tax dollars rather than hard dollars."[43] Recall also that limited partnerships avoided the type of binding regulatory constraints that ARD had endured. They were private entities exempted from the more onerous reporting standards associated with publicly traded investment vehicles.

DGA was established with a $6 million fund (about $50 million today)—small by current standards—and was analogous to an early-stage modern-day fund focused on "seed" or "Series A" investments. DGA's limited partners included the investment banking house Lazard Frères & Company, members of the Rockefeller family, and Edward H. Heller and his family. (Heller had made his money in investment banking in San Francisco.) DGA's general partners added $700,000 ($5.8 million today) to the fund, or about 12 percent of the total amount raised.[44]

By virtue of its limited partnership agreement, DGA had just a five-year fund life. Of particular interest is the way that DGA thought about investment incentives. Modern venture capital revolves around the canonical 2 percent annual management fee on committed capital, and a 20 percent profit share to the VC general partners—the purpose of which is to align the incentives of passive limited partners and active general partners. Although the management fee is not known in the case of DGA, senior partner annual salaries were capped at $25,000 (about $200,000 today) and junior partners typically received about $10,000 (about $80,000 today).[45] With four general partners and five associates being paid at these levels, DGA's wage bill alone accounted for as much as 2.5 percent of the fund's value. By comparison, in 1964, salary and consulting costs as a share of funds being managed by SBICs were 1.04 percent for small SBICs, 1.39 percent for medium SBICs, 1.41 percent for large SBICs, and 1.23 percent for the very largest SBICs. At ARD in 1966, the share was 0.77 percent.[46]

The general partners of DGA were especially well remunerated on a profit-sharing basis relative to modern conventions, receiving 40 percent of the fund's realized profits, with that share in turn being split among the general partners according to the capital they had contributed to the fund.[47] The limited partners received the remaining 60 percent, which is only three-quarters of what they would have received under the now-conventional "two and twenty" rule.

The payoffs to the general partners of DGA were extremely high, especially when compared to two prominent contemporary examples. In 1949, at the age of forty-eight, Alfred Winslow Jones set up what is generally regarded as the first hedge fund, which he converted into a limited partnership in 1952. He paid 100 percent of salary costs and 80 percent of other expenses, and he received 20 percent of the realized profits.[48] In 1956, at twenty-five years of age, Warren Buffett formed Buffett

Partnership, Ltd., with seven limited partners contributing $105,000 ($1 million today), most of them family. Buffett charged no management fee and received 25 percent of the returns only after his limited partners had received 6 percent per annum.[49] Of course, neither Alfred Winslow Jones nor Warren Buffett had a track record at the outset. Hence, the favorable economics for DGA's general partners relative to the limited partners probably reflected the prestige and command of the founder group. Notably, *Businessweek* described DGA as a "Blue-Ribbon" venture capital firm.[50]

Because of the reasonably small size of DGA's fund, the firm was not able to write big checks to startups for the simple reason that a large single investment would have created too much exposure to the fund. Hence, it focused on investments of $100,000 to $200,000 ($1 million to $2 million today).[51] To leverage its position in negotiations with portfolio companies over equity, beyond what it could get for a pure cash infusion, DGA agreed to act as a loan guarantor to allow portfolio firms access to growth capital. Thus, DGA was described as operating "in the twilight zone between investment banking and commercial banking with primary interest in budding technological fields."[52]

DGA attempted to exploit the growing expansion of science-based industry around the academic institutions of Northern California, and especially in close proximity to Stanford University. Although the nexus of university-business relations was relatively underdeveloped in the Palo Alto area at this particular point in time, the Stanford Industrial Park was authorized for development there in 1951 as an entity "where business, academic, and government interests could come together in a synergistic vision of the future."[53]

DGA's investment approach followed several of the basic principles of the private capital entities discussed in Chapter 3. It was codified into six main criteria:[54]

1. The company must have an unusual product line or service.
2. The product or service must have been substantially developed, and the time or cost of bringing it to the market should be predictable.
3. A ready market for the product or service must be visible.
4. The company must have qualified management either on the payroll now or readily available.

5. There must be prospects for substantial growth in sales and earnings in the foreseeable future.
6. Ownership of the company must be limited and its securities privately held.

These investment criteria emphasize that DGA sought minority equity stakes in companies developing breakthrough innovations with strong market potential, whose management teams also had the capabilities to govern them through their life cycles. In this context, being able to observe potential investing opportunities and monitor portfolio firms in close geographic proximity also clearly mattered for DGA. Four-fifths of its portfolio ended up consisting of companies that were located in California, specifically in the San Francisco Bay Area and around Los Angeles.[55]

DGA aimed to invest in firms developing radical ideas for large, accessible markets. While some of its portfolio companies were in lower-tech areas, such as camshaft bearings, it also targeted medical electronics, which became a hot area for investment in the 1950s and 1960s. Technological advances after the Second World War brought revolutionary concepts like miniature electronics for diagnosing, treating, and monitoring human health into the realm of practical possibility. DGA invested in Corbin-Farnsworth, a health devices company founded in Palo Alto in 1960 and an early developer of the external defibrillator. Smith, Kline & French (today part of GlaxoSmithKline) acquired Corbin-Farnsworth in 1964 for $1.5 million in Smith, Kline & French stock.[56] US companies dominated this sector. Medical electronics was projected to become a billion-dollar industry within a decade, given the potential for strong innovation, growth, and earnings.[57]

Yet DGA's overall portfolio performance was poor. The firm suffered from Rowan Gaither's 1961 death by cancer, the withdrawal of some of its key limited partners, and Frederick Anderson's declining health. Furthermore, William H. Draper, Jr. left and so did his son, who first started an SBIC and subsequently the VC firm Sutter Hill Ventures. By this time, DGA had exited from eighteen of the forty-six firms in its portfolio, realizing a return approximately one-third of what a passive investor could have earned from the S&P Composite. Furthermore, the investments DGA held on to had an approximate mark-to-market value of $7.8 million, just $200,000 more than their original cost.[58]

The efforts of three new general partners—Don Luca[s?], Cooley, promoted from associates in 1961, and Pete Ba[ncroft] in 1963—led to a reversal of fortune in portfolio pe[rformance?]. [New?] policies were instituted for investing such as making capi[tal?] [commitments?] to portfolio companies conditional on their meeting m[ilestone?] [require]ments. Turning DGA around was a matter of pride—an[d incentivized?] by the fact that DGA general partners still received 40 percent of the fund's realized profits. Of the total profits, 12.8 percent went to Duerig, one of the original founders, 12.2 percent to Cooley, 12.2 percent to Lucas, and 2.8 percent to Bancroft.[59]

The impact of the new partners was noticeable. When DGA completed its fund life in 1967, following a three-year extension, it had made $5.9 million on $7.6 million of capital invested (the original fund of $6 million plus another $1.6 million raised in 1962), equating to an 8.5 percent IRR. Still, by comparison, over the same time period the S&P Composite returned an annualized rate of return of 6.4 percent, or 9.8 percent with dividends included. While DGA had established an important blueprint for the VC industry through its organizational structure based on the limited partnership, it had also highlighted the perennial challenges of generating outsized returns from a long-tail investment strategy.

For its fund size, DGA maintained a relatively large number of portfolio investments, which it could not adequately govern. To compound matters, DGA also found it difficult to liquidate the poorly performing firms in its portfolio in a timely manner. Finally, the historical context acted against DGA because "the markets, particularly for young technology companies, exploded in 1968"—the year after DGA wound down.[60] Intel was founded that year, for example, and its IPO in 1971 was successful. DGA was at least partly a victim of bad timing, given the difference a few years of fund life could have made.

Greylock Partners

While DGA struggled to achieve the type of performance preeminence ARD had attained, another nascent venture capital firm, founded by ARD veteran William Elfers in 1965, managed to successfully generate VC-style returns using the limited partnership structure. Initially called Greylock & Company, it subsequently became Greylock Partners and survives to this day as a leading VC firm.

Elfers graduated from Harvard Business School in 1943 and joined ARD after serving as a US Navy lieutenant during the Second World War. He quickly became a prominent source of ARD deals as well as the executive largely running the firm operationally. In 1951, Elfers was made senior vice president at ARD, reporting directly to Georges Doriot. He had high standing in the investing community. In 1958, he provided testimony to Congress on the Small Business Investment Act, which created the small business investment companies discussed in Chapter 4. Because Doriot looked likely to stay on indefinitely as ARD president, Elfers's enthusiasm for staying waned. Faced with the choice between more years as a subordinate or exploring new opportunities, Elfers decided after discussions with confidants to seek financial backing for his own firm. "With enthusiastic support by my wife, some regrets over leaving my boss and colleagues, and no little fear," he later recalled, "I decided to try to form a small private venture capital partnership."[61] Rather than use his own name to mark the firm, as the founders of DGA had done, Elfers chose "Greylock" after the street on which he lived in Wellesley Hills, Massachusetts.

Unlike ARD, which operated as a closed-end investment fund, Elfers followed DGA's organizational structure and made Greylock a series of limited partnerships, composed of a select group of wealthy US families (and their investment agents) and, later, university endowments. Although Elfers could have raised the entire fund from one family, he declined, and instead opted to raise funds from a set of limited partners. By his account, "Greylock was one of the first private venture capital organizations to use a multifamily approach rather than a single limited partner, as with J. H. Whitney & Co." He believed that "what success Greylock has enjoyed is the direct result of [its] . . . general and limited partners and their advisors and . . . how they all came together."[62] By the end of October 1965, Elfers had formed a group of limited partners willing to invest in young technology companies with significant growth potential. Most of the limited partners were old friends or business associates from Elfers's years at ARD.

Like DGA, Greylock adopted a multifamily approach to assembling limited partners. These included Warren Corning, head of the Corning family that made its fortune in the railroad and oil industries. Joined by a set of cousins in California, Corning invested $2 million ($15.2 million today). Edwin Thorne, who controlled an investment banking fortune along with his brother Landon, also signed on. Another scion of a wealthy family to join was Louis F. Polk, Jr., who had been Elfers's classmate at Harvard Business School. To this group, Elfers added several prominent industrialists, including inventor and entrepreneur Sherman Fairchild. Rounding out Greylock's initial limited partners were Thomas J. Watson, president of IBM, and Arthur K. Watson, president of IBM's international sales subsidiary, IBM World Trade Corporation. In 1966, Elfers welcomed the Ayers family as Greylock's final limited partner. The Ayers fortune had been built on the sale of patent medicines in the nineteenth century, with earnings profitably invested in the textile mills of Lawrence and Lowell, Massachusetts. Fairchild, Polk, and Thorne all knew the Watsons, and the Cornings and Polks knew each other from Ohio. Thus, even beyond all their individual ties with Elfers, this was a tight-knit network of investors.

Greylock was far more structured and professionalized as a venture capital firm than DGA had been. To provide governing oversight, Elfers created Greylock Management Corporation "to provide each limited partner family an informational conduit to the general partners through its director representative on Greylock Management's board."[63] Yet, Elfers still restricted the role of limited partners so that they were not involved in setting strategy or choosing portfolio companies. "A partnership atmosphere must be created at the outset between a company's management and its board," he insisted. "The managers must manage, not the directors. The directors can only help set policy and monitor its execution." Only general partners therefore held investment decision rights. In fact, legal documents stated that "no investments will be made or sold without unanimous consent of general partners."[64]

After a thorough interview process involving his limited partners, Elfers added Boston investment manager Daniel S. Gregory in 1966 as a second general partner and cofounder of the firm. In 1967, Charles Waite became the third general partner and, in 1973, Henry McCance became the fourth. All held Harvard MBA degrees, as Elfers did. Another key member of the firm, Howard E. Cox, Jr., joined Greylock in 1971 after his own 1969 graduation from Harvard Business School.

Greylock was socially interconnected at both the limited partner and general partner levels. The board meetings of Greylock Management Corporation served as the primary communication medium and solidified that social connection. In these meetings, directors approved annual budgets, compensation decisions, the partnership value, and the audited financial statements prepared by the general partners. Initially, Greylock Management Corporation held board meetings with limited partners in New York and Boston eleven times a year, a practice that continued into the mid-1970s. Thereafter, the schedule was reduced to eight and then to four meetings per year.

Greylock's 1965 offering memorandum gives real insight into its investment strategy. Under the rubric of *General Investment Policy*, the memorandum details the types of investment opportunities it seeks:

1. Young growth companies, in all promising fields, which require developmental capital
2. Established small or medium size companies which are embarking on new programs, taking the first steps to outside ownership, or the assumption of control from an inactive founder
3. Speculative new companies based on new products, new processes, new services, or new ideas, usually of a technological nature
4. Undervalued securities, which appear to offer considerable promise because of imminent operating improvement

Offering further detail on *Specific Investment Characteristics*, it provided the following set of guiding questions:

1. Is the venture in which the investment is proposed managed by people of outstanding competence and integrity?
2. Does the financial basis of participation offer a realistic opportunity for substantial capital gains?
3. Does the proposed dollar investment represent a significant participation in the venture?
4. Do the other owner partners, including the management, appear to be compatible in objectives?
5. Does the situation offer unusually attractive sales growth possibilities?
6. Are the products or processes, if a new company, developed at least through the early prototype stage and are they adequately protected during the formative years, either by patents or sophisticated technological know-how?

7. Can an important contribution in the form of business counsel and participation by the investor be made which will advance the successful development of the situation?

While these lists mirror many of DGA's chief criteria, several aspects are worth highlighting because they make Greylock's approach unique. First, while Greylock included "speculative new companies" in its investment policy, its focus was on "developmental capital," buyouts, and the public stock of unrecognized companies. Unlike modern VC firms, funding was aimed principally at going concerns seeking additional capital for growth—not at start-ups early in their life cycle. This made sense given the risks of new ventures. ARD's investment in DEC had provided proof of concept of an early-stage investing model, but that model had not been successfully replicated since. As Elfers pointed out, Greylock's strategy "was intended to produce a good financial record to justify continued support from the limited partners. Developmental capital is somewhat more predictable and safer, if that word is appropriate, than other paths of venture investing."[65] This sentiment was echoed in Greylock's partnership meetings, where most of the focus was on optimizing the performance of portfolio companies and the discussion of new deals happened later on the agenda.

Second, the investment strategy revolved around the oft-cited modern venture capital refrain of investing in "people, technology, and markets"—a combination that is discussed at great length in Chapter 6. Although ARD was doing as much, here the emphasis was explicit, being codified into the investment strategy. Greylock specifically sought out ventures that were "managed by people of outstanding competence and integrity." Ability mattered, but Greylock also emphasized the *types* of people the firm targeted for financing, valuing honesty, decency, and "compatible objectives."

In line with ARD's approach, Greylock was also interested in technology ventures where patent protection had been secured, or ventures where the tacit technical knowledge created a competitive advantage. Finally, the importance placed on market size is evident in the requirement that an investment candidate have "unusually attractive sales growth possibilities." All of these factors, it is reasonable to assume, had to be in place for Greylock to see a "realistic opportunity for substantial capital gains."

Third, even though Greylock was de-risking its investments by going later-stage, it did not see itself as a passive investor. Rather, a main objective was to realize greater value through "business counsel and participation by the investor." To provide this, Greylock realized it needed "significant participation in the venture." Furthermore, it needed the right investment personnel. As Elfers emphasized while he was still at ARD, "perhaps most important of all—and I don't think anybody can stress this too much—is the quality of the management for a small business investment company." He went on to say "there is no substitute for full-time experienced personnel" to undertake due diligence, select investments, and assist in the governance of portfolio firms. He cautioned that, "if an investment company of this type is set up on an extracurricular basis, there is real danger that you will be sending a boy on a man's errand."[66]

Given this emphasis on governance, it was understandable that Elfers would be extra careful about the selection of his general partners. His experience at ARD, where Doriot had been the unambiguous decision maker, also likely shaped the more collaborative environment Elfers fostered at Greylock. Unlike Doriot, Elfers was willing to step aside for the next generation, recognizing that "productive young partners should be given added responsibility and recognition as soon as practicable."[67] In 1976, Elfers relinquished important operational roles. Gregory became CEO and chairman of Greylock Management Corporation, while Waite became president, replacing Elfers, who moved to chair the board's executive committee. This nurturing of the right talent paid off in the long run. Elfers never lost a general partner or saw a colleague leave Greylock to start his own venture capital firm.[68]

All these factors combined to spur the development of another key area of importance to VC investing: deal flow. Early on, Greylock's primary source of investment ideas was other venture capital organizations, followed by friends, and investment bankers "who often were also friends." Elfers noted that very few came from his old firm, ARD, and "none fell out of the mail chutes."[69] To explore deal-making opportunities, Greylock joined a small consortium of similar investors in many entities, including Bessemer Securities (the investment arm of the Phipps family, discussed in Chapter 3), the Gardner family office, and the Massachusetts Small Business Investment Corporation. Greylock benefited from these co-investing relationships as its own investment strategy and identity simultaneously developed. "A venture capital program is not a one-transaction, one-year, isolated kind of thing," Elfers stated; "rather it is an ongoing stream of technical, commercial, and financial managers and directors, their changing and developing friendships and relationships, and experience."[70]

Despite its later stage focus and the professional approach to investing, Greylock was still in the risk capital business, with all the downside problems this approach entailed. Several of Greylock's first investments were unsuccessful. For example, a large investment in Rixson, a Chicago-based maker of high-end door closers, led to a mediocre return despite a seasoned management team, "enticing financial parameters," and an excellent client reputation. Greylock acquired over half of Rixson's equity, and brought in Fidelity Ventures as a co-investor. "We flooded the board with our representatives," Elfers later recalled, but despite an extensive effort to broaden Rixson's product base and a small IPO to raise cash for acquisitions, no acquisitions took place. Management was fundamentally opposed to straying beyond its existing niche. Rixson was ultimately sold to a NYSE-listed firm at a price just above its IPO value.[71]

Some of Greylock's underperforming investments may have been caused by its "generalist" approach to investing. It covered an extraordinarily wide array of sectors—from "peripheral data-processing equipment" to "leisure time consumer products" to "oceanography"—hoping for breadth and cross-industry capital allocation efficiencies while sacrificing depth in any particular area of expertise. This approach may have increased the number of problem investments in the portfolio; as it turned out, it was impossible to govern adequately across such a wide range of areas. As Elfers pointed out, the strategy became costly both in terms of money and in time because "a successful company . . . runs along with less assistance than a problem company, which demands days and sleepless nights of rescue activity." He went on to say that "a managing partner must assure that sick companies do not dominate the attention of the organization and that healthy companies do receive the attention of the partnership so that they can achieve success and exploit their assets."[72] This was difficult to do with such a generalist investment approach, which required of its partnership both extensive breadth of expertise and depth of domain knowledge. During the 1980s, Greylock took corrective action by specializing in information processing, telecommunications, software, and health care investments.

Still, the performance of Greylock's first fund, which lasted from 1965 to 1977, was extremely favorable. Among its big hits was Damon-IEC, which involved an initial management buyout of International

Equipment Company, a medical centrifuges firm based in Needham, Massachusetts, and then a merger of that firm with a nearby electronics leader, Damon Engineering. Such investments offset more problematic ones, such as Rixson.

Greylock invested in fifty-eight companies during this time period on the basis of a $9.8 million fund ($74.5 million today). It returned $10.7 million in cash distributions, $25 million in distributions in kind, and $4.6 million in return-of-capital distributions. While Elfers noted that his initial partnership's experience with pure start-ups was "disappointing and inconclusive," its record at buyouts was better.[73] Based on reported data, and making certain assumptions, the net IRR of the fund was perhaps 16.3 percent. By comparison, the S&P Composite returned just 0.89 percent on an annualized basis during that period, and even with dividends included, only 4.5 percent.

Greylock's initial success acted as a spur to further fundraising and deal flow. Over later funds, Greylock increased its risk appetite and became more "adventuresome" with start-up investments, despite the inherent variability in outcomes associated with long-tail investing. Elfers emphasized that "start-ups are the most dangerous part of the game," because "you obviously can lose or win big."[74] Alluding to the importance of governance, Elfers commented that "start-ups can be spectacular when they succeed. Yet commitment and digestion of start-ups require tremendous partnership time."[75]

Greylock further noted that its investment strategy required limited partners with a longer-term mindset. Greylock drew the attention of the Harvard Management Corporation, which manages Harvard's endowment with long-term goals in mind. Once Harvard's counsel had approved venture investing as appropriate for a small portion of endowment assets, other universities followed. Harvard—and subsequently, Dartmouth, Duke, MIT, Stanford, and Yale—invested with Greylock. Indeed, from the late 1970s, universities accounted for about half the new capital in each Greylock partnership.[76] Greylock became a recognized player in venture capital because of the returns it had generated, the relationships it had created with prominent co-investors, and its strong base of limited partners.

Venrock Associates

Just as Greylock became a model east coast venture capital firm, another prominent limited partnership—Venrock Associates, founded in 1969— was steeped in east coast "old money" and a strong tradition of activity in the market for entrepreneurial finance. Venrock was established to arrange the VC activities of Laurance Rockefeller, who had started engaging in this form of investing during the late 1930s (as discussed in Chapter 3). Venrock followed the guiding principle of Laurance's grandfather, J. D. Rockefeller, who asserted that "if you want to succeed, you should strike out on new paths rather than travel the worn paths of accepted success."[77] Venrock was colocated with the family office at 30 Rockefeller Plaza in New York where a staff of around 150 people engaged in three forms of investing: standard (that is, in equities and bonds), real estate, and venture capital.

Laurance Rockefeller had initially brought family members into investments on an as-needed basis, but Venrock was designed to systematize matters and be a single entity that would act as the core of the Rockefeller family's activities in venture finance. The Rockefeller family naturally grew in size with the passing of generations; there were about eighty-four descendants by the time Venrock was founded. With a systematic pool of funds, family members could diversity their investments, and at the same time receive statutory protection from creditors by virtue of the limited partnership structure.

Venrock started out with $7.7 million in capital ($50.4 million today), including about $3.5 million in investments and $4.2 million in cash. Laurance's personal investment in Venrock amounted to $1.2 million in securities, $600,000 in cash, and a commitment to invest a further $400,000. Beyond this infusion of additional funds for investment, the partnership was given the right to call on key family members for a further $1.7 million. Like Laurance, David Rockefeller committed $400,000, while John III, Winthrop, and Abby each committed $300,000.[78] The remaining sibling, Nelson Rockefeller, was engaged in politics at the time, becoming the forty-first vice president of the United States from 1974 to 1977, during the Ford administration. His political activity meant his ability to invest was more restricted.

Unlike DGA or Greylock, Venrock was structured as an evergreen fund with permanent capital, akin to ARD's closed-end structure. Limited partners could add capital without being tied to a particular schedule. Likewise, Venrock's general partners could focus on investing without the constraint of being in capital-raising mode for new funds every few years. Through the backing of the Rockefeller family, a steady stream of capital was accessible, which meant financing was always available for follow-on investments. Because of its stable limited partners (which Greylock had to work hard to achieve), Venrock was also insulated against the risk of having to repatriate deployed capital at mid-investment. By 1974, Venrock held $9.6 million of assets contributed by thirty-three family members and forty trusts.

Over time, Laurence took much less of an active role in the investment process as his interests focused more on environmental issues and philanthropy. Venrock was therefore managed by a core group of general partners. Venrock cofounder Peter Crisp had been active with the Rockefeller family since he joined in 1960. Ted McCourtney joined Venrock in 1970 from McKinsey & Company. Anthony Evnin joined in 1974 as a physical and life sciences expert, having worked at Story Chemical and Union Carbide. Henry Smith, described as a "California dropout" with "full beard and mustache," joined in 1974 as the information and communications technology expert, with prior work experience at Intel, Fairchild Semiconductor, and IBM.[79] Anthony Sun joined in 1979 with expertise in software and artificial intelligence. And David Hathaway joined in 1980 with computer system, electronics, and software expertise. Venrock did not have a fixed fee structure. Instead, it had a budget for expenses, and general partners received carried interest. As McCourtney later recalled, "the carried interest should provide the incentive for us to make good investments so that if our limited partners make attractive returns, we as general partners can share in those returns."[80]

Archival evidence shows that Venrock arranged its investment strategy with basic objectives, activities, and criteria for portfolio companies in mind. The following is an outline of the firm's investment strategy:[81]

1. Objectives:
   a. Seek long-term capital gains through investments in innovative enterprises
   b. Foster the development of new businesses and new technologies which generate social, technical, and economic benefits

2. Activities:
   a. Screen new investment proposals
   b. Make investments after extensive review
   c. Monitor and assist portfolio companies
3. Investment Criteria:
   a. Quality and competence of management team
   b. Technology advance with more than one product application
   c. Sound business plan
   d. Rate-of-return targets
   e. Visibility of a route to liquidity

The first of these objectives, to seek "long-term" capital gains, was very much in the tradition of Laurance's early investment approach. For example, he was actively associated for over four decades with Eastern Airlines, a firm in which he first invested in 1938. Once an investment decision had been made, Venrock was described as being "grimly tenacious," often persisting with portfolio firms for long periods of time. Venrock was proud of the fact that none of its portfolio firms had ever gone bankrupt.[82] Yet, this tendency to stick with investments in portfolio companies may have reflected east coast conservativism and too great an aversion to failure. As a further reflection of conservatism, it was not until 1984 that Venrock and Greylock opened VC offices in Silicon Valley, fifteen and nineteen years after the firms were founded, respectively.

The second of these objectives, to develop businesses with "social, technical, and economic benefits," followed Laurance's initial aim of prioritizing societal and private returns jointly. Venrock was in line with Greylock's early "generalist" approach to investing. Unlike Greylock, however, which was late to add general partners with industry backgrounds, Venrock's general partners had domain expertise across a wide range of industries from early on in its history. A 1975 Venrock memo, "Outline of Venture Capital Review," suggests that a division of labor existed among the general partners for sourcing deals in high-tech growth areas. McCourtney was heavily involved in energy-related investments; Evnin focused on microbiology and fermentation as well as analytical and diagnostic instrumentation; Smith focused on computer peripherals.[83] Interestingly, technology areas were selected if they had a "high rate of technological advance," created "a business opportunity rather than merely scientific advance," and offered a "specific opportunity for a new small innovative company." In other words, Venrock fashioned a basic blueprint for early-stage, high-tech investing.

The activities and investment criteria outlined above share many common characteristics with Greylock's approach. Investments needed to be extensively screened. Sun, who was noted as one of the more detail-oriented Venrock general partners, kept up with a multitude of industry periodicals and journals to be able to undertake due diligence on venture opportunities at the "far fringes of science."[84] Like Greylock, Venrock stated that its purpose was to "monitor and assist," or govern, portfolio investments—hence the focus on the "quality" and "competence" of the company's management team. Technologies with multiple applications in the context of a "sound business plan" were arguably better than technologies with a narrower focus, because the portfolio company could then have multiple opportunities to realize a high rate of return. The final point, "visibility of a route to liquidity," is self-evident in the industry today, but it was not in the early history of VC. Recall that this was an area of weakness for DGA.

On the basis of this investment strategy, Venrock made money on about two-thirds of its investments, losing money on the other third.[85] That is, it followed the economics of the long tail, where a subset of outsized returns compensate for other, loss-making investments. Venrock was a first-round investor in Intel in 1969. The firm invested $300,000 ($19.6 million today) and exited the investment in 1978 with a gain of $13.6 million ($50 million today). Not only did this produce a healthy financial return for Venrock, it connected the firm to Intel's "old-boy network" of investors, entrepreneurs, and associates. This ultimately led to one of the most important venture capital investments in Venrock's history: its 1978 investment of $288,000 (upped to $499,998 in a later round) in the fledgling Apple Computer, which yielded a gain of $116.6 million ($289 million today) just three and a half years later.[86]

Given Venrock's stunning success with Apple, it is interesting to learn that the investment decision was close to accidental. While Venrock maintained an interest in what became microcomputing, the technology was still in its infancy and Apple's trajectory was highly uncertain. The 1977 private placement memorandum Apple sent out to potential investors made clear that it had only "applied for one patent" and gave "no assurance that this patent will be granted or, if granted, will be enforceable, and no assurance that this patent will be valuable." Moreover, Apple had only what Crisp described as an "incomplete management team" at the time.[87]

Steve Jobs, Mike Markkula, and Mike Scott (then president of Apple) attended a pitch meeting at Venrock's offices in Rockefeller Plaza with Smith, Venrock's domain expert in this area. Smith later recalled that he favored the investment largely because he knew and trusted Markkula, having worked with him at Fairchild Semiconductor and Intel. Once the investment was made, Smith was appointed to Apple's board of directors and Crisp took over his position in October 1980. At the time of Apple's IPO in December 1980, according to its prospectus, Venrock owned 7.6 percent of its common stock. When IBM announced the introduction of its rival personal computer in August 1981, Apple's product became part of a rapid and wide diffusion of the minicomputer, which had profound societal impact. Retrospectively, the Apple investment epitomized Venrock's philosophy to finance companies with combined "social, technical, and economic benefits."

The significance of the Apple investment to Venrock's portfolio is vividly displayed by Figure 5.1, which shows an estimate of the annualized returns on thirty-one investments made in the first decade of Venrock's existence. These investments were made between 1969 and 1978, and the exit value of each investment is documented between 1971 and 1993. Note that Venrock made no investments in 1973 and 1974, as those years' oil-price shocks produced confusing economic uncertainties. The Apple investment stands out as a huge hit in a long-tailed distribution of payoffs because the gross IRR on all the investments illustrated in Figure 5.1 is 26.8 percent including Apple, but just 3.4 percent excluding it. Following the public market equivalent (PME) method, Venrock generated a staggering market-adjusted multiple of 13.3 on these thirty-one investments, representing a return that was more than thirteen times what a hypothetical investment in public equities would have achieved. Without the Apple investment, however, the PME is 2.3, implying that Venrock would have done approximately twice as well as investing in public equities. Looking across the whole period from 1969 to 1996, during which time Venrock made 214 investments in total, the PME is 3.9, implying that Venrock strongly outperformed public equities over the long run.

As Figure 5.1 illustrates, the Apple investment was important because Venrock also had failures and mediocre portfolio companies it needed

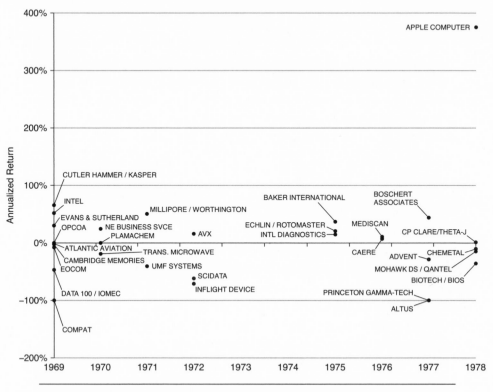

Figure 5.1 Returns on Venrock Investments from 1969 to 1978.

Based on data in Peter Crisp Papers, Baker Library Business Historical Collections, Business Manuscripts Mss 784 1946–2008, Harvard Business School.

to compensate for, including the $1 million investment ($6.6 million today) it made in 1969 in Compat Corporation, a producer of continuous magnetic tape loop for data retrieval for minicomputers, and a $423,358 ($1.7 million today) investment in 1977 in Altus Corporation, a maker of high-energy lithium batteries. Like ARD's Digital Equipment Corporation investment, Venrock's Apple investment more than offset the underperformance associated with the remaining investments in its portfolio.

The fact that Venrock exited its investment in Apple after only a few years is noteworthy because it is indicative of a shifting time horizon, and the notion that a "visible route to liquidity" really did matter. While Venrock could still be active with a company after its formal investment had ended, the average time period from formal investment to exit of its investments between 1969 and 1978 was 5.8 years, within the frame of a VC fund life. Moreover, most of these investments were in early-stage ventures, so the risks were particularly high. Of the thirty-one investments made between 1969 and 1978, sixteen (51.6 percent) were seed investments, eight (25.8 percent) were second-round investments and seven (22.6 percent) were third-round investments. In sum, Venrock exhibited investing and return dynamics that look very much like a successful modern-day venture capital limited partnership.

The Enabling Role of Government: Pension Funds and the Supply of VC Finance

These examples of the limited partnership in practice reveal how the industry was evolving during the 1960s and 1970s. But although the limited partnership structure had become the dominant form of organization following DGA's lead, the industry had yet to develop extensively. By the mid-1970s, there were still no more than about thirty fairly substantial VC firms around the country. And even the substantial ones, including Greylock and Venrock, had reasonably small pools of investment capital by modern standards. During the late 1970s, this situation began to change when the supply side of venture capital was strongly influenced by a key government policy shift regarding the use of pension funds for investment purposes.

The issue of pensions had become prominent in political debates, and concerted efforts were being made to strengthen pension funds by changing the areas to which their assets were allocated. By giving pension funds greater latitude to invest in alternative areas, including venture capital, the government helped to spur the supply of entrepreneurial finance.[88] Although ARD had successfully unlocked institutional capital, limited partnerships had not done so to the same extent. Inevitably, this restricted the size of the industry.

Much of the drive for this pension-policy shift came from Lloyd Bentsen, a Democratic Senator from Texas with experience in the insurance industry who became a key proponent of reform. In 1977, during Congressional testimony before the Senate Finance Committee's Subcommittee on Private Pension Plans and Fringe Benefits, and the Senate's Select Committee on Small Business, he argued that "private pension assets are managed by a very small number of financial institutions located in a very few localities." Bentsen's rhetoric on this concentration in finance is remarkably close to that of Merrill Griswold, chairman of the board of trustees of the Massachusetts Investors Trust, in the years immediately prior to the founding of ARD, in the late 1940s. As noted in Chapter 4, Griswold had railed against the fact that almost half of New England's wealth was concentrated in the hands of trust and insurance companies. But Bentsen saw more nefarious consequences than Griswold had, noting that concentration gave these institutions "a disturbing amount of power over the Nation's economic life." He went on to argue in his testimony that "dominant stock market trading by the investment committee of a single pension fund manager can substantially influence or even virtually set stock market prices."[89]

While Bentsen's testimony mainly advocated the implementation of safeguards to protect against this concentration of pension fund power in public equity markets, he also argued for much wider reform. Bentsen sought to change the strict interpretation of the "prudent man" rule contained in the 1974 Employee Retirement Income Security Act (ERISA), a piece of legislation that was designed to sets fiduciary standards to protect individuals holding private pension and health plans. The prudent man rule was derived from an 1830 Massachusetts common law ruling concerning due diligence and process. It states: "All that can be requested of a trustee is that he shall conduct himself faithfully and exercise sound discretion. He is to observe how men of prudence, discretion and intelligence manage their own affairs, not in regard to speculation, but in regard to the permanent disposition of their funds considering the probable income, as well as the probable safety of the capital to be invested."[90]

ERISA made it a federal offense to violate the prudent man rule. It set uniform fiduciary standards that required fund managers to act "with the care, skill, prudence, and diligence under the circumstances then prevailing that a prudent man acting in a like capacity and familiar with such matters would use in the conduct of an enterprise of a like character and with like aims." Two problems followed from this piece of legislation. First, a fund manager could be held liable for breach of fiduciary duty for investing in a venture capital fund if that fund acted improperly. Previously, pension fund managers had been subject only to state laws, which they could creatively bypass by contracting on the basis of exculpatory clauses. Second, the standard of "prudence" was not clearly spelled out as it pertained to the practice of investing. With such great uncertainty over what constituted a breach of fiduciary duty, fund managers with career concerns rationally avoided risky investing. As Bentsen put it, "no one is going to bring a suit against a manager because the stock of General Motors or IBM went down the tube, but they might if he had invested in Widget Corp."[91]

While the rule was designed to make investing safer and less speculative for plan participants and beneficiaries, the rule was actually counterproductive because it flew in the face of some fundamental principles associated with optimal investment strategies. Principally, it treated investments as single assets rather than as collections of assets in a portfolio that could be optimized to maximize expected return for a given level of market risk. Relatedly, it neglected to appreciate the benefits of diversification. Finally, it prioritized the preservation of capital and the avoidance of speculation. To the extent that this led to overinvestment in "safe" securities like government bonds, pension funds were highly susceptible to inflation risk.[92]

Bentsen presented evidence to suggest that the prudent man rule as interpreted by ERISA severely curtailed the flow of investment into venture capital both in terms of pension funds making direct investments and through their intermediary relationships with venture capital firms. Another expert provided quantitative evidence, arguing that "since the passage of ERISA, pension funds have made virtually no investment in venture capital. To our knowledge, the level was zero in 1974 and 1975 and there was a matter of somewhere between $5 and $6 million believed to have been invested in 1976."[93]

More generally, Bentsen's arguments read similarly to the arguments presented two decades earlier in favor of SBICs. He stated that "in recent years it has become particularly difficult for small businesses . . . [to] simply get off the ground. We may never know how many potential 'Xeroxes' or 'Polaroids' have failed to get started . . . for lack of startup capital." Bentsen argued for the modification of the prudent man rule that would permit pension funds to invest 2 percent of their assets in companies with a paid-up capital of less than $25 million, or in venture capital firms that invested in firms of this nature.[94]

At the Congressional hearing, Bentsen was supported in his efforts to encourage reform by a range of industry experts including a key figure, David T. Morgenthaler, senior partner and founder of Morgenthaler Associates, a venture capital firm based in Cleveland, Ohio.[95] Notably, at the time, Morgenthaler was president of the National Venture Capital

Association, which had been founded in 1973 as an industry association to represent the interests of both the venture capital and private equity industries.

At the time of Morgenthaler's testimony, that association had about seventy members. The fact that it existed at all suggested that the VC industry was evolving beyond its nascent stage. In his testimony, Morgenthaler entered into record a report written by the association, pointedly titled "Emerging Innovative Companies: An Endangered Species." The main theme of the report was that entrepreneurial businesses were the most powerful engine of growth and employment in the US economy, but that the startup sector was shrinking due to various factors, including ERISA's application of the prudent man rule. The National Venture Capital Association also pushed for modifications to tax legislation to enhance capital formation and create incentives for investors. Its report was significant because it highlighted that the market for venture capital did not exist in isolation from the broader regulatory environment. Indeed, it suggested that attention to public policy was an important prerequisite for the venture capital industry to thrive. Most importantly, the association's report heralded that venture capitalists would continue to be active lobbyists.

Despite two failed attempts in 1977 to introduce formal legislation to permit pension funds to invest in venture capital, in the summer of 1979, a clarifying amendment to ERISA was quietly introduced.[96] This allowed for a more flexible interpretation of the prudent man rule. So long as a "particular investment" was calculated "to further the purposes of the [pension] plan . . . taking into consideration the risk of loss and the opportunity for gain . . . associated with the investment," then the fiduciary responsibility had been satisfied.[97] Put another way, this made it possible for pension plans to use a total portfolio approach to managing aggregate risk exposures, rather than subject single investments to risk analysis in isolation. By clarifying investing rules, the ERISA amendment created a path for pension funds to engage in higher-risk asset classes.

The result of the new laws was that pension fund investment in venture capital increased sharply. Between 1978 and 1979, the share of pension fund commitments to venture capital more than doubled. Paul Gompers and Josh Lerner show that ERISA's clarification correlates with a sizable increase in real pension fund commitments to the VC industry in the period of 1979 to 1994, relative to the pre-amendment period.[98]

While some VCs viewed this development with disdain—because pension fund managers still emphasized short-term performance, which militated against creating sustainable startups—it represented a major shift in the history of the industry. It also came at an opportune moment given contemporaneous growth in entrepreneurial opportunities in high-tech; this was the era when innovations including the semiconductor chip and the microprocessor were commercialized. The demand side and the supply side of the VC industry were converging, and over the next few decades they would increasingly move in lock-step.

The Effect of Changes in Capital Gains Taxation

Government policy acted as a further boost to the limited partnership structure during the late 1970s and early 1980s as a consequence of changes to capital gains tax policy. While Morgenthaler had appeared before the Congressional subcommittee considering pension plans, much of his testimony focused on the desirability of securing lower rates of capital gains taxation to spur venture capital investing. As an addendum to his association's report, he presented a set of proposals for federal tax revision. Most of these centered on the idea that, unless something was done to correct for the fact that "the investor is receiving back less and less after taxes in return for taking the high risk of starting and backing new and growing enterprises," venture capital—and therefore employment growth in the United States—would stall.[99]

Pension funds were not liable to taxation, so varying the capital gains rate would have no impact through that channel. Still, there were at least two other relevant mechanisms. First, as noted earlier, the 1954 Internal Revenue Code defined partnership tax rules and the payouts general partners in a venture capital firm could receive. A carried interest in a partnership's profits, collected in exchange for performing services for that partnership, was deemed to be subject to capital gains taxation and not to ordinary income taxation. A lower rate of capital gains taxation was therefore advantageous to general partners who received a large part of their compensation through the VC fund's "carry" as a form of performance-related pay. Second, in terms of occupational choice, lower capital gains taxation could make potential entrepreneurs more willing to switch out of wage-work and into entrepreneurial activities, and in turn expand the pool of opportunities that venture capital firms could invest in. The combination of these mechanisms was potentially powerful.

The argument that capital gains taxes could affect entrepreneurship, invention, and economic growth had long been made. In 1953, G. Keith Funston, President of the New York Stock Exchange, argued eloquently that "taxation of capital gains and double taxation of dividends are Federally-erected twin dams holding back the free flow of life-giving venture capital into American industry."[100] In 1963, President Kennedy asserted that "the tax on capital gains directly affects investment decisions, the mobility and flow of risk capital from static to more dynamic situations, the ease or difficulty experienced in new ventures in obtaining capital, and thereby the strength and potential for growth of the economy."[101] Nevertheless, Congress had raised the top tax rate on capital gains and lengthened the qualifying holding period. The maximum personal rate on capital gains increased as a consequence of changes to the tax laws in the 1969 Tax Reform Act. It peaked at 35 percent during the 1970s.[102]

William Steiger, a young Republican congressional representative from Wisconsin, became a key proponent of capital gains tax reform. In his testimony before the Subcommittee on Taxation and Debt Management in June 1978, he cited the favorable stance toward lower capital gains taxes taken by the Kennedy administration. Since then, as he saw it, the tax code had favored consumption over investment: it had cut personal income taxes for middle and lower income families while raising the burden on capital. "Today our tax system discourages the formation of capital," he declared, "and it is little wonder that our economy is suffering from insufficient investment, inflation, and slow growth."[103] Steiger advocated for a 25 percent capital gains rate—the same rate that had prevailed before 1969.

Steiger was joined in his 1978 testimony by a bevy of expert witnesses, many with strong links to the venture capital industry. Among the more notable of these was the highly respected Robert Noyce, cofounder and then chairman of Intel. Noyce argued that, since its foundation in 1969, Intel had created 8,100 jobs and paid $105 million in taxes. He even advocated for the elimination of the capital gains tax altogether. Most importantly, he offered a counterfactual scenario that suggested Intel might not exist if more onerous tax policies had been in place at its founding. "We were fortunate in founding our company at a time before the 1969 Tax Law was passed," he said, "when venture capital was readily available for new companies."[104]

E. F. Heizer, Jr. was the chairman and president of Chicago-based business development firm, Heizer Corporation, founded in 1969. He also argued that a capital gains incentive was crucial for a vibrant startup sector.[105] Perhaps the most revealing testimony, however, came from B. Kipling Hagopian, a founding partner of the Los Angeles VC partnership Brentwood Associates (founded in 1972) and a director of the National Venture Capital Association. He posed three questions: "Who will make the needed investments if not those with capital? How can we stimulate those with capital to invest greater sums if we don't offer them the potential for higher rewards? Why should we care if, in the process of serving the overall public interest, a few wealthy persons also benefit?"[106] Hagopian's last question was a remarkably candid statement and its implicit avarice went against the progressive principles of then-incumbent Carter administration. But despite President Carter's personal opposition to a reform that would benefit "almost exclusively the very wealthy," the Steiger Amendment drew bipartisan support. The capital gains rate was cut from 35 to 28 percent.

How common Hagopian's views were in the venture capital industry can be seen from a 1985 report, "Venture Capital and Innovation," presented to the Joint Economic Committee of the US Congress.[107] Published at a time when the capital gains rate had been lowered further to 20 percent, the report contained results from a survey of 277 VC firms, about half the nation's total number. Though these firms were hardly the most objective observers when it came to promoting lower levels of capital gains taxation, one of the report's key conclusions was that "the capital gains tax differential was and continues to be a major factor behind the post-1978 surge in venture capital availability."[108] It also emphasized as determining factors improved pension fund regulations (alluding to ERISA and clarification of the prudent man rule), reduced SEC reporting regulations for small businesses, and a generally better IPO environment.

Figure 5.2 presents the report's survey results regarding just how significant a weighting venture capitalists attached to capital gains taxation. When asked to rate on a scale of ten (high) to zero (low) the potential of each action to aid the creation of startups, further reductions in capital gains taxation got an average score of 9.2, the highest of all the actions listed. The further relaxation of ERISA requirements came in third, with a score of 8.2. To be sure, these individuals had the most to gain from

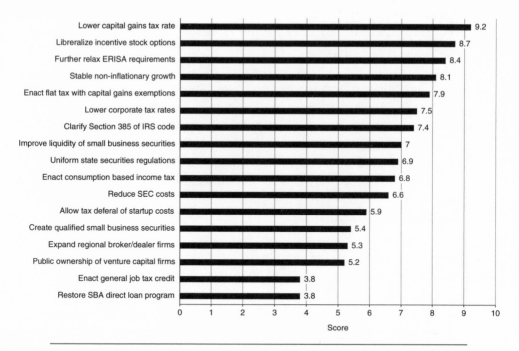

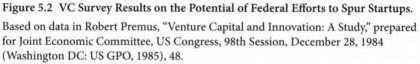

Figure 5.2 VC Survey Results on the Potential of Federal Efforts to Spur Startups.
Based on data in Robert Premus, "Venture Capital and Innovation: A Study," prepared for Joint Economic Committee, US Congress, 98th Session, December 28, 1984 (Washington DC: US GPO, 1985), 48.

revisions to the tax code, so it is no surprise that factors related to government subsidies or loan programs targeted to the small business sector got smaller scores, and were even considered by many to be "inappropriate and counterproductive." This survey's results suggested that the government's role was *purely* to create a favorable regulatory structure in which the startup ecosystem could function. In the eyes of venture capitalists, that role involved creating incentives for venture capital investment in the form of higher net-of-tax payoffs. Morey Greenstein, founder and managing partner of the Silicon Valley tax and accounting firm Greenstein, Rogoff, Olsen & Company recalled that he was frequently asked by leading venture capitalists, "tell me the tax effects if I do it this way or that way."[109]

Empirically, the evidence is mixed on the extent to which capital gains taxation mattered in the way that venture capitalists perceived that it did.

The responsiveness of venture capital provision to changes in capital gains tax rates may not be especially high. James Poterba's analysis shows that groups least expected to be sensitive to changes in tax rates—untaxed investors—accounted for an increasing share of the venture capital pool of funds over time. Their share grew from 11 to 34 percent during the period 1977 to 1987, whereas the share contributed by individual investors—who would be most likely to be influenced by changes in capital gains tax rates—actually fell from 18 to 15 percent. On the demand side, however, Poterba's analysis indicates that lower capital gains tax rates might have induced an increase in the supply of entrepreneurs and employees seeking the opportunities provided by venture capital funding.[110] This idea receives further support by recent empirical evidence showing that "superstar" inventors, who are often the source of startup ideas, can be extremely sensitive in terms of their location decisions to variation in the tax exposure they face.[111] For venture capitalists at the time, however, the issue was more instinctual. They followed the basic principle of "the more you tax something, the less of it you generally get."

Increasing Institutionalization

The development of the US venture capital industry from the late 1950s to the 1970s involved three interrelated changes. First, the limited partnership organizational form was adopted. While there was nothing especially new or novel about this structure, it would become ubiquitous over the ensuing decades, representing a major departure from the closed-end form chosen by ARD. Importantly, limited partnerships offered tax advantages and were subject to much less regulatory scrutiny. These factors appear to have been important drivers of the choice of organizational form.

Second, gains from long-tail investing were becoming less elusive than they had been in the early years when ARD first proved the concept. DGA's returns were modest, but both Greylock and Venrock generated superior payoffs. Although major technology shifts, exemplified by Venrock's investment in Apple, created opportunities for outsized returns, both Greylock and Venrock exceeded the returns that could be achieved by investing in an index of public equities. Both firms systematically used long-tail investing techniques by attempting to select the right early-stage investments through extensive due diligence and engaging in post-investment governance. The history of both limited partnerships reflects the growing professionalization of the VC firm.

Third, the context in which venture capital firms functioned changed as a consequence of government policy shifts, which became more conducive to the flourishing of early-stage investing activity and the limited-partnership structure. The increased supply of venture capital commitments coming from pension funds, as a result of changes to the ERISA regulations, led to explosive growth in the industry, while lowering the capital gains rates (according to venture capitalists) increased incentives for entrepreneurs on the demand side through boosting net-of-tax payouts. The venture capital industry itself was not a passive bystander in these changes. Rather, it actively lobbied the US government for pro-VC policies.

These changes meant that the venture capital industry became increasingly institutionalized as an attractive area of finance for individuals willing to engage in the search for the kinds of startups that would enhance a long-tail portfolio. Echoing a main theme of this chapter, Chapter 6 will show that this continuing development was not independent of government influence, either. Unique venture capital investing styles began to emerge, and these were chiefly visible during the evolution of Silicon Valley—a place where public investment played a critical role in both creating and nurturing a cluster of VC-backed startups.

6

Silicon Valley and the Emergence
of Investment Styles

IN HIS 1977 CONGRESSIONAL TESTIMONY on possible modifications of the rules for pension fund investing (discussed in Chapter 5), David T. Morgenthaler made a perceptive observation about the venture capital industry and how its development should be considered in a much broader economic context. He argued that investment opportunities tend to "occur largely around university and research centers" and therefore that venture capitalists "are always concerned when our states fail to keep up in the research and development activities, or especially fail to get their share of Federal funds for research and development." According to Morgenthaler, such funding failures disadvantage the VC industry because they often mean "there will be a falling off in the availability of venture opportunities."[1]

In the spirit of Morgenthaler's comment, no account of the history of the venture capital industry in the United States would be complete without emphasizing the powerful and pervasive role of Silicon Valley and of government influence in its rise. Currently, Silicon Valley accounts for the vast majority of US venture capital funds, and most of the leading venture capital firms are located there. Yet, a century and a half ago, the area we now know as Silicon Valley was mostly orange groves, wild flowers, and farmland. It was far from the place Don Hoefler, a publicist for Fairchild Semiconductor, would famously describe as "Silicon Valley" in a series of articles in *Electronic News* in 1971.

The history of Silicon Valley has already been well documented.[2] This chapter weaves this narrative into the history of venture capital. While the seeds of success enjoyed today by the larger, five-county San Francisco

Bay area colloquially known as Silicon Valley were first sown in the late nineteenth century, the process of expansion, with respect to venture investing, owed much to the intersection of three main factors: direct and indirect benefits from universities, government military expenditures as a boost to high-tech, and a special cultural, legal, and physical climate. The formation of a strong innovation cluster created a demand for venture capital to finance unproven people, technologies, and products.

Silicon Valley powerfully affected the culture of the VC industry as specific investment styles started to emerge during the 1960s and 1970s. It is often argued that venture capital means investing in three areas: people, technology, and markets. Although Greylock, Venrock, and other early VC firms had acknowledged the significance of these in determining their investments, three key individuals really defined the people-technology-markets taxonomy. Arthur Rock, a pivotal venture capitalist responsible for some of Silicon Valley's most influential investments, focused largely on the people side. Tom Perkins, cofounder of Kleiner & Perkins, filtered investments through the lens of technology. And Don Valentine, founder of Sequoia Capital, emphasized the importance of market size. Their abilities to generate high payoffs from long-tail portfolios, using the limited partnership structure, added to the momentum created by the increased supply of VC finance coming through pension fund reform.

Preconditions for Silicon Valley Venture Capital

Some of the main historical links between academic institutions and the types of investment opportunities that Morgenthaler considered key to the growth of venture capital have already been sketched out in Chapter 3. It is important, however, to take a step back in time and elaborate further on the contribution of Frederick Terman, a 1922 Stanford graduate who returned to his alma mater three years later, after receiving his PhD in electrical engineering from MIT. By 1941, Terman was dean of Stanford's engineering school and by 1955, he was the university's provost. In these roles, he developed a strategy for achieving academic and practical excellence by connecting science to engineering and academia to local firms. Terman is often singled out as one of the principal figures in Silicon Valley's evolution.[3]

Terman's motives at Stanford were not without institutional self-interest. He encouraged entrepreneurs to visit campus with an eye to buttressing Stanford's then limited finances. But crucially, he combined this need for fundraising with an effective universitywide strategy. In 1937, he secured agreement from the board of trustees that the university should own any patents granted to its researchers.[4] That initiative was important because Terman believed in the provision and sharing of physical space to allow for university-industry ties. That year, brothers Russell and Sigurd Varian were invited to use the physics lab, where they began the joint work that would become the basis of radar technology. Working along with them was their academic friend William W. Hansen, close colleague to Felix Bloch, an immigrant quantum physicist who would go on to become Stanford's first Nobel Prize winner in 1952. Stanford provided space and lab supplies and got licensing income to patents, including the famous klystron vacuum tube patent for generating high-powered microwaves for use in airborne radar-detection techniques.[5] Stanford had incubated a pivotal twentieth-century innovation. It got about $2 million ($18 million today) in royalties for its support.[6]

During the early 1950s, in a continuation of the emphasis on physical proximity between academia and private industry, Terman designated a portion of undeveloped university land as the Stanford Industrial Park. It sought electronics and high-tech companies as tenants. The Varian brothers were the first to locate there in 1953, when they opened Varian Associates. The Hewlett-Packard Company (which had Terman as one of its first investors) followed a short time later. By 1961, more than twenty-five companies employing eleven thousand people filled the 650-acre park, and eventually even well-established east coast firms, including General Electric, Eastman Kodak, Lockheed, and Xerox, opened branch offices there. (In Xerox's case, this was the Palo Alto Research Center known as PARC.) To bring the companies closer still to Stanford's faculty and students, Terman initiated in 1954 the Honors Cooperative Program, which permitted engineers in local electronics firms to enroll directly in graduate courses. By 1961, thirty-two companies were sending more than four hundred employees into Stanford classrooms. Off campus, Terman furthered his vision of Stanford sharing space with industry in nearby Menlo Park. There, the Stanford Research Institute, founded in 1946, was populated by faculty pursuing "science for practical purposes" and "assisting West Coast businesses" in ways that "might not be fully compatible internally with the traditional roles of the university."[7]

During the post-Terman era, university leaders built on this strong and valuable tradition of Stanford-industry relations. In 1964, for example, Stanford convinced an engineer from Shockley Semiconductor to open a new Integrated Circuits Laboratory and help the school incorporate the new technology into the technical curriculum.[8] A few years later, the university expanded the "Stanford Industrial Affiliates Program," which for a modest fee granted companies access to academic labs, research meetings, students, faculty, and special recruiting events. For the new inventions that came out of these joint affiliates programs, the university established a licensing office in 1969, which helped commercialize the new products. Even the smallest tech firms were able to thrive in an environment where technical ideas were discussed and refined. Beginning in 1975, Stanford started hosting the meetings of the Homebrew Computer Club in the university's Linear Accelerator Center. The club served as a gathering point for fledgling tinkerers and entrepreneurs, including Steve Jobs and Steven Wozniak, who wanted to showcase their latest tech inventions and share their ideas.[9]

Venture investors emphasized the significance of this growing regional advantage because "despite the excellence of MIT and Harvard, Boston by the mid-1960s had lost its preeminence as a center of technology based entrepreneurship to the semiconductor wizards of Silicon Valley."[10] Looking back on the causes and consequences of this geographic shift, Arthur Rock, the prominent venture capitalist, had a theory: "All of the energetic scientists were forming around Stanford. The reason for that, in my opinion—although some people will differ—is because of Fred Terman. He was the head of the engineering school at Stanford, and he encouraged his students, especially the doctoral and post-doctoral students, to form companies and continue to teach at Stanford. That was an unknown concept at any other school in those days—it certainly wasn't happening at MIT, Harvard, or Princeton, or any of the good engineering schools. People got fired from MIT in those days if they started companies."[11]

It could be argued, however, that Terman was as much a product of the electronics industry in the San Francisco Bay area as he was a catalyst for its development.[12] Notably, during the early 1920s, prior to entering his PhD program at MIT, Terman had spent a summer internship at the Federal Telegraph Company, a pivotal Palo Alto radio transmission technology startup (discussed in Chapter 3). Moreover, while Stanford was clearly important to the evolution of Silicon Valley's regional advantage, it was not alone in its influence. California's flagship system of higher education institutions also created centers of excellence in high-tech areas. UC Berkeley emerged as a powerhouse in science following the 1939 award of a Nobel Prize to the physicist Ernest Lawrence. The Lawrence Berkeley National Laboratory became a hub for frontier developments in basic science. Gordon Moore, the revolutionary Silicon Valley engineer and entrepreneur attended San Jose State University before transferring to UC Berkeley where he received an undergraduate degree in chemistry in 1950.[13] During the 1970s, San Jose State University was graduating more scientists and engineers than Stanford or Berkeley, while local community colleges within the California system provided crucial access to technical training programs.[14]

The impact of these educational institutions meant that capital, expertise, and ideas were attracted to the region, creating a cluster of economic activity and an excess of potential venture-based opportunities. Once venture capitalists started locating there, these forces became self-reinforcing. During the 1980s and 1990s, the probability that a venture capitalist would make an investment declined significantly as geographic distance rose between the location of that VC firm and a given startup, although syndicated investing between different location-specific firms did provide a channel through which portfolios could be geographically diversified.[15] Generally, it was easier to govern investments in close physical proximity.

While the positive impact of universities helped Silicon Valley to establish itself as a premier high-tech center, a sizable and unexpected shock to the demand for its specialized products permitted further expansion and innovation. As a result of a boost from the US military during the Second World War and Korean War, the region's electronics firms rose to national prominence, compounding earlier advantages. During the First World War, Federal Telegraph had created the Poulsen Arc long-wave radio for the US Navy, a product that quickly became "the Navy's darling of the WWI period."[16] Magnavox, a Federal Telegraph spinoff, invented a public address system for battleships and anti-noise microphones for the US Navy's flying boats. Between June 1940 and September 1945, the scale of federal involvement increased sharply, with California receiving $16.4 billion in wartime supply contracts and more than $2.5 billion for investment in military and industrial facilities. During this "Second Gold Rush," as the *San Francisco Chronicle* described it, California came behind only New York and Michigan in terms of total spending.[17]

California received a large share of funding for a variety of reasons, including the fact that it was adept in technology areas related to wartime demand. Military purchases of microwave tubes, one of the Bay area's technology specialties, soared from a few million dollars in 1940 to $113 million by 1959. This dramatic increase in military purchases helped double California's share of prime military contracts from 13 to 26 percent from 1951 to 1953, which catapulted the state into the top spot in terms of total military contract spending, overtaking the previous leader, New York.[18] Between 1955 and 1959, armed forces transistor acquisitions increased from $1.8 million to $99 million and the Department of Defense quickly became the largest consumer of such products.[19] In fact, until 1967, the US military consumed more than half of all integrated circuits produced by Bay area firms.[20] Given that the military acted as an early adopter, it imposed strict technology performance standards on contracting firms. It also effectively financed movement up the learning curve to the point where costs of production, and therefore prices, fell to a reasonable level. Military demand was an important precursor for the consumer market to expand. For example, between 1963 and 1968, the price of an integrated circuit fell from $31.60 to $2.33.[21]

Entrepreneurs responded to the increased military demand for high-tech products by continuing their tradition of new firm foundation. Funding often took place through informal mechanisms akin to those discussed in Chapter 3. In 1944, Alexander Poniatoff, a Russian-born electrical engineer, was an employee at the wartime-booming San Carlos submarine antenna manufacturer Dalmo-Victor. He used $25,000 from his boss, $5,000 of his own savings, and a loan from the First National Bank to start Ampex, a company that would design antennas for military aircraft. Poniatoff was so successful he had to relocate Ampex to a larger facility less than two years later. The Varian brothers raised the original $120,000 for Varian Associates in 1948 from friends, employees, and nearby investors and it became a springboard for entrepreneurship.[22] Employees of the firm started over twenty high-tech companies in the second half of the 1960s.[23]

Despite the relative security of military contracting, Bay area firms made concerted efforts to improve productivity. In 1942, Federal Telegraph engineers devised a novel vacuum-tube production technique that enhanced yields from 35 percent to above 95 percent. This allowed the firm to scale up production and revenues from $47,000 per month to over $600,000 per month.[24] From 1941 to 1944, Hewlett Packard retooled its line of electronic measuring devices and receivers to increase output by twenty-seven times, from $37,000 to $1 million, while increasing employment by only eleven times, from nine people to one hundred.[25] Varian Associates raised klystron sales by a factor of one hundred and twenty-five, between 1949 and 1959 while only quadrupling its staff size. This made Varian the largest US maker of microwave tubes, bigger than General Electric, Raytheon, or RCA.[26]

With an influx of federal dollars came an influx of human capital. Between July 1940 and July 1945, California as a whole gained 1,987,000 people through net migration.[27] Employment in the high-tech sector grew to more than 58,000 by 1960 as firms scaled up to meet military production demands.[28] In the two counties of San Mateo and Santa Clara alone, employment in electronic components manufacturing climbed from less than one thousand to ten thousand workers.[29] This would eventually make San Jose the densest US metropolitan area in terms of highly skilled workers.[30] Some of the very best innovators came to work in the Bay area and they most likely attracted further high-skilled migrant flows. For example, Nobel Prize winner William Shockley, who was raised from an early age in Palo Alto, had moved back to the Bay area to care for his mother after a career at Bell Telephone Laboratories in New York and New Jersey, where he had been part of the team that invented the transistor. In 1955 (the year prior to his Nobel Prize award in physics), Shockley had founded Shockley Semiconductor Laboratory in Mountain View, California, to commercialize the new technology.

The staying power of Bay area entrepreneurial activity was exemplified when military contracting started to be scaled back. During the 1960s, Defense Secretary Robert McNamara reduced military spending on high-tech devices. Department of Defense purchases of microwave tubes, for example, fell from $146 million in 1962 to $115 million in 1964. The lucrative cost-plus contracts (contracts paid for all production expenses as well as a guaranteed fixed fee) that had helped build the local area manufacturing base dropped from 35 to 15 percent of all contracts from 1960 to 1965.[31] As a testament to the region's innovation capabilities, incumbent firms quickly adapted to the new reality by altering their product lines. Eitel McCullough Corporation (Eimac), a 1934 spinoff from custom radio equipment manufacturer Heintz & Kaufman, developed a new line of power-grid tubes designed to improve FM radio.[32] Litton Engineering Laboratories, founded in 1932 by Charles Litton (holder of two Stanford engineering degrees, having completed mechanical in 1924 and electrical in 1925), modified its microwave tube division to produce microwave ovens. Varian Associates began producing scientific and medical instrumentation, to the point that the firm's sales to the military dropped from 90 percent to 40 percent in just eight years.[33]

This kind of within-firm reallocation in the Bay area signaled a level of adaptability that was missing elsewhere. Boston's Route 128, home to important firms such as Digital Equipment Corporation (see Chapter 4), did not manage to adjust in the same way. Incumbents were slower to shift product lines. For example, Raytheon, one of the east coast's most military-dependent firms, still sold more than 55 percent of its output to the military by the late 1960s. Nor did a post-1960 startup wave sweep through Route 128 on the scale of the Bay area's. Whereas more than forty new semiconductor firms were established in Northern California from 1959 to 1976, only five opened in Massachusetts.[34] Combined with incumbent firm inertia, this resulted in more than thirty thousand high-tech sector job losses in Route 128 during the early 1970s.[35] By the mid-1970s, the Route 128 technology recession was so severe that the balance of employment and output had shifted strongly westward. It is no accident that venture capital gravitated to a region where high-tech opportunities were greatest.

If universities and military investment were tangible contributors to the proliferation of startup opportunities, the culture of Silicon Valley was more intangible. Culture is difficult to define, but it manifested in many ways and attracted certain types of people who subscribed to—and in turn helped to establish—a different commercial ethos from that of the east coast. AnnaLee Saxenian argues that "the region's culture encouraged risk and accepted failure" and that "there were no boundaries of age, status, or social stratum that precluded the possibility of a new beginning."[36] Practical universities—along with rolling, sun-soaked hills in a temperate climate—appealed to individuals interested in technology, many of them uninterested in the brutally cold winters and more structured order associated with the east coast. In Congressional testimony on how to foster a "Climate for Entrepreneurship and Innovation in the United States," Robert Noyce of Intel emphasized the geographic advantages of Silicon Valley. "What attracted us to this area?" he asked. "First of all it is one of the best climates in the world. We have good weather and an unspoiled—at least at the time—terrain nearby."[37] Employees at Intel could pick pears in the orchard of their Mountain View workplace.

Silicon Valley attracted people who wanted to work at the frontier of technical know-how, but in more flexible and less hierarchical organizations. Some of the earliest examples were the ham radio enthusiasts of the 1910s and 1920s. Devotees of short-wave radio established in the nascent Bay area electronics industry a culture of friendship, collaboration, and openness. Clubs were formed, such as the Santa Clara County Radio Club of the mid-1920s, that paid no heed to traditional distinctions of class or education. New technical findings were openly published in newsletters like the San Francisco–based *Radio*. Ralph Heintz, cofounder of Heintz & Kaufman, recalled that in the electronics industry "we learned from each other."[38] Budding entrepreneurs could write their own rules on a new cultural canvas uncluttered by decades of east coast precedent.

Cultural openness can be a powerful driver of creativity and innovation.[39] In the Bay area, it helped to cultivate the technological progress that can come with immigration. Paradoxically, given the emphasis on links to military technology outlined above, immigrant inventors played a key role in the development of private sector industry precisely because of their limited access to defense-related employment. In his Congressional testimony, Noyce declared that, at Intel in 1985, 80 percent of its newly hired PhDs and 50 percent of its master's degree–level hires were foreign born. Noyce even quipped that these individuals tended to be "better prepared than our students here." He went on to list a series of high-tech discoveries made by immigrants. "Let me just mention that the first microprocessor was done by an Italian engineer, namely, Federico Faggin, who went on to form Zilog, one of the major companies in the area," he began. "The first EPROM at Intel, which was one of the most important products that we have done, was developed by an Israeli working at Intel. A Japanese engineer designed the 8080 microprocessor. Aryeh Finegold, an Israeli, started Daisy Systems, which is one of the major computer-aided design / computer-aided engineering companies. Philip Hwang of Korea started Televideo, which is one of the most successful terminal and microprocessor / microcomputer outfits in the valley. Sirjang Lai Tandon from India started Tandon Computers."[40]

The culture of business was distinctively democratic. Back in the late 1940s, the Varian brothers purposefully chose the name "Varian Associates" to emphasize that their organization would be an "association of equals" rather than a company of owners and employees.[41] Varian Associates had no elaborate reporting charts, and each engineer was a part owner. Employees voted for a group of colleagues who sat on a "Management Advisory Board," which helped senior engineers design firm policy. Similarly, Hewlett-Packard maintained a nontraditional, decentralized organizational structure based on the belief that it encouraged teamwork, openness, and creativity. Senior executives, including the two founders, frequently engaged in project work with new engineers. Managers were taught to "wander around" and be accessible. They nurtured informal, unplanned conversations with employees, who were also encouraged to pursue their own ideas.[42] As such practices spread, a new model of management emerged. According to Tom Wolfe's widely-read *Esquire* piece on Silicon Valley in December 1983, "the atmosphere of the new companies was so democratic, it startled businessmen from the East."

Bay area tech firms were among the first to offer nonmonetary fringe benefits—and the most ambitious in designing them. In 1939, Eimac set up an on-site medical unit and a subsidized cafeteria for its workers. Litton Industries (incorporated in 1947) went a step further in 1949 by purchasing a large tract of land surrounding Jackson Lake in the High Sierras for employees to use as a vacation spot. Profit-sharing and employee stock ownership plans became common, in part as a way of retaining talent. When Electro Dynamics, a major microwave tube maker, purchased Litton in 1953, it offered each Litton manager stock options as an incentive to stay with the merged entity and participate in its profitability.[43] Option-based pay was uncommon at the time.[44]

Because they built up a capacity for employee loyalty, such management practices had profound effects on the labor market. At the same time, employees wishing to leave firms to start their own enterprises were not constrained from doing so. The California regulatory environment created a labor market in which truly free movement was possible. Going back to a landmark decision in 1872 as part of California's Civil Code, the state provided more rights to labor, and denied corporations the right to enforce any restrictive labor contracts they might devise—such as noncompete agreements forbidding employees to enter into competition with the firm for some period after their employment by it. While this legislation arose accidentally as a consequence of California's mix of Spanish, Mexican, and English legal traditions, it had long-lasting legacy effects. Section 16600 of the California Business and Professions Code mandates that "every contract by which anyone is restrained from engaging in a lawful profession, trade, or business of any kind is to that extent void." This represented a departure from many other states, where corporations were permitted to enforce restrictive labor market practices.[45] Empirical evidence suggests that the absence of these restrictions on employee movement in states like California has been a spur to innovation and entrepreneurship.[46] Certainly, many key Silicon Valley firms were established in circumstances in which a non-compete agreement with a former employer could have seriously impeded the new venture's establishment—and the region's economic development.

Investing in People: Arthur Rock and Fairchild Semiconductor

Given the attractiveness of the west coast for entrepreneurship, it is hardly surprising that one of America's most renowned venture capitalists would make his career there. Arthur Rock began his life and work on the east coast, having been born in Rochester, New York, in 1926. His Russian immigrant father and first-generation American mother owned a candy store and ice cream shop there, and Rock grew up stocking shelves and sales clerking. After graduating from high school in 1944, he was drafted into the US Army, but never served overseas because the war had ended by the time he finished basic training. Next, he enrolled at Syracuse University on the GI Bill, graduating in 1948 with a bachelor's degree in political science and finance. He then spent a year in Manhattan working in finance before attending Harvard Business School. As a newly-minted MBA in 1951, Rock went back to New York to join the corporate finance department of securities firm Hayden, Stone & Company as a securities analyst.

As Rock participated in a number of Hayden Stone's new stock underwritings, he became known for his expertise in the high-technology sector. In 1955, he played a key role in financing the major electronics firm General Transistor Corporation. Following the work of Shockley and his colleagues at Bell Telephone Laboratories, transistors had been introduced to the market in 1951. General Transistor had been formed as a spinoff from Radio Receptor Corporation, and was one of twenty-six firms active in this commercial space by the mid-1960s. With military demand during the immediate postwar period providing the impetus, the technology advanced, the sector learned, and productivity improved. Although the industry was at an early stage of expansion, Rock saw vast potential for industrial applications: "I knew something in a business sense about semiconductors and appreciated their possibilities."[47]

As illustrated by firms like General Transistor, the semiconductor industry in those early years was rife with spinoffs from incumbent firms, as talent remained highly mobile in an environment devoid of restrictive employment contracting.[48] Famously, in 1957, a letter landed on Rock's desk from a group of scientists asking for help; they wanted to split from their company and be hired as a group by another firm. The eight scientists—Robert Noyce, Gordon Moore, Eugene Kleiner, Jean Hoerni, Sheldon Roberts, Jay Last, Julius Blank, and Victor Grinich—had all been recruited as young PhDs by William Shockley to work at Shockley Semiconductor Laboratory in Mountain View, but had come to resent their boss's harsh managerial style and frequent changes of direction. Within a year of establishing the Lab, Shockley had abandoned the idea of making silicon transistors, preferring to pursue other projects. Shockley Labs had been founded with the backing of Beckman Instruments, so the frustrated scientists first pleaded with Arnold Beckman, as Shockley's boss, to put someone else in charge so that they could finish their work on silicon transistors. As relationships deteriorated from there, Kleiner summed things up: "we don't like him and he doesn't like us, but we like each other."[49] The group began exploring options. "It was Gene Kleiner," Moore would later recall, "who wrote a letter to his father's investment house saying, 'A lot of us like working together. Do you think there's a company that would hire the whole group?' The investment house was Hayden Stone. And they sent two people out, one of whom was Arthur Rock."[50]

At that first meeting in California, Rock was impressed by the group of scientists that Shockley would later allegedly label the "traitorous eight." Instead of migrating together to a new employer, he encouraged them to form a new company. A ten-page business plan was put together with a financing requirement of $800,000.[51] And while Rock initially struggled to raise capital, he ultimately succeeded with Sherman Fairchild of

Fairchild Camera & Instrument, based in Syosset, New York. Fairchild agreed to help the group found Fairchild Semiconductor as a division of his company. Fairchild Camera provided a $1.5 million loan, almost double what the business plan had specified, in exchange for a key option: he could buy the company for $3 million if it maintained net earnings of more than $300,000 for three successive years, or buy it for $5 million if the option was exercised between years three and eight. Each of the scientists held a 7.5 percent interest in the new concern, Hayden Stone held 17 percent, and the remainder was left as a pool of equity for new hiring.[52]

In 1957, Fairchild Semiconductor opened in Mountain View in close proximity to Shockley Labs. The company planned to develop the technology of placing transistors on small pieces of silicon, rather than adopting the prevailing germanium-based transistor method used by companies like General Transistor. Fairchild Semiconductor was profitable after just six months. In 1959, sales exceeded $3 million and the firm generated a net profit margin of 10 percent.[53] Fairchild Camera bought the company, as agreed. Fairchild Semiconductor quickly won large contracts from the government to pursue silicon transistors for the space industry. The vast majority of its sales were military-related.

Figure 6.1 shows that the founding of Fairchild Semiconductor coincided with a remarkable shift in the nature of Silicon Valley innovation. In 1957, the Silicon Valley area accounted for 2 percent of all information and communication technology patents granted to inventors living in the United States, and a decade later it accounted for 8 percent. It went on to dominate that space, accounting for over 20 percent of information and communication technology patents by US inventors by the end of the twentieth century. In 1968 and 1969, twenty-four new semiconductor companies were formed, thirteen of which were in Silicon Valley. Eight of these were founded by former employees of Fairchild Semiconductor.[54] Just as the "traitorous eight" were motivated to leave Shockley and go it alone, other firms were spawned by Fairchild employees. In the words of one observer, "a typical scenario would be that as a product was introduced a small group of the Fairchild development team would leave to start a separate company."[55] Six months after Fairchild introduced a new series of integrated circuits in March 1961, for example, Signetics was formed by a group led by one of its chief development engineers. Then, in 1963, General Microelectronics was

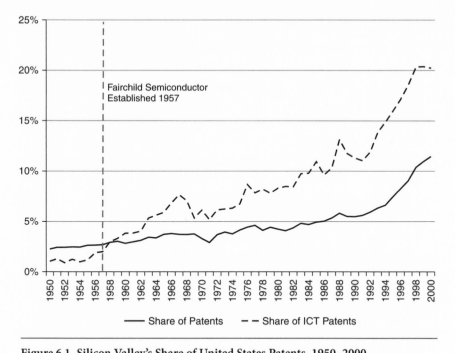

Figure 6.1 Silicon Valley's Share of United States Patents, 1950–2000.

Based on patent data from the United States Patent and Trademark Office. ICT refers to information and communication technology.

formed by another group of Fairchild employees, and in 1967, yet another group left to rescue the flailing National Semiconductor—citing, among other factors, Fairchild Camera's frugality with granting stock options.

It is important to remember, however, that although the Fairchild investment has a legendary status in accounts of the rise of Silicon Valley, this was not a VC-style arrangement. The nature of the original contract to buy between Fairchild Camera and the founders meant that the financial upside was capped at between $3 million and $5 million, regardless of the degree of success. There would be no outsized payoff for the founders. When Fairchild Camera acquired Fairchild Semiconductor under the terms of the original agreement, the eight scientists received publicly traded shares in the parent company and became employees.[56] Furthermore, although Rock kept in contact with the eight founders, he was not involved in any governing capacity at Fairchild Semiconductor. Hayden Stone was not a VC-style intermediary. It was not like the early venture capital firms described in prior chapters, such as Draper, Gaither & Anderson or Greylock or Venrock.

Still, Rock's assistance to those eight scientists represents an early indication of his people-based approach, which did become an important feature of his emerging VC investment style. Although the technology side clearly mattered to the Fairchild Semiconductor investment, Rock's ability to spot the value and capabilities of the Fairchild team is noticeable. These were recent PhDs, still young and largely unproven at the time, yet Rock persisted even as he encountered difficulties in fundraising. "I really liked the eight of them," he would later state, "and thought they would accomplish something."[57] In what would become a hallmark of his investment style, Rock emphasized that "good ideas and good products are a dime a dozen . . . good *people* are rare," and explained: "I generally pay more attention to the people who prepare a business plan than to the proposal itself."[58]

For Rock, the decision to migrate from the east coast to the west coast was inevitable given the potential for value creation and capture that he saw in this fledgling industry and beyond. He found that "people were a lot more adventuresome in California than they were in the East. In the East, it's the old establishment and old money. . . . I found that the brighter, more imaginative, adventuresome people were out [West]."[59]

Davis & Rock, 1961–1968

Rock entered the venture capital industry explicitly when he established a limited partnership with Thomas (Tommy) J. Davis, Jr., a lawyer and financier he met through mutual friends in San Francisco. Davis had been mentored on technology investments by Frederick Terman. Davis and Rock could not have had more opposite personalities. Davis struck people as "open and friendly with a talent for conversation" while Rock was perceived as "silent and brooding, a keen listener who rarely offers a sentence or two of reaction."[60] Rock required high standards of excellence and could be extremely intimidating. One associate indicated: "I was scared to death of him for the first ten years I knew him."[61]

Davis and Rock started by securing $5 million from about twenty-five investors, largely through existing connections. Several of the "traitorous eight" were investors in the fund. So was Henry Singleton, whom Rock had helped to finance in 1960, during his days at Hayden Stone. Singleton had left Litton Industries that year to form Teledyne, which became a conglomerate of technology and science-related businesses, and Rock served on Teledyne's board of directors from 1960 through 1994. Although the limited partners, by construction, were not directly involved in the business, they did often help out with due diligence and deal flow. Kleiner, for example, said he evaluated "four or five companies a year." Davis & Rock invested in fifteen companies over its seven-year limited partnership lifespan, including Teledyne, which became one of its most influential investments. The limited partnership was structured so that Davis and Rock as general partners received 20 percent of the funds profits as carried interest.[62]

An insight into the investment strategy of Davis & Rock can be gained from the details of an important document in the history of the venture capital industry. In September 1966, Davis delivered a speech to the Western Electronic Manufacturers Association in Palo Alto on "How to Pick a Winner in the Electronics Industry." This document appears to have been widely read and circulated. A copy held by Venrock's Peter Crisp was annotated in the following way: "I think this is well done, perceptive, coherent, and well worth reading at least as a 'focus-sharpening' device."[63] Davis starts the speech by outlining what actually constitutes a "winner." In a financial sense, it meant "a situation in which our initial investment would appreciate at least ten times in five to seven years"—a criterion that some might incorrectly call "too stringent." He argued there was often a failure to realize that "the risks in small companies are so enormous" and that "some would fail for practically unforeseeable causes" while "others would only putter along." Davis commented that the overall portfolio return would depend on "the few that did exceed the ten times criterion" and that the "up-side potential is to us much more important than the downside risk." He also acknowledged that Davis & Rock's investment strategy went beyond startups to include firms "in business long enough to have a market of some kind." For these types of investments, he argued, a multiple of "four or five times" seemed reasonable given the lower level of risk.

On the question of how to select portfolio company investments, Davis was unequivocal: "back the right people." Fundamentally, he said, "people make products; products don't make people" and furthermore, "only a tiny percentage of people possess the managerial and motivational capabilities to build extraordinary growth companies." He went on to list six criteria for identifying the "right people":

1. *Integrity.* This is basic, but too often overlooked or assumed. It implies more than financial honesty. It includes the guts to take responsibility, admit mistakes, face the facts.
2. *Motivation.* This is the key criterion. Do the people want to build the largest and best company that can possibly be built without reckless haste and foolish risk? Or, do they want to have a nice, comfortable company that moves conservatively along? Or, do they want prestige from esoteric developments that may not achieve volume sales for years and years, if ever? Or, do they want company cars, large salaries, perquisites . . .
3. *Market Orientation.* The man I like to back is completely market orientated. He has interest only in things that people are going to buy, buy soon, and buy in quantity. He starts there—not with an idea of a product he likes because it would be a fine creation, a magnificent solution to a problem only a few people want to have solved . . .
4. *Skills and Experience.* The man to back in starting a company must have the technical capability to create in his chosen fields. In addition, he should have had experience in actually managing operations of substantial size. And, the operation he plans should be of the type he has managed. It is costly for investors to have a manager learn at their expense.
5. *Accounting Ability.* A real manager has a deep appreciation of the role inspired accounting can play in his company. Without accurate information on costs, the really astute manager knows he cannot price his product appropriately, or bid on contracts with any assurance. And he cannot tell where to place his efforts in cost reduction . . .
6. *Leadership.* He must have this quality to a very high degree. I won't try to describe this quality. So many books and articles have tried, mostly without success. But you can usually get a pretty good feel for this quality, given a little time and propinquity.

Rare though it might be, Davis argued, "all the above-mentioned qualities sometimes come together in a man who really can manage" and this was "the man to back." In terms of sectors where such entrepreneurial individuals might be active, Davis said he preferred manufacturing to services, because "the more you sell, the more profitably you can produce." He targeted innovative "sophisticated products" aimed at "existing markets" on the order of "around $100 million and which are still growing rapidly." Although backing the "right people" therefore meant simultaneously backing the right technologies and markets, Davis was unambiguous about his people-first approach.

This was the approach behind Davis & Rock's 1962 investment of $280,000 to help start computer maker Scientific Data Systems.[64] Davis sourced the investment and Rock chose to support it at least partly because of its founder, Max Palevsky. Born in Chicago to immigrant parents, Palevsky had previously run the computer division at Packard Bell. When that company started to face financial difficulties, he decided he should venture out on his own. Rock claimed some degree of prescience: "I was convinced [Palevsky] was going to make money. Very few people turn me on the way he did."[65] On another occasion, Rock would say that "Max was, and is, a very interesting man. . . . He was a very, very good manager. But his style was different than most people's style. His was an easygoing, slap you on the back, put your feet up on the table [kind of style]. I think he was the first executive I ever came across who didn't wear a tie."[66]

In the same way that the eight defectors from Shockley had faced difficulties contracting for finance, Palevsky ultimately ceded 80 percent of his firm for $980,000 in capital.[67] With venture capital investment also came governance. Rock sat on the board at Davis's insistence, subsequently becoming chairman. In 1965, Scientific Data Systems had sales of about $45 million and $3 million in net profits. Three years later, it had sales of $100 million and was double the size of Digital Equipment Corporation. Xerox, taken at the time by the rash notion that it must diversify into computers (because its major competitor IBM was diversifying into copiers) saw it as an acquisition possibility. Xerox went ahead with the acquisition in exchange for a stratospheric $990,000,000 of its stock. Rock soon left the board. Unfortunately for Xerox, the early 1970s recession compounded the problem of its strategic blunder of diversifying into an area where it lacked core capabilities. Xerox ended up shuttering Scientific Data Systems over the next few years at a total loss of around $2 billion.[68] For Davis & Rock, however, the transaction worked out spectacularly. As Rock recalled: "Davis & Rock owned 415,000 shares of SDS according to the prospectus dated June 16, 1967, which represented 10.8 percent of the fully adjusted shares outstanding. Xerox exchanged about $990,000,000 of their stock for SDS shares. So it looks like Davis & Rock made about 380 times their money. There may have been some adjustments, which I don't recall, so say 300 times."[69]

Beyond Davis & Rock, the Scientific Data Systems investment was significant to the venture capital industry more generally. Davis and Rock had verified that the limited partnership structure of portfolio venture investing could deliver great value to both its limited partners and general partners in a reasonable time frame and in a systematic way. Managing a set of investments with a long-tailed distribution of payoffs, they had secured one of the hits that would assure the overall success of the fund. Davis and Rock were regarded as careful investors; indeed, they gave so much personal attention to picking the right investments that they did not even invest about $2 million of the original $5 million. The fund ultimately distributed about $90 million to investors as capital gains. Davis & Rock received over $16 million in carried interest.[70]

The Intel Investment

If Scientific Data Systems was among the most important investments in venture capital history, what was to come next was to have even more significance to the growing development of venture capital, and Rock's reputation as a people-based investor. In 1968, Davis & Rock dissolved their partnership as it had come to the end of its seven-year lifespan. In 1969, Davis went on to cofound the Mayfield Fund, another prestigious west coast venture capital firm. Meanwhile, Rock revisited his longstanding relationship with members of the traitorous eight.

By the mid-1960s, the east coast management style at Fairchild Camera had become increasingly problematic for the founders of Fairchild Semiconductor, which itself was struggling to compete in a world where integrated circuit prices were falling sharply. By the late 1960s, Noyce and Moore were the only ones of the original eight who remained. Although Noyce was the de facto head of Fairchild Semiconductor, and the division generated virtually all of Fairchild Camera's profits, Noyce was passed over for promotion to CEO of the parent company. He and Moore decided at that point to sell their equity and leave. Moore was head of research and development at the time and had grown frustrated with a lackluster product pipeline.[71]

Rock and Noyce had remained close friends since the initial Fairchild Semiconductor investment and had talked on and off about business options for some time. In fact, Rock had actually encouraged Noyce to leave Fairchild Semiconductor. Rock later remembered: "In 1968, Noyce called me and said, 'Gee, I think maybe Gordon and I do want to leave Fairchild Semiconductor and go into business for ourselves.' And so we talked about it for a while and I asked him how much money they needed and he said $2.5 million. And I said, 'Well how much money are you guys willing to put up?' He thought about it for a while and said, 'Well, we'll each put up $250,000' which represented a fairly good portion of their net worth at the time."[72]

The idea Noyce and Moore had was to make computer memory from silicon devices, an area of R&D that Moore had already been working on at Fairchild. But it was yet to be commercialized even though other firms, including IBM, were interested in the space. Both Noyce and Moore felt the idea was technically and economically feasible and that it could form the basis of a standalone company. In 1965, Moore had articulated what became known as "Moore's Law" based on the observation that the number of transistors per square inch on integrated circuits had doubled every year since their invention. This level of increasing sophistication meant that integrated circuits could potentially act as memories for computers. Rock realized how difficult the task would be, yet, he later recalled, "I was absolutely 100 percent sure [the new firm] would be a success because of Moore and Noyce."[73]

In July 1968, NM Electronics was incorporated, soon to be renamed Intel as shorthand for "integrated electronics." Noyce was forty years old and Moore was thirty-nine. Rock, just short of 42, became chairman. At the beginning, Noyce and Moore each held 45 percent of the shares and Rock held 10 percent. Cash flow was secured through a $1.5 million loan arranged by Noyce and Rock. Salaries were set on par with what founders in Silicon Valley would receive today: Noyce was paid $30,000 (about $200,000 in today's terms), which amounted to about one-third of his Fairchild pay.[74] To secure further funding for the venture, Noyce and Rock wrote up a short business plan and Rock set about raising $2.5 million in convertible debentures, convertible at $5 per share. The use of convertible debentures gave investors some protection in event that the company failed, while providing financial upside benefits through conversion into common stock. Such was the excitement associated with the investment that Rock secured the financing within forty-eight hours from a select group of investors including the remaining six founders of Fairchild Semiconductor.[75]

Several aspects of the investment and its structure shed light on the development of the venture capital industry. First, although Rock was not, strictly speaking, a venture capitalist at the time (because his partnership with Davis had been dissolved), he did act like a VC intermediary. He did not receive a fee for the transaction. Instead, his equity purchase of $300,000 of the convertible debentures on his own account made him the largest investor after Noyce and Moore.[76] The fact that he was able to raise the financing so swiftly suggests the immense value of his intermediation. Noyce reflected later that he might have been able to disintermediate the transaction and raise the financing by himself, but he "had no idea how to go about it."[77] Moreover, Rock brought additional value because he was among the first VCs to certify investments through his personal involvement. As Mike Moritz, an outstanding investor from Sequoia Capital, later wrote, "a telephone call from Arthur Rock was viewed by other venture capitalists, underwriters, commercial bankers, and stockbrokers as the financial equivalent of white smoke emerging from a Vatican chimney."[78]

Second, the Intel investment showcased the importance of repeat entrepreneurship, deal flow, and incentive compensation in a VC-style startup. Noyce and Moore had had to sacrifice a great deal of ownership for financing when they and their colleagues started Fairchild Semiconductor. Now, however, they were experienced entrepreneurs with a track record, which they could use to command a higher ownership share. The Rock convertible debenture financing plan for Intel states clearly that "the investors will own 50 percent of the company for which they will have paid $2,500,000 and the founders 50 percent for which they have paid $500,000." Intel maintained a pool of equity to incentivize key employees. Andy Grove, who was employee number three when he joined Intel in 1968 in his early thirties, would see his net worth rise to several hundred million dollars on the basis of the equity he held in the firm.[79]

Third, Rock's involvement with Noyce and Moore went beyond venture financing into the realm of governance. Rock mentored the founders at an early stage of the enterprise and he also governed more formally by sitting on Intel's board. The structure of Intel's board exemplified how startup finance intersected with VC-style governance. At the outset, the board had six members, three of whom were non-operating: Max Palevsky from Scientific Data Systems, Gerard Currie who led Data Technology, and Charles B. Smith, a representative of the Rockefeller family. (As noted in Chapter 5, Venrock invested in Intel, too.) The board had outside majority representation; it was large, formal, highly active, and legitimate; and it consisted of individuals who had excellent domain expertise. It was also tolerant of early losses, with directors expecting that gains would ultimately be realized.[80] Thus, the startup of Intel is fully recognizable as a VC-backed startup, having all the practical elements one would see today.[81]

Finally, Intel was the kind of classic hit in a long-tail investment portfolio that attracted other entrepreneurs and venture capitalists to Silicon Valley to seek out wealth-making opportunities. Over a thousand startups were established in the area between 1975 and 1983, and many of the founders went on to become fabulously wealthy on the basis of their high-tech innovations. Noyce and Moore each had a stakes in Intel valued at $147 million eleven years after the firm was established.[82] For Rock, however, such numbers were immaterial at a personal level. Although his fortune in the early 1980s probably exceeded $200 million, he said, "I don't like people to count my money. That isn't what turns me on."[83] Alluding to his hobby in a 1970 *Businessweek* article, he claimed: "I'd rather be known as a skier."[84]

Apple Computer, Inc., and Diasonics, Inc.

Rock formed another limited partnership, Arthur Rock & Company (ARC), in 1969. To serve as junior general partner he enlisted Richard Kramlich, a recent Harvard Business School graduate who had been mentored by Georges Doriot and who would go on, in 1977, to cofound New Enterprise Associates (see Chapter 7). ARC raised $10 million, invested approximately $6.5 million, and distributed about $30 million in capital gains.[85] Both Noyce and Moore were among the limited partners. ARC made many investments, but two of them—Apple Computer, Inc., and Diasonics, Inc.—were most notable from the perspective of long-tail returns.

Regarding Apple, Rock continued his emphasis on personal networks and relationships. He was introduced to the startup through his friend Mike Markkula, who had been a marketing manager for Fairchild Semiconductor, then Intel's vice president of marketing. A few years after

Intel's IPO in 1971, Markkula had retired early, at age thirty-four, already wealthy from his stock options. In 1977, his investment of $91,000 in Apple Computer made him a one-third owner with Steve Jobs and Steve Wozniak.[86] Operations were financed through loans by Markkula and the Bank of America.[87] Markkula encouraged Rock to meet Apple's founders and consider making an investment.

When Jobs and Wozniak pitched their idea to Grove and Moore, Rock was unenthusiastic. In a 2001 interview, he recalled that Jobs and Wozniak "kind of turned me off as people." He noted that "Steve had a beard and goatee, didn't wear shoes, wore terrible clothes, hair down to his collar, and probably hadn't had a haircut in twenty years." His interest was later piqued, however, at the Homebrew Computer Show in San Jose, where Jobs and Wozniak were in attendance.[88] He described the scene: "There was a big auditorium full of people with circuit boards and makeshift computers. No one was actually making a computer. Many booths were empty. I walked over to the Apple booth, and I couldn't get close to it. People were piled up behind the booth. I began to figure maybe there was something to this. I stood around there for quite a while, and listened to people talking about it, and I thought, there's really something here and if Mike is going to be really serious about this company, I guess I'll make an investment."[89]

As Venrock was spearheading the financing for Apple (see Chapter 5), Rock made a $57,600 investment and joined the board, though in a much less active capacity than he had at Intel. Further financing arrived in stages. When Apple issued its IPO in December 1980, that investment was worth a staggering $14 million.[90] Rock's governance efforts included helping to infuse Apple with managerial talent, and he was involved in the 1983 hiring of John Sculley as CEO. Later, Rock sided with Sculley and others on the board in removing Jobs from the company, typifying the VC view that founders are often unsuited to firms' requirements later in their life cycles. Rock stepped down from the Apple board in 1993.

While Apple proved to be a big hit in Rock's portfolio of investments, and did much to cement his reputation as the most exceptional venture capital investor in Silicon Valley, the same could not be said for his backing of Diasonics, Inc. He would describe his 1978 investment in this developer and manufacturer of medical instruments as "his biggest failure." In fact, to this day, Rock keeps a Diasonics plaque in his San Francisco office because, he says, "I don't want to forget that one."[91] About its genesis, he ruefully quips that the entrepreneur might have "found me in the phone book under venture capital."[92]

Rock made the investment in Diasonics as a standalone investor after his partnership with Kramlich expired. In keeping with his approach of actively governing his portfolio investments, he chaired the company's board. Diasonics grew quickly and in February 1983 went public. Over the following year, however, the company's stock price dropped sharply, from $29 a share to $6.50, as it struggled with technology choices and competition. In February 1984, *Forbes* published a disparaging article ("Solid as a Rock?") claiming that Rock had unscrupulously profited to the tune of around $3.1 million by selling some of his shares at the IPO. Noyce, also an investor, had cashed in a share of his equity for $2.5 million.[93] The article declared that "the real loser is the public" because "many of Diasonics founders sold their shares when the price was high, making hefty profits." Diasonics taught a lesson in the levels of moral opprobrium and ethical controversy that can surround VC investing. On the other hand, in January 1984, *Time* celebrated Rock's career by putting his face on the magazine's cover next to a bold headline: "Cashing in Big, the Men Who Make the Killings." This was eleven months into the Diasonics implosion.

Investing in Technology: Tom Perkins and Kleiner & Perkins

Like Arthur Rock, Tom Perkins considered the people running a startup to be critical, but his emphasis on this factor was quite different. Once, when Perkins was asked what made for a successful venture capital investment, he summed it up: "if you have good people, proprietary technology, and a high growth market sector, you'll win every time."[94] Undoubtedly he saw the collective importance of these three factors, but in practice, it was often observed that his primary filter was technology. Perkins earned his electrical engineering degree at MIT in 1953, and his MBA from Harvard four years later. Although in business school he studied the softer side of general management in Georges Doriot's classes (and Doriot even offered him a job at ARD), he was at his core a technologist, and that gave him distinctive insights as a VC investor.

Upon graduating from Harvard Business School, Perkins joined Hewlett-Packard, then left there to work briefly as a consultant for Booz

Allen Hamilton, from 1959 to 1960. From 1960 to 1963, he worked at Optics Technology, Inc., an optical science startup financed by Draper Gaither & Anderson to the tune of a few million dollars.[95] Both David Packard and William Hewlett also had a personal investment interest in the company. Perkins, however, soon developed an acrimonious relationship with Narinder Kapany, the physicist who had founded the company, and he returned to Hewlett Packard from 1963 to 1972. There he became an administrative manager of HP Laboratories; then general manager of HP's new computer business, reporting directly to Packard; and finally, director of corporate development, reporting to Hewlett, while Packard was off in Washington, DC, leading the Department of Defense.

At Optics Technology, Perkins had been marketing director, but he increasingly developed an interest in the science of laser technology. With encouragement from Packard, he established University Laboratories, Inc. in Berkeley in 1965—at the same time that he was building HP's computer business. Packard, revered by Perkins as a mentor and "substitute father," had encouraged his startup ambitions.[96] Perkins founded University Laboratories with Richard Jaenicke, an electrical engineer from Optics Technology, and Henry Rhodes, described by one journalist as a "long-haired, pot-smoking glassblower."[97] To found the company, Perkins used his life savings of about $15,000, took out loans, and raised $200,000 in venture capital. University Laboratories, in possession of valuable patent rights on lasers, went into direct competition with Optics Technology. As an insight into his personality, Perkins admitted that his founding of University Laboratories was an act of retribution: "Sure, I wanted to make some money" he said. "But I really wanted to put Optics Technology out of business, because I really detested Narinder Kapany in, I suppose, a very vindictive way."[98] When University Laboratories was acquired by Spectra Physics in 1970, Perkins got about $2 million in cash and equity and joined Spectra's board. Four years later, Optics Technology was out of business.

In addition to having an overtly hostile relationship with Kapany, Perkins also had a series of major disagreements with executives at HP. In one case, he used proceeds from the University Laboratories sale to purchase a red Ferrari, just to annoy an HP executive who had taken away his company car.[99] Most importantly, he disagreed with Hewlett and Packard over the direction HP should take. His first argument was with

Packard over how HP's newly developed minicomputers should be sold. He advocated a strategy of offering discounts to original equipment manufacturers (OEMs) to spur sales, whereas Packard resisted discounting. Perkins won—and was proved right, as OEM discounting was a key factor in HP's subsequent success. His second big conflict was with Hewlett, who was scornful of the counterculture Perkins had established within HP's computer division. In its Cupertino offices, employees worked flexible hours and wore blue jeans and sandals, in contrast to HP's more conservative work practices and dress code. Finally, Perkins, as director of corporate development, clashed with both when he attempted to realign HP using Boston Consulting Group's influential strategic framework to identify "star" products with future potential to dominate markets and cross-subsidize their growth with the revenues of declining "cash cows." Packard was opposed to this approach, given his emphasis on excellence across all of HP's product lines. So intense was the disagreement over the strategic direction of the firm that, even though his relationship with Hewlett and Packard remained cordial and respectful, Perkins felt he had no option but to leave.[100]

Perkins's entry into the venture capital industry was a consequence of a contact he made with Eugene Kleiner through Sandy Robertson, an eminent San Francisco investment banker. Kleiner, one of the eight who left Shockley Semiconductor to start Fairchild Semiconductor, had left that firm in 1961. During the early 1970s, Robertson became aware that Kleiner was working to raise a fund at the request of the Hillman family, whose wealth had its origins in Pittsburgh heavy industry. Kleiner had been an investor both individually in Silicon Valley electronics firms and as a limited partner in Davis & Rock. Despite their opposing personalities—Kleiner was said to be calm and balanced in his approach whereas Perkins was considered restless, egotistical, and even prone to moments of complete derangement—Robertson connected the two believing they would be "terrific together" as venture capitalists.[101] Kleiner was nearly fifty years old at the time, and Perkins had just turned forty.

Perkins considered his approach distinct from other players in the venture capital space. There were essentially three types of venture-style investors at the time—east coast firms such as ARD (in its twilight years), Greylock, and Venrock that were often steeped in "old money"; west coast entities like Davis & Rock and Sutter Hill; and individuals who acted like modern-day angel investors. An example of the latter would be Reid

Dennis, William Bowes, John Bryan, and Bill Edwards, who formed a Bay area investment syndicate colloquially known as "the Group."[102] While all of these venture-style investing types helped to manage their portfolio companies to one degree or another, Perkins felt they were making "Las Vegas place-your-bets-and-take-your-chances" investments when the real opportunity was in "controlling the game itself."[103] Following on his experience of managing technology at Hewlett-Packard and University Laboratories, Perkins aimed to develop his own venture investing style by providing a more systematic approach to seed capital deployment and governance in high-technology industries. This was described as a "new style of participatory, value-added investment."[104]

The structure of the original limited partnership and the investment strategy of the firm are outlined in an illuminating 1972 prospectus: "Kleiner & Perkins: A Venture Capital Limited Partnership, Statement of Philosophy." This appears to have been the basic document used in Kleiner & Perkins fundraising. The title page includes a reference to the investment bank Robertson, Colman & Siebel (RCS), which acted as an agent to help Kleiner and Perkins raise about $3.7 million of the fund, for which RCS would be paid a 3 percent commission. This is unusual from a modern VC perspective because general partners in venture capital firms typically approach their limited partners without an intermediary. The size of the fund was set at $8 million. Interestingly, the prospectus states that $2 million could be added through a loan from the Small Business Administration and Kleiner & Perkins would then own the resulting SBIC. This aspect of the financing never actually materialized.

The prospectus states that Eugene Kleiner and Tom Perkins "are investing an aggregate of $300,000, of which $100,000 will be invested by them as general partners, and $200,000 will be invested by them as limited partners." Presumably, financial involvement by the operating general partners was a way of contractually aligning their own incentives with their investors' interests, especially considering the prospectus's warning that "there can be no assurance that the partnership will be profitable, or that investors will recover their investment."

The limited partnership had a life of seven years, with 80 percent of the profits allocated to the limited partners and 20 percent to Kleiner and Perkins. The prospectus is revealing in its attention to distribution rules determining when Kleiner and Perkins were to receive their shares of the profits. Distribution rules are central to venture capital limited partnership agreements.[105] The partnership operated under a "return first" rule whereby the operating general partners received profits on the termination of the partnership only after their investors had received distributions equal to their capital contributions. The prospectus states that "upon liquidation, after payment of expenses, the limited partners will receive first the amount of their capital contribution, and the general partners will receive the amount of their capital contribution, in each case reduced by amounts previously paid to partners. The value of any assets then remaining will be distributed 80% to the limited partners and 20% to the general partners."

Kleiner and Perkins were named alone as general operating partners, with additional staff members (to a total of five) expected to be added within a few years as investments were made. Kleiner and Perkins were each to receive a salary of $50,000 (about $285,000 today) and the fund's operating expenses were "not to exceed $300,000 annually." This latter figure is important because it would correspond to a 3.0 to 3.75 percent management fee, much higher than the 2 percent annual fee on committed capital that modern venture capital firms typically charge. Yet, Kleiner and Perkins specifically chose that particular fund size because this scale made sense from an investment strategy perspective. According to the prospectus, the fund was set at this level because it was "large enough to support a few very significant growth corporations, and not too large to be cumbersome through forcing too large, or too many investments."

The prospectus states that the partnership would focus on early-stage high-tech investments, typically of "a few hundred thousand dollars," because these were the situations in which the greatest multiples could be achieved. Kleiner & Perkins would stage its investments across funding rounds based on the "merits" of portfolio firms. Furthermore, the size of the fund would permit Kleiner & Perkins to provide a rich menu of financing by engaging in venture debt–type activities to "provide working capital for a growing firm which is contemplating public issues." All investment decisions would require joint approval of the general partners, and an advisory board was to be set up to provide oversight and help with the formulation of strategy. The prospectus shows the planning behind Kleiner & Perkins to be thoughtful and highly systematized.

The objective of the limited partnership was to "maximize return through an active venture capital fund managed by seasoned and successful investor / managers." The prospectus goes on to outline the preconditions for success in venture capital investing, noting in particular that "the experience, judgment, and management capability of the operating general partners is key." To succeed, the partnership planned to invest according to three main principles:

1. *Exposure* to a wide variety of investment opportunities.
2. Excellent *judgment* in selecting only the best situations.
3. The *ability to develop* the investment.

To Kleiner and Perkins, "exposure" meant access to networks and deal flow, which they were in a privileged position to exploit as individuals who were "widely known within their industries." For this reason, the prospectus emphasizes their involvement with Stanford University "and the associated circle of contacts." It stresses that "their own names should be a magnet to future potential opportunities" and explains that "it is for this reason that they are identifying the Fund with their own names, rather than some less recognizable title." The assumption was that the Kleiner & Perkins name alone would be an important source of credentialing for portfolio companies.

The second item, "judgment" was another way of saying that, as investors, Kleiner and Perkins both had track records. A favorable track record of prior investing is a first-order determinant of fundraising ability.[106] By outlining ways in which both men had shown good judgment through their own investing and startup experiences, the prospectus suggested their record of past successes was an "important factor in their future judgment."

Finally, the "ability to develop" reflected an ardent belief that venture capitalists had particular abilities to add value if they had operating backgrounds. Citing Georges Doriot at ARD as an exemplar investor who believed in the power of good governance, the prospectus stresses that both Kleiner and Perkins had the special talent to "work with the management of fledgling investments" and to "understand the entrepreneur." Because governance was facilitated by close proximity, Kleiner & Perkins would locate in the Northern California area, and "concentrate their activity in the West, with emphasis on the San Francisco Bay Area and the Los Angeles Basin."

Yet, despite the methodical way in which the prospectus is written, Kleiner & Perkins found it difficult to raise a fund.[107] The VC industry was still small and largely unproven. Venture capital commitments amounted to around $10 to 20 million per year in the late 1960s and the total pool of funds was no more than a couple of hundred million dollars.[108] Perkins quipped about VC that "all the practitioners could be assembled into a moderately sized room."[109]

Furthermore, the macroeconomic environment deteriorated. Growth in the stock market slowed down, capital gains taxes went up (the maximum rate was 25 percent until the late 1960s, when Congress increased the rate to 40 percent), and there were fewer entrepreneurial startups. Although the prospectus had done a good job of outlining the highly promising investing capabilities of Kleiner & Perkins, Sandy Robertson said fundraising was "like pulling teeth."[110] Even Kleiner's friends Robert Noyce and Gordon Moore invested only a "couple hundred thousand dollars"—and only then on the condition that general partner salary costs would be capped.[111]

Following a wide search for limited partners across the United States, an $8 million fund was eventually raised. Unusually from the perspective of a modern VC firm, where capital calls to limited partners are made over time as investments are made, Kleiner & Perkins's entire $8 million fund was drawn down immediately. In 1972, Kleiner & Perkins opened offices at a newly developed office complex at 3000 Sand Hill Road in Menlo Park, California. The Sand Hill Road area soon became the most important cluster of venture capital firms in the world. Although Kleiner & Perkins relocated to San Francisco's financial district between the mid-1970s and mid-1980s, it ultimately moved most of its operations back to Sand Hill Road. The performance of that first venture capital fund contributed significantly to Sand Hill Road's locational preeminence.

Kleiner & Perkins quickly earned a reputation in the Silicon Valley startup community as a highly knowledgeable technology investor, though Perkins's dominant personality was often a source of friction. Although investment opportunities were difficult to identify, the first fund made seventeen investments between 1973 and 1980. Most of these were unsuccessful or generated mediocre returns. Breakeven and loss-making investments made up 41 percent of the portfolio; they included

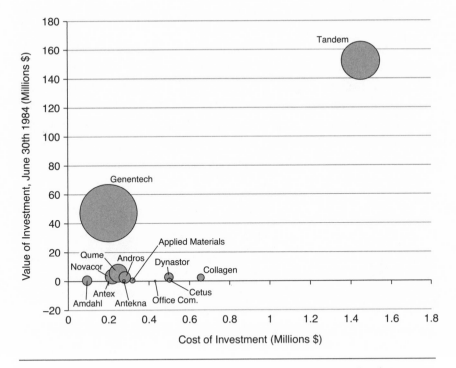

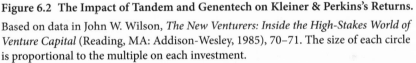

Figure 6.2 The Impact of Tandem and Genentech on Kleiner & Perkins's Returns.
Based on data in John W. Wilson, *The New Venturers: Inside the High-Stakes World of Venture Capital* (Reading, MA: Addison-Wesley, 1985), 70–71. The size of each circle is proportional to the multiple on each investment.

such epic failures as Advanced Recreational Equipment Corporation, which produced a kit to transform motorcycles into snowmobiles, and American Athletic Shoe Corporation, which attempted to market the "retreading" of rubber-soled tennis and other athletic shoes. Nevertheless, these failed investments had the positive effect of considerably sharpening Kleiner & Perkins's investment focus. Perkins would come to acknowledge that "we bring little to the party outside the high technology area."[112]

Crucially for Kleiner & Perkins, 24 percent of the portfolio investments generated multiples of greater than ten on their total investment. And while these investments accounted for 30 percent of the total cost of the portfolio, they generated a staggering 93 percent of the gross return. Figure 6.2 shows the outsized influence of two key investments: Tandem Computers and Genentech. In line with the long-tail distributions seen in other eras (for example, ARD's as described in Chapter 4, or Venrock's in Chapter 5), these two investments dramatically lifted fund performance. Excluding them, the fund yielded a gross compound annual return of 16 percent. But including them, the annualized return was 51 percent. For perspective, the stock market returned a compound annual return of 2.9 percent from the S&P Composite index, or 7.8 percent including dividends, over the same time period. These results underscore the appeal of the long-tail investing model. And the manner in which the investments were developed also set precedents for how VC firms would develop portfolio companies.

Tandem Computers

Kleiner & Perkins's investment in Tandem Computers can be best described as an incubated startup. While it is common today for venture capital firms to incubate startups, back then it was rare.[113] Perkins was approached in early 1973 by James Treybig, a young engineer with an MBA from Stanford who had worked for Perkins in HP sales and marketing. The idea was for a "fail-safe" computer startup, whereby multiple computers would work in tandem to prevent microprocessing breakdowns. Both HP and IBM had solutions to this problem, but their systems were ad hoc, expensive, and inefficient. Treybig convinced Perkins that the idea for a cost-efficient, off-the-shelf solution was feasible. Obviously, too, he said, it would have widespread applications in bank fund transfers and ATM transactions, where it was imperative to process continuously, reliably, and safely. Perkins hired Treybig to work on this new venture idea and assist with other aspects of managing the Kleiner & Perkins fund. Treybig soon worked solely on Tandem.

Three specific aspects of the Tandem investment are noteworthy. First, Perkins was heavily involved in the initial design stages, applying his capabilities as a technologist. In fact, Treybig stated that Perkins was instrumental over the course of the first eighteen months in developing the technical aspects of the idea, although they both lacked the expertise to make the technology fully operational. Second, Kleiner & Perkins provided $50,000 to take the idea beyond its nascent stage, which required a dedicated search for technical talent. Two HP engineers—Michael Green and James Katzman—were brought in to advance the software and hardware side. John Loustaunou, an HP cost-accounting expert recently hired by Kleiner & Perkins, also joined. Third, Kleiner & Perkins was explicit about using milestones and staged financing. The initial $50,000 of seed capital to recruit Tandem's team was followed by a $1 million first round of financing, once the proof of concept had been shown, for 40 percent of Tandem's equity.[114] A second round of financing was raised in December 1975, when Kleiner & Perkins added an additional $500,000 and other venture investors contributed $1.5 million.[115] In sum, Perkins was true to his vision of providing active governance and participatory-style VC investing in the realm of high-tech startups. Kleiner & Perkins helped to assemble the perfect founding team with technical, financial, and selling capabilities. Tandem was effectively incubated through a process of financial and technological experimentation.

Tandem represented Kleiner & Perkins's first substantial investment hit and deepened its commitment to long-tail investing. But, because a $1.5 million total investment was a nontrivial amount from Kleiner & Perkins's $8 million fund, the investment entailed substantial risk. Failure would have been catastrophic, but equally, as Perkins would later note, Tandem's success put Kleiner & Perkins "on the map" as investors.[116] From a risky 1974 high-tech startup initially located in a Cupertino warehouse, Tandem launched its IPO in 1977 on the basis of $7 million in sales, largely to financial sector clients. Sales stood at $100 million by 1980, and exceeded $1 billion by 1987. Perkins was extensively involved, writing the prospectus and shepherding the company through its roadshow. At the IPO, Kleiner & Perkins's investment was worth $12.5 million, which would become $152.2 million assuming the investment was held until June 30, 1984.[117]

Tandem became one of the most successful computer firms in the United States. In 1983, it held a 98 percent market share in the "fail-safe" computer sector. Perkins continued on as chairman of the board until it was acquired by Compaq in 1997, although not without considerable cost to his personal relationship with Treybig. Perkins commented that "it became my duty to replace him in order for the company to merge into Compaq."[118] By happenstance, given that half its founding employees had worked at HP and Perkins had a strong relationship with that firm, Tandem became a de facto part of HP in 2002 when HP, in turn, acquired Compaq.

Genentech

The Tandem investment was related to Kleiner & Perkins's next big hit, Genentech, by another quirk of fate. Because Treybig had left Kleiner &

Perkins to concentrate on his startup, that left an opening for a new hire. Bob Swanson joined the firm in 1975 and went on to cofound Genentech. Swanson was educated at MIT in the late 1960s and graduated with degrees in chemistry and management. *New Scientist* noted in its 1978 "Profile of a Genetic Engineer" that he had a confident-bordering-on-arrogant demeanor.[119] Prior to his career in venture capital, Swanson had worked as an investment officer in New York with Citibank. He moved to San Francisco in 1973 where, first with Citibank and later as an independent consultant, he came into contact with Kleiner in local investment circles. Swanson joined Kleiner & Perkins at Kleiner's request.

The Genentech investment was revolutionary as a template for VC investing, especially as it created a lean biotech startup decades before that very notion became talked about conceptually in the venture capital industry. Biotech became an industry only later, in the 1970s and early 1980s, when Genentech and others in a first wave of new companies were established. Opportunities for VC investing in the closely related pharmaceuticals industry were more limited as large, established firms such as Eli Lilly and Company dominated. Firms like this used their own internal cash flows to fund research and were fully-integrated operations. Pharmaceutical companies profited using intellectual property rights to protect and license their inventions, and they also made simultaneous investments in R&D, organizational, production, marketing, and regulatory capabilities.[120]

Furthermore, although science was being conducted extensively in universities and nonprofit foundations at the time, there was little interaction between the proprietary and "open science" worlds. In the not-for-profit sector, scientists focused largely on grant-funded basic science, and research output was disseminated for the most part through peer-reviewed publications. Few patents were ever filed. Companies such as Genentech in the emerging biotechnology industry offered the promise of challenging the "Big Pharma" model. They would do this principally by changing the organizational structure of the industry by inducing interactions between large incumbents, entrepreneurial entrants, and not-for-profit enterprises.[121]

Genentech was not the first biotech-related venture in which Kleiner & Perkins held an equity stake. Cetus Corporation, a startup established in Berkeley, California, in 1971, proposed to develop scientific instruments to automate certain screening functions that laboratories performed. By the mid-1970s, it was also exploring genetic engineering. Stanford Professor Stanley Cohen, an eminent geneticist, was recruited to Cetus's large scientific advisory board. Kleiner & Perkins had invested $500,000 in the company, but Perkins worried about the direction in which Cetus was moving, its governance structure, and its slow speed to market. Swanson was given the task of ensuring that Kleiner & Perkins would receive a return on its investment, but Perkins became disillusioned both with the Cetus investment and with Swanson. Within twelve months of joining Kleiner & Perkins, Swanson was encouraged to find alternative employment opportunities, though his relationship with Perkins remained cordial. Swanson was still permitted to use Kleiner & Perkins's office space.

Swanson maintains that he took the idea for commercializing the science behind recombinant DNA technology to Cetus, but was turned down.[122] Most scientists and practitioners agreed that a marketable product from the new science was at least a decade away, perhaps more, especially given the obvious regulatory hurdles that a commercial endeavor would face. Swanson's breakthrough came when he pursued the idea in collaboration with Herbert Boyer, who had been on the faculty at the University of California at San Francisco (UCSF) since 1966, and a full professor since 1976. His research focused on *Escherichia coli* bacteria, more familiarly known as *E. coli*, and specifically on why it was so resistant to viruses. Scientists had observed that *E. coli* replicated either by splitting in two or by the exchange of genetic information between cells. Boyer conjectured that, if different genes could be introduced into *E. coli* cells, then he could gene-engineer the bacteria. This idea would become an important part of the recombinant DNA technology, as a form of genetic engineering.

To be precise about this underlying technology, the first step related to what we now call gene splicing, discovered by Stanford University scientist Paul Berg in 1971. Gene splicing involved cutting the DNA of a gene and introducing new characteristics from another entity. The second step was Boyer's observation that *E. coli* enzymes were able to cut DNA into smaller fragments with "sticky ends," allowing foreign DNA to be inserted into *E. coli* in such a way that the foreign DNA would replicate. The third step involved Stanford's Stanley Cohen, who was working on small rings of DNA called plasmids that helped to pass genes between bacteria. Boyer and Cohen met at a conference in 1972 and their joint efforts were integral to pushing the research program forward. Boyer's DNA fragments could be joined together with Cohen's plasmids, and genetic material could be manipulated and reproduced.[123]

Swanson felt the combination of these ideas was much closer to commercial reality than many scientists assumed. His ultimate objective was to clone human insulin. Eli Lilly held 80 percent of the US market of animal pancreas-derived insulin, so the potential payoff of developing replicable recombinant insulin was enormous. After drawing up a list of potential technical cofounders (and initially approaching Paul Berg), Swanson found Boyer most receptive but still skeptical about the commercial possibilities. Boyer and Swanson bootstrapped, contributing $500 each to incorporate Genentech in April 1976.[124]

Swanson approached Kleiner & Perkins for financing. The six-page business plan he put together with Boyer "to engage in the development of unique microorganisms that are capable of producing products that will significantly better mankind" outlined a need for nearly $2 million dollars' worth of laboratory space, equipment, and salaries. Perkins pushed back, encouraging Swanson to consider financially leaner alternatives. Swanson returned to Perkins with a plan to subcontract out to local universities and research centers. Perkins agreed to invest $100,000, which gave Genentech nine months of funding.[125]

At the same time, Swanson showed his shrewdness as a founder, shopping the business plan around to alternative venture investors. For Kleiner & Perkins's $100,000 investment, Swanson gave up just 25 percent of Genentech's equity.[126] In the new corporation, Swanson became president and treasurer, receiving an annual salary of $30,000 (about $125,000 today) and Boyer became vice president and secretary on a salary of $12,000 (about $50,000 today). Boyer would still earn his salary as a UCSF professor, in the region of $50,000 (about $210,000 today). Both took board seats alongside Perkins, who became chairman.[127]

Swanson and Boyer followed through on their subcontracting strategy. Genentech began negotiating contracts with UCSF; City of Hope, a private research institution and hospital in Duarte, California (close to Los Angeles); and Caltech. Each was to perform a distinct function: Boyer's UCSF laboratory had expertise in gene splicing and he had developed a good network of scientists working there; City of Hope had capabilities in the area of gene synthesis; and Caltech was a first-rate testing facility. Although the subcontracting strategy ceded significant financial claims to the contracting entities, it created overwhelming benefits to Genentech in terms of exploiting each institution's specialization. Still, Swanson and Boyer did not have a product they could sell. By December 1976, Genentech reported losses of $88,601 on assets of $88,421.[128]

Between December 1976 and February 1977, Genentech raised a second funding round, with Kleiner & Perkins investing an additional $100,000 and a further $750,000 coming from other investors. The venture's fate rested on making breakthroughs. Genentech decided to experiment with producing the human protein *somatostatin* in *E. coli.* Although the ultimate objective was to clone human insulin, *somatostatin* was a step along the way. Boyer explained that "it was much more straightforward as a model than doing insulin."[129] Perkins emphasized that the somatostatin experiment was designed to generate "proof of principle first."[130]

The strategy worked and the experiment also produced patents and scientific articles that signaled Genentech's commitment to world-class basic research. Perkins pointed out that somatostatin had done something critical, which was to "remove much of the risk from the entire venture. . . . For next to nothing we had removed a world class question about risk."[131] Swanson articulated this sentiment in his address to shareholders in April 1978. "I am pleased to point out," he announced, "that the two year start-up of the company, including the completion of our first research goal, the production of the human hormone somatostatin, and the first commercial demonstration of our new technology, was accomplished for a total of $515,000. We plan to approach future growth in the same lean but effective manner."[132]

Genentech went on to raise a third round of financing of $950,000 for 8.6 percent of the equity in March 1978. The higher valuation reflected the fact that, through experimentation, distinct milestones had been achieved. In June 1978, Eli Lilly, fearing potential disruption, agreed to provide $50,000 a month to Genentech in support of its research efforts. Consequently, Genentech began to build out laboratory capabilities at a warehouse in South San Francisco. On August 21, 1978, scientists working at Genentech's facility and City of Hope managed to synthesize the insulin gene and clone it in bacteria, producing the world's first genetically engineered form of human insulin. Genentech signed a licensing agreement with Eli Lilly. For an upfront fee of $500,000 and commitments to fund further R&D, Lilly received an exclusive worldwide license.

Genentech secured a 6 percent royalty on sales, and City of Hope, a 2 percent royalty. The agreement stipulated that Eli Lilly could use Genentech's technology only to manufacture human insulin, not other products, and Genentech retained ownership of the intellectual property rights.[133]

In 1980, Genentech went public through an IPO raising $35 million, with a first-day spike from $35 to $89 a share. It was a heady time for Kleiner & Perkins. "We were the hot guys," Perkins recalled, "with the best this, the most aggressive that, the best science, the best patents, the best financial relationships, the best publicity."[134] The new firm's founders, Swanson and Boyer, instantly became very wealthy, each worth $65.7 million on the basis of the shares they held and the closing price on Genentech's first day of trading. On March 9, 1981, Boyer's ebullient face graced the cover of *Time* under the heading "Shaping Life in the Lab: The Boom in Genetic Engineering." Genentech went on to become a multibillion dollar company.

Kleiner & Perkins's involvement with Genentech showed how the discipline of venture capital could play an important role in the early stages of a new enterprise and in its subsequent success. Four factors are worth emphasizing. First, this was an important moment for the VC industry in terms of its ability to create valuable businesses through the deployment of risk capital in high-tech industries. In a world of bank-based financing, it is unlikely that such a risky venture would have been funded. The nature of the product—insulin—made the potential social benefits enormously high. By intermediating and governing the Genentech investment, Kleiner & Perkins could capture private returns while also producing vast social benefit.

Second, Kleiner & Perkins's association with Genentech epitomized what good governance meant from the standpoint of a professional venture capital firm. Perkins had advocated the lean startup approach, insisting on outsourcing, experimentation, and staged financing as a way of de-risking the business. He showed that a lean business model could work even in a highly capital-intensive industry. Furthermore, good governance meant being able to exert some degree of control over the founders, even though Kleiner & Perkins did not have a controlling equity stake. As a condition of Kleiner & Perkins's original investment, Perkins joined the board, performing a post-investment monitoring role and setting milestones. Year after year, he spent an afternoon a week at

Genentech. Good governance meant faultless execution. On reflection, Perkins said: "I honestly think that if we had to do it all over again, we'd do it the same way . . . subcontracting the experiments, then licensing to Lilly . . . I don't think we could have done it better."[135]

Third, achieving success in a VC-backed startup was conditional upon being able to leverage existing capabilities in the local area. Note that the scientific basis for recombinant DNA technology was largely developed by star academics at universities in California, operating with the aid of government funding, and Genentech's own staff included many scientists trained at these institutions. While the collaborative nature of the relationships blurred the boundaries of attribution (and Genentech engaged in litigation with UCSF over precisely this issue), these institutions were undoubtedly essential to Genentech's and Kleiner & Perkins's success. Reinforcing points made earlier in this chapter, these contextual factors were the important preconditions that allowed Silicon Valley VC to develop.

Fourth, the Genentech investment, like the Tandem investment that preceded it, helped Perkins refine his investment style and his strategic approach to venture capital investing. Conspicuously, Kleiner & Perkins did not significantly "up" its investment in Genentech during later funding stages. Once the business had been de-risked, Genentech was able to raise money at much higher prices. It became too expensive. Furthermore, in light of his investing experiences, Perkins established his own "law." It states that "market risk is inversely proportional to technical risk." The best startups, he argued, would push the frontier of technology, thereby guaranteeing market power and selling opportunities for their products. If a product were easy to develop, competition would quickly erode any excess returns. Perkins sometimes got investment decisions wrong on this basis, but he at least had a consistent viewpoint and perspective. He rejected the hypothesis that VC investing was simply about embracing randomness.

For Kleiner & Perkins, the first fund's successes with its Tandem and Genentech investments were a boon to additional fundraising efforts. The venture capital cycle was renewed. In 1978, Kleiner & Perkins raised $15 million to accommodate two additional partners, Brook Byers and Frank Caufield—and as a firm, it assumed their names. Byers, a Georgia Tech–educated ham radio enthusiast and consummate Silicon Valley technologist, had been under the mentorship of local investor Pitch

Johnson and became an early investor in Tandem on his own account. Caufield, who had turned down the opportunity to invest in Tandem, had redeemed himself by deftly managing the Menlo Park–based Oak Grove Ventures fund, navigating a $5 million VC fund to a 40 percent compound annual return.[136] Kleiner, Perkins, Caufield & Byers raised a $55 million fund in 1980, and in 1986, a very substantial fund of $150 million.[137]

Perkins went on to become president of the National Venture Capital Association, and testified before Congress in support of the US venture capital industry. Both Kleiner and Perkins withdrew from running Kleiner & Perkins in the 1980s. Kleiner spent more time on personal investments, while Perkins continued with board duties—among them, a controversial stint at HP, which involved the 2005 firing of CEO Carly Fiorina. Perkins also embraced his wealth during his well-earned retirement, splitting his time between a residence in Marin County and a manor house in the English countryside. In 2006, his $130 million, 289-foot megayacht *The Maltese Falcon* was completed. Harvard Business School gained a small insight into his lifestyle when, in 2013, he politely rejected an invitation to discuss the Genentech investment. His email read, "Sorry, but I will be in Tahiti, leaving this weekend and not returning until late April. I am going to try to capture video of big sharks at depth using my submarine. I was the first to do this with Humpback whales in Tonga in September."[138]

Investing in Markets: Don Valentine and the Pathway into Venture Capital

Arthur Rock and Tom Perkins had very different personalities and investment styles. While Rock was the consummate "people picker," Perkins was fundamentally a frontline technologist. To complete the taxonomy of styles, Don Valentine was distinctive, too. As a venture capital investor, Valentine focused mostly on markets where he saw great potential. In his words, "my position has always been you find a great market and you build multiple companies in that market."[139] Of course, neither Rock nor Perkins ignored markets when making choices about the portfolio companies they backed, but this was not their primary filter. And likewise, Valentine explained that his investment decisions involved an assessment of "people risks, market risks, product development risks, and finance risk"—and that three out of these four needed to be understood comprehensively for an investment decision to be made. Yet, he went on to emphasize: "the risk that I'm least willing to take is market risk."[140]

In terms of family backgrounds, Rock and Perkins were positively patrician compared to Valentine. In 1985, a writer for *Inc.* noted that "he speaks like the New York street kid he used to be," while his partner at Sequoia, Mike Moritz, described him as "a weathered version of the frat brother who organized the weekend football pool."[141] Valentine was born in 1933 and raised in Yonkers, New York. His father drove delivery trucks and was a member and official of his local Teamsters Union. Almost all of Valentine's education was in Jesuit schools. He graduated from Mount St. Michael Academy and Fordham University. In 1952, he was drafted into the US Army, where he studied and taught electronics, then was transferred to the US Navy on the west coast. The geographic advantages of Silicon Valley were not lost on him: "I discovered there were places where it didn't snow in your driveway and I decided I was not going to live in New York State any longer. I was eventually going to live in California."[142] Like Perkins, he had a volatile temper, though probably more outsized. Often abrasive to the point of being downright obnoxious, he is once said to have reprimanded a subordinate so severely that the person in question fainted.[143]

After Valentine completed his time in the military, he joined Sylvania Electric Products, Inc., in upstate New York. He chose Sylvania at least partly because it had west coast facilities. Valentine started with various factory assignments in Sylvania's main business units: cathode-ray tubes, semiconductors, and vacuum tubes. He eventually moved into a sales position and, after a short stint at the military and commercial electronics company Raytheon, went back to Sylvania and was transferred to California. When he arrived in California, he felt that markets would move away from vacuum products and toward semiconductors. Sylvania was not, however, embracing the new technology. Valentine left in 1960 to join Fairchild Semiconductor, based in Los Angeles, as one of their first salesmen on the west coast.

While he was working for Fairchild, Valentine improved his knowledge of sales and marketing by taking late afternoon classes on the subject at the Anderson School of Management at the University of California, Los Angeles. He never studied for an MBA, however; it was a degree he disdained. Valentine became an expert practitioner and outstanding salesman at Fairchild. He kept abreast of the technical details of Fairchild's technology offerings and he knew how to sell their products. His customers in Los Angeles were mostly defense and aerospace firms that were building complex weapons systems requiring advanced electronic capabilities. Valentine was quickly promoted to head of sales for Fairchild in Los Angeles, and then to run sales for the entire west coast region. Before long, he was moving to Mountain View to manage all of Fairchild's sales efforts.

Valentine's next stop was National Semiconductor, where he joined a team of managers, many from Fairchild, attempting a turnaround. Valentine was brought in by Charlie Sporck, to whom he had reported when Sporck served as Fairchild's general manager. The company, a publicly traded Santa Clara–based firm, was struggling: it made approximately $7.2 million in sales in 1966, but virtually no profit. National Semiconductor was targeting industry customers with its products, which was a very different proposition from targeting large military customers. Rather than relying largely on an internal sales force, as most firms in its industry did at the time, Valentine spearheaded a distributed sales strategy involving the use of a large network of independent distributors who received commissions on sales of five to seven percent. To equip these distributors with the requisite practical knowledge of the products they were selling, he deployed highly trained "field applications engineers" to supply the technical know-how. Moreover, these engineers often consulted with companies directly during the sales process, which meant that end users started to design their architecture around National Semiconductor's products.[144] It was a creative, entrepreneurial approach, and it worked effectively—both by freeing up cash flow for National Semiconductor and by motivating the network of independent distributors to sell. Just as Perkins had by outsourcing much of the lab work at Genentech, Valentine kept National Semiconductor's costs down with his selling strategy. By 1970, sales had shot up to $41.9 million and the workforce had expanded from 300 to 2,800 people. Valentine, along with the rest of the management team, had transformed National Semiconductor into an industry powerhouse.

These experiences helped to shape Valentine's investing style and his ultimate entry into venture capital. At Fairchild and National Semiconductor, he learned about companies that were addressing very large markets undergoing significant technological changes. He became incredibly "product smart" and analyzed the nature of these opportunities in as precise and scientific a way as possible. That focus on market potential provided an opportunity to create comparative advantage in venture investing. He later summarized this perspective:

> The great thing about evaluating markets first is that usually there are very poor data sources. So you have to create these scraps of information, and most people don't do that—they prefer to make a judgment on some other basis: whether the product is patentable, whether the technology is differentiated, whether the people are world-class. To us, you can scrape and push and dig and find out tidbits of information which, when you put them together, you get a conviction about when something will happen. You talk to people in distribution; you talk to all of the sources of information that you can, and you make a judgment.[145]

Valentine also learned at National Semiconductor about governing under operating constraints. He emphasized that "lack of money is a terrific discipline."[146] Moreover, with his own limited pool of funds, he was tinkering as a venture capitalist by investing in "small companies, some of which were customers of both Fairchild and National."[147] This activity and his growing reputation drew the attention of outside investors. Valentine was approached to start a venture capital entity by a group working under the umbrella of the Capital Group, an influential financial investment firm headquartered in Los Angeles. He left National Semiconductor to join an arm of the Capital Group in 1971 as a principal investment manager.[148] By this time, the Capital Group had already made some investments, including one in Advanced Micro Devices, a startup established by a group of Fairchild Semiconductor employees that would become Intel's main competitor.

Sequoia Capital

Valentine's move set the seeds for the foundation of Sequoia Capital. Key protagonists working within various entities inside the Capital Group were interested in venture capital as a way of conducting "market intelligence" on the high-tech sector with a view to enhancing investment performance in the publicly-traded sector. Because the Capital Group was involved in asset management activities, this posed certain organizational issues. Specifically, Capital Group focused on major stock market firms, not fledgling companies with nonexistent revenue streams. As such, venture capital could be a distraction from its core activities. Moreover, investing in venture capital would mean embracing a different compensation structure. The idea of a dedicated venture capital fund was initially rejected by power brokers at the Capital Group who were eager to avoid internal conflicts—only to be revived on a narrow vote of the board when the issue was revisited. A venture capital arm, called Sequoia, was subsequently sanctioned. This approval, however, came with the caveat that it could not use Capital Group client money.[149] Sequoia would have to engage in fundraising independently.

The proponents of venture capital within the Capital Group eventually raised $1 million from a variety of sources. Valentine took this fundraising further by going to institutional investors. As part of the process, he invited the New York investment banking firm Salomon Brothers to act as an intermediary, but was rebuffed, he says, due to his lack of pedigree.[150] As Valentine struggled to raise additional capital, in a time when venture capital was not recognized as an area of investment, he was coached in his efforts by Robert Kirby of Capital Guardian Trust, a subsidiary of the Capital Group. Valentine was introduced to potentially receptive investors. The Ford Foundation agreed to invest $3 million— warning, however, that it would withdraw its capital if other institutional investors did not join. After some time, General Electric Pension invested $3 million. Alcoa, Armco, and Yale University followed. Valentine never forgot that "without Bob's introductions and guidance on pitching institutional investors, there would be no Sequoia Capital."[151]

In 1975, Valentine took what was now named Sequoia Capital and re-established it as an entity independent from the Capital Group. For the Capital Group, the synergies with other areas of asset management arising from "market intelligence" had never really materialized. One senior figure noted that the sphere of investing in public firms in a mutual fund capacity was simply too different from venture investing—the former being principally a fee and relationships business, the other being about startup investments.[152] The challenging experience of the Capital Group was something of a test case; to this day, limited partners who attempt to disintermediate venture capital firms by doing direct investments in startups frequently run into similar problems.[153] At the same time, the Capital Group never fully disassociated from Sequoia Capital. Several of its key personnel maintained longstanding relationships with Valentine whereby they would get privileged access to Sequoia's investments through side-funds, without having to sacrifice a share of their gains due to being exempted from Sequoia's customary carried interest rate.[154]

Investments, Philosophy, and Returns

Across Valentine's early investments at Sequoia, common patterns can be identified. Access to networks mattered, especially as Valentine relied on connections made at Fairchild Semiconductor. In 1974, for example, he learned from a Fairchild connection about Atari, a startup founded by Nolan Bushnell in 1972 that made its mark by developing the first arcade video games. Its early hit, *Pong*, developed by star engineer Allan Alcorn, a UC Berkeley graduate, was a simulated tennis game. The first versions were made from television sets purchased at a nearby Walgreens, with a milk carton inside to collect coins, and placed in a local bar. The game quickly caught on. To finance home entertainment versions of *Pong*, Valentine put up $600,000 and by mid-1975 he had raised a further $1.5 million from the Mayfield Fund, Time, Inc., and Fidelity Associates. In September 1976, Atari was sold to Warner Communications for $28 million. In the span of about a year, Valentine had gained a fourfold multiple on his investment.[155]

The importance of access to the right networks was proved again when Valentine came into contact with Steve Jobs through his investment in Atari. Jobs had worked at the firm as an engineer. Bushnell suggested that Jobs approach Valentine for capital, and Valentine, in turn, connected Jobs with Mike Markkula, whom he knew from his time at Fairchild Semiconductor. Valentine felt that Jobs and Wozniak needed help with business plan development, especially pertaining to sales. Markkula had those capabilities. Although Venrock, not Valentine, led the first-round financing for Apple (see Chapter 5), Valentine took a $200,000 stake and obtained a seat on the board. When offered $6 million for this stake in a private placement prior to Apple's IPO in 1980, Valentine took the exit opportunity. With the benefit of hindsight, this stands as one of the biggest mistakes in venture capital history. Valentine still, however, gained a multiple of thirty on his investment within a year and a half.[156]

Deciding when to exit early-stage investments demands careful assessment of the complexities associated with the risk-reward tradeoff. Atari went on to become a hugely successful business in a billion-dollar market, so it could be argued that Valentine exited prematurely, as he did with Apple. On the other hand, in 1983, Atari suffered a large loss of $536 million in the face of game console competition from new entrants coming into the market. As Valentine noted, "when the world badly wants what we have and is willing to pay us twenty or thirty times what we paid for it, our inclination is to let them take it."[157]

Furthermore, Valentine was mindful that venture capital limited partnerships had a reasonably short duration and, at the time of the Atari and Apple investments, Sequoia Capital was a relatively new entity. A track record of successful investing and returns was critically important because it helped to establish a reputation, which in turn would facilitate future fundraising. Valentine also noted that Sequoia typically provided funding in stages to resolve uncertainty and manage the tradeoff between risk and reward, but he was quite robust in ending the funding cycle. When milestones were not achieved, the firm was quick to cut its losses.

As an insight into his personality and approach, Valentine once quipped at a speech at Stanford University in October 2010 that "I had a special advantage going into the venture business . . . I knew the future. And if you don't think knowing the future is a great advantage, it is a phenomenal advantage."[158] In reality, however, it was difficult to pick the winners *ex ante*. Don Valentine, like Rock and Perkins, faced the challenge of trying to identify novel product categories and market developments and anticipate future trends in entrepreneurship.

To manage unpredictability, it made most sense to have a rigorous viewpoint on what constituted a good investment opportunity. For Valentine, that meant effectively screening the market for novel sources of value creation, to connect products with the anticipated desires of consumers. Valentine was enthusiastic about the Atari investment because he saw a large shift in the market for electronic entertainment from bars and cafes to inside the home. By the same token, he was initially reluctant to invest in Apple because neither Jobs nor Wozniak "had any sense of the size of the potential market."[159] While Perkins saw potential in biotech investments, Valentine would later recall his conclusion at the time that "there is no market . . . [and] we were 90 percent right."[160] He put Sequoia's money where he considered market potential would be large. For example, he invested in LSI Logic, a software and integrated circuits developer. It was founded by Wilfred Corrigan in 1981, after Corrigan had served as president and CEO of Fairchild Semiconductor, and went public in 1983. Sequoia also invested, along with other venture investors including Kleiner Perkins Caufield & Byers, in the home software company Electronic Arts—which had a successful IPO in 1989, continuing its push toward global market expansion.

While Valentine viewed the market-dimension of investments differently than Rock or Perkins, he faced the same sorts of governance challenges. Specifically, founders tend to view control of their firm as a first-order priority, whereas investors tend to think more about returns. Valentine emphasized that "our first responsibility is to our limited partners," and for this reason he played a crucial role in persuading a reluctant Bushnell to sell Atari to Warner. He recognized that "it was his first company . . . and he did not want to give it up."[161] In following his fiduciary obligations, however, he often created antagonism. Oracle cofounder Larry Ellison lamented what he described as the "Mephistophelian" terms under which VCs provided funding for new startups, and their common practice of replacing founders with professional management. Oracle was founded in 1977 and Sequoia invested in 1983. Although Ellison and Valentine enjoyed a mutually respectful relationship, Ellison gave speeches on the theme of "Just Say No to Venture Capital," where he criticized the proliferation of baseless founder replacements in venture-backed investments.[162]

One of Valentine's most controversial governance decisions came as a consequence of a 1987 investment in Cisco, which had been founded in 1984 by the husband-and-wife team Len Bosack and Sandy Lerner. The couple started the company while working as computer support staff in two different departments at Stanford University. Bosack had devised a way to communicate via computer with Lerner at work by connecting the local area networks in their offices. Based on that technology, they decided to start Cisco (named as shorthand for San Francisco) to develop internetworking routers with software automatically determining the most efficient data transfer paths between networks. Bosack and Lerner resigned from Stanford, mortgaged their house, deferred salaries, and ran up credit card debt to bootstrap their new company.

Cisco first brought their routers to market in 1986 at price points ranging between $7,000 and $50,000. Within a year, revenues grew to over $250,000 a month—with only eight employees—but Bosack and Lerner were unable to fund further expansion. While they approached a multitude of VC firms without success, Valentine agreed to invest $2.5 million for a 32 percent stake.[163] Unbeknownst to anyone at the time, the internet was poised for a remarkable explosion in growth. In 1984, when Bosack and Lerner started Cisco, about a thousand hosts existed on the internet. By December 1987, the year they got funding, there were 28,174. By January 1998, there were 29.7 million.[164] As Valentine put it, Cisco "filled a desperate need."[165]

Unfortunately for Bosack and Lerner, they agreed to Sequoia's financing terms without fully appreciating what the various positive and negative covenants meant. Valentine became chairman of the board and effectively took control of Cisco's managerial development. Valentine believed "there is one set of management skills needed to start a company and another set needed to manage a bigger company. They are rarely resident in the same person."[166] He hired John Morgridge, a Stanford MBA from Grid Systems Corporation, and replaced several executives who had been friends of Lerner and Bosack with more experienced managers. Bosack was chief technology officer and Lerner served as vice president of customer service.

While the company continued to grow rapidly, targeting mainstream corporations and developing products that supported an even broader array of protocols, there were major fractures internally. Lerner repeatedly came into conflict with Valentine and the rest of the management team. While the two sides each have their own accounts of what happened, Lerner's experience has often been interpreted as an early example of the struggles faced by female founders in Silicon Valley high-tech firms. In August 1990, six months after Cisco had gone public, Lerner was fired and Bosack left, too. Both cashed out their equity. Sequoia held onto its interest, reaping the benefits of Morgridge's talents as a professional manager. At the inception of his tenure, Cisco had $5 million in annual revenues; that increased to $1.2 billion by the end of his tenure as president and CEO in January 1995.[167]

Valentine's investment approach created a record of exceptional VC returns for Sequoia Capital. The firm's first fund generated a net IRR of 51 percent from 1974 to 1980, a period when the S&P Composite returned 4.8 percent, or 10 percent including dividends. The second fund performed even better in absolute terms, generating a net IRR of 71 percent from 1979 to 1983. Figure 6.3 shows the returns to a series of Sequoia Capital funds, with Kleiner Perkins Caufield & Byers's fund performance for similar vintage years also included. It powerfully illustrates how significant the early funds were, because they created a track record of success, leading to momentum for further fundraising and

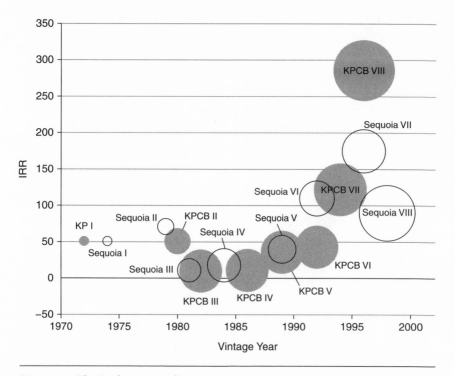

Figure 6.3 The Performance of Sequoia Capital and Kleiner Perkins Caufield & Byers Funds.

Based on returns reported in Preqin Venture Capital Database and disclosures under states' public records laws regarding investments made by entities such as the California Public Employees Retirement System. The size of each circle is proportional to the size of each fund.

returns. The status of both Sequoia Capital and Kleiner Perkins Caufield & Byers attracted some of the very best investing talent and entrepreneurial ideas. They increasingly solidified their positions as marquee VC limited partnerships during the 1980s and 1990s, in a setting where the overall pool of funds invested in the US venture capital industry grew significantly. Valentine stepped down from his management responsibilities at Sequoia Capital in 1996.

Poised for Takeoff

This chapter started with a history of Silicon Valley and ended with an analysis of some of the venture capital industry's most influential pioneers. The region and the talent were not independent of each other, but developed together as Silicon Valley offered an unparalleled environment

for the exploitation of entrepreneurial opportunities. What began in the late nineteenth century as a place populated mostly by fruit farms became a powerful cluster of high-tech firms from the 1950s and 1960s due to the pervasive influence of universities, government technology expenditure, semiconductors, and geography. Arthur Rock, Tom Perkins, and Don Valentine were all born and educated on the east coast, but they migrated to the west coast because it offered better prospects for new firm foundation. In doing so, they channeled the deployment of risk capital, helping Silicon Valley to maintain its regional lead.

While Rock, Perkins, and Valentine all realized enviable returns from their long-tail investing, providing even more proof that the venture capital "hits" model could work, they also maintained fundamentally different perspectives on the sequencing of the link between people, technology, and markets. Their investment styles were as different as their personalities, indicating that the early venture capital industry was far from homogenous. What they did have in common, however, was a heavy dose of what Valentine once described as "intelligence equity" based on their extraordinary understanding of how to make early-stage investments work.[168] They supplied capital, provided governance support in terms of business plan development and access to contacts, and certified the quality of startups through their involvement.

Finally, the importance of the overall environment that attracted Rock, Perkins, and Valentine to the west coast must be emphasized. The Silicon Valley ecosystem consisted of high-growth companies like Fairchild Semiconductor, a pool of potential entrepreneurs eager to spin off their own startups, and professional managers whose training had been incubated inside large, high-tech firms. Founders intersected with venture capitalists and professional managers to create innovation powerhouses like Intel, Genentech, and Apple in time frames that were incredibly short. Venture-backed success stories like these were highly visible, and acted as catalysts to the development of additional startups and talent pools. By the late 1970s and early 1980s, the US venture capital industry was poised for an unprecedented takeoff.

7

High-Tech, an Evolving Ecosystem, and Diversity during the 1980s

DURING THE EARLY 1980S, venture capital and high-tech business became inextricably linked, especially as a consequence of the revolution in personal computing. When Sequoia's Don Valentine was asked why his investments were so biased toward the computer industry, he said, "we probably have less to offer to companies outside the wide embrace of technology."[1] The US venture capital industry had a long history of supplying entrepreneurial finance to startups in high-technology industries. Going back to American Research and Development Corporation (see Chapter 4), Georges Doriot maintained a preference for investing in innovative portfolio companies with patent protection. But during this decade, the link with high-tech ventures grew stronger. While at the Mayfield Fund, Tommy Davis noted that, relative to opportunities in nontechnical areas or in services, new technologies produced large returns very quickly. Greylock's William Elfers explained further that "new technology is usually protected by patents and thus more immune to quick competition from rivals."[2]

Venture capital grew considerably in importance during the 1980s, even though the amount of active capital in the VC industry was dwarfed by the amount of later-stage capital deployed as a result of the leveraged buyout boom.[3] The model of VC investing became increasingly verified and the ecosystem of early-stage finance widened to support this growing industry. Banks and insurance companies developed capabilities as intermediaries, enabling VC-backed portfolio companies to raise further funds for growth. A group of investment banks, including San Francisco–based Hambrecht & Quist, developed expertise in underwriting IPOs.

The combined effect of these changes was large, especially alongside the favorable government policies discussed in Chapter 5. Annual new commitments to VC funds had been about $100 to $200 million during the 1970s, but they exceeded $4 billion annually during the 1980s.[4]

As the industry grew in size, different varieties of venture capital entities formed through a process of stratification and specialization. Corporate venture capital increased in importance, and the nexus of public-private financing evolved beyond the SBICs covered in Chapter 4. The Small Business Innovation Research (SBIR) program was launched in 1982, based on funding promising early-stage ideas using some of the basic principles associated with the VC model. This changing scale and scope in the structure of the industry was unprecedented. Organizing and governing ever larger VC limited partnerships meant overcoming new challenges.

Finally, in this historical context, both VC firms and their lead investors generated distinct identities. Limited partnerships fell into segments by fund size, region, and industry of focus. The certification effect of being financed by one of the marquee firms, such as Sequoia Capital or Kleiner Perkins Caufield & Byers, was powerful and a new generation of investors joined these firms as they underwent leadership transitions. Notably, women began to make their marks as venture capitalists. Yet, by the end of the 1980s, venture capital continued to be a socially homogenous occupation, underscoring that the lack of diversity in today's VC industry is a long-standing issue. Overall, the decade of the 1980s was one of the most formative ones in the history of US venture capital.[5]

Boom and Bust in the High-Tech Sector

In 1982, *Time* broke with tradition by not announcing a "person of the year." Instead, it heralded a product. The cover of its January 3, 1983 issue named the personal computer (PC) as "Machine of the Year." The accompanying article, "The Computer Moves In," noted that "the 'information revolution' that futurists have long predicted has arrived, bringing with it the promise of dramatic changes in the way people live and work, perhaps even in the way they think. America will never be the same." The first IBM PC was sold in 1981, and the rapid diffusion of that product would have immense social and economic benefits. IBM had introduced the PC in response to Apple's success with the Apple II, originally targeted at small and medium-sized businesses. A basic IBM PC model

5150, mated to Microsoft's DOS operating system with 64K of RAM and an Intel 8088 processor speed of 4.77 MHz, could be purchased for $1,565. A top-of-the-line IBM PC could be had for $3,000. At these price points, the PC had mass-market appeal. With its strong manufacturing capabilities, IBM could produce a new PC every forty-five seconds.[6]

Of course, IBM was a large incumbent rather than a venture-backed entrepreneurial entity, but as shown in Chapter 6, the venture capital industry was involved in financing some of the fundamental innovations associated with the microcomputer industry. Bill Gates and Paul Allen sold a 5 percent stake in Microsoft in 1981 to a Menlo Park VC firm, Technology Venture Investors. David Marquardt, general partner of that firm, became a long-standing member of Microsoft's board and gained renown as a strategic thinker.[7] While venture capital did not have much to do with many of the first wave of microcomputer firms in the 1970s—including Polymorphic Systems, Imsai, and Digital Group (all of which went bankrupt)—it played a role in financing the second wave. This included companies such as Compaq, founded in February 1982, which received funding from a newly established Texas-based VC firm, Sevin-Rosen, and from Kleiner Perkins Caufield & Byers.[8]

Venture capital was also crucially involved in the link between computer hardware and software. It was not always a source of startup financing. For example, Ashton-Tate, the California firm behind the path-breaking database management system dBASE, received no venture capital funding at all. But in many instances, the role of early-stage finance was pivotal. Sales of the Apple II computer were boosted by its ability to run VisiCalc, an electronic spreadsheet that became known as the original "killer app." VisiCalc was developed by VisiCorp, which had attracted venture financing from Arthur Rock and Venrock. Soon after it had invested in Compaq, Sevin-Rosen financed Lotus Development Corporation, which developed the famous Lotus 1-2-3 spreadsheets for the IBM PC. Rosen recalled that Compaq had expected to have sales of $30 million in its first year according to its business plan, but spectacularly "ended up doing $111 million." Lotus projected sales of about $3 million but "the company did $53 million . . . seventeen times more than forecast."[9]

Another software success owed much to the governing capabilities of Fred Adler, a New York lawyer who turned his hand to venture capital. Adler had some experience in the industry, having made a 1968 investment of $150,000 in a Route 128 (Massachusetts) enterprise called Data

General Corporation, which was worth around $22 million by 1984. In 1981, Adler invested in MicroPro International, developer of WordStar, a full-featured word processor program representing an advance over word processing on dedicated machines. Despite some early success, the company began to falter a few years later due to management problems. Adler took over operational control and "figured out who the egoists were and cut them to pieces." During this process, Adler replaced MicroPro's founder with an experienced professional manager. From losses of $1.5 million in Q1 of 1983, MicroPro went on to a successful IPO in 1984 at a valuation of $125 million, before ceding growth to new competition from WordPerfect and Microsoft Word.[10]

So extreme was the enthusiasm for venture capital investing during the early 1980s that, in a September 1981 special report by *Inc.*, the magazine could confidently state: "anyone with more than a passing knowledge of business and finance knows that venture capital is 'hot.'"[11] The report emphasized five main factors driving high-tech investments: (1) "experienced venture capital fund managers who can identify promising investments"; (2) "the increased flow of money into the venture business . . . particularly pension funds freed from past legal shackles"; (3) "stable long-term public policy commitments to venture capital," including the importance of SBICs; (4) "further capital gains tax relief"; and (5) "the booming market for new public stock offerings." At the same time, the report recognized the potential for a "bursting of the bubble" because, it argued, "venture capital will remain a cyclical business." Those words would prove prophetic.

High-tech markets did indeed collapse sharply during 1983 and 1984, signaling a major tech-based boom and bust cycle in the industry. From June 1983 to December 1984, the tech-heavy NASDAQ was down 28 percent. By contrast, the broader S&P Composite index lost a more modest 5.9 percent of its value. This era showed that, when expected payoffs were high, capital would flow into the industry at an accelerating rate—a phenomenon clearly on display in the NASDAQ boom and bust of the late 1990s and early 2000s, associated with internet-related startups. It was common during the early 1980s to see venture capitalists quoted in newspaper stories, commenting on "too much money chasing too few deals"—by now, a very common aphorism in the industry.

During the stock market run-up in public equity values, VC activity was concentrated in the high-tech sector. One estimate suggests that about 40 percent of venture capital money went into workstation ventures.[12] By 1984, venture capitalists had helped to start approximately three hundred such firms, many of which eventually failed in a crowded marketplace.[13] In a famous case of investment mania, the early "Winchester" disk drive industry (based on a type of storage device introduced by IBM with 30MB of fixed storage and 30MB of removable storage) attracted a flurry of venture-backed entrants and a race for market share. Forty-three firms received over $400 million in funding from 1977 to 1984.[14]

This level of investment could have destructive consequences. In December 1984, a *Wall Street Journal* headline blared: "Silicon Valley's Grim Reaper is a High-Tech Auctioneer with a Bumper Harvest." Yet, opinions remained divided. Gordon Moore argued, at Intel's annual meeting in 1984, that "the sopping up of resources by multiple startups trying to solve the same problem is detracting from the competitiveness of US industry."[15] Alternatively, as the *Inc.* special report implied, it might be more true that competition fosters innovation, and competitiveness rises when the "real winners are sorted out by the market."

This period highlighted the intense cyclicality associated with the VC investing model. While the PC revolution seems passé from the perspective of the modern networked economy, few predicted just how rapid the take-up of PCs would be. Difficulties associated with predicting new technology trajectories created the long-tail distribution of returns, which VCs fully embraced. When California-based Gavilan Computer—hoping to be an early pioneer in laptops—filed for bankruptcy in September 1984, leading to the loss of $31 million in venture capital money, the situation was lamentable. But tellingly, a New Enterprise Associates venture capitalist who had been one of the lead investors offered a more optimistic perspective. "The most you can lose in any company is 100 percent of your investment if it fails," he noted, "but you can gain up to 1,000 or 2,000 percent if the company succeeds."[16] Accepting that early-stage venture capital investing was truly about the deployment of high-risk capital in expectation of a long-tailed distribution of payoffs became even more fundamental to the industry during this era.

The boom-and-bust cycle of the early 1980s created industry fervor. One commentator noted that "every MBA thought venture capital was the next hot thing to get into," but that, as a result, "the quality of venture capitalists is dropping."[17] When money flowed in, there was simply an inadequate supply of individuals who could successfully put the new capital to work. The frenzy of venture capital activity led to "companies being launched with management teams that are woefully inexperienced."[18] Manuel Fernandez, founder of Gavilan Computer, was good at raising VC money and at sales, but he could not get his product to market. The clearest manifestation of this problem was the rush on the part of many venture capitalists and entrepreneurs to "cash out" through IPOs. According to Benjamin Rosen of Sevin-Rosen, in 1983, "anything that wiggled went public."[19] And with a number of newly entering VC firms, this problem was exaggerated. Young venture capital firms can tend toward "grandstanding," bringing portfolio companies to IPOs quickly to enhance the perception of their credibility.[20]

This context highlighted a major issue that would become central in the venture capital industry during the late 1990s and early 2000s NASDAQ bubble—namely, the conflict between the fiduciary duty to deliver returns to limited partners and the ethical responsibility to finance and develop viable businesses. The term *vaporware* came into popular usage at this time to describe imaginary high-tech products announced with fanfare before they actually existed. The innovation promised by Massachusetts-based Ovation Technologies was a well-known example. It spent $6.5 million of venture capital on the development of a sophisticated office productivity suite and promised delivery to market, but the software never shipped.

Public markets provided an opportunity to exit from investments and generate returns for limited partners, but Sequoia's Don Valentine estimated that, of the firms that did go public in 1983, "only 50 percent had a real need to."[21] In 1984, Reid Dennis, a well-respected venture capitalist at the Menlo Park firm Institutional Venture Partners, cautioned a National Venture Capital Association audience that the "public securities of venture-backed companies are the product of the venture investment process . . . the public is taking a shellacking and this will ultimately impact the venture capital industry."[22] When venture capitalists brought recently established firms to public markets prematurely, the industry faced a backlash. During the market crash, financial journalists—like the *Boston Globe* reporter of "Tough Times Ahead for Venture Capitalists"—suggested that the venture capital industry's problems were largely self-inflicted.[23]

While a number of venture capital firms did disappear, and limited partners became more discerning over where to put their capital, overall commitments to the industry were still higher at the end of the decade than they had been at the beginning. Outside the formal VC investing channel, the amount of capital available for entrepreneurship was even larger. William E. Wetzel, Jr. estimates that, by the late 1980s, about 250,000 angel investors existed and roughly 100,000 of them were active at any specific point in time. These individuals typically had net worths of at least $1 million, and collectively they accounted for a pool of capital at least twice the size of that managed by organized venture capital firms.[24] The informal market was plagued, however, by inefficiencies. Wetzel notes how angels frequently lacked the necessary skills and experience to make a material different to the startups in which they invested. By contrast, formal VC became increasingly professionalized, attracting additional financing from institutional investors.

Banks, IPO Intermediation, Mezzanine Finance, and Venture Debt

It would have been impossible for the VC industry to achieve scale without a broader development of the ecosystem of VC-backed finance. As noted in Chapters 5 and 6, the role of government policy was paramount. A key part of the market for early-stage finance was also created by the banking sector. Indeed, it is important to note that, among formal sources of capital for startups, bank loans are quantitatively important relative to venture capital. In the late 1980s, a much larger share of the fastest-growing private firms in America relied on bank loans and mortgages for finance as opposed to formal venture capital.[25]

A central area in which the banking sector became critical to the functioning of the venture capital industry was through intermediation in the IPO process. The existence of a robust market for IPOs is important to the venture capital cycle because it creates opportunities for liquidity. In 1983, a peak year of high-tech activity, there were 451 IPOs, and 173 (or 38 percent) of these were technology related. VC-backed IPOs accounted for a quarter of the total.[26] During the 1980s, acquisitions were more frequent than IPOs, but as a general rule IPOs yielded higher rates of return than did alternative exit routes.[27] A 1988 study by *Venture Economics* suggests that an investment in a VC-backed IPO firm could yield almost 1.4 times as much as an investment in an acquired firm over roughly equivalent holding periods.[28]

One of the most important intermediaries in the sphere of the high-tech IPO market was Hambrecht & Quist (H&Q) a San Francisco–based investment bank. H&Q was cofounded in 1968 by William R. Hambrecht, who had headed the west coast corporate finance office of Du Pont & Company, and George Quist, who had worked at Bank of America's SBIC arm. It got started in high-tech ventures as a "low-end disruptor," by persuading leading firms like Lehman Brothers to allow it to do the underwriting in the smaller and much less lucrative high-tech segment. Typically, the brokerage fee for such transactions was 7 percent, so the size of the public share offering mattered. Because H&Q was closely connected to leading Silicon Valley venture capitalists, it got privileged access to some of the most important IPO deals of the 1980s. Tom Perkins of Kleiner-Perkins was an investor both in H&Q and in Genentech. When Genentech underwent an IPO in October 1980, H&Q did the underwriting along with Blyth Eastman Paine Webber. In December 1980, H&Q was one of the main underwriters for the Apple Computer IPO, along with Morgan Stanley.

As an indication of H&Q's significance, in 1981 it underwrote twenty-five issues, and that year there were seventy-two technology IPOs.[29] In 1983 it did fifty-six deals, worth $2.2 billion. Although H&Q suffered in the high-tech downturn in 1984—the *New York Times* declared in March 1985 that "Hambrecht & Quist Loses Its Edge"—the firm rebounded, helping to take the publishing software company Adobe Systems, Inc., public in 1986.[30] In fact, along with Alex Brown & Sons of Baltimore, L. F. Rothschild, Unterberg, Towbin of New York, and Robertson, Colman & Stephens of San Francisco, H&Q was part of a small, powerful group that became known in the 1980s as the "four horsemen" of high-tech underwriting.

Together, these firms represented something fundamental in terms of IPO intermediation because they developed unassailable domain expertise in due diligence, valuing high-technology companies, and taking them public. Prior to their being subsumed into larger banks during the merger wave of the 1990s, they constituted a key link between high-tech venture capital portfolio firms and exit opportunities created by the IPO market. They also interacted with another key part of the VC ecosystem: the influential law firms, including Cooley, Crowley, Gaither, Godward, Castro & Huddleson and Wilson Sonsini Goodrich & Rosati, which were highly active in venture capital financings, serving as counsel to either portfolio companies or venture capital firms.

Unusually, H&Q became active as both an underwriter and an organizer of VC funds. During the 1970s, it was among the first investment banks to set up VC funds and, by the early 1980s, it was managing capital of over $200 million. It was also engaged in corporate venture capital. An H&Q affiliate managed a dedicated venture fund for Adobe. While many venture capital firms had reputations for culling their investments quickly, H&Q had a longer-term approach. In particular, it frequently used a professional manager, Quentin T. Wills, to "turn around" portfolio companies. Wills garnered such a reputation that he was even deployed into firms where H&Q had a limited equity stake. Notably, he was sent to Diasonics, one of Arthur Rock's struggling investments (see Chapter 6). Rock also happened to be an investor in H&Q, and H&Q had co-managed the Diasonics IPO in 1983. Although H&Q held less than 1 percent of Diasonics's stock, the signaling value was important. As Hambrecht stated, "we're trying to tell the marketplace, hey, we're in this for the long run; we're not going to walk away from companies that we back. We're going to do everything we can to make them work."[31]

Following the death of George Quist in 1982, Wills became chairman of the firm, but he struggled to adapt to this new leadership role. H&Q raised larger pools of venture capital in line with its growing reputation, but it did not have the capabilities to manage a portfolio of VC investments at this scale. During the mid- to late 1980s, H&Q financed over a hundred early-stage companies but neglected to fully nurture and govern all of them. Performance returns suffered. *Forbes* described the portfolio as being "littered with walking corpses."[32] For his part, Hambrecht was criticized for promoting unscrupulous underwritings because shares in companies H&Q took public so frequently traded below their initial offering price in the following years. Hambrecht remained optimistic in the face of this criticism, however. He saw H&Q's waning reputation as only a temporary reaction to cyclicality in the stock market and the declining value of technology stocks after the peak in 1983.

H&Q was also involved, like the other four-horsemen firms, in the provision of mezzanine finance, which represents another important function performed by banks and related financial institutions. In the venture capital vernacular, this refers to investments in portfolio companies that are about to go public but still need funds to finance sales growth or capital projects. Sometimes the mezzanine stage could be financed by a variety of different investment entities, including banks, corporations, and individuals. In 1979, just prior to its IPO, Apple raised $7.2 million from sixteen investors, including L. F. Rothschild, Unterberg,

Towbin; Brentwood Capital Corporation, a Los Angeles–based boutique investment banking and venture capital house; Xerox Corporation; and Fayez Sarofim, an individual investor and friend of Arthur Rock.[33] As a general rule, however, mezzanine finance became much more institution-alized in the VC context during the 1980s, being performed by special-ized financial intermediaries. For example, the insurance powerhouse Cigna provided a range of portfolio companies with mezzanine capital as they approached their IPOs.[34]

During the hottest IPO markets, such as the late 1960s, 1983, and 1986, mezzanine capital was in high demand. Because mezzanine finance came later in the life cycle of the firm, it was considered "medium-risk capital." The borrowing firm would receive a loan—subordinated debt with a fixed interest rate—in the region of $500,000 to $5 million for a period of about 5 to 7 years.[35] Most of the time, the loan contract would come with warrants entitling the provider of the debt to acquire equity in the borrowing firm. Mezzanine finance tends to offer lower but more stable returns than dedicated early-stage venture funds do. For that reason, the number of mezzanine investors increased in the 1980s. Banks established dedicated funds that crossed over between VC and private equity operations. For example, in 1989, Citicorp raised a $650 million fund to invest solely in mezzanine securities, to be managed by its ven-ture capital arm.

The 1980s also witnessed the emergence of specialized commercial banking operations that would evolve into key venture debt lenders. These entities provided "starter" lines of credit and debt financing to new firms to support cash flow, operations, and growth. Venture debt could be raised on top of venture capital to provide financing for capital equip-ment purchases, such as computer systems and R&D laboratory infra-structure. For early-stage and emerging high-growth companies without profits or positive cash flows, this became an opportune way to raise capital in an equity-efficient manner. Capital injections would help to achieve milestones and thereby enable entrepreneurs to raise new rounds of formal VC financing at higher valuations.

The most notable of the new niche players in this area was Silicon Valley Bank (SVB). It was incorporated in 1983 by William Biggerstaff, a Harvard MBA, who had held a senior position at Wells Fargo Bank. Roger Smith, who had spent a career in banking, became CEO.[36] SVB opened its first office in San Jose, California, and while it also engaged in real estate and corporate lending, it quickly became defined by its innovative lending practices to early-stage firms. It provided equipment financing, working capital, and asset acquisition loans, as well as bridge financing to high-tech startups with varying degrees of security. On the basis of a 1986 agreement, it would syndicate more substantial loans to its large partner in the northeast, the Bank of New England.

SVB's approach was attractive to founders who were reluctant to cede equity to venture capitalists, and it filled a gap in the market for entrepreneurial finance left by traditional commercial banks, who were less likely to want to engage in high-risk lending. Smith explained SVB's unconventional strategy in this way: "We want to know the company at its birth. . . . Many banks say they like companies to be three years old. We think new isn't bad."[37] As it turned out, the failure rate was indeed much lower in this sector than had widely been anticipated. From 1983 to 1987, SVB "charged off" as bad debt just $150,000 in loans to technology companies.[38]

As a result of its effective business model, growth was explosive. SVB provided $7.6 million in loans in 1983, and that number rose to $286 million in 1989.[39] In 1987, about 28 percent of SVB's loan portfolio was devoted to high-technology firms. In 1989, SVB opened an office in Menlo Park, California, in the venture capital hotspot of 3000 Sand Hill Road. This was a natural step, given its growing emphasis on providing debt-financing to high-tech startups that had raised funds from reputable VC firms. By the mid-1990s, SVB was heavily focused on VC-backed technology lending. In addition to interest payments and fees, SVB would receive equity warrants in these startups, meaning it, too, could access the kinds of returns associated with long-tail investing. It also became a limited partner in some VC funds. For their part, VC firms got access to reciprocal relationships from SVB.

Corporate Venture Capital

Another important shift in the structure of the VC industry occurred during the 1980s, with the growth in corporate venture capital arms. Corporate venture capital first began to take off in the mid-1960s. During that decade, about 25 percent of *Fortune* 500 firms started corporate venture capital arms to pursue new business development opportunities as part of their diversification strategies.[40] Sometimes these efforts led to large firms' financing "spinoff" companies to commercialize innovations which had been developed in-house but did not support existing product lines. From 1969 to 1973, General Electric's Technology Venture Operation funded six spinoffs in areas from integrated circuit production to membrane filters. By the early 1970s, the equity in these spinoffs was worth around three times the book value of the original investments, although this did not take into account General Electric's heavy initial R&D costs in the preliminary development of these products.[41]

In other cases, corporate venture capital arms acquired new portfolio companies. During the 1970s, Exxon Enterprises invested $100 million in information systems startups, though the program was ultimately unsuccessful.[42] A key issue was whether it made more sense for corporations to initiate standalone venture capital operations, or to outsource to private venture capital firms. A lot depended on the underlying motivation—that is, whether the initial entry into venture capital had been driven by the pursuit of financial returns or strategic benefits. The greater the importance of strategic benefits, the more likely it was that corporations would start up their own corporate venture capital programs. By monitoring the market for innovation through these entities, corporations could attempt to reduce the risk of competitive threats posed by new startups.

The market for corporate venture capital has always tended to be highly cyclical. During the early 1970s, around the time of the oil crises, there were about thirty corporate venture capital entities with total capital of $160 million.[43] By 1983, however, in light of the high-tech boom, the pool of funds available to corporate venture capital had grown to $2.5 billion.[44] Some of the most influential corporate venture capital entities increased their investment activity, having been encouraged by earlier successes. During the early 1970s, Monsanto had set up InnoVen, a venture investing operation with another Missouri-based firm, Emerson Electric, to invest in chemicals and microelectronics businesses. Through an InnoVen fund, Monsanto acquired equity in a range of biotech firms including Genentech, Biogen, Collagen, and Genex, as it considered expanding into pharmaceuticals. Through its corporate venture capital arm, the large specialty chemicals firm Lubrizol gained a board seat at Genentech by investing $10 million in 1979.[45]

During the 1980s, Xerox established two venture capital funds which, although themselves unsuccessful, were important precursors to the wildly successful Xerox Technology Ventures (XTV) established in 1989.

As a $30 million fund, operating almost exactly like an independent venture capital limited partnership but within the boundaries of a parent company, XTV made a series of hit investments. One, for example, was Documentum, an enterprise software firm that underwent an IPO in 1996 at a $351 million market capitalization. XTV represented a highly successful attempt to generate VC-style returns. Indeed, XTV generated a staggering net IRR of 56 percent, compared to just 13.7 percent for the mean venture capital fund and 20.4 percent for an upper-quartile fund from the same vintage year.[46]

Because XTV had mimicked a venture capital structure, however, its partners received carried interest in amounts far in excess of normal corporate compensation. XTV portfolio companies also had privileged access to Xerox customers, so some of the exit value of XTV's portfolio was due to its association with the parent company. XTV partners were judged to be receiving a disproportionate share of the financial gains, and XTV was terminated in 1996—to be replaced by a new, more conservative organizational entity called Xerox New Enterprises. Compensation in Xerox New Enterprises was more aligned with corporate practices and it was also given far less autonomy than XTV over investment decisions.

The XTV experience highlighted that corporate investment principles and venture capital principles were largely incompatible.[47] Bringing venture capital inside large firms offered high-potential opportunities, but a change in organizational culture would be required for it to work, especially regarding compensation. If a firm opted to avoid internal conflict by operating corporate venture capital as a "normal" corporate division, at associated compensation levels, it ran the risk of losing the very best investors to venture capital limited partnerships. Both Exxon and General Electric lost talented people in this way.

In this context, it is easy to see why independent venture capital investing was so attractive to some corporations. It offered the benefits of strategic interaction between corporate limited partners, and removed the costs and conflicts associated with separate corporate venture capital arms. Notably, 3M committed about $75 million to twenty-seven venture capital limited partnerships during the 1980s. It opted to acquire VC-backed portfolio companies from the funds in which it held an interest, under the assumption that this would create complementarities with its own internal business units. 3M's net IRR on its venture capital investments exceeded 20 percent.[48] In other words, 3M did what very few corporations involved in venture capital were able to do in the 1980s: it simultaneously generated both financial and strategic upside. In a 1991 survey of corporate venture capital practices, 3M was voted as the standout firm by its peers.[49]

Public-Private Entities

As an additional boost to the developing VC ecosystem, a new government effort to support high-tech startups came into existence under the Small Business Innovation Research Development Act of 1982. Debate over the introduction of the Small Business Innovation Research (SBIR) program has clear parallels with debate over the introduction of SBICs under the Small Business Investment Act of 1958. Recall from Chapter 4 that the perception of a "funding gap" for startups was the main impetus for federal support for the financing of small businesses. Similarly, an influential May 1980 report, "Small High Technology Firms and Innovation," argued that a funding gap existed because small business owners were often reluctant to cede equity to venture capital firms, and SBICs were not in the business of deploying early-stage risk capital. High-tech innovation was particularly constrained, the report stated, because it was excessively expensive and time consuming. Among its policy proposals, the report recommended that the "National Science Foundation's Small Business Innovation Research (SBIR) Program should be expanded."[50]

The National Science Foundation's program was heavily influenced by the methods of the venture capital industry. It was designed by Roland Tibbetts, a Harvard MBA who, before going to work in government administration, had been both a venture capitalist, having founded the Washington, DC–based firm Allied Capital Corporation, and an operational executive, serving two high-tech firms as a vice president.[51] The program called for a three-phase funding structure. Phase I was a "proof of concept" stage, where ideas were refined through experimentation. Under the National Science Foundation's version, awards of up to $30,000 (about $80,000 today) were made in this phase. Phase II provided further funding for refinement of the idea, assuming applicants could show they had "a commitment for follow-on venture capital or other funding." Phase III facilitated transition of the idea to the commercial marketplace on the basis of Phase II financing. This structure was clearly analogous to the VC model of using milestones and staged financing to mitigate investment risk.

The public-private component of the program was appealing because it placed an emphasis on small firms' development of ideas with commercial relevance. This was a government-funded platform designed to encourage creative technological development through the supply of seed money. Crucially, one proponent argued in Congressional testimony that "the program serves as a pre-screening of investment opportunities for venture capitalists seeking to invest in small, technology-oriented growth companies."[52] This de-risking of early-stage investments meant that venture capital would potentially flow into high-tech ventures at a much higher rate.

Early successes by the program in creating a pathway to successful VC-backed firms suggested it was gaining traction. For example, Omex Corporation, a Santa Clara–based laser optics and computer firm, received a total of $172,000 in federal grants, which subsequently attracted $4 million in venture capital funding. Collaborative Research, based in Waltham, Massachusetts, received between $8 million and $9 million in follow-on venture capital financing in its pursuit of industrial applications of recombinant DNA techniques. Over a period of more than four years, the National Science Foundation's SBIR program spent a total of $15.4 million, funding about three hundred proposals.

The 1982 SBIR program was much larger because it mandated that the major R&D agencies of the US government, including the Department of Defense, allocate a share of their budget to nurture creative small-business innovation projects. From 1983 through fiscal year 1988, twelve federal agencies awarded over $1.35 billion; the Department of Defense accounted for 55 percent of that total. Over the same time period, new commitments to the venture capital industry equaled about $14.5 billion, so SBIR spending represented 9.3 percent of that amount. Like a venture capital firm screening portfolio companies, the SBIR funded only a small share of proposals. In 1987, just 15 percent of Phase I proposals received an award, and only 35 percent of Phase I projects went on to receive Phase II awards. Although a study of 120 Phase I award recipients in 1983 showed that about 45 percent had failed, it also argued that "a handful of successes in these programs more than compensate for all the failures."[53]

In line with the distributions of returns that venture capitalists were familiar with, the SBIR program led to some spectacular successes— among them, IG Laboratories, which became a subsidiary of Genzyme Corporation. Genzyme itself got started in 1981 because its founder,

Henry Blair, received contract financing as an academic scientist from the National Institutes of Health to produce modified enzymes. Generally, SBIR-financed firms grew at a faster rate than otherwise equivalent firms that did not receive SBIR grants.[54] Recent research, focusing on small high-tech firms and analyzing data from some $884 million worth of awards by the Department of Energy from 1983 to 2013, reveals the principal mechanism by which the SBIR program had its impact: it encouraged "technology prototyping." Early-stage awards lowered innovation risk, thereby increasing the appeal of the recipient firms to venture capitalists.[55] The SBIR program provides strong evidence that government-sponsored VC-style initiatives can be effective, especially in spurring experimentation in energy innovation and other high-risk areas that tend to be less attractive to private markets.

Tiering, Performance Benchmarks, and Investment Stages

Within the private venture capital market, different types of firms began to be identifiable. National firms sat at the top of the hierarchy, given the size of the funds they could raise. These included Kleiner Perkins Caufield & Byers, Sequoia Capital, Mayfield, and Greylock, with their capacity to raise funds in the region of $100 million or more. Other national firms, but with smaller capital bases, included Boston-based Battery Ventures, which raised a $34 million fund in 1984 and a $42 million fund in 1988. Other new entrants during the 1980s included Matrix Partners, which excelled during the 1990s specializing in high-tech investing, and Accel Partners, founded in 1983 by James Swartz and Arthur Patterson (both formerly of Adler & Company) in Princeton, New Jersey. Accel quickly moved to the upper tier, closing a $100 million fund in 1989. Draper Fisher Jurvetson, founded in 1987, continued a long family tradition in venture capital. Cofounder Timothy C. Draper is the son of William Draper III, who founded Sutter Hill Ventures in 1965, and he in turn is the son of William Henry Draper, Jr., who cofounded Draper, Gaither & Anderson in 1959 (see Chapter 5). Draper Fisher Jurvetson went on to manage a $636 million fund in 2000.

Specialty venture capital firms focused on certain regions or industries typically existed at a lower capital base, but some could also be extremely large. At the smaller end, in 1986, ARCH Venture Partners was founded with a $9 million fund to commercialize the most creative ideas emerging from the University of Chicago and the Argonne National

Laboratory.[56] Various biotech and healthcare specialty funds were formed during the 1980s, inspired by successes like Genentech (see Chapter 6) and Amgen—a company founded in 1980 when William Bowes, who sat on the board of Cetus Corporation, coaxed eminent UCLA scientist Winston Salser into the emerging world of biopharmaceuticals. In 1981, Bowes cofounded US Venture Partners, which became a leading Silicon Valley venture capital firm.

HealthCare Ventures, founded in New Jersey in 1985 with a $60 million fund, went on to become one of the largest venture capital firms in this sector. Its 1989 fund was $100 million, and its 1992 fund stood at $217 million. In 1986, HealthCare Ventures made an investment in Genetic Therapy, Inc., returning $50 million to its limited partners based on a $5.2 million investment when the company was acquired in 1995.[57] The growing size of the funds in this area reflected the increased complexity of getting biopharmaceutical products to market. Whereas an early-1980s biotech startup could be funded with $10 million to $20 million, one a few decades later might require $100 million to $200 million to make it through clinical trials and reach commercialization.[58]

Across all of these categories, venture capital firms were judged by a variety of performance standards. When *Inc.* listed the "50 Most Active Venture Capitalists" in 1981, its emphasis was on fund size and the time it took to raise fund commitments. By contrast, *Venture's* 1982 ranking of venture capital firms was by the dollar amount of risk capital they invested.[59] Returns, of course, also served as an indicator. On that basis, a 1985 survey of the VC industry calculated that private venture capital firms outperformed SBICs and corporate venture capital arms.[60]

Although returns were a natural part of the dialogue surrounding performance, the modern notion that the very best venture capital firms consistently generate "top-quartile" returns came much later on. During the 1960s, SBICs were categorized by profitability quartiles in Congressional reports relating to the Small Business Investment Act, and during the 1970s, other investment vehicles, including mutual funds, were grouped by quartiles. The number of venture capital limited partnerships, however, was still not large enough to be bracketed in the same way. Although databases were available, such as VentureXpert, which originated as the SBIC Reporting Service in 1961, discrepancies in reporting and data meant that rates of return were difficult to evaluate systematically during the 1980s.[61] The "top-quartile" terminology became common only during the 1990s, when VC funds started to be more methodically benchmarked by the performance of funds with the same vintage year.

Despite these measurement issues, tiers of VC firms started becoming discernible to investors. Reputation mattered most. In 1984, *Institutional Investor* wrote about the "Two-Tier Market for Venture Firms," reporting that some firms "can raise money for partnerships just by letting pension funds know that a new one is open," but that "the myriad of new entrants are finding that [fundraising] is much more difficult."[62] The article profiles the relative ease with which leading firms like Menlo Ventures (founded in 1976) and Adler & Company could raise funds because they had substantial commitments from long-standing limited partners. A natural response of the firms lower down in the hierarchy was to opt for a strategy of differentiation to fill particular niches, giving further impetus to the rise of specialized entities.

Venture capital firms also attempted to fundraise from new types of intermediaries, including those that developed "fund-of-funds" vehicles to hold portfolios of individual VC funds. For example, in 1982, the Boston-based insurer John Hancock Financial Services raised a $148 million fund both to invest in a range of venture capital limited partnerships and to invest directly in firms. While the fund-of-funds approach succeeded for other institutional investors by increasing diversification into different venture capital pools, direct investing proved more problematic. As one entrepreneur emphasized, "the last place you [want] to get your money from [is] an insurance company like John Hancock" because "they just [aren't] sophisticated like other venture capitalists."[63]

But while venture capitalists had domain expertise in early-stage investments, they also got caught up in later-stage activities—specifically, the leveraged buyout boom of the 1980s. Leveraged buyout transactions in the US economy increased almost eightfold from 1979 to 1988.[64] Kohlberg Kravis Roberts & Company was founded in 1976, and two other major players in private equity, Blackstone Group and Carlyle Group, were founded in 1985 and 1987, respectively.

Although the expected return on an early-stage VC investment was higher than a leveraged buyout transaction, the long-tail distribution typical of early-stage investing made it considerably riskier. Add to this the need to deploy increasing amounts of capital coming through the influx of dollars from pension funds into VC (discussed in Chapter 5), and the appeal of leveraged buyouts is clear: they offered an opportunity to generate favorable returns in a short time frame. Whereas, in 1980, zero percent of VC investments were in leveraged buyouts, 23 percent were by 1986.[65] Venture firms faced a demanding challenge: how to scale their activities while simultaneously maintaining a focus on early-stage investments.

Scaling: New Enterprise Associates

A long-standing issue in the VC literature is the extent to which performance can be maintained as fund size increases.[66] A prominent venture capitalist remarked: "This business is just not set up for big bucks."[67] New Enterprise Associates (NEA), which became a top-quartile venture capital performer, provides an ideal lens through which to consider scaling and, more broadly, the evolution of the venture capital industry during the 1980s. Established in 1978 with a $16.4 million fund (approximately $60 million today), it subsequently grew into the largest venture capital firm in the world. While NEA II (a $45.3 million fund raised in 1981) was about equivalent to the average fund size, NEA V, a $199 million fund raised in 1990, was approximately 2.5 times larger than the average fund size from the same vintage year. Adjusting for inflation, NEA V was six times larger than NEA I.

NEA was founded by Richard "Dick" Kramlich, Charles "Chuck" Newhall, and Frank Bonsal. Kramlich had been influenced by two key figures in the early history of the venture capital industry. First, he knew Georges Doriot from his time pursuing an MBA at Harvard Business School—in fact, his firm was named New Enterprise Associates at Doriot's suggestion. Second, Kramlich had worked as a junior partner in Arthur Rock & Company on the west coast during the 1970s. Beyond his associations with these major venture investors, Kramlich had a strong track record on his own account. For example, he was an early investor in Apple Computer. His connection with Newhall and Bonsal came as he sought more autonomy and wound down his partnership with Rock. He became a managing partner in NEA in 1982, a position Newhall had offered him from the very beginning.

Newhall also had connections with the history of venture capital. His father, Charles W. Newhall, Jr., was an Army Air Corps colonel who, after the Second World War, worked with well-known venture capitalist Laurance Rockefeller (see Chapters 3 and 5). Newhall earned his MBA in 1971, five years after Doriot's retirement. He then joined what was still, at the time, a small investment company, T. Rowe Price Associates, headquartered in Baltimore, Maryland.

The third of the trio, Bonsal, graduated with a degree in American Studies and Economics from Princeton, and did not pursue an MBA. Bonsal initially joined the Baltimore investment banking firm of Robert Garrett & Sons as a retail salesman. In 1965, he joined the Baltimore-based Alex Brown & Sons as an investment banker, specializing in IPOs. He remained at the firm until 1977. Bonsal was an archetypal dealmaker.

Kramlich, Newhall, and Bonsal did not always get along. "Frank feels the only thing that counts is finding the investment," Newhall once mused, whereas "Dick feels that what counts is making a difference as a board member." Despite their differences, Newhall said, the three "together somehow" were able to "make a collective peace."[68] Through their social networks and business connections, Kramlich, Newhall, and Bonsal raised an initial $5.5 million in committed capital from lead investors. Of this, $1 million came from T. Rowe Price, through the support of its CEO, Curran Harvey. Such lead investors paved the way for further capital inflows. In return, NEA's general partners agreed to cede nine of their twenty-five carried interest percentage points to the lead limited partners. In one of NEA's founding documents, they announced their goal:

> The objective of NEA is to invest in and assist emerging innovative companies with exceptional management and outstanding growth and profit potential. In essence we finance change. The objective of NEA is to achieve a superior investment return over the life cycle of the Partnership for our Limited Partners. Capital appreciation will be an earned reward for providing risk capital and assisting in the creation of real economic value. . . . The goal of NEA is to retain the venture art form while directing substantial resources toward company creation.[69]

This description reveals the motivation behind NEA. The words "*we finance change*" were very much in the spirit of Doriot's belief that venture capital money should be deployed "to do things that have never been done before."[70] Providing "risk capital" and "assisting in the creation of real economic value" was aligned with one of Laurance Rockefeller's guiding principles—namely, to finance companies that made a real difference. Finally, and perhaps most pertinently, the description of the venture business as an "art form" recognized that this was not a scientific endeavor. Achieving returns from a long-tail portfolio would depend on the general partners' tacit knowledge.

Despite this emphasis on venture capital as an "art form," Kramlich, Newhall, and Bonsal designed NEA with systematic rigor, creating a "vertical network" of resources linking limited partners, general partners, associates, portfolio companies, and industry analysts from T. Rowe Price, who analyzed and flagged potential investment opportunities.[71] NEA was also formally designed to be a bi-coastal firm. At the time, venture capital was beginning to spread geographically, but it was predominantly regionally concentrated in California, New York, and Boston. NEA chose to set up offices in Baltimore and San Francisco and to be national in focus. By the mid-1980s, it also operated an affiliated partnership in Dallas, Texas. Kramlich noted an implication of this increased scope: "we had to synthesize what we were doing into a clear and understandable *modus operandi*."[72]

Given the need for efficient communication, NEA designed a protocol of weekly conference calls and a system to transfer data seamlessly among offices. But the link between the east and west coast gave NEA a platform that went beyond these functions. How much general partners matter relative to the firm in which they work is an important question in the venture capital literature.[73] One way to address it is to ask whether the organizational structure of a firm adds value. In NEA's case, the answer was often yes. In 1981, Bonsal identified an investment opportunity with Digital Communications Associates, a struggling telecom and information technology firm based in Atlanta. Kramlich identified a turnaround manager from his networks and bi-coastal communications ensued through the protocols that NEA had set up. This investment ultimately generated a multiple of six on the original investment. Kramlich emphasized, "that's a case where had we not been on the two coasts and had this proliferation of resources, the deal would not have come together nearly as smoothly as it did."[74]

NEA built additional organizational capabilities by harnessing close relationships with its limited partners. Corporate limited partners, such as the multinational conglomerate 3M, accounted for a large share of NEA's capital—about 20 percent, as compared to the average venture capital firm's 14 percent. These limited partners provided financing services and investment analysis, including technology evaluation and due diligence. Newhall later recalled an instance of this: "In NEA I, we had an opportunity to invest in Tandon [a disk drive and PC manufacturer]. We had about a week to react to the investment opportunity. 3M at the time was the largest customer of Tandon. 3M's customer knowledge was extremely useful and allowed us to materially reduce the due diligence time. . . . Having active LPs with a good deal of industry knowledge can be very beneficial . . . and can dramatically help the venture capitalist achieve a superior return."[75]

NEA's limited partners also assisted portfolio companies in recruiting, marketing relationships, and customer acquisition. Newhall noted: "When 3M made an investment, internal rate of return was not the only concern. What 3M was also interested in was the variety of other interactions that it could have with portfolio companies of the venture partnership." NEA did not violate the principles of a limited partnership agreement because technically its limited partners did not engage in "day-to-day" activities of the firm. A vice president of strategic planning at 3M stated unequivocally, "we don't want to have responsibility for investment decisions; we don't want to take the general partner's role."[76]

Because there was a potential for overreach with these relationships, Kramlich, Newhall, and Bonsal set up an investment committee composed of NEA's most prominent investors, and on top of that, an advisory committee to provide higher-level governing oversight. Newhall recalled an occasion when the investment committee weighed in: "In 1980, we were approached by Merck to see if NEA would be interested in setting up a dedicated life sciences fund with Merck as the only LP. We took the proposal to the investment committee to discuss the subject. It was tempting to have access to Merck's life sciences knowledge, but the IC had concerns. It became immediately clear that Merck as a corporation may want to do an investment for strategic scientific purposes rather than for pure economic gain. Who would have the first call on a health-care investment: NEA or the dedicated life science fund? The potential number of conflicts of interest was so enormous that we declined the opportunity."[77]

Both the investment and advisory committees could also deal with any conflicts between general partners and limited partners; they could approve values of portfolio assets and distributions; and they could make judgments about the expenses of the partnership, including general partner salaries. As Newhall put it, the IC "subjected us to the same governance that our companies were subjected to." Most venture capital firms at the time felt that NEA had created organizational bureaucracy.[78] But this structure made sense because it was consistent with NEA's strategy of creating an environment of mutual trust.

Kramlich's observation was that organizational oversight meant NEA could operate with exceptions rather than rules. This approach was beneficial in the case of Forethought, a California software company founded in 1983. Forethought went through a series of financings and, on the last round, Kramlich was outvoted by his partners. With the investment committee's approval, Kramlich invested in the company himself, with the proviso that NEA could buy out his position at a later time. Forethought went on to be successful, developing the software that became PowerPoint. Microsoft acquired Forethought for $14 million in 1987. True to his original commitment to NEA's governance principles, Kramlich did indeed sell his shares back to NEA at his original cost. NEA made a multiple of three on the total amount it had committed to this investment.[79]

NEA's management fees were normally around 1.5 percent, which was based on the cost of administering the partnership. While NEA fees were lower than the 2 percent industry norm, the share of the investment gains collected by the general partners was 25 percent—higher than the 20 percent norm. Later, NEA funds gravitated to the highest carried interest rate in the industry: 30 percent. According to Newhall, the intuition was to "optimize the number of investments made, enhance the internal rate of return of LPs, and align the interests of LPs, GPs, and entrepreneurs."[80] Collecting a smaller fee meant that more of a limited partner's committed capital could be deployed into actual investment at the initial stages of the fund. Because carried interest came at the end of the fund's life, it created effective contracting incentives. Kramlich, Newhall, and Bonsal were essentially signaling their superior capabilities as investors by their willingness to forego current fees in favor of later and more variable carried interest compensation.

Newhall noted that NEA advocated a wide distribution of carry to younger partners to facilitate an orderly transfer of leadership. A newly promoted general partner would have typically spent three to six years at NEA as a special partner (an interim step) and three years before that as an associate. The intention of the founding partners to create an enduring venture capital firm is reflected in changes in the distribution of carried interest. In NEA's first fund, the founding partners received 100 percent of the total carried interest of the partnership. As new partners were brought in or promoted, this share fell. In NEA II, the founding partner share of total carried interest was 66 percent. In NEA III, it was 52 percent, and in NEA IV, 38 percent.

In terms of selecting associates, NEA targeted a set of skills and attributes, but it did not impose a specific formula. The best general partners Newhall said, possessed a mix of investment banking, investment management, and high-technology operating skills, which is consistent with empirical evidence showing that venture capitalists who outperform tend to have industry experience.[81]

NEA actively governed; indeed, selecting portfolio companies willing to accept business counsel from the general partners was written into NEA's philosophy. At the same time, governance at scale created its own set of challenges. Bonsal remarked that "governing portfolio companies takes a lot of time. It's very time intensive. . . . It's easy to put the money out, but it's not easy to manage it."[82] Newhall recalled of NEA's investment in Queue Systems, a West Virginia manufacturer of cryogenic preservation equipment for biotech research, "we did not lose much money, but I lost 25 percent of my life for five years and I wasted months in exhausting, useless travel."[83] Board seats were taken in 90 percent of investments in NEA I. That portion fell to 68 percent in NEA II and to 77 percent in NEA III, and rose again to 85 percent by the time of NEA IV.

In line with the skewed distribution of long-tailed returns, NEA experienced successes and failures during its early years. As noted above, the firm suffered major losses through its investment in Gavilan Computer, but this was accepted as part of the risk with a portfolio of uncertain investments. Although seed and startup investments accounted for only 38 percent of the portfolio in NEA I, they accounted for 75 percent of the portfolio by NEA IV. Further highlighting the uncertainties of early-stage investing, NEA also passed on some of the most important investment opportunities of the time period, including Home Depot and Staples. Both became spectacular successes.

Yet, NEA's big hits compensated for these loses and missed opportunities. Giga-tronics, a specialized electronics firm located in Pleasant Hill, California, was one of NEA's most influential investments. In 1981, the five founders of Giga-tronics sought $600,000 of investment capital, a purposefully small amount because they wanted to retain control. Several marquee venture capital firms countered with offers in the region of $1 million, conditional on a significant ownership share. All were rejected. Because Kramlich believed in the technology and the founding team, he

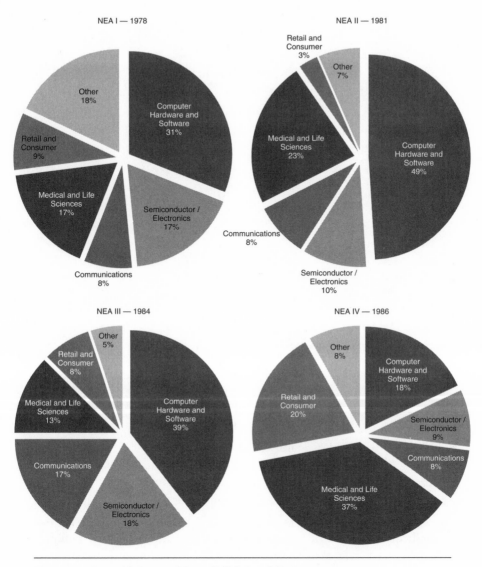

Figure 7.1 Sectoral Composition of NEA Portfolio Investments.
Based on data in NEA annual reports, NEA Archives, provided by Chuck Newhall.

took a more holistic approach and agreed to meet the founders' terms. He accepted a smaller share of the firm and invested $480,000 for 29 percent.[84] Giga-tronics produced a multiple of thirty-two on NEA's investment.

NEA shifted investments by sector when it anticipated changes in opportunities. As Figure 7.1 shows, following the boom and bust era of the

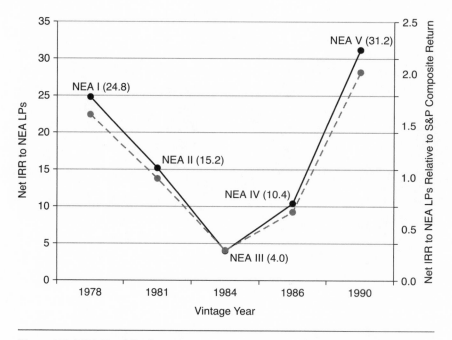

Figure 7.2 NEA Fund Performance.

Based on data in NEA annual reports, NEA Archives, provided by Chuck Newhall. The dashed line is the return on each NEA fund relative to a contemporaneous return on the S&P Composite.

early 1980s, capital increasingly moved from the crowded computer hardware and software space to other sectors, such as medical and life sciences. NEA invested in Immunex Corporation, a startup based in Seattle, which became a leading biotech company in immune system science. It was ultimately acquired by Amgen for $10 billion in July 2002. In 1978, just 17 percent of NEA I investments, by dollar amount, had been in medical and life sciences, but by NEA V, the portion rose to 37 percent. By 1986, NEA was also heavily into retail and consumer-related investments, which accounted for 20 percent of the portfolio—more than double the level in 1978.

Over time, NEA showed that a VC firm could overcome scaling limits, as illustrated in Figure 7.2. Although returns declined initially as the firm scaled from NEA I to NEA III, returns increased with later funds, whether measured in absolute terms or by benchmarking relative to returns in public equities markets to control for changing market circumstances.

NEA's founders each had their own distinctive view of what drove this success. Kramlich credited personal drive: "I have an unlimited amount of energy. I'm willing to take chances to reach certain goals, push the envelope. I know what I can do. I'm straightforward with people so they tend [to] believe me, which allows me to lead in what I believe is the proper direction."[85] Bonsal spoke of self-assurance: "to be in the venture business, I guess you've got to feel confident in yourself. You have to have self-confidence to get up in the morning and go do it. If you don't have that ability to go do it, it won't happen."[86] Newhall was characteristically philosophical: "You can know all the rules of venture investing and yet have nothing of value. . . . Rules must be part of a natural instinct. Not a checklist formula. What is really important varies in each situation. Skill is only maintained and improved by continuous immersion in the art and hard work. Success comes from knowing that which is important before, rather than after, the fact."[87]

A New Generation of Outstanding Investors

Kramlich, Newhall, and Bonsal were ultimately the key assets at NEA, even though the firm's organizational capital also contributed to investment performance as the firm scaled. Across the venture capital industry, empirical evidence suggests that, as a general rule, the contribution of a firm's investors matters most to explaining performance differences.[88] Being a top-tier venture capital firm was obviously important to fundraising during the 1980s because of the associated branding and reputational benefits. For that reason alone, the marquee firms really existed because of the investment opportunities identified by their most influential investors.

The 1980s represented an important period of transition in the VC industry, as a first generation of key investors passed on leadership positions to a new generation. In 1980, John Doerr joined Kleiner Perkins Caufield & Byers after earning his bachelor's degree in electrical engineering from Rice University and his MBA from Harvard, and working a short time at Intel. While Tom Perkins had incubated Tandem, Doerr was involved with the incubation of Silicon Compilers, Inc., a startup in integrated circuit design. Kleiner Perkins Caufield & Byers provided the financing and Doerr spent half his time on the project until Silicon Compilers was up and running.[89]

In 1981, James Lally, who graduated from Villanova University with a degree in electrical engineering, joined the firm from Intel. Doerr and

Lally were responsible for some of Kleiner Perkins Caufield & Byers's most prominent 1980s investments, including Symantec, which at the time was heavily oriented toward data management tools grounded in the new field of artificial intelligence.[90]

In January 1988, the *Wall Street Journal* devoted a large section to the hiring of thirty-two-year-old Vinod Khosla as the ninth general partner of Kleiner Perkins Caufield & Byers, describing him as an "astute technology entrepreneur." Doerr referred to him as "an aggressive and tenacious investor, highly successful at incubating companies."[91] Khosla had been trained as an engineer at the Indian Institute of Technology and Carnegie Mellon, earned an MBA from Stanford, and cofounded two major high-tech firms: Daisy Systems and Sun Microsystems.

The pattern was a consistent one. Like Eugene Kleiner and Tom Perkins, general partners at Kleiner Perkins Caufield & Byers were all fundamentally technologists. That was the lens through which they viewed investments. Brook Byers even quipped that "sometimes we lose patience with Frank [Caufield] because he doesn't really understand the technology."[92] Kleiner retired from the firm in 1982. In 1986, Caufield and Perkins announced that they would pass management of the funds to Byers and Doerr.[93]

Sequoia Capital also underwent a transition of leadership. As the firm grew in size as a consequence of its success, it began to add staff and take on new partners. During its earlier years, Valentine recruited many of his former colleagues. Gordon Russell joined Sequoia as a general partner in 1979, having worked with Valentine at a unit of the Capital Group. Russell developed Sequoia's healthcare practice.

In 1981, Pierre Lamond became a general partner. Prior to joining Sequoia, Lamond had a distinguished career in the high-tech industry, managing product development at Fairchild Semiconductor, for example, and helping to run National Semiconductor. At Sequoia, he focused on semiconductors and became a trusted advisor to Valentine.

Sequoia's new general partners had some similarities, but they were also an idiosyncratic bunch. Valentine noted that he looked for people with industry and startup expertise because "we pride ourselves on our differences and the methodology by which we develop our individual opinions." He underscored the point: "I look for people that are different than I am, because we do things here on the basis of consent among the partners. I don't like having a homogenized set of opinions. I want as much confrontation and different thinking as possible."[94]

Mike Moritz was certainly different. Moritz studied history at Oxford University before going on to get his MBA from Wharton. He went to work for the magazine *Time* and "quickly became known as a guy who could cut through business speak." In 1984, after writing a profile Arthur Rock that described him as "The Best Long Ball Hitter Around," Moritz became intrigued by venture capital. He left *Time* to help start a venture capital industry newsletter. Moritz approached Don Valentine as well as Tom Perkins, Dick Kramlick, and a couple of others because he wanted to be in the venture capital business. In 1986, Moritz convinced Valentine to hire him at Sequoia.

Doug Leone, like Moritz, quickly became a full and influential partner at the firm. He joined Sequoia in 1988 following a cold call to Valentine. Leone had worked in sales and sales management at Sun Microsystems and Hewlett-Packard. In terms of education, he had various engineering degrees from Cornell University and Columbia University, and a degree in management from MIT's Sloan School. Leone was mentored by Valentine, who counseled him to learn and develop a point of view. It took three years for Leone to make his first investment at Sequoia. In 1996, control transitioned from Valentine to Moritz and Leone.

Across the venture capital industry, leadership transitions were common. Two old-guard figures who planned to hand their businesses over to successors were Reid Dennis of Institutional Venture Partners and Pitch Johnson of Asset Management Company. In 1987, Benjamin Rosen, at fifty-four years of age, and L. J. Sevin, at fifty-seven years of age, reduced their roles as active investors in Sevin-Rosen, transitioning to forty-seven-year-old Jon Bayless. Bayless had left a professorial position at Southern Methodist University's Institute of Technology in Dallas, Texas in 1969 to work in the high-tech industry before becoming a VC. Peter Brooke, founder of Boston-based TA Associates, increasingly left day-to-day management of the private equity and venture capital firm to Kevin Landry, whom he had hired in 1967. At the Mayfield Fund, founders Thomas Davis and Wally Davis mentored a group of successors.

Although the individuals who took over the top-tier venture firms quickly gained reputations as outstanding investors in the media and from their peers, they were not immune from failure. Despite their pedigrees as entrepreneurs and investors, Doerr and Khosla at Kleiner

Perkins Caufield & Byers lost money on a laptop computer company they incubated during the 1980s called Dynabook. For Doerr, this was simply an inevitable risk in a long-tail investing business that required "swinging for the fences." He shrugged off Dynabook as "the one in four deals that fails."[95] Sequoia's Moritz appropriately described venture investing as a "giant step into the unknown."[96]

To mitigate downside risk, it was important from an investing perspective to develop a point of view. Yet many of the most prominent investors had very different points of view, as well as styles and personalities that were impossible to codify in a systematic way. Some were brash, others were more thoughtful and reflective. A *New Yorker* journalist once described John Doerr as a "highly caffeinated Clark Kent."[97] Chuck Newhall at NEA describes himself as hypomanic, claiming it is also a trait of most of the entrepreneurs he knows.[98] No single pattern of behavior or investment style stands out, only adding to the difficulty of replicating VC success, whether during the 1980s or now.

The Origins of a Diversity Problem

Despite variability in investment styles and personalities, one inescapable fact about venture capital during the 1980s was its lack of racial and gender diversity. The investors profiled so far in this chapter have been mostly white males, with a smattering of immigrant talent. Indeed, NEA's Newhall recalled that he did not know of any black venture capitalists during the 1980s; neither did he remember anyone in that racial category applying for a job at his firm.[99] Broader societal trends did not help, with discrimination and liquidity constraints creating large barriers to entry into entrepreneurship. According to the 1980 US Census, the rate of entrepreneurship among employed blacks was about one-third of the rate of their white counterparts.[100]

Similarly, women venture capitalists and entrepreneurs were significantly underrepresented relative to their population share. A 1983 US Commission on Civil Rights report, "Women and Minorities in High Technology," found that in Silicon Valley, about 86 percent of the managers and 83 percent of the professionals working in high-tech businesses were male, whereas about 88 percent and 84 percent, respectively were white. Venture capital was not necessarily any better, or worse, than other areas of finance like investment banking and private equity. But the historical origins of the diversity problem in this industry are particularly intriguing.[101]

Despite the level of underrepresentation, there were several well-known female investors during the 1980s, suggesting that at least some progress toward gender equality was being made. In 1989, Ann Winblad cofounded Hummer Winblad Venture Partners in San Francisco with John Hummer, a Princeton undergraduate and Stanford MBA. Winblad became one of the most important female venture capitalists of her generation, even though Hummer Winblad's fund performance was unspectacular. She grew up in Farmington, Minnesota, where she was valedictorian of her high school class, then earned her bachelor's degree at St. Catherine University, where she took classes in mathematics and computer science. Notably, as a reflection of the time, Winblad was one of the first three women to get a business degree at St. Catherine's. She then became a systems programmer at the Federal Reserve in Minneapolis, while also studying to earn a master's degree in education from the University of St. Thomas, with a concentration in economics.[102]

In 1975, with a group of cofounders, Winblad bootstrapped an accounting software company called Open Systems starting with $500, around the same time that industry giants like Microsoft, Apple, and Oracle were getting started. Winblad worked closely with Microsoft and has always been candid about her relationship with Bill Gates during the 1980s. While she did not receive venture capital financing, Winblad came into contact with Don Valentine. This was thanks to the fact that Open Systems sold software through vendors, including California-based CADO Systems—a company Valentine had financed. Open Systems was acquired in 1983 for $15 million (about $36 million today) and a year later Winblad gave a remarkably open interview in which she spoke about the role of women in the computer industry.[103] "There are a lot of women programmers; women, in fact, make good programmers," she said. "Because they are good at programming, though, they get into a technical rut and stop there; they don't learn the business skills, the people skills, they need. A lot of the successful men in the industry have no wives or children. It's hard for women who have spouses or children to go it alone and put their business first. Men have clearly put their business first, and it's easy for them, but a difficult focus for women."

She elaborated further: "It helps if you are in the network and the network is mostly male . . . but it's not a barrier to entry . . . [because] the venture capitalists don't discuss if you're male or female." Regarding the importance of female aspirational role-models in high-tech, she had this to say: "I think that what hasn't emerged is some woman who is an advanced technical designer. There is no female equivalent of Bill Gates and we're waiting to see one." Of her newfound wealth, Winblad noted: "I don't have financial worries so I can think in a broader mode. And the few people who intimidated me don't anymore."

Following the sale of Open Systems, Winblad did indeed think more broadly. She undertook a major project on the computer hardware and software industry for Price Waterhouse, coauthored a textbook on object-oriented software, and consulted for various venture capital firms. At one of these engagements she met John Hummer, who had been in the venture business for a few years, and with whom she agreed to explore the possibility of starting a specialty firm focused on software-related investments. With initial backing from Don Valentine and Pitch Johnson—and also William Edwards, another prominent old guard Silicon Valley venture capitalist—Winblad and Hummer were able to secure additional commitments, including from St. Paul Insurance and 3M Corporation, to raise a $35 million fund. The connection with Valentine proved to be important. One of the first investments Hummer Winblad made was in a company called Control Point Software, which it co-led with Sequoia. Compounding the Sequoia connection, Winblad said, "one of the next deals we did was with a younger partner, Doug Leone."[104]

Winblad was not the only female venture capitalist during the 1980s who made her mark. In a December 1984 article on high-tech investing, *InfoWorld* prominently featured a picture of Jacqueline Morby, a managing director at TA Associates. Don Valentine was pictured also, but only on the second page.[105] Ann Lamont, recently a managing partner at Oak Investment Partners in Westport, Connecticut, began her career as an analyst at Hambrecht & Quist and joined Oak in 1982. Ginger More was a prominent partner at the time. In fact, in 1986, two of Oak's general partners and three of its four associates were women.[106]

Shirley Cerrudo was a partner at Burr, Egan, Deleage & Company, a Boston-based venture firm founded in 1979. Like Winblad, she focused on computer software. Cerrudo went on to become a founding partner of Novus Ventures, which started out in 1994 in Cupertino, California. Deborah Smeltzer, an accomplished scientist, led Baltimore-based Rockland Capital Group's biotech venture capital investing. Mary Jane Elmore became a trailblazer at Institutional Venture Partners in Menlo Park, California, as did Joy London at Adler & Company. In 1987, *Businessweek* wrote about a "Cigar Chomping Venture Capitalist Named Francine."[107] Francine Sommer started her own fund, Communication Ventures, and when it failed she was hired by the Gabelli Group, a New York investment firm, to run their venture arm. All were consummate professionals. Ginger More said, "I think of myself as a venture capitalist, not as a woman in venture capital."[108]

Patricia Cloherty became especially prominent, having cofounded the venture capital firm Tessler & Cloherty Inc., based in New York, with her husband. In 1985, the *Chicago Tribune* described Cloherty as "one of the country's most respected women in the field." Cloherty had been a career VC, becoming a partner in Alan Patricof Associates, Inc., at just twenty-eight years of age. (She returned there in 1988.) As a mark of her impact, Cloherty became deputy administrator of the US Small Business Administration in the late 1970s. Cloherty said in the mid-1980s, "the time is great for women" given that "the economy today is more gender-neutral than ever."[109]

Most male VCs concurred. One analysis concluded that "male venture capitalists are almost unanimous in their belief that their industry is unbiased, and female venture capitalists equally deny that their gender hinders their careers."[110] One man argued, "if you make money, people don't care if you have two heads."[111] NEA's Dick Kramlich went so far as to say that VC "is a great industry for women."[112] Yet, in reality, women were significantly underrepresented. Despite Kramlich's encouraging sentiment, none of the eleven partners at his VC firm were women. Just 7 percent of the associates and partners listed in the 1986 directory of the National Venture Capital Association were women.[113] Recent research by Paul Gompers and Sophie Wang shows that the share of women venture capitalists was between 6 and 9 percent from 1990 to 2015.[114] In other words, not much has changed in the last thirty years.

Three factors are worth mentioning in this lack of progress. First, Winblad noted the cost of having a family for a professional pursuing a career in high-tech, which is striking in its ubiquity as an explanation for the gender gap in wages.[115] Time taken away from a career in progress probably has a major effect on performance in the venture capital industry, where networking is such an important determinant of identifying investment opportunities. Furthermore, it is not unusual for 60 percent of a venture capitalist's time to be spent traveling to portfolio companies to aid with governance—time on the road that is disproportionately hard for a woman with a young family to spend.[116]

Second, Winblad was one of very few women who chose a high-tech career. Insofar as the leading venture firms focused on hiring associates and general partners with industry management experience, few women in high-tech management meant a thin pipeline into the venture capital industry. As Jacqueline Morby put it, the "criteria that some of the firms use make it likely a woman won't be hired—several years [of] operating experience and a technical background. That's hard. Most women don't have that."[117] Furthermore, a high-tech career was stymied at the educational entry point because the "STEM" disciplines of science, technology, engineering, and mathematics were heavily male-dominated. In 1980, women made up 42 percent of the workforce but just 14 percent of employment in STEM fields.[118]

Finally, although causation is difficult to pinpoint, Harvard Business School should share in the blame. Several leading venture capitalists of the 1980s were educated by Professor Georges Doriot there and, as discussed in Chapter 4, he epitomized the School's institutional sexism—largely barring women from taking his class even after women were officially admitted into the MBA program in 1963. Harvard MBAs became a mainstay of American VC, with recent data showing they still account for about a quarter of all venture capitalists at the top firms.[119] Perhaps it is not surprising that there is so little diversity in the industry, when so many entering their venture capital careers were conditioned at an impressionable age to associate with individuals of the same race and gender. While they may not have done so purposefully or maliciously, unconscious biases can be powerful.[120] Any attempt to explain the venture capital industry's current diversity problem should recognize that its history matters a great deal.

Opportunities Ahead and Warning Signs

The 1980s were a watershed era in the history of the venture capital industry. At the start of the decade, venture capital was still a relatively small-scale activity. By the end of the decade, the *Wall Street Journal* was reporting that "proven venture capitalists are raising large sums at a rapid rate."[121] Although venture capital investing was subject to cycles and uncertainty, plenty of hits had materialized to make long-tail distributions pay off. The VC model of investing was facilitated by an influx of capital, especially from pension funds.

As venture capital grew in size and significance during the 1980s, firms divided into segments and the industry saw increasing specialization. Top-tier firms stood out in terms of their fundraising capabilities, giving rise to additional pressures to professionalize the deployment of risk capital. While the organizational structure of firms mattered to performance, prominent individual investors garnered most attention. The fact that most of these were white males clouded the narrative of a sector of finance that has otherwise yielded spectacular achievements by supporting innovative change.

The alignment between venture capital and innovation in the high-tech sector grew closer over subsequent decades. Venture capital was suited to high-tech investing because it involved making long-term projections of the rate and direction of technological progress, and venture capitalists could appropriate large payoffs from their investments when their visions of the future turned out to be right. Venture capital investors gained growing domain expertise in governing high-tech startups and bringing new innovations to market, creating an insatiable demand for entrepreneurial finance.

At the same time, growing scale in the industry could be seen as a sign of overexuberance. In an address to the National Venture Capital Association in 1987, Pete Bancroft issued a warning: "Today I see our industry as over-financed and under self-disciplined." He lamented the increasing shift of VC dollars toward later-stage investments, which he saw as antithetical to the purpose and skills of the "true" venture capitalist, who should have been "in the role of building and developing people and companies."[122] As Chapter 8 explains, throughout the 1990s and into the early 2000s, the VC industry did in fact reorient itself toward early-stage high-tech investing. This shift owed much to the extraordinary rise of technological opportunities associated with the commercialization of the internet.

8

The Big Bubble

THE 1990S AND EARLY 2000S are truly the standout period in terms of the growing size and impact of the venture capital industry. By 2000, there were more than ten times as many VC firms engaged in active investing as there had been in the mid-1980s. In 2000, venture capital fund commitments stood at $104.7 billion and some of the top venture capital firms generated truly astonishing fund-level returns.[1] Matrix Partners V, for example, a 1998 vintage year fund, generated a net IRR for its limited partners of 514.3 percent.[2]

Venture capital helped to fuel economic growth. By the end of the twentieth century, Paul Gompers and Josh Lerner estimate, VC-backed firms accounted for 20 percent of publicly-traded US firms or 32 percent of market capitalization.[3] Although the performance of these firms can be explained by other factors as well as venture finance, including managerial talent over the life cycle of the firm, it is undeniable that a vibrant VC industry had a sizable economic effect. VC-based startup finance especially facilitated entrepreneurial dynamism in information and communications technology, a sector that became crucial to the functioning of the American economy. In an oft-cited statistic, six high-tech powerhouses in this area—Microsoft, Intel, IBM, Cisco, Lucent, and Dell—had combined market value of $1.79 trillion at year-end 1999, equivalent to almost 20 percent of US GDP.

It was at this time that a fundamental shift occurred in the focus of the VC industry that would have profound implications for the present day. Many of the VC investments covered in previous chapters focused on "real" technology including semiconductors, computers, and biotech products. Starting in the 1990s, however, the industry moved increasingly toward software and online services, as a consequence of developments related to the internet.[4] A distinct mentality of rapid expansion and the acquisition of controlling consumer market share also pervaded the industry as VCs concentrated their investments in these particular areas. Online pet supply retailing, as one contentious market, offers a useful lens for examining the venture capital industry's dynamics. The pet supply retailing sector had an estimated worth of $31 billion in 1997, and in the late 1990s, several online-only startups as well as existing "brick and mortar" firms launched commercial websites, each hoping to become the premiere online pet supply retailer. Oakland-based Petstore.com and San Francisco–based Pets.com became signature VC investments of the era. In many respects, these investments were precursors to Uber, Airbnb, and others of today's market disruptors.

Yet, Pets.com became a symbol of the 2000 to 2001 crash in VC-backed firms, and the ensuing crisis in the stock market signaled a major inflection point for the venture capital industry as a whole. Returns fell precipitously. Matrix Partners, whose late 1990s performance returns made it one of the outstanding firms, generated a net IRR of 2.5 percent on its 2000 vintage year fund, VI. One venture capitalist described 2001 as akin to a "nuclear winter."[5] The high-tech sector as a whole faced turmoil as market valuations started to reverse. The group of firms mentioned above (Microsoft, Intel, IBM, Cisco, Lucent, and Dell) saw its collective market capitalization plunge to $678.9 billion at year-end 2002, a fall of 89 percent from 1999.

New commitments to venture capital plummeted to $11.4 billion in 2003, a fall of 62 percent from 2000.[6] Amid the heavy crash of public markets, questions were raised about the legitimacy of the venture capital model. Venture capitalists were discredited as startup investors for bringing firms with fatally flawed business models and inexperienced management teams to public markets. Also founded, however, were enduring high-tech companies like Amazon and Google, in a financing atmosphere that rewarded experimentation and creative innovation. Axiomatic of the long-tail investing model, the few spectacular hits from this era arguably compensated for the losses. In situations where risk capital can be seamlessly deployed, society tends to be made better off by the handful of key firms that are ultimately created. According to William Sahlman, "the societal return on venture capital has been, and remains, very high."[7]

The High-Tech Revolution of the 1990s

The information and communications technology (ICT) revolution of the 1990s materialized as an outgrowth of a long sequence of historical developments in high-tech, many of which were accelerated by VC-style finance. Vacuum tubes were invented in the early 1900s, creating a pathway for the introduction of radio and telecommunications and critical innovations like radar during the Second World War. William Shockley and his team at Bell Labs invented the transistor in the late 1940s, and Shockley codified the knowledge in his famous 1950 book *Electrons and Holes in Semiconductors, with Applications to Transistor Electronics.* That new technology steadily displaced vacuum tubes starting in the mid-1950s.[8] Then came mainframe computers, the integrated circuit, and the microprocessor. Digital Equipment Corporation, funded by ARD (see Chapter 4) introduced radical computer systems in the 1960s, and Intel (see Chapter 6) made the first commercially available microprocessor when it introduced the "4004" in 1971. In 1968, Robert Dennard, an electrical engineer at IBM, was granted a patent for Dynamic Random Access Memory, creating one of the building blocks of high-density RAM storage. The introduction of the PC, along with software and hardware innovations of the 1980s, created a foundation for the ICT revolution of the 1990s. The "triumph of the new economy," to borrow the title of Michael Mandel's frequently cited 1996 *Businessweek* article, was the culmination of generations of innovation and technological progress.[9]

Figure 8.1 illustrates the significance of changing technology trajectories. It shows, for the years 1950 to 2000, how all the patents granted by the United States Patent and Trademark Office to inventors residing in America have been distributed across domains. While the ICT share stood at around 4 percent in 1950, it was almost 20 percent fifty years later. Much of the increase occurred during the 1990s, with the ICT share more than doubling between 1990 and 2000. Figure 8.2 shows the substantial increase in the number of ICT patents granted, especially during the late 1990s. Some of the surge in high-tech patenting during this time period reflected pro-patent legislative changes, which had a particular effect on firms in the semiconductor industry, but a fundamental increase in innovation has also been documented.[10]

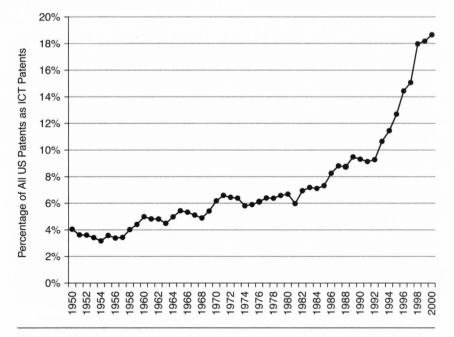

Figure 8.1 The Share of Information and Communication Technology Patents, 1950–2000.

Based on patent data from the United States Patent and Trademark Office.

Figures 8.3 and 8.4 illustrate the relationship between the distributions of total ICT patents and total venture capital investments across US states between 1990 and 2000. ICT patents were heavily geographically concentrated. California accounted for 25,942 ICT patents, reflecting the dominance of Silicon Valley firms, whereas Massachusetts accounted for just 5,046 ICT patents—a signal of the decline of the high-tech corridor Route 128. Texas is noticeable, too. It has a long tradition of innovation in this sector. Texas Instruments, founded in Dallas in 1951, became a major player in integrated circuit technology. L. J. Sevin of the venture capital firm Sevin-Rosen was an engineering manager there, and Sevin-Rosen backed the group of Texas Instruments engineers who founded Compaq in Houston in 1982. Although Dell Computer, founded in Austin in 1984, was not started with venture capital backing, it contributed to regional high-tech advantage, which did attract venture capitalists. Both Dell and Texas Instruments developed substantial corporate venture capital arms during the 1990s.[11] Texas accounted for $17.9 billion

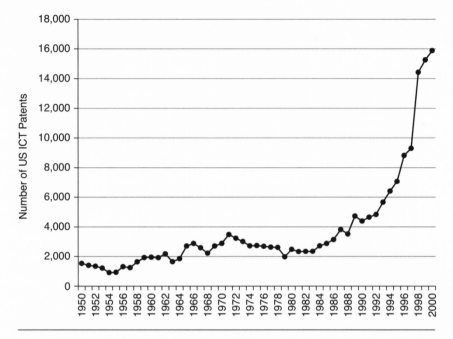

Figure 8.2 The Number of Information and Communication Technology Patents, 1950–2000.

Based on patent data from the United States Patent and Trademark Office.

of venture capital, in today's dollars, between 1990 and 2000, putting it on par with New York, which accounted for $18.1 billion. Massachusetts accounted for $30.5 billion, but that amount was dwarfed by California's total of $128.1 billion. Within California, Silicon Valley accounted for over three-quarters of total venture capital investment.

The commercialization of the internet represented a profound technological breakthrough and an opportunity for VC-backed investments.[12] By the late 1950s, the US Department of Defense funded research into networking for use in the military, and its efforts led to novel developments like COBOL, the programming language for data processing.[13] During the 1980s, the National Science Foundation and other agencies funded networks for use in universities. As a consequence of various innovations, including the PC during the 1980s, and the development of the World Wide Web by Tim Berners-Lee and his collaborators at CERN in 1991, the internet was devised. It was catapulted into the public domain when the National Science Foundation made a series of decisions

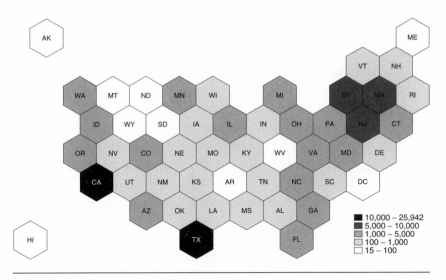

Figure 8.3 The Geography of Information and Communication Technology Patents, 1990–2000.

Based on patent data from the United States Patent and Trademark Office. Maps compiled using the maptile program in Stata developed by Michael Stepner using code for state hexagons provided by Paul Goldsmith-Pinkham. Legend categories reflect the number of patents from 1990 to 2000.

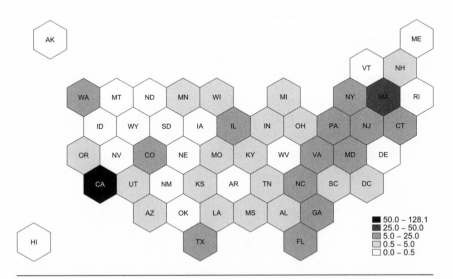

Figure 8.4 The Geography of Venture Capital Investments, 1990–2000.

Based on patent data from the United States Patent and Trademark Office. Maps compiled using the maptile program in Stata developed by Michael Stepner using code for state hexagons provided by Paul Goldsmith-Pinkham. Legend categories reflect the total amount of investment from 1990 to 2000 in today's billions of dollars.

in the 1990s to privatize access. After that, the number of internet hosts increased at a staggering rate, from 313,000 in 1990 to 43.2 million by 2000.[14]

The diffusion of the internet was rapid. Protocols established early on helped to spur innovation. The development of the TCP/IP protocol suite ensured interoperability by creating a basis on which computer systems of different platforms could seamlessly communicate with one another. Web pages could be designed with relative ease using HTML and HTTP, and documents could be located using the URL resource locator. Each of these innovations had been implemented by Berners-Lee at CERN.[15]

Crucially, a team at the University of Illinois, working within the National Center for Supercomputing Applications and funded by National Science Foundation, incorporated this architecture into Mosaic, a prototype internet browser that ran on UNIX and Windows operating systems. One member of that team was Marc Andreessen, who subsequently cofounded Netscape Communications Corporation, a pivotal VC-inducing startup. The Java programming language was released in May 1995 and integrated into the Netscape browser. Open-source Apache server software was released in December 1995, often to be used in conjunction with the server scripting language PHP and with MySQL to integrate relational databases with the web. By 2001, Apache ran on over 60 percent of the world's web servers.[16]

Web hosting services like Geocities and Tripod were launched in the mid-1990s as precursors to today's flourishing social networks. Web-based email started in 1995. In 1996, Microsoft introduced ActiveX in an effort to compete with Java applets—the small programs that could be embedded into web pages. Macromedia introduced Flash the same year, which added dynamic capabilities to web pages by providing a plug-in for delivering animated content. These and many other innovations opened up web-based interactions as a new standard for worldwide communications.

The 1990s also brought a revolution in telecommunications technology. The 1996 Telecom Act deregulated markets, creating competition in local telephone service and opening up internet services to a wider geographic array of American consumers.[17] In network communication systems, the demand to process and move electronic information increased substantially. For example, Cascade Communications, cofounded in 1990 by Gururaj Deshpande in Massachusetts, became a leader in

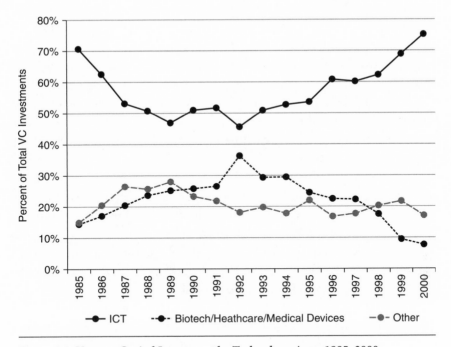

Figure 8.5 **Venture Capital Investment by Technology Area, 1985–2000.**

Based on data in NVCA, *The National Venture Capital Assocation Yearbook 2014* (New York: Thomson Reuters, 2011), 45.

network switching technology. Deshpande believed the value of computers would be limited "unless they can connect to every other computer in the world."[18] Cascade's innovations enabled networks to cope better with the flow of data across the internet. A number of new entrants became successful in this sector, including California-based Juniper Networks in 1996 and Massachusetts-based Sycamore Networks in 1998. The latter, also a Deshpande enterprise, was founded after Cascade was acquired by Ascend Communications for $3.7 billion in 1997. At its peak in March 2000, Sycamore had a market value of almost $45 billion. Juniper peaked at about $78 billion.

Because ICT was such a "hot" technology area during the 1990s, it led to the redirection of venture capital investment away from other areas of activity. Figure 8.5 illustrates the changing share of venture capital dollars going in to ICT relative to other technology areas between 1985 and 2000. Although the ICT share hovered around the 46 to 52 percent range until 1992, by 2000 it had increased to 75 percent. By contrast, while there had been much excitement about venture capital investment in biotechnology, healthcare, and medical devices during the 1980s, these areas experienced declining shares of investment during the 1990s as opportunities in ICT flourished.

This does not mean that these areas were devoid of the hits that justified long-tail investing. The Human Genome Project, initiated in 1990, increased the scope for new startups to commercialize the science relating to the makeup of human DNA. Millennium Pharmaceuticals, founded in Cambridge, Massachusetts in 1993 with $8.5 million in VC funding, created a platform of technologies to enable drug companies to do more effective genomics work on product discovery.[19] One of its founders, Mark Levin, had been a partner at Mayfield Fund from 1984 to 1987 and a serial entrepreneur. Mayfield was one of four venture capital firms (including Greylock, Kleiner Perkins Caufield & Byers, and Venrock) providing the Series A financing in April 1993.[20]

In another example of entrepreneurship in this sector, MIT star scientist Robert Langer founded eight medical-engineering startups during the 1990s, leading to a long-standing relationship with the Boston-based venture capital firm Polaris Partners, established in 1996. As a general rule, however, these types of investments became increasingly incompatible with the time frames of venture capital fund lives. A biotech investment in new drug discovery could take a decade or more to come to fruition, with high levels of capital outlay and considerable levels of uncertainty along the way.[21] One of Langer's enterprises, Acusphere, founded in 1993, faced extremely protracted challenges with clinical trials in relation to its lead product, a drug for detecting coronary heart disease. ICT, on the other hand, could deliver investment returns through exits in much shorter time frames. Between 1995 and 2000 there were 1,396 ICT-related IPOs, compared to just 169 in biotech.[22]

Venture Capital Returns and Compensation Payoffs

Figure 8.6 shows the spectacular returns generated by venture capital funds with points of inception, or vintage years, during the 1990s. Returns are reported net of fees and carried interest; therefore, they reflect what limited partners would have received. Averages for all funds are presented, along with the top-quartile threshold and the average return for top-quartile funds.

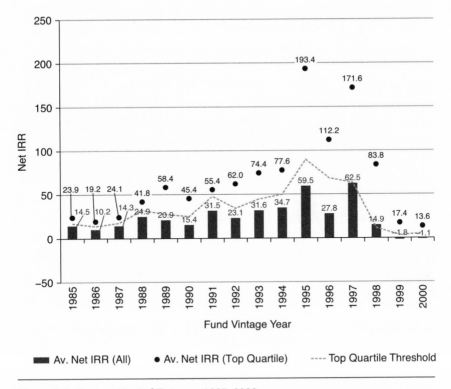

Figure 8.6 Venture Capital Returns, 1985–2000.
Based on data from Preqin Venture Capital Database, accessed March 2016.

The high level of returns across the mid- to late-1990s is striking. Although returns for the "hot" high-tech market of the early 1980s (examined in Chapter 7) are missing from the commercial databases, this period stands out relative to that one. Using available data for the 1980s, 1987 appears to be the peak year, with an average net IRR on funds of 24.1 percent. Yet, during the peak year in the 1990s, the average 1995 vintage year fund returned a net IRR of more than double that amount: 59.5 percent. That year, the top-quartile threshold was a net IRR of 89.7 percent, and within that quartile, average net IRR was an astounding 193.4 percent. Note, however, the dramatic attenuation of returns on venture capital funds with late 1990s and 2000 vintage years. By this point, the collapse in high-tech valuations was having clear adverse impacts on the returns these funds earned over their life cycles.

A large body of literature has attempted to benchmark the returns illustrated in Figure 8.6 against returns that would have been otherwise achievable if limited partners had deployed their capital in public equities. The "public market equivalent" (PME) test has become the standard method of directly comparing the returns from venture capital funds to contemporaneous hypothetical returns from investing in public equities. Using the most comprehensive data on fund-level cash flows, Robert Harris, Tim Jenkinson, and Steven Kaplan find average public market-adjusted multiples of 0.98 for funds with vintage years from 1984 to 1989, 1.99 for the 1990s, and 0.91 for the 2000s, when using the S&P Composite as a benchmark. A PME greater than unity indicates that venture capital outperformed relative to the public market, whereas a PME less than unity signifies underperformance. Their analysis shows venture capital outperforming public equities only during the 1990s, albeit by a substantial amount. The PME for later-stage buyout funds in that decade was lower, at 1.27.[23]

Average VC fund performance was heavily skewed, with a long right-sided tail. Figure 8.6 shows that funds in the top quartile of the return distribution generated truly exceptional returns, especially in vintage years from 1995 to 1998. For example, Matrix Partners IV (vintage year 1995) generated a net IRR of 218.3 percent. Even this was dwarfed, however, by the 514.3 percent net IRR from Matrix Partners V. Matrix had substantial success in 2000, when one of its portfolio companies—ArrowPoint Communications—was acquired by Cisco Systems in a stock transaction valued at $5.7 billion. ArrowPoint, a Massachusetts-based firm started by serial entrepreneur Cheng Wu, developed innovative web switching technology to ensure that web page "hits" were handled by the most appropriate server. This had enormous value at a time when internet traffic was skyrocketing.

These return characteristics had profound implications for fundraising and compensation. Institutional money flowed to venture capital and especially to firms perceived to have the best general partners. According to the National Association of College and University Business Officers, the percentage of university endowment money invested in non-marketable securities, including venture capital, increased from 3.6 percent in 1990 to 7.2 percent in 1999. Growing demand for venture capital, plus a high level of persistence in the VC limited partnerships achieving the best returns, led to a shift in the balance of power between limited partners and venture capital firms. Yale University was forced to accept higher fees to access the most attractive funds.[24] As Harvard Management Company's Jack Meyer put it in 2000, "Ten years ago Harvard had little trouble putting as much money in [venture capital] as we'd like [whereas] today we'll say $70 million and they will take $25 million." Harvard Management Company's focused on top-tier firms with proven track records.[25]

In addition to fee income on committed capital, which could account for as much as half of total compensation, carried interest naturally offered large upside potential.[26] Additionally, beneficial distribution rules with respect to carried interest meant that VCs could receive their shares of profits from successful investments during the life of the fund, as if they had contributed the investment capital in the same way that limited partners did. Their proper share—20 percent of the profits, after deducting the original investment capital—was only fully settled out on the liquidation of the fund. In effect, this created remuneration in the form of interest-free loans from limited partners to venture capitalists during the life of a fund.[27]

Overall, the payoffs could be substantial. In 2001, the average salary for a general partner in a venture capital firm was $1.1 million, consisting of $785,400 in base salary and $342,000 in bonuses.[28] These figures do not include carried interest payments, which were heavily skewed, given the very uneven distribution of fund returns. Court filings from an IRS tax dispute involving Todd Dagres, who joined Battery Ventures in 1996, provide unique insight into the upper tier of VC compensation at this time. Between 1999 and 2003, Dagres received $10.9 million in wages and salary. These came to him through Battery Management Company, which provided management services to Battery Ventures funds. Over the same time period, Dagres received a substantial $43.4 million in capital gains, that being his proportionate share of the 20 percent carried interest Battery Ventures generated on its funds. Thus, his total compensation from 1999 to 2003 stood at a remarkable $54.3 million. Dagres received 80 percent of that amount ($2.6 million in wages and salary plus $40.6 million in carried interest) in 2000 alone, at the peak of the high-tech boom.[29] Dagres was involved in a number of key investments, including the influential Akamai Technologies.[30] Founded in 1998 in Cambridge, Massachusetts, it created new technology and efficient algorithms that sped up the operations of the internet. Battery invested

$4 million for 17 percent of the equity in November that year.[31] Akamai became a well-publicized high-tech IPO when it began trading on the NASDAQ in October 1999.

Pivotal Investments

The types of returns highlighted above derived from a set of pivotal investments, which also reflected the changing nature of the US venture capital industry. In a 1997 interview, John Doerr of Kleiner Perkins Caufield & Byers explained that "Silicon Valley isn't about silicon anymore. . . . It's about networking." He described himself as a "glorified recruiter," by which he meant that the key to his firm's success was not necessarily the amount of capital it could raise, but rather its ability to attract the most capable individuals with domain expertise either to engage in startup activity or to aid the process of governing inexperienced management teams.[32] Because venture capital firms syndicated, the power of the network was cumulative in terms of being able to leverage a wider array of contacts and resources to increase the likelihood of a favorable valuation at exit.[33] Kleiner Perkins Caufield & Byers was an important firm at the center of the Silicon Valley network.

Doerr's networking capabilities led to one of the most important venture investments of the 1990s: Netscape Communications. Although the Netscape investment has been extensively chronicled, it is important to emphasize why it was so pivotal for the venture capital industry at the time.[34] Netscape (first named Mosaic Communications) had been founded in 1994 by Jim Clark and Marc Andreessen to commercialize the Mosaic browser, which as noted above, built on research done at the University of Illinois. In 1982, Clark, a former Stanford computer science professor, had cofounded Silicon Graphics, which developed high-powered computer workstations with three-dimensional imaging capabilities. Mayfield and NEA led the financing. Andreessen had worked on Mosaic as a student, relocated to California after graduating, and then joined with Clark to cofound Netscape in Mountain View. Clark put in $3 million of his own money and owned all of the Series A shares.[35] Andreessen was paid a $60,000 salary, with a further $280,000 being granted in stock options.[36]

When the new startup consumed cash at a rate that exceeded what Clark wanted to cover with his own financial resources, Doerr was one of the few venture capitalists he called in his search for additional financing. While Clark had a disdain for venture capitalists, describing them as "velociraptors" (highly intelligent but rapacious dinosaurs), he chose to approach Doerr because they had known each other from Clark's time at Stanford. Clark noted that Doerr "was the star at the most successful and influential venture capital firm" and following his firm's culture of recruiting general partners with technical expertise, he was also "technologically savvy."[37] Given Doerr's network, Clark felt he could also attract talent. Andreessen concurred, emphasizing Doerr's exceptional talent "in attracting superstar engineers and executives."[38] As Clark put it, this meant that dollars from Kleiner Perkins Caufield & Byers were "worth more than other dollars."[39]

Despite the fact that Clark had a favorable track record as an entrepreneur, he was considered to be a difficult founder, to the point of being arrogant and stubborn. Furthermore, Doerr's decision to invest was also subject to sizable uncertainty, especially at the $18 million valuation Clark had proposed. Both Mayfield and NEA were provisionally approached before Kleiner Perkins Caufield & Byers, and initially declined the opportunity—NEA on the basis of the high valuation. Clark had learned his lesson in equity negotiations: he had given up 40 percent of Silicon Graphics for just $800,000 to Mayfield's Glenn Mueller, and much to his annoyance, saw further financing rounds dilute his ownership to the point that he ultimately owned less than 3 percent of the company.[40] While Doerr agreed to Clark's valuation terms, effectively shutting out Mayfield and NEA, the relationship was still fraught. Clark said, "I didn't entirely trust John" because he feared Doerr might poach Andreessen for another startup. Indeed, Clark believed that Doerr had done so previously, with one of his key collaborators in the run-up to the founding of Silicon Graphics.[41]

A tragic event occurred the day Netscape was officially founded as Mosaic Communications, April 4, 1994, when Mayfield's Glenn Mueller committed suicide while on vacation in Mexico. He and Clark had had a friendly but fractious relationship going back to their dealings at Silicon Graphics. Some have connected the suicide with Clark's denying Mueller access to the Netscape investment. (Mayfield had tried to get in, reversing its earlier reluctance to participate.) Clark believes, however, that this was not a factor. Mueller had an unfortunate history of mental health challenges.[42]

When Netscape became a public company on August 9, 1995, just sixteen months after its founding date and eight months after Navigator

1.0 had been released, it demonstrated the power of long-tail investing for both founders and investors. Doerr had joined the board and used his network to help Clark find a CEO—James Barksdale—who joined in January 1995. Figure 8.7 illustrates the changing valuation of the startup over the funding rounds and its IPO valuation. Clark owned the Series A shares as the sole investor at $0.75 per share and added additional investment in Series B. Kleiner Perkins Caufield & Byers came in at $2.25 per share in Series B, with another major investor, Adobe Systems, investing in the Series C round at $9 per share. The IPO price was set at $28 per share—a thirty-seven-times multiple over the Series A price and a twelve-times multiple over Series B—giving Netscape a market capitalization of $1.1 billion. The staggering $58.25 closing market price on the first day of trading valued the firm at $2.4 billion.

At the end-of-day IPO price, Clark's shares were worth $566 million. Andreessen, at age twenty-four, held equity worth $58.3 million. Barksdale held $223.7 million. The equity held by Kleiner Perkins Caufield & Byers was worth $256.3 million, providing a significant financial boost to its limited partners. Its general partners benefited too, obviously from their profit share but also from the cachet of being associated with the Netscape investment. Going forward, the firm's preeminence allowed it to command 30 percent carried interest on its funds.[43]

The Netscape IPO acted as a significant catalyst to the development of further internet-related innovations in software and services. On May 26, 1995, Bill Gates sent his famous memo titled "The Internet Tidal Wave" to Microsoft executives, calling the growth of the internet "the most important single development to come along since the IBM PC was introduced in 1981." This led to an upsurge of innovation in web-browser technology and strong competition for market share. In 1996, Microsoft acquired VC-backed Vermeer Technologies for $130 million to leverage its FrontPage software tool for web design on Internet Explorer; this was during the famous browser wars that culminated in the 2001 *United States v. Microsoft* antitrust case. Just as VCs had directed risk capital to the PC industry during the 1980s, it is logical that they saw opportunities in web-related startups during the 1990s.

Yet, while the potential social value of these innovations was high, given the large impact of communications technology on a wide range of consumers and industries, considerable uncertainty remained about the direction of technological change. Yahoo! was incorporated

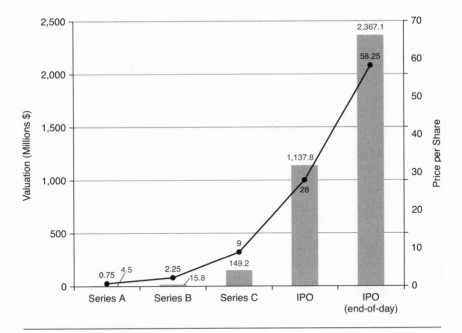

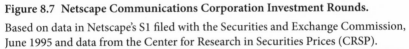

Figure 8.7 Netscape Communications Corporation Investment Rounds.
Based on data in Netscape's S1 filed with the Securities and Exchange Commission, June 1995 and data from the Center for Research in Securities Prices (CRSP).

in January 1995 by Stanford electrical engineering students Jerry Yang and David Filo, who envisioned a web-based navigational guide. But Kleiner Perkins Caufield & Byers passed on this opportunity, along with other firms. Sequoia's Mike Moritz, on the other hand, made an initial $1 million Series A investment for 25 percent of the equity, thereby valuing Yahoo! at $4 million.[44] Sequoia added another $1 million of investment in a Series B funding round. On April 12, 1996, Yahoo! had a market capitalization of $867 million based on its closing price of $33 a share at its IPO, and became a billion-dollar company in June 1997.

In another pivotal moment for the venture capital industry with respect to ICT, Draper Fisher Jurvetson funded a startup called HoTMaiL, cofounded by Sabeer Bhatia and Jack Smith, to develop email over the web. At the time, AOL had an email system, but it was limiting because it tied users to the AOL gateway. The odd use of capitalization in the firm's name reflected its proposal to use an HTML interface for its email service. Aware that the idea would be easy to replicate, the two founders, who had first connected as engineers at Apple, approached venture capitalists with some degree of care. They ultimately linked up with Draper Fisher Jurvetson, who agreed to a $300,000 investment for a 15 percent equity share, giving the firm a $2 million valuation. Draper Fisher Jurvetson had originally wanted 30 percent for its $300,000 investment, but ceded to the entrepreneurs' lower proposed equity share.[45]

HoTMaiL launched on July 4, 1996 as a free service with a two-megabyte limit, and astoundingly, within six months had one million registered users, mostly students at universities. It had twelve million users by the end of 1997. At that point, Microsoft acquired the company for $400 million in stock to integrate it into the Microsoft network. The investment was significant not only because it represented a hit for Draper Fisher Jurvetson, but also because it proved two things: browser-based email could work, and users could be acquired en masse for trivial marketing costs. Bhatia spent a year at Microsoft before leaving to start a number of other enterprises. Smith also went on to be a repeat cofounder, though his Akamba Corporation, a server-side product infrastructure venture, ultimately went out of business in September 2001.

Perhaps the most important venture capital investment from the standpoint of its effects on serial entrepreneurship was PayPal. PayPal started out as Confinity, Inc., a Silicon Valley firm founded in late 1998 by Max Levchin, Peter Thiel, and Luke Nosek. It was subsequently funded largely by Nokia Ventures, the corporate venture capital arm of the telecom powerhouse Nokia, which invested $3 million of the $4.5 million first-round funding. When Confinity was officially launched in July 1999, a representative from Nokia Ventures "beamed" that amount to Peter Thiel's Palm Pilot III using a prototype of the electronic service it would call PayPal.

In March 2000, Confinity merged with X.com, a financial services site founded by Elon Musk. Prior to X.com, Musk and his brother Kimbal had cofounded Zip2 Corporation, a VC-backed software firm financed by Mohr Davidow Ventures, which was sold to Compaq in a cash deal for over $300 million. It is thought that Musk received $22 million for his 7 percent share of the equity.[46] In 1999 X.com secured financing from Sequoia and Mike Moritz joined the board of directors. The 2000 merger with Confinity helped to cement the new entity (which subsequently took the name PayPal) as a leading person-to-person electronic payment facilitator. PayPal successfully went public in February 2002 and was acquired by eBay in August 2002.

PayPal represented more than a high-tech company. It was a hotbed of entrepreneurial talent. Its impact was analogous to that of the Brush Electric Company on Cleveland in the 1880s and 1890s (see Chapter 2), the Federal Telegraph Company on Bay Area entrepreneurship in the early 1900s (Chapter 3), or Fairchild Semiconductor on Silicon Valley entrepreneurship in the 1960s (Chapter 6). Several PayPal founders and employees went on to start up other successful ventures (among them, YouTube, Yelp, LinkedIn, Tesla, and SpaceX) and became known as the "PayPal Mafia"—a moniker popularized by a 2007 *Fortune* article. Several of these startups involved relationships with VCs. For example, David Sacks, former chief operating officer at PayPal, founded Yammer, a first mover in social networking tools for enterprises. Its Series A backing came from Founders Fund (which itself was founded by several PayPal alumni) and Charles River Venture Partners. Yammer was acquired by Microsoft in 2012 for $1.2 billion.

In these investments, and many others, it is possible to see four key factors that drove much of the venture capital industry's evolution at that time. First, venture capital was heavily relationship-dependent, in terms of both risk capital deployment and opportunity identification. While relationships matter in most areas of finance, there was something different about how the venture capital industry operated. Syndication of venture capital investments across firms helped to cement the power of networks, but being able to independently identify the best investments was also critical. In John Doerr's case, he constantly monitored the market for new technology. He got to know Jim Clark because he was a regular visitor to the engineering department at Stanford University. Not only did he get to know Clark there, he also met the future founders of Sun Microsystems, another investment success for his firm. He had strategic intelligence and this carried over into future investments. When Jeff Bezos sought finance to support the development of Amazon, he decided to go with Doerr and, in 1996, Kleiner Perkins Caufield & Byers invested $8 million for a 13 percent equity stake. Amazon's valuation back then was $60 million.

Leading investors, through their intersecting relationships, tended to tie up a large share of the best prospective startups. When Mike Moritz invested in the Yahoo! founders, Sequoia's first internet-related investment, it set in motion a sequence of events leading to Sequoia's 1999 investment in Google. Moritz had first met Larry Page and Sergey Brin through Yang and Filo when they were all students at Stanford. He recognized the entrepreneurial talents of Page and Brin, but saw Google primarily as a potential vendor for Yahoo! in the search engine space.[47] At the same time, Doerr was attracted to the technology behind Google, and had a connection to the founders by virtue of his relationship with Bezos, himself an original investor in Google and an advisor to Page and Brin. Google represented one of the rarer instances in which the highly competitive Sequoia and Kleiner Perkins Caufield & Byers both invested in the same startup—sharing equally between them a $25 million investment announced in June 1999. Sequoia made over $4 billion from its $12.5 million investment, with about $2.8 billion going to its limited partners and $1.2 billion to its general partners through their carried interest share.[48]

Second, technological uncertainty remained high, as evidenced by the fact that some venture capitalists missed opportunities that seem obvious in retrospect. David Cowan, a leading investor from Bessemer Venture Partners, counts Google as a missed opportunity, having declined to meet Page and Brin early on because he did not see market value in another search engine.[49] Shane Greenstein notes in his history of the internet that "many of the key innovations fell outside known forecasts and predictions and were unanticipated by established firms in computing and communications."[50] Of Yahoo! Moritz said, "Nobody took the company seriously at first, because the conventional wisdom around the Valley was that you couldn't make a business with a product that was being given away. People were asking: How are you ever going to make money on this thing?" Consequently, several venture capital firms made investments that at the time seemed highly speculative. Benchmark Capital, founded in 1995, made *the* deal of the 1990s when it turned a $6.7 million investment in eBay into $6.7 billion.[51]

Third, the availability of startup finance, and the attraction of pecuniary gain, acted as a powerful inducement to entrepreneurs to found high-tech companies. The environment favored experimentation, and Silicon Valley flourished because of its dynamic entrepreneurial sector. After Netscape, Andreessen cofounded the web hosting company Loudcloud, investing independently, and then became a successful venture capitalist in his own right. He founded Andreessen Horowitz with Ben Horowitz in 2009. Elon Musk and his brother got their start because Mohr Davidow Ventures were willing to take a chance on two unknown South Africans. From there Musk became one of the most important and controversial entrepreneurs in the modern era.

Equally, the venture capital industry was known for its frictions with entrepreneurs. Jim Clark learned along the way about the perils of dealing with venture capitalists in terms of equity dilution. While Page and Brin successfully prioritized their control at Google, Scott Kriens and Pradeep Sindhu, cofounders of Juniper Networks (funded by Kleiner Perkins Caufield & Byers and other firms), were together left with just 11 percent of equity after their IPO in 1999.[52] Venture capital was often crucial to the growth of a startup, but it habitually came at a high price.

Finally, it is important to emphasize that, for all it achieved, the venture capital industry had a much darker side. Returns sometimes came at the expense of retail investors in public equity markets as venture capitalists exploited opportunities to take their portfolio companies public. As *Fortune* magazine put it on October 26, 1998, "The dirty little secret of the venture business is that VCs can be enormously successful even though most of their portfolio companies may tank in the public markets."[53]

Venture capitalists won out because they could exit firms at a public-offering price well above what they paid for their equity interest in the initial stages of a startup investment. Although this was the return for taking early-stage risk, the journalist behind the *Fortune* article estimated that of the seventy-nine high-tech companies taken public by Kleiner Perkins Caufield & Byers between 1990 and 1997, fifty-five of them lost money based on a return calculation at a price per share "immediately after the first day of trading." A $100 dollar investment in these seventy-nine firms underperformed relative to the NASDAQ index by about 25 percent. As Reid Dennis of Institutional Venture Partners had cautioned the industry during the early 1980s high-tech boom-and-bust cycle, venture capitalists had a responsibility to bring productive companies to market to avoid reputational backlash (see Chapter 7). In 1987, Pete Bancroft cautioned further that "the inevitable subsequent failures and losses by public stockholders create long memories in a chastened public to the detriment of future initial public offerings."[54] Often during the exuberance of the 1990s, this sentiment appeared to get lost in the relentless search for outsized returns.

Venture Capital Structure, Strategy, and Methods

The US stock market experienced one of the most extreme run-ups in its history between 1995 and 2000. The NASDAQ exceeded 500 for the first time in April 1991. By the time of the Netscape IPO in August 1995, it exceeded 1,000. It then reached 2,000 in July 1998 and went on to peak at over 5,000 in March 2000—a tenfold increase in less than a decade. Given that public markets represented one of the most important exit opportunities for venture-backed startups, the changing economic environment had a profound effect on the way that venture capitalists selected portfolio companies, thought about governance and business model development, and captured economic value from high-tech startups.

Following the success of the Netscape IPO, internet-related investments dominated venture capital activity in the technology sector. Scale increased significantly. In 1995, 1,864 venture capital investments were made, totaling $7.2 billion. Just five years later, 7,974 investments were made, totaling $98.6 billion. Silicon Valley accounted for 27 percent of these investments by number, and 32 percent by value. Average fund size stood at around $130 million, and just over a thousand venture capital firms (including corporate venture capital arms) were actively investing.[55]

While the top-tier firms had advantages in terms of relationships with limited partners and their ability to attract entrepreneurs, a wave of new entries also took place, sometimes in the form of spinoffs from the leading firms. In 1995, Menlo Park–based August Capital was founded specifically to exploit ICT investments. One of its cofounders, David Marquardt, had been a cofounder of Technology Venture Investors, an early-stage investor in Microsoft (see Chapter 7). Internet-focused Redpoint Ventures was founded as a limited partnership, also in Menlo Park, in 1999 by general partners from two well-established entities: Brentwood Venture Capital and Institutional Venture Partners. Redpoint raised a $550 million fund in 1999, and a truly substantial $1.2 billion fund in 2000.

Corporate venture capital took off again in the mid-1990s. SoftBank Capital was founded in 1995 as the VC arm of SoftBank Corporation, the Japanese telecom giant. In a joint venture agreement, SoftBank and Yahoo! set up Yahoo! Japan in 1996. Corporate venture capital operated in search of strategic as well as financial benefits, as it had done in the 1980s (see Chapter 7). Intel Capital invested in the open-source software company Red Hat in 1998 because Red Hat developed products and services for Linux, which threatened Microsoft's market share and therefore Intel's own position as a leader in the computer industry ecosystem. With rapid technical change threatening many incumbent industry leaders with disruption, the growth of corporate venture capital made sense. Indeed it grew at a faster pace over this period than independent venture capital, in terms of annual investments made.[56] An active group of angel investors also provided startup finance. For example, Ram Shriram invested $100,000 in Google in 1996, and owned 2.2 percent of Google's shares when it went public in 2004.[57]

In this context, venture capital strategy and methods changed in a number of crucial ways. The Netscape IPO created excitement about the possibility of excess returns in internet investments, spurring more rapid deployment of capital into startups. Typically, capital from a fund would be deployed into portfolio companies over a three- to five-year period, to allow the companies to grow and generate returns by the end of the fund's life cycle. During the late 1990s, however, several venture firms were deploying the capital within six to nine months. Benchmark III, a 1998 vintage year fund, was largely deployed in nine months into ICT and internet-based investments. They included Collab.net, a provider of open-source software development services; Epinions.com, an online buying guide based on consumer reviews; Guild.com, an online art marketplace; Living.com, an e-commerce platform for home products and services; and Respond.com, an online shopping service. SoftBank Capital invested its entire 1999 $600 million Fund V within about twelve months, in forty-eight startups, mostly e-commerce ventures.[58] Overall, internet startups accounted for about 68 percent of VC dollars invested in 1999.[59]

The problems associated with deploying capital so quickly were at least twofold. First, it did not leave much time for due diligence, which venture capitalists had traditionally relied on to identify the best portfolio investments. In a May 1999 article about Draper Fisher Jurvetson, the *Financial Times* reported that "investment decisions have to be made very rapidly, in as little as 48 hours in some cases." Consequently, valuations for high-tech firms rose steeply. In late 1999, the median pre-money valuation (that is, the value of a startup before the investment was made) on a VC-backed startup was $30.6 million, and the median amount raised in a financing round stood at $10.5 million.⁶⁰ While downside risk could be mitigated by contracting provisions, such as convertible preferred stock (senior to common) and liquidation preference (a multiple of the original investment the venture capitalist would receive in the event of a startup's dissolution), it was not uncommon for VCs to write heavily pro-entrepreneur contracts, because competition for investments was so intense.

Second, if a fund was quickly exhausted, little was left over to govern portfolio companies on their paths to growth. This did not matter so much with a booming NASDAQ, because retail investors were willing to put additional capital at risk. When the market faltered, however, VC firms attempted to fill the gap by propping up ailing portfolio companies using cross-fund investments. Benchmark, for example, used fund IV capital to finance fund III firms.⁶¹ That practice risked alienating limited partners who had invested in one fund but not the other. Exuberance had created a severe problem as the financial management of portfolio companies was deferred from present to future. In sum, venture capitalists lost sight of the investment selection and governance emphases which had traditionally been hallmarks of the industry.

Not all venture capitalists were so shortsighted. Richard Burnes, for example, cofounder of Charles River Ventures, had a different mindset. He told *Red Herring* that "a lot of thinking these days is much too oriented toward money and cashing out rather than building a strong organization with good people, good products, and a defensible strategy."⁶² After the market had started to decline in November 2000, Crosspoint Venture Partners decided to forego around $1 billion in limited partner commitments for a new fund because it felt the capital would be difficult to deploy in an increasingly volatile and overvalued early-stage venture market.⁶³

Because it was difficult to be a contrarian, few venture capital firms had engaged in conservative investing earlier. The theory of career concerns proposes that decisions are driven by individuals' worries about how their current performance will affect future compensation. For a VC investor, this might have meant that the downside risk of missing out on another Netscape, eBay, Yahoo!, or Amazon outweighed the threat of seeing a fund perform badly, along with all the others. Also, because the initial selection of portfolio companies signaled something about the ability of a venture investor, there was reputational incentive to continue with portfolio companies even if a VC's private information sug-gested that abandonment would be a better option.[64] Probably all these mechanisms added to the unbridled optimism in internet startups seen in the late 1990s.

An E-Commerce Dogfight: Pets.com versus Petstore.com

The story of online pet products retailing teaches a great deal about the changing nature of venture capital strategies and methods during the late 1990s. The opportunity to migrate the pet category from brick-and-mortar stores to online commerce became a focus of attention for venture capi-talists. A survey by the American Veterinary Medical Association showed that in 1996 almost one-third of US households had a dog or a cat—these households were home to 52.9 million dogs and 59.1 million cats. Moreover, dog and cat ownership was growing rapidly in the late 1990s, at about three times the rate of growth in the population.[65] Given the potential size of the market, online pet supply retail became one of the most heavily financed and fiercely contested sectors of e-commerce. It was estimated at $3 billion to $6 billion in revenues, comprising 10 to 20 percent of the total pet retail market.[66]

Two startups—Pets.com and Petstore.com—were the earliest to receive major venture backing. Petstore.com, established in October 1998 in Oakland, California, started out as Pet Projects and was rebranded in March 1999 with the acquisition of the Petstore.com domain name. Cofounder and CEO Josh Newman was a 1988 Harvard Business School graduate who had worked a few years at the Boston Consulting Group and then been an executive at Amerigon, Inc., which designed and pro-duced components for electric vehicles. In April 1999, Petstore.com re-ceived $10.5 million in funding from Battery Ventures and Advanced Technology Ventures. At the time, Amazon had started to gain trac-tion in book retailing, and E-Toys was about to go public—it did so a month later with a market value of about $7.7 billion, 35 percent higher than its brick-and-mortar counterpart, Toys "R" Us. According to Newman, online pet retailing was the archetypal target area for ven-ture investment.[67]

In early 1999, Hummer Winblad, the VC firm cofounded by Ann Winblad (profiled in Chapter 7), acquired the Pets.com site and domain name from Greg McLemore, an internet startup incubator, and ap-proached Julie Wainwright, then an executive at e-commerce site Reel

.com, inviting her to run the company and develop the Pets.com online store. Wainwright, a graduate of Purdue University, had a substantial background in high-tech startups. In 1997, she was made CEO at Berkeley Systems, a software company whose computer game "You Don't Know Jack" became one of the best-selling games of the 1990s. There, she designed and executed the firm's internet strategy. When Berkeley Systems was sold in 1997, Wainwright took the president and CEO job at Reel .com, the first e-commerce site that sold movies, where she led the growth of the two-year-old start-up. Within eighteen months, the company had raised venture financing, including from Microsoft cofounder Paul Allen's Vulcan Ventures, and was generating strong revenues. Reel.com was acquired by Hollywood Entertainment in October 1998.

Wainwright began work at Pets.com in San Francisco in March 1999, with the Pets.com website scheduled to be launched in August 1999. She was paid a salary of $185,000 and exercised the right to purchase equity, which equated to 4.4 percent of the company prior to the Pets.com IPO in February 2000. Wainwright recruited high-profile talent familiar with the pet supply retailing industry. John Benjamin, from the brick-and-mortar chain Petco, joined as merchandising vice president, and John Hallon, with a background at *Dog Fancy* and other magazines, became VP of editorial content. Amazon's announcement, in late March, that it was acquiring a stake in Pets.com was vital in giving the fledgling business credibility. Having Amazon as a strategic partner would also provide access to the retail sector and increase brand recognition. Between Hummer Winblad and Amazon, Pets.com had secured about $10 million in funding. In June 1999, Pets.com received an additional $50 million from Amazon, Bowman Capital Management, and Hummer Winblad. By the time of the IPO, Amazon held 43 percent of the equity, Hummer Winblad owned 22.4 percent, and Bowman owned 6.6 percent.[68]

The business model was straightforward: build an online presence to tap the multibillion-dollar pet products market, set up distribution centers to get product to customers efficiently, and quickly build unassailable market share with heavy advertising. While VC-backed businesses in the online pet retailing space were accused in the aftermath of the stock market crash of irrational exuberance, the original business plan for the company that would become Petstore.com was perfectly well thought out and compelling. Its sophisticated unit-economics analysis, estimates of customer lifetime value, and customer acquisition cost estimates would not look out of place in a startup's pitch today.

The team at Petstore.com showed that, if a customer purchased pet food online, the product could be shipped at a reasonable rate, and anticipated that in many cases the pet owner would add other items to the order, such as the kinds of toys and treats they traditionally purchased in brick-and-mortar stores. As Newman explained, profits materialize because "the margin on the dog food pays for the net shipping on the entire bundle, and then there's 100 percent markups, 50 percent margin on the other things that people buy." He went on to say that "the essence of the analysis on the business plan was really built around those two discoveries: The shopping cart margin and weight data, and the shipping costs analysis married to it."[69]

The two startups went into head-to-head competition. From a distribution center in Emeryville, California, Petstore.com's website debuted in May 1999, featuring a full line of cat and dog supplies amounting to some 1,200 items. In September, Pets.com opened a 140,000-square-foot distribution facility in Union City, California. To match the advantages Amazon brought to Pets.com as a strategic partner, Petstore.com formed a financing and strategic partnership with Discovery Communications. Under the terms of the contract, Discovery became the largest equity holder and Petstore.com received promotion on television and on Discovery's website, as well as a license to the Animal Planet trademark. Petstore.com also established a promotional relationship with Safeway, the grocery chain. In their efforts to gain market share, both startups used cutthroat pricing tactics.

In December 1999, Pets.com filed preliminary documentation for an IPO with the SEC. Its prospectus was quite candid about the potential business risks: "we believe that we will continue to incur operating and net losses for at least the next four years, and possibly longer, and that the rate at which we will incur these losses will increase significantly from current levels."[70]

Table 8.1 shows the reported financials from its February 2000 filing. While the startup had grown rapidly in terms of net sales between September and December 1999, gross margins remained negative. Pets.com spent inordinate sums on marketing and sales activities, including its famous sock puppet ads, to acquire customers. In 1999, Pets.com spent $42 million to generate just $5.8 million of revenue, a strategy that was

TABLE 8-1
Pets.com Financials

	Quarter Ended 6/30/1999	Quarter Ended 9/30/1999	Quarter Ended 12/31/1999	Period from 2/17/1999 (Inception) to 12/31/1999
Net sales	$39	$568	$5,168	$5,787
Cost of goods sold	76	1,766	11,570	13,412
Gross margin	($37)	($1,198)	($6,402)	($7,625)
Operating expenses:				
Marketing and sales	$1,122	$10,693	$30,676	$42,491
Product development	1,624	2,194	2,646	6,481
General and administrative	838	1,205	2,211	4,254
Amortization of stock-based compensation	—	1,139	979	2,118
Total operating expenses	$3,584	$15,231	$36,512	$55,344
Operating loss	–3,621	–16,529	–42,914	–62,969
Interest income, net	123	577	491	1,191
Net loss	($3,498)	($15,852)	($42,423)	($61,778)

Based on data in Pets.com's S1 filed with the Securities and Exchange Commission, February 2000, 8.

common during the era.[71] But with negative operating margins, Pets.com only lost money as it grew.

At its pinnacle in January 2000, Pets.com bought advertising time during the Super Bowl at a cost of around $1.2 million. When Pets.com went public on February 11, 2000, its share price opened at $13.50, above its initial $11 offering price, and rose as high as $14 before falling back to $11. By June, however, a few months after the stock market had begun its deep decline, Pets.com's share price was hovering around $2. Some relief came that month when Discovery announced a divestiture by which Petstore.com would go to a new owner—Pets.com—but any respite was short-lived. In November 2000, Pets.com traded at a low of just $0.22 a share. It announced that it would be shuttering its operations, laying off 255 of its 320 employees, and liquidating all its assets. In December, Pets.com sold its domain name, www.pets.com, to competitor PetSmart, Inc., the leading brick-and-mortar pet retailer. In January 2001, the company's shareholders approved a formal liquidation plan.

The Importance of Historical Perspective

The decline in Pets.com's share price was part of a wider collapse in the US stock market. From its March 2000 peak to its October 2002 trough, the NASDAQ lost 77 percent of its value. Companies like Pets.com had shown signs that online sellers could reshape consumer preferences and purchases, but the reality was that anticipated cash flows had failed to materialize. For their part, venture capitalists were blamed for financing founders with lackluster business models. A startling and oft-cited statistic from a March 2000 *Barron's* article revealed that about three-quarters of internet companies had negative cash flows.[72]

Even the very best investors had been susceptible to exaggerated optimism. For example, John Doerr repeatedly described the internet as "under hyped" and suggested that Silicon Valley's VC-fueled innovation advantage reflected "the largest legal creation of wealth in the history of the planet."[73] In another case of overexuberance, Geoffrey Yang, cofounder of Redpoint Ventures, exclaimed in a December 1999 *Fortune* article: "What risk? If the company doesn't work out, we'll sell it for $150 million. If the company kind of works out, we'll sell it for $500 million, and if it really works out, it'll be worth between $2 billion and $10 billion. Tell me how that's risk."[74]

Naturally, such statements sounded brash and oblivious when the stock market crashed, but history provides a different perspective. Although Doerr prudently amended his observation in the aftermath of the crash to saying the United States had witnessed "the largest creation (*and evaporation*) of wealth in the history of the planet," with the passage of time his initial perspective seems more astute than ever. His 2003 prediction—"I believe we're still in the early stages of the Internet transformation"—turned out to be true. Marc Andreessen's widely-read 2011 *Wall Street Journal* piece, "Why Software Is Eating the World," emphasizes the economic significance of the changes Doerr foresaw as "more and more major businesses and industries are being run on software and delivered as online services."[75]

Many of Doerr's investments continued to flourish. Google transformed internet-related services and products in ways that could not have been imagined on its founding in 1998.[76] Similarly, Amazon revolutionized e-commerce far beyond book retailing, targeting numerous consumer segments, including pet products. Google had revenues of $961.9 million in 2003, and that year also saw Amazon turn its first full-year profit, on $5.3 billion in revenues. In 2016, Google's revenues stood at $89.5 billion, a ninety-three-fold increase over 2003, while Amazon's revenues were $136 billion, a twenty-seven-fold increase. Ironically, Willoughby's 2000 *Barron's* article had highlighted the value of cash-strapped Amazon as an example of internet irrationality.

In the end, online pet products retailing during the 1990s serves as an emblematic case of how long-tail investing works. In a portfolio of investments with highly uncertain outcomes, some companies need to be spectacularly successful to compensate for the majority of loss-making ones. Although Hummer Winblad held equity in Pets.com through its fund III (a 1997 vintage), which ended up as a bottom-quartile performer with a net IRR of just 0.9 percent, Battery Ventures still managed to generate a top-quartile net IRR of 8.2 percent on its fund V (a 1999 vintage) even with Petstore.com among its investments.

Moreover, the basic ideas behind many of the discredited late-1990s dot-com enterprises came to fruition in new startups in subsequent years. The online grocery-delivery service WebVan, initially venture-backed by Benchmark Capital and Sequoia Capital, was ridiculed in the aftermath of the crash, but the idea lived on to become a mainstay in e-commerce. In the business of pet products, PetFlow.com was founded in 2010 with a leaner version of the business models used by Pets.com and Petstore .com. Whereas Wainwright estimated that it cost about $7 million to $10 million to set up the infrastructure for Pets.com, excluding inventory, PetFlow.com was established with only around $50,000. That precipitous drop in cost owed much to the diffusion of the enabling technologies developed by previous high levels of investment in internet startups. Innovations like Amazon Web Services, introduced in 2006, enable the outsourcing of functions that Pets.com and Petstore.com had to build in-house. In a further verification that online pet products retailing now generates healthy margins, in April 2017, PetSmart, Inc., agreed to acquire Chewy.com in a multibillion-dollar transaction.

A decade after Petstore.com's initial funding, Newman thought back on his 1990s startup, wondering aloud: "In a world of disruptive internet technologies, how do you know if your business model is crazy or brilliant?"[77] We now know that e-commerce was as revolutionary as many VCs had predicted it would be. US Census Bureau figures show that online retailing spending increased by 215.8 percent from 2002 to 2008, while offline retail spending increased by just 23.6 percent.[78]

Beyond direct impact, the spillovers into the real economy generated by venture investing during the 1990s were powerful and pervasive. The VC industry was part of a wider capital-deepening process in which investments in broadband, DSL, and fiber optic cable facilitated the high-volume transmission of data that internet businesses demanded. Limited bandwidth hampered early firms like Pets.com and Petstore.com in their efforts to access markets, but communications companies responded by investing heavily to meet growing user requirements, and in doing so, generated the network infrastructure that would be harnessed by a new generation of startups. By the year 2000, 204,463 fiber optic *real* route miles were in place, compared to just 82,647 a decade earlier. Most of the investment in network route miles occurred from 1998 to 2000.[79]

While it could be argued that this period saw significant overinvestment in the infrastructure surrounding the internet, that same argument can be made more positively. Ramana Nanda and Matthew Rhodes-Kropf argue that during "hot" markets many more experimental and ultimately innovative projects receive funding.[80] The software startup Endeca provides an example. Endeca was founded in 1999 in Cambridge, Massachusetts, based on its revolutionary approach featuring advanced "faceted" search to clarify and refine online navigation queries. This breakthrough was especially relevant for e-commerce enterprises. It was acquired by Oracle in a reported billion-dollar transaction in 2011. But cofounder Steve Papa later reflected, "if it wasn't for the internet bubble, we wouldn't have pursued this opportunity."[81] In normal times, Nanda and Rhodes-Kropf argue, capital tends to dry up in novel areas like this, and there are insufficient funds for the necessary research required to carry experimental projects to full fruition. Consequently, the nature of the ideas being developed at any point depends on investors' perceived level of "financing risk"—that is, the likelihood that projects that will need additional investment from other sources in the future to proceed *but not be able to get it*, even though the ideas behind them may be fundamentally sound. Reinforcing this argument, Bill Janeway shows that novel technologies tend to be disproportionately funded in hot markets because an active marketplace for venture capital during bubbles allows for innovation through trail-and-error entrepreneurship. The benefit of this, he argues, outweigh the costs of a crash. Put simply, "it took the wastage of a bubble to fund the exploration that would yield Amazon and eBay and Google."[82]

Finally, this era helped to create a flourishing pool of serial entrepreneurs who could experiment, and sometimes fail, in their efforts to innovate. Julie Wainwright was widely chastised as a symbol of everything that was wrong in the dot-com era, yet her talent came through in repeat entrepreneurship. Following a failed startup in the area of women's health, Wainwright established The RealReal, an online luxury goods consignment business, in 2011. It attracted VC financing and has proved highly successful. A decade and a half after the dot-com debacle, a *Forbes* profile portrayed her as rising phoenix-like from the ashes of Pets.com.[83]

Venture Capital in the Aftermath: A Legitimacy Crisis

These positive long-run implications of the dot-com era were of little solace to venture capitalists in the aftermath of the crash, or many others affected by the decline in the stock market. The venture capital industry faced the most significant crisis in its history. At no time before had there been such a reversal in returns. Firms failed and opportunities for liquidity events diminished. The IPO market dried up and so did the market for trade sales. The National Venture Capital Association estimated that, in 2000, VC-backed firms raised $67 billion in merger and acquisition transactions and $24 billion through the IPO window. By contrast, in the first half of 2001, the former accounted for $9 billion raised, and the latter, $1.7 billion. More uncertainty rocked the markets following the September 11, 2001 terrorist attacks on American soil. Cyclical downturns had adversely affected the VC industry in the past, but the effects of the dot-com crash had the appearance of something more structural. In May 2002, Ray Rothrock, managing general partner at Venrock, said, "It's the worst we have ever seen and we don't expect much liquidity for four or five years."[84]

Venture capitalists came in for some hard knocks. Retail investors felt duped by losses in high-tech investments. For example, Sycamore Networks had been valued at $14.4 billion when it went public in 1999, but by the end of 2002 it was worth just $598 million. Akamai had been valued at $13.3 billion at the end of its first day of trading in 1999, compared to $65.9 million at the end of 2002. Red Hat's first-day IPO percentage gain had been the eighth-largest in US stock market history, valuing it at $3.5 billion in 1999, but it fell to $598 million by the end of 2002. While Red Hat went on to exceed its valuation in the dot-com era by some margin (and the online travel aggregator Priceline.com also rebounded to success), for many of the key high-tech firms, large shares of their market values were permanently wiped out.

Many retail investors perceived that there had been collusion, explicit or otherwise, among venture capital firms and investment banks as both IPO intermediaries and suppliers of market intelligence through their stock analysts. Overly optimistic reports, such as those written by Henry Blodget, the much-maligned Merrill Lynch internet stock analyst, and Jack Grubman, who covered telecoms at Salomon Smith Barney, did much to fuel "irrationality" in the startups that venture capitalists were bringing to public markets. Though she was never charged with any wrongdoing (unlike Blodget and Grubman), Mary Meeker, an internet stock analyst from Morgan Stanley Dean Witter, was also heavily criticized for unduly fanning exuberance in the stock market.[85] Meeker became a partner at Kleiner Perkins Caufield & Byers in 2010.

Conflicts of interest were rampant, especially due to interlocking relationships. In a well-reported instance, Frank Quattrone, an investment banker at Credit Suisse First Boston, set up "Friends of Frank" accounts so that certain individuals would be allocated shares in companies going public (normally a few percent of the total) and make healthy gains in the equity appreciation typical on the first day of trading. One "Friends of Frank" beneficiary was a VC firm, Silicon Valley–based Technology Crossover Ventures, which received shares in VA Linux Systems. It made a healthy paper profit on the shares during the IPO day in December 1999, even though the stock lost money later on. There was nothing illegal about this transfer of shares to Technology Crossover Ventures. To many observers, however, it had the putrid stench of a kickback, given that Credit Suisse First Boston acted as an IPO intermediary in an unusually large number of the firms that were taken public from Technology Crossover Ventures' portfolio.[86]

Retail investors incurred disproportionately large losses. According to a 2003 study in the *Journal of Finance* by Eli Ofek and Matthew Richardson, retail investors were heavily concentrated in internet stocks relative to institutional investors.[87] Lock-up provisions had prevented insiders, including venture capitalists, from selling their equity—but when these began to unwind, especially in the latter half of 2000, there was a flurry of selling. Pessimism began to overwhelm optimism. As stock market prices declined, retail investors lamented their excess losses; but these same investors had been responsible for driving the prices of internet stocks higher during the boom because of their overly optimistic beliefs.

Entrepreneurial teams in venture-backed startups were another constituency affected by the dot-com crash. Due to the nature of contracting for finance, venture capitalists had liquidation preference—meaning they would get paid before founders and employees in the event of a liquidation event. Once these were exercised, there was often not much left over to be distributed to the management team. The "down round" became commonplace, referring to a round of financing for a portfolio company that was not shuttered, which was completed at a fraction of the prior round's price per share. Unemployment shot up in Silicon Valley's Santa Clara Country, exceeding the state average for the first time since reliable records started to be kept in 1983. Between December 1999 and August 2001, there were 34,200 layoffs in dot-com companies in California (mostly in Santa Clara county and San Francisco), which accounted for about 36 percent of total dot-com layoffs nationwide.[88]

Layoffs meant major dislocations. Frequently, individuals and families were forced to relocate. In 2002, a billboard near San Francisco airport that had been displaying an ad for the online gardening retailer Garden.com (it failed a week after Pets.com) was papered over with a new one for Allied Van Lines' household moving service. At the same time, these employment losses should be put in some perspective. Labor had flooded into Silicon Valley in anticipation of capturing enormous short-term financial gains from startups, and layoffs, while unfortunate, may have been an inevitable part of the entrepreneurial cycle. Petstore.com's Josh Newman was relatively upbeat about the whole experience. He took some time out to reassess before turning his attentions to entrepreneurship in the area of education technology.[89]

Venture capital firms were put under immense pressure. Rather than spending resources on searching for new startups, many shifted their attention to salvaging investments in existing portfolio companies. Annex funds were raised by firms that still had credibility. For example, Accel Partners raised a $50 million fund to support portfolio companies in its 1998 fund VI. NEA raised a $150 million annex fund for the same reason.[90] Limited partners, however, put pressure on venture firms to reduce the size of funds to lessen their management fee obligations, because they were paying fees on committed capital, not on capital actually invested. Several VC firms, including Kleiner Perkins Caufield & Byers, announced they would call on limited partners for less than anticipated because investment opportunities for new funds had diminished.[91] Likewise, in April 2002, Charles River Ventures decided to reduce the size of its planned $1.2 billion year 2000 fund XI by $450 million, foregoing management fees in the region of $150 million.

Some venture capital firms were forced to defer management fees on their funds, while others were caught in a bind because of the distribution rules they had followed. Often, a VC firm took its carried interest only at the end of a fund's life, after returning to its limited partners all the principal they had contributed. Sometimes, however, a firm took carried interest as it accrued. Battery Ventures, in its fund V, had taken out $44 million in carried interest sequentially, as its portfolio companies exited.[92] After the crash, given the much lower likelihood that remaining portfolio companies would undergo liquidity events, this opened up Battery to the "clawback" provision in the limited partnership agreement, meaning that money would have to paid back to the extent that it turned out, on final accounting, to exceed the appropriate carried interest share.

To maintain credibility and to avoid future liability, Battery Ventures announced it would waive its management fee to net out the carried interest it had already received. While fund V did ultimately perform well, planning ahead still meant cutbacks. Headcount was reduced sharply, a common practice. In December 2002, Battery let go of nine employees, including two general partners who had invested heavily in the telecom sector. Further shakeout was expected in the industry as poorly performing firms would be unable to raise future funds. The reduction in capital commitments had major implications. The *Financial Times* felt that the dot-com crash signaled a turning point in the VC industry. "What is clear is that the glamour surrounding the venture capital industry in general and Silicon Valley in particular has dissipated," it concluded. "It will be a long time before it recovers and many moons before a venture capitalist graces the cover of a business magazine for the right reasons."[93]

Arthur Rock, who had memorably graced the cover of *Time* in 1984, bemoaned how the mindset of the industry had changed over the last few decades. In the past, he commented, "we just built companies to be listed on the New York Stock Exchange. . . . It was a time when VCs still had time to think, because institutional limited partners weren't part of the picture, pressing GPs for big numbers. . . . There wasn't this need to produce returns, returns, returns." Lamenting the contrast with his famous Intel investment, he said that back then, "we weren't interested in how soon you could get your money out."[94] As one venture capitalist focused on internet investments conceded, "We realized only once it was too late that we forgot to pay attention to this one important factor called profitability."[95]

Such was the turmoil in the venture capital industry following the dot-com crash, and especially after September 11, 2001, that the National Venture Capital Association issued an important statement. As would be expected from an industry organization, it remained upbeat about the future while noting the challenges ahead. The statement provided select quotes from its members. For example, Jim Breyer, Managing Partner of Accel Partners, said "risk is woven into the fabric of the venture capital industry. On September 11th the world just got riskier and venture capitalists will need to maintain discipline and continue to do what they do best—take calculated risks that help fuel our economic engine." The terrorist attacks had also hit the industry on a personal level. Danny Lewin, cofounder of Akamai Technologies (backed by Battery Ventures and others), was on American Airlines Flight 11, the first plane to hit the World Trade Center. So were David Retik and Christopher Mello, general partner and associate, respectively, from Boston-based Alta Communications. For the whole venture capital industry, this was a tremendously challenging time. The VC field felt great uncertainty about the future. It seemed that any step forward would be choosing to go further into the unknown.

Creating Value, Financial and Social

The dot-com era was the most turbulent period in the history of the venture capital industry. It epitomized everything about the allure of long-tail investing. It is a time period often associated with the failure of dot-com and telecom startups, and with trillions of dollars of lost stock market value. With historical perspective, however, the era appears far more productive. Experienced venture capitalists recognized patterns from the past. NEA's Dick Kramlich, for example, noted that 2002 was not too dissimilar to the "wasteland economy" he faced with Arthur Rock when they invested during the 1970s. He said that venture capital "was and always will be a super cyclical industry. It is marked by long periods of illiquidity in the past, as now. It may seem like this won't be over, but it will be."[96]

Indeed, investment cycles have always had their booms and crashes, given the uncertainties associated with technological changes plus the risk of intermittent systemic crises. When Sequoia Capital distributed its famous "R.I.P. Good Times" presentation in October 2008, a month after Lehman Brothers had failed, it was hard to predict that several multibillion dollar exits (including Sequoia's own investment in WhatsApp) would materialize within a small number of years—or that Marc Andreessen would soon be writing about the preeminence of software in the future growth of the US economy "with scars from the heyday of Webvan and Pets.com still fresh in the investor psyche."[97] Clearly, immense social value can be created when high-tech ventures are financed, and financing happens more readily when investors can expect overall attractive returns from long-tail portfolios. The fact that so many innovations have been launched in this way says a lot about the economic benefits of a vibrant and unconstrained venture capital industry.

Epilogue

THE VENTURE CAPITAL INDUSTRY has an extensive history, certainly stretching back much further than the moment commonly identified as the industry's genesis—the foundation of the American Research and Development Corporation (ARD) in 1946. Long before ARD was founded, the United States was marked by dynamic capital markets and many efforts to capture financial returns from the intermediation of early-stage risk capital. The concept of long-tail investing has existed in America from the early whaling industry to the multitude of venture firms associated with entrepreneurial finance today. Over time, individuals and firms created pathways to the institutionalization of the modern venture capital industry, providing a significant catalyst to entrepreneurship and innovation. Nowhere else in the world has the skewed distribution of returns associated with early-stage finance been embraced with so much impact.

Four main stages in the industry's evolution can be identified, which extend back to the early history of the United States. During the first stage, venture finance was directed into entrepreneurial activities in ways that are historic precedents for today's VC-style investing. Capital was intermediated in the whaling industry in the search for high returns from pooled investing (Chapter 1), and contracting similarities between capital providers and entrepreneurs are clearly evident in the rise of high-tech industries and Silicon Valley–like innovation hotspots in the nineteenth and early twentieth centuries (Chapter 2). Private capital entities as precursors to modern VC first emerged through the investing activities of wealthy families (Chapter 3). In the second stage, from around the mid-1940s, specialized firms emerged—most notably, ARD, as a pioneer in the intermediation of risk capital (Chapter 4). The limited partnership, which itself has a long and firmly established history, was adopted in the venture capital industry during the late 1950s and grew in popularity to the point that it was embraced as the dominant organizational structure for firms seeking right-skewed returns (Chapter 5). The third stage in the history of venture capital spanned the late 1960s, 1970s, and 1980s, when proof came that the venture capital "hits" model could be managed in a systematic and repeatable way. By the 1980s early-stage VC investing was fully institutionalized in America (Chapters 6 and 7). Finally, the fourth stage in the history of venture capital started in the 1990s, culminated in the crash of 2000 to 2001, and featured the extensive application of the VC investing model in the high-tech sector. During this volatile period, as the industry reached unprecedented scale, many of today's high-tech powerhouses were founded as VC-backed startups (Chapter 8).

Across all these stages, a major theme of this book has been the importance of historical perspective. History matters because it helps to explain how things came to be what they are. Lines of continuity or change can often be traced from the past to the present. The venture capital industry was not an isolated mid-twentieth century invention, but rather a continuation of a deep-seated tradition in the deployment of risk capital in the United States going back to early instances of entrepreneurship. Historical perspective can also discipline a better understanding of future directions and possibilities. In particular, it can illuminate several challenges the VC industry faces today.

Long-Tail Returns

The most obvious of these modern challenges is the extent to which outsized financial returns can be achieved systematically. In 2005, David Swensen, the well-respected manager of Yale University's endowment, concluded that, on average, "over long periods of time, venture investors receive no more than market-like returns with demonstrably higher levels of risk."[1] This insight can be confirmed by data. Although VC funds on average performed better than US public equities during the 1990s, they underperformed both during the mid- to late-1980s and during the early 2000s.[2]

Historical evidence shows that attractive returns from long-tail portfolios have always been difficult to generate. Figure E.1 presents data on *absolute* performance using examples drawn from earlier chapters. These

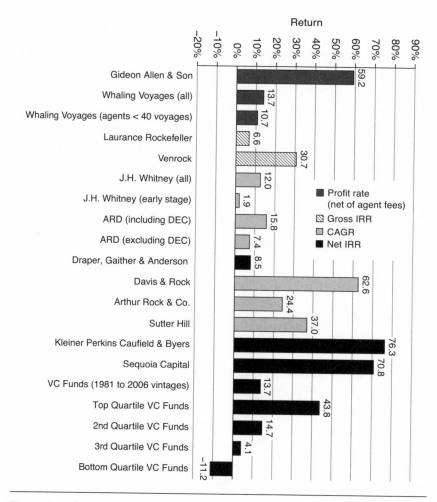

Figure E.1 Absolute Performance: From Whaling Ventures to Modern VC Funds.

Based on data in the following sources: *Whaling:* Lance E. Davis, Robert E. Gallman, and Karin Gleiter, *In Pursuit of Leviathan: Technology, Institutions, Productivity, and Profits in American Whaling, 1816–1906* (Chicago: University of Chicago Press, 1997), 405, 429, 448–450. *Laurance Rockefeller* and *Venrock:* Peter Crisp Papers, Baker Business Historical Collections, Business Manuscripts Mss 784 1946–2008, Harvard Business School. *J. H. Whitney:* Briefing Session on the Small Business Investment Act of 1958, sponsored by the American Management Association, New York, December 1–2, 1958; Committee on Banking and Currency and Select Committee on Small Business 117 (1959), Testimony of Charles Wrede Petersmeyer. *American Research and Development:* Patrick R. Liles, *Sustaining the Venture Capital Firm* (Cambridge, MA: Management Analysis Center, 1977), 83. *Draper, Gaither & Anderson:* Leslie Berlin, "The First Venture Capital Firm in Silicon Valley: Draper, Gaither & Anderson," in *Making the American Century: Essays on the Political Culture of Twentieth Century America,* ed. Bruce J. Schulman (New York: Oxford University Press, 2014), 16. *Davis and Rock and Arthur Rock & Co.:* Personal correspondence with Arthur Rock. *Sutter Hill:* Peter Henig, "The Old Guard," *Venture Capital Journal,* October 2002, 27. *Kleiner Perkins Caufield & Byers and Sequoia Capital:* Based on returns reported in Preqin Venture Capital Database and disclosures under states' public records laws regarding investments made by entities such as the California Public Employees Retirement System. *VC Funds (1981 to 2006 vintages):* Preqin.

return estimates do not always reflect "like-for-like" performance comparisons because the economic details of each fund are not always observable. Sometimes the available data means an IRR can be calculated; in other cases the return is expressed as a compound annual growth rate, or related metric. Sometimes the unit of analysis is the fund, but in other instances, the available data allows for average returns to be estimated across funds. Unfortunately, "public market equivalent" (PME) calculations cannot be performed in each of these cases, due to lack of data about capital calls and distributions between limited partners and VC firms, but Figure E.2 does attempt to show the returns from Figure E.1 *relative* to the return on public equities. The interpreting intuition is approximately the same as a PME. A ratio greater than one indicates outperformance relative to a contemporaneous return on public equities, whereas a ratio below one indicates underperformance.[3]

Figures E.1 and E.2 show clearly that profiting from long-tail investing has been difficult irrespective of time period. Going back to the analysis of whaling ventures in Chapter 1, the mean return that the whaling agent Gideon Allen & Son was able to generate on sixty-four voyages over the period 1830 to 1897 was spectacular in historical perspective. The profit rate represented a multiple of 7.89 over the compound annual return (including dividends) on the New York Stock Exchange during the same time period. But Gideon Allen & Son was unquestionably an outlier compared to the average return on all whaling voyages. Less experienced agents who organized fewer than forty voyages generated much lower average returns. Recall also from Chapter 1 that whaling ventures had significant exposure to downside risk. Around six percent of voyages from New Bedford resulted in the total loss of a vessel, and a substantial share of voyages (in some years as high as two-thirds) returned to port unprofitable.

Leading examples from the early history of the emergent private capital entities covered in Chapter 3 highlight further the challenges associated with generating systematic payoffs from long-tail portfolios. Laurance Rockefeller invested heavily in new and emerging industries and was particularly active in the area of aviation, a high-tech sector of the early to mid-twentieth century. Yet, Figure E.2 shows that his investments underperformed relative to public equities. The ratio of his return relative to the return on public equities is 0.59, which is directionally similar to the PME on his portfolio of investments of 0.86, from Chapter 3. Similarly, J. H. Whitney & Company struggled to generate

Multiple over Benchmark Return

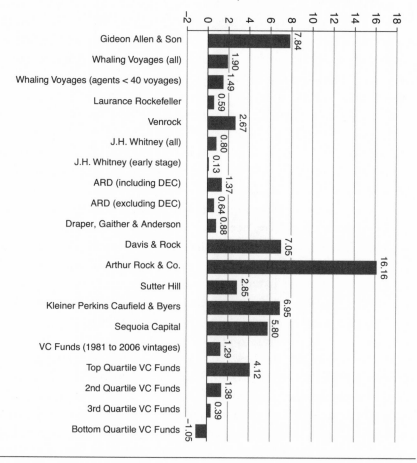

Figure E.2 Relative Performance: From Whaling Ventures to Modern VC Funds.

This figure scales the returns in Figure E.1 using the return of a contemporaneous benchmark investment. The benchmark for whaling voyages is calculated as the return on the NYSE with dividends included using data in William Goetzmann, Roger G. Ibbotson, and Liang Peng, "A New Historical Database for the NYSE 1815 to 1925: Performance and Predictability," *Journal of Financial Markets* 4, no. 1 (2001): 1–32. Otherwise, the benchmark is calculated as the return on the S&P Composite with dividends included for a comparable time period.

VC-style returns, especially on a portfolio of early-stage investments. The firm reacted to the uncertainties associated with startups by changing its orientation over time increasingly toward more mature investments. This helps to explain the origins of the separation between venture capital (early-stage) and private equity (later-stage) investing.

Notably, however, returns were not a first-order concern for either Rockefeller or J. H. Whitney, given their levels of wealth accumulation. By the 1950s, Rockefeller was worth upwards of $200 million and Whitney's wealth was estimated to be "in excess" of $100 million—about $2 billion and $1 billion today, respectively. Both Rockefeller and Whitney were motivated by a strong social responsibility to invest their capital productively in small and medium-sized enterprises. As a hint of that mindset, Laurance once said: "I like doing constructive things with my money rather than just trying to make more."[4]

ARD presents a clear historical illustration of the long-tail model. As discussed in Chapter 4, ARD's 1957 investment in Digital Equipment Corporation showed that it was possible to build a portfolio of high-tech investments such that a substantial "hit" in the positive skew of the distribution of returns would compensate for the lesser returns in the remainder of the portfolio. Figures E.1 and E.2 reveal that, without that one investment, ARD would have generated a return lower than what could have been achieved by an investment in public equities. The investment performance of Draper Gaither and Anderson (see Chapter 5) shows the "hits" model was hard to replicate.

In this context, the results posted by Davis and Rock and Arthur Rock & Co., discussed in Chapter 6, are especially revealing. Tommy Davis and Arthur Rock invested in entrepreneurial teams that created spectacularly successful returns, as did Rock and Dick Kramlich. The annualized returns from these investment partnerships are striking in Figure E.1, but they stand out even more in Figure E.2, which attempts to control for the investing context. The life of the Arthur Rock & Company fund spanned the early 1970s, a profoundly depressed era for the US stock market and the economy more generally. Regarding the venture approach to investing, these partnerships established proof of concept, which in turn proved a significant impetus to industrywide development. Momentum was also fueled by other early entities, including Venrock, an outgrowth of Laurance Rockefeller's investing (see Chapter 5), and Sutter Hill, founded in 1964 (see Chapter 4). As marquee firms in the history of VC, Kleiner Perkins Caufield & Byers and Sequoia Capital both generated outsized mean returns when these are measured over successive funds from the 1970s through the late 1990s (see Chapters 6, 7, and 8).

While data limitations mean that it is impossible to gauge what average returns looked like on an industrywide basis for anything earlier than the 1980s, more modern fund-performance data indicates a highly asymmetric distribution of returns. Figures E.1 and E.2 show that, among funds with vintages between 1981 and 2006, top-quartile funds outperformed bottom-quartile funds by a considerable margin. The literature's various explanations for these performance differences are contested, especially the relative importance of skill and luck.[5] In general, however, return differences are likely to be large and persistent due to high variations in general partner expertise, access to early-stage investment opportunities, and momentum created by initial investment successes.[6]

Finally, it is worth noting that the way in which "returns" are conceptualized has changed fundamentally over time. Long-tail investing implies that the returns of the biggest hits matter most; however, as one observer noted, "Arthur Rock & Co.'s investment style was as much about singles and doubles as it was about home runs."[7] Although venture capital is unequivocally a returns-centric industry today, it has not always been so. At ARD, Georges Doriot set out to be "creative" versus "remunerative" with venture capital. Daniel Gregory, Chairman of Greylock from 1976 to 1990, saw the 1980s as an unfortunate turning point (see Chapter 5), declaring in that decade that "the quest of the institutions for rates of return is very counterproductive for achieving the long-term results that we are supposed to be after."[8] Recall, too, Arthur Rock's comment on his career as a venture investor during the 1960s and 1970s: "We just built companies to be listed on the New York Stock Exchange ... there wasn't this need to produce returns, returns, returns."[9] For Rock, returns were a byproduct of building sustainable firms. They would naturally materialize when the aim was to finance high-impact entrepreneurial startups with potential to create societal value.

Organizational Structure and Strategy

The most appropriate organizational structure for long-tail investing has traditionally been the limited partnership form (Chapter 5). Yet, this structure has limitations. ARD's closed-end fund approach, with permanent capital and tradeable shares on public markets, entailed costs in terms of regulatory compliance—but it also offered opportunities, because it meant that ARD had relatively "patient" capital. Had ARD been organized as a limited partnership with a seven- to ten-year fund life, it probably would have failed. ARD's long-tail investment in Digital Equipment was made in 1957, eleven years after it was founded, and that firm did not IPO until 1966, nine years after the initial investment was made. Avoiding short-termism within the limited partnership structure requires choosing institutional investors carefully. Paul Wythes was cofounder of Sutter Hill, an evergreen fund—that is, one in which investors could roll over their realized gains into further investments by the same fund, or withdraw their investment after a specified number of years. Wythes said he "favored foundations and university endowments" as limited partners because "they don't come and go."[10] These institutions could endure illiquidity, were less likely to withdraw funds in the face of underperformance shocks, and were therefore more aligned with Sutter Hill's long-term view.

This is not to say that the limited partnership model is an incorrect choice of organizational structure, but it does emphasize that the adoption of this form can dictate the types of startups that are financed. Venture capital returns from the clean energy sector, for example, have typically been lackluster because these investments require high levels of initial capital and sustained financial support to grow. The VC model is largely incompatible with these characteristics.[11] John Doerr asserted in 2007 that "green technology—going green—is bigger than the Internet. It could be the biggest economic opportunity of the twenty-first century"—but his firm's portfolio of green investments failed to deliver attractive returns. As the eminent business historian Alfred D. Chandler always emphasized, strategy should be aligned with organizational structure.[12] Venture capital investments in "cleantech" in recent years appear to be a classic case of strategy-structure misalignment.

As the VC industry faces the future, an important question is whether firms' organizational structures will ever add as much value as their "partner capital." Michael Ewens and Mathew Rhodes-Kropf find that the human capital of the general partners in a venture capital firm is between two and five times more important than its organizational capital to explaining its returns.[13] The fact that partners' talent matters most is an important finding, and it is consistent with the fact that the VC industry has been remarkably devoid of organizational innovation since Draper Gaither and Anderson was founded as a limited partnership in 1959.

This makes it all the more interesting that, when Marc Andreessen and Ben Horowitz established their eponymous venture capital firm as a limited partnership in 2009, they introduced an important organizational change. Unlike most venture entities, Andreessen Horowitz offers a rich "platform" of services to entrepreneurs, from human resources to marketing. This was an idea that first emerged in the late 1990s, when several VC firms developed recruiting and operating help for startups, but it was abandoned when the market crashed. Andreessen Horowitz finances these services in part by redirecting management fees (above what it costs to administer a fund) away from payoffs to general partners into more productive activities designed to enhance the performance of portfolio companies. The platform facilitates future deal flow and it disciplines investing. The strategy of Andreessen Horowitz is thus reflected in its organizational structure. One interpretation of this organizational change is that it simply represents a variation on the value of partner capital, given that both Andreessen and Horowitz have strong track records as early-stage investors. Another interpretation, however, is that this organizational structure is a new and important step in the professionalization of VC firms.

The relationship between organizational structure and strategy takes on added significance given the scale of venture funds currently being raised. Recall from Chapter 7 that NEA started in 1978 with a $16.4 million fund, yet its 2017 fund closed at $3.3 billion, a 201-fold increase in nominal terms over forty years, or a 54.6-fold increase in inflation-adjusted dollars. Early on, NEA's founders realized they needed to put in place structures to enable the firm's funds and portfolio companies to be effectively managed at scale. SoftBank's recently raised Vision Fund, at close to $100 billion (more than double the total amount raised by all US venture capital funds in 2016), marks a renewed industry-wide dedication to fundraising at ever higher levels. This may simply reflect the fact that startups are now staying private much longer and the capital demands of operating in an increasingly connected world are much higher. Historically, however, as one study noted, "an influx of capital into VC funds is associated with lower subsequent performance."[14]

Scale economies are notoriously difficult to capture. They failed to materialize in the whaling industry because good agents, captains, and crew could be spread across only so many voyages.[15] By the same token, as a venture firm scales, the additional requirements of moving a larger number of portfolio companies through the pipeline can become burdensome. The supply of capital may be out of sync with demand, which can militate against successful exits in the timeline of a limited partnership. Scale also creates challenges of governance. During the late 1990s, when megafunds were being raised for the first time, a general partner at the west coast firm Crosspoint Venture Partners was expected to sit on twelve portfolio company boards, versus the five or six that would be typical in normal times.[16] Motivations also potentially change at scale because the management fee, as an annual percentage of committed capital, can create unproductive incentives to fundraise. William Janeway notes of the late 1990s that "firms went from raising $100 million funds to raising $1 billion funds . . . and a tenfold increase in management fees provided a powerful incentive against returning to pre-bubble scale."[17] Agency concerns can be exaggerated during financial market booms, because compensation tends to be less tied to performance outcomes when capital is easy to raise.[18]

Finally, in terms of the overall structure of the venture capital industry, the informal market for startup finance, which has operated throughout history (see Chapter 3), has become increasingly professionalized and integrated into the formal market for venture finance. The 2007 founding of AngelList, a platform to link entrepreneurs with investors, represented an important turning point in seed investing, as did Y-Combinator, founded in 2005 as an early-stage accelerator of ideas that provided seed money as well as business advisory and networking capabilities. Both helped to democratize access to startup capital and both have generated their share of hits. Airbnb's founders were admitted to the Y-Combinator program for startups in 2009, for example, having agreed to $20,000 in financing in return for 6 percent of their startup's equity.[19] The model proliferated. By 2013, around 170 seed accelerators were active in America.[20]

At the other end of the spectrum is the recent resurgence in corporate venture capital arms as incubators in the market for ideas. Google Ventures, for example, was founded in 2009. This shows how risk capital deployment can be seamlessly shifted to different organizational forms in early and later-stage investments. On the one hand, these structural changes might increase the scope of startups that get financed, rather than narrowing the space in which venture capital limited partnerships typically operate. On the other hand, they might threaten the margins and the hegemony that VC firms have traditionally enjoyed.

Silicon Valley as a Venture Capital Hotspot

A third issue is the possibility that regional or global advantage in the deployment of risk capital might shift. Put another way: Will Silicon Valley survive? History shows that no place has enjoyed greater geographic domination in VC than Silicon Valley (Chapter 6). Unlike New Bedford whaling, where coastal proximity was key, the proliferation of startup finance in Silicon Valley was not tied closely to geographic resource endowments, other than perhaps the weather. That creates some degree of permanence. Furthermore, when Silicon Valley faced obsolescence as military funding dried up during the 1960s, the region adapted by reorienting product lines like silicon transistors and integrated circuits toward a more commercial customer base. A tradition of dynamic capital markets helped to facilitate that process of change as venture capitalists directed investment funds toward entrepreneurs with the best ideas and capabilities.

A complementarity between venture capital and high-tech has been pivotal to Silicon Valley's development. The venture-financing model works best when technological uncertainty is high. At that point, the long-tail model is most compelling because venture capitalists can deploy startup finance into high-tech growth areas that they expect to yield the largest payoffs. As Tommy Davis once said, "a new technical product is much more likely to produce a big and fast return on investment than a nontechnical product or service."[21] While there are other regions of the United States where venture capital and high-tech powerfully intersect, including the east coast corridor from Boston to Washington, DC, and key cities like Austin, Texas, the historical primacy of Silicon Valley is underscored by the decisions made by so many key venture capitalists and entrepreneurs to locate there. Arthur Rock, Tom Perkins, and Don Valentine (see Chapter 6) moved to Silicon Valley from the east coast to exploit better entrepreneurial opportunities. Likewise, in the late 2000s, Greylock (as noted in Chapter 5) moved its main location from its founding state in Massachusetts to Silicon Valley. Jessica Livingston, cofounder of Y-Combinator, described moving the pioneering seed accelerator from the east coast to Silicon Valley as "one of the best things we've ever done."[22] Facebook's Mark Zuckerberg found Palo Alto, California, to be a more compelling place to build an entrepreneurial venture than Cambridge, Massachusetts.

Entrepreneurs and venture capitalists are attracted to Silicon Valley because of what economists describe as agglomeration advantages, the benefits to firms and people that grow when they are in close proximity to one another. Three factors help to keep Silicon Valley a vibrant venture capital and entrepreneurial hotspot: value-chain relationships among firms, the expertise resident in a deep high-tech labor pool, and the relatively free flow of intellectual ideas. These have been known as "Marshallian" factors since the prominent economist Alfred Marshall created the basis for their study in his 1890 book *Principles of Economics*—and they tend to be magnified in high-technology industries where the benefits of clustering are quite pronounced. These advantages have remained remarkably persistent even as the costs of transacting over distance have declined.

Importantly, these agglomeration benefits did not emerge in isolation or at an identifiable point in time, but rather arose over time through the long-run evolution of Silicon Valley. Combining to create indelible advantages were strong returns to scale from a deep-seated history of university-led innovation and human capital development; spillovers from military investment; pivotal firms such as Fairchild Semiconductor; a highly competitive but open entrepreneurial culture; amenable weather; pools of high-skilled immigrants; and a flourishing venture capital sector. New England did not have all of these. Nor did Cleveland, Pittsburgh, or Detroit.

At the same time, shifting regional development throughout US history indicates how ephemeral such advantages can be. Chapter 1 traced the rise of the whaling industry in America but it experienced relentless decline from around the 1860s. Similarly, the New England cotton industry, once an important driver of industrialization, waned after the 1920s. Cleveland and Pittsburgh, both innovation hotspots of the Second Industrial Revolution, were next to lose their entrepreneurial edge (Chapter 2). As regional advantage moved westward, Detroit also rose to prominence through automobile manufacturing (Chapter 3) before Silicon Valley took over as a high-tech center.

Given these precedents, it could be argued that Silicon Valley's advantage in VC is overdue for collapse. Globally it faces threats from Beijing and other fast-growing technology hubs where governments and investors are less devoted to the idea of copying the American model. Indeed, a large number of government-sponsored efforts around the world to kick-start Silicon Valley VC clusters have failed precisely because they attempted to replicate a US-specific environment in a short time frame.[23] The new pathways being created globally suggest that Silicon Valley may not always be the magnet it is today for capital, people, and ideas.

The Importance of Government

In the history of Silicon Valley and the VC industry more generally, government has played a defining role. Its importance is frequently neglected as an explanation for the rise of the venture model in the United States. A key question, then, is how government will influence the industry moving forward. The Federal Telegraph Company, the early-twentieth-century Palo Alto communications enterprise that was a focal point for entrepreneurship, just as Fairchild Semiconductor was in Silicon Valley many decades later, was heavily dependent on naval contracts and government support (Chapter 3). Military spending was vital to the growth of Silicon Valley during the 1940s and 1950s (Chapter 6). During the 1970s and 1980s, too, the government changed the course of VC with legislative changes that permitted pension funds to invest in venture capital (Chapter 5). Government investments in basic science at universities have spurred innovation and entrepreneurship, and the benefit can be seen in companies like Genentech (Chapter 6).

From a societal perspective, keeping the startup sector vibrant is perhaps the most important function the VC industry performs. Venture capitalists generate private value in the form of fund-level returns, but the social value they create surely exceeds that. That social value is equivalent to private value plus all other returns realized from the technological change that venture financing enables. Numerous innovations developed by VC-backed firms, from memory chips to recombinant insulin (Chapter 6), have moved society forward—and in turn, stimulated additional waves of technological development with immense collective impact. New startups, by introducing important product and process innovations, challenge change-resistant industry incumbents and bring about the creative destruction, in Schumpeter's famous phrase, that is critical to economic growth.

Mounting evidence suggests that the forces of creative destruction may not be as powerful as they once were. Superstar firms like Google, Facebook, Apple, and Amazon have emerged from being fledgling VC-backed startups to dominating their markets, with limited threat of displacement.[24] Markups (the difference between the price a firm charges for products and the marginal cost to produce them) have increased dramatically over time, indicating growing market power. Average markups were about 21 percent over marginal cost in 1980, but rose to 61 percent by 2016.[25] The recent uptick in markups is especially noticeable. It could be the case that increasing markups are the reward for existing firms' stepped-up innovation. And some evidence indicates that incumbents have excelled at improving on their own offerings, outweighing the contributions to economic growth brought about through startup-driven creative destruction.[26] Another view suggests there has been a significant decline in business dynamism since around 2000, measured along three lines: the share of firms in the economy that are young (aged five years or less); the number of jobs created by young firms; and those firms' total share of employment.[27] This decline in business dynamism echoes the NVCA's remarkable and influential 1970s report, "Emerging Innovative Companies: An Endangered Species" (discussed in Chapter 5). As corporate venture capital has become more significant in recent years, it is plausible that incumbent firms engaging in it will be increasingly able to fend off creative destruction by making strategic investments in areas where they face competition.

Government has various levers at hand to affect the supply of and demand for venture capital, and policies with regard to taxation, immigration, and labor law have historically been key influences. During the late 1970s and early 1980s, the venture capital industry successfully lobbied for tax breaks, and the reduction in capital gains taxation was seen by venture capitalists as a major driver of the industry's success (see Chapter 5). While, on the supply side, there is no evidence that more favorable capital gains treatment of carried interest leads to greater venture capital commitments, broader tax policy may increase the demand for venture capital by affecting occupational choice. Faced with a lower capital-gains threshold, ceteris paribus, talented managers find entrepreneurship more attractive, and the likelihood increases that they move away from wage work.[28] Furthermore, the superstar inventors who often engage in startup activity tend to be highly sensitive to top tax rates in making decisions about where to locate. This suggests that tax levers can affect labor mobility, especially in a world where talent flows are more global than they have ever been before.[29]

Immigration policy has obvious implications for the startup ecosystem given that around a quarter of workers engaged in innovation and entrepreneurial activity in the United States are high-skilled immigrants.[30] Immigrants have had large impacts on the American economy throughout its history, going back to at least Samuel Slater, the entrepreneurial immigrant whose ingenuity helped kick-start industrial development in New England cotton textiles in the eighteenth century (see Chapter 2). Immigrants have routinely teamed up with native-born entrepreneurs to create truly impactful ventures. Two members of the "traitorous eight" who established Fairchild Semiconductor were born abroad—Eugene Kleiner in Vienna, Austria, and Jean Hoerni in Geneva, Switzerland. During the 1980s, another member of this eminent group, Robert Noyce, emphasized that foreign-born individuals represented the bulk of the intellectual talent working at Intel, the firm he cofounded in 1968 (see Chapter 6). The very fact that Intel was launched owed much to the venture capital expertise of Arthur Rock, whose father was a Russian immigrant—and Andy Grove, Intel's much celebrated CEO, was a Hungarian immigrant. The NVCA estimates that a third of the American VC-backed startups that underwent IPOs between 2006 and 2012 had at least one immigrant as a founding member.[31] While immigrants make up about 15 percent of the US workforce, they constitute about a quarter of US entrepreneurs.[32]

High-skilled immigrants tend to be attracted to places where they can freely pursue entrepreneurial opportunities. It is logical that Silicon Valley has thrived in a legal context favoring the free movement of labor. Indeed, many of the firms that figure prominently in the history of VC—including Fairchild Semiconductor, Intel, Genentech, and the series of startups emerging from PayPal—were established in situations where enforceable noncompete agreements would have obstructed venture capitalist activities or a firm's founding. Places where noncompete clauses are common impose large adjustment costs on labor mobility and entrepreneurship.

To be sure, direct government involvement in the venture capital industry has not always been favorably received.[33] Yet, historically, direct efforts have created benefits that are difficult to overlook. The SBICs (discussed in Chapter 4) may not have generated financial performance returns in line with the very best private VC firms, but they helped to establish large pools of capital and various intermediary services, building infrastructure essential to the modern VC industry's development.[34] The SBIR program of the early 1980s (see Chapter 7) provided further impetus to entrepreneurship by subsidizing research and development efforts in new high-tech startups.[35] Overall, government has had major impacts, both direct and indirect, on the various mechanisms and incentives that led to the rise of the venture capital industry in the United States.

Diversity

A final question for the present and future is the one brought up when women first gained a foothold in the industry during the 1980s (see Chapter 7): Can the VC industry reverse its abysmal record on diversity? This book's narrative has been largely a story of white males. Although the VC industry has succeeded at tapping into immigrant talent, gender disparities have persisted. A 2014 analysis of leadership in the US venture capital industry shows that, in the vast majority (52 percent) of top firms, women did not occupy *any* senior positions.[36] Ellen Pao's unsuccessful 2012 lawsuit against Kleiner Perkins Caufield & Byers drew attention to the workplace culture problems associated with this lack of diversity. Although the 2018 *Forbes* "Midas List" of the hundred best venture capitalists includes 50 percent more women than the 2017 list, and Mary Meeker of Kleiner Perkins Caufield & Byers is ranked highly at number six, there are still only nine women on the 2018 list. Black and Hispanic venture capitalists are vastly underrepresented in the industry.

In many respects, this lack of diversity is paradoxical because venture capital is based on the premise of financing radical, often revolutionary, change by nonincumbents. Some of the most successful venture capitalists, moreover, come from nontraditional backgrounds, suggesting a willingness on the industry's part to embrace differences. For example, Sequoia Capital's Mike Moritz was a journalist for *Time* before entering the VC industry. Given that the characteristics of a "great VC" are not easily observable *ex ante*, it is hard to imagine that venture capital firms are engaging in "statistical discrimination" by using race or gender to infer the expected returns of new hires. One explanation, therefore, is that there is some perceived disamenity associated with hiring women, and therefore a "taste-based discrimination" in favor of hiring men. This would relate to what sociologists call homophily, or a preference for interacting with those "coming from the same group."[37] If an industry started out with a pronounced set of personality attributes or profiles, homophily could cause those characteristics to persist long into the future.

Historical figures have not been innocent bystanders with respect to these disparities. Georges Doriot, for example, played a pivotal role in the early development of venture capital, as discussed in Chapter 4, but he chose to exclude women from his popular elective class at Harvard Business School. His misogynistic tendencies did not help prepare the industry for a future in which a deep commitment to diversity would serve it better. Inevitably, people's thinking is conditioned by the cultural environments in which they operate. Silicon Valley, in many ways an open place, as detailed in Chapter 6, has never been devoid of sexism and "clubbiness." Through the lens of Leslie Berlin's analysis of Robert Noyce's extraordinary career as a cofounder of Fairchild Semiconductor and Intel, for all its entrepreneurial brilliance, Silicon Valley could be a hotbed of machismo and chauvinism.[38]

Importantly, the women who did become noted venture capitalists during the 1980s did not owe their careers to positive discrimination. They were celebrated by their male counterparts for their expertise as investors—and criticized as harshly as their male counterparts when their investments underperformed. At a macro level and within the venture capital sector more specifically, a growing body of research suggests that diverse teams make better decisions and that performance outcomes improve with greater diversity.[39] This evidence implies that the VC industry could benefit by embracing more diverse talent pools—not as recompense for its past inadequacy, but in order to enrich the stock of human capital required to produce attractive returns.

Final Thoughts

This book has attempted to narrate the long-term development of the US venture capital industry in a way that stresses the importance of historical perspective. Venture capital in America arose out of a long-running orientation toward risk capital and entrepreneurship, which can be seen in the earliest expressions of economic growth and development. The allure of the long tail represents the prospect of outsized returns with a right-sided skew that rarely materializes in reality. Just as crews on whaling voyages in the nineteenth century, in spite of low odds of success, were willing to set sail from New Bedford and navigate to distant seas, venture capital firms continue their pursuits despite the fact that the vast majority of funds underperform public equities.

VC's history, then, is a story about something far more encompassing than a model of startup finance that has been so difficult to replicate in other countries. It signifies a cultural appetite for risk-taking that celebrates entrepreneurship's spirit of adventure, that accepts unbridled avarice, and that encourages the insatiable pursuit of material financial gain. In many ways, the history of the venture capital industry is a window into the larger history of America.

Notes

Introduction

1. Spencer E. Ante, *Creative Capital: Georges Doriot and the Birth of Venture Capital* (Boston: Harvard Business Press, 2008).

2. Paul A. Gompers and Josh Lerner, *The Venture Capital Cycle*, 2nd ed. (Cambridge, MA: MIT Press, 2004); Peter Thiel, with Blake Masters, *Zero to One: Notes on Startups, or How to Build the Future* (New York: Crown Business, 2014).

3. Daniel Kahneman and Amos Tversky, "Prospect Theory: An Analysis of Decision under Risk," *Econometrica* 47, no. 2 (1979): 263–291; Charles P. Kindleberger, *Manias, Panics and Crashes: A History of Financial Crisis,* 3rd ed. (New York: Wiley, 1996).

4. Kenneth J. Arrow and Gerard Debreu, "Existence of an Equilibrium for a Competitive Economy," *Econometrica* 22, no. 3 (1954): 265–290.

5. Diego Puga and Daniel Trefler, "International Trade and Institutional Change: Medieval Venice's Response to Globalization," *Quarterly Journal of Economics* 129, no. 2 (2014): 753–821.

6. Avner Greif, *Institutions and the Path to the Modern Economy: Lessons from Medieval Trade* (Cambridge: Cambridge University Press, 2006).

7. Lance E. Davis, Robert E. Gallman, and Karin Gleiter, *In Pursuit of Leviathan: Technology, Institutions, Productivity, and Profits in American Whaling, 1816–1906,* (Chicago: University of Chicago Press, 1997); Eric Hilt, "Incentives in Corporations: Evidence from the American Whaling Industry," *Journal of Law and Economics* 49, no. 1 (2006): 197–227; Eric Hilt, "Investment and Diversification in the American Whaling Industry," *Journal of Economic History* 67, no. 2 (2007): 292–314.

8. Tom Nicholas and Jonas Peter Akins, "Whaling Ventures," HBS no. 813-086 (Boston: Harvard Business School Publishing, 2012).

9. Steven N. Kaplan and Per Stromberg, "Financial Contracting Theory Meets the Real World: An Empirical Analysis of Venture Capital Contracts," *Review of Economic Studies* 70, no. 2 (2003): 281–315.

10. Alfred D. Chandler, "Samuel Slater, Francis Cabot Lowell, and the Beginnings of the Factory System in the United States," HBS no. 792-008 (Boston: Harvard Business School Publishing, 1995), 21.

11. Naomi R. Lamoreaux, Margaret Levenstein, and Kenneth L. Sokoloff, "Financing Invention during the Second Industrial Revolution: Cleveland, Ohio, 1870–1920," NBER Working Paper No. 10923, National Bureau of Economic Research, November 2004.

12. David Cannadine, *Mellon: An American Life* (New York: A. A. Knopf, 2006).

13. Eric Hilt and Katharine O'Banion, "The Limited Partnership in New York 1822–1858: Partnerships without Kinship," *Journal of Economic History* 69, no. 3 (2009): 615–645.

14. Leslie Berlin, "The First Venture Capital Firm in Silicon Valley: Draper, Gaither & Anderson," in *Making the American Century: Essays on the Political Culture of Twentieth Century America*, ed. Bruce J. Schulman (New York: Oxford University Press, 2014).

15. William Elfers, *Greylock: An Adventure Capital Story* (Boston: Greylock Management Corporation, 1995).

16. Paul A. Gompers and Josh Lerner, "What Drives Venture Capital Fundraising?"*Brookings Papers on Economic Activity, Microeconomics* 1998 (1998): 149–204.

17. Shane M. Greenstein, *How the Internet Became Commercial: Innovation, Privatization, and the Birth of a New Network* (Princeton: Princeton University Press, 2015).

18. Tom Nicholas and David Chen, "Dot.Com: Online Pet Retailing," HBS no. 809-117 (Boston: Harvard Business School Publishing, 2015).

19. Peter Temin, "The American Business Elite in Historical Perspective," NBER Historical Working Paper No. 104, National Bureau of Economic Research, October 1997.

1. Whaling Ventures

1. Tom Nicholas and Jonas Peter Akins, "Whaling Ventures," HBS no. 813-086 (Boston: Harvard Business School Publishing, 2012).

2. W. J. Snelling, *The Polar Regions of the Western Continent Explored; Embracing a Geographical Account of Iceland, Greenland, the Islands of the Frozen Sea, and the Northern Parts of the American Continent* (Boston: Printed for W. W. Reed, 1831), 77.

3. C. W. Sanger, "The Origins of British Whaling: Pre-1750 English and Scottish Involvement in the Northern Whale Fishery," *Northern Mariner* 5, no. 3 (1995): 15–32.

4. Lance E. Davis, Robert E. Gallman, and Karin Gleiter, *In Pursuit of Leviathan: Technology, Institutions, Productivity, and Profits in American Whaling, 1816–1906,* (Chicago: University of Chicago Press, 1997), 19.

5. Jennifer Herman, *Massachusetts Encyclopedia* (Hamburg, MI: State History Publications, 2008), 310.

6. Davis, Gallman, and Gleiter, *In Pursuit of Leviathan,* 513–522.

7. Thomas Nickerson, and others, *The Loss of the Ship Essex, Sunk by a Whale: First-Person Accounts* (New York: Penguin, 2000).

8. William R. Kerr, Ramana Nanda, and Matthew Rhodes-Kropf, "Entrepreneurship as Experimentation," *Journal of Economic Perspectives* 28, no. 3 (2014): 25–48, 31.

9. "Account Books and Other Material Relating to the Whaling Industry, Chiefly from New Bedford and Nantucket, 1774–1922," Baker Library Special Collections, Harvard Business School, Harvard University, Mss 252.

10. Davis, Gallman, and Gleiter, *In Pursuit of Leviathan,* 425.

11. Preqin gets its data largely from limited partners like public pension funds that make public disclosures. Other sources include voluntary disclosures from VC firms and SEC filings. Some funds, however, are clearly not captured because VC firms typically impose reporting restrictions on their performance.

12. The voyage is the unit of analysis in the whaling data set and the fund is the unit of analysis in the VC data. The VC net IRR represents the return on a fund after fees and carried interest have been paid out, whereas the profit rate on a whaling voyage nets out agent fees

and other costs but does not account for the timing of cash flows. For a full explanation of the profit rate calculation see further, Davis, Gallman, and Gleiter, *In Pursuit of Leviathan,* 429.

13. Alexander Starbuck, *History of the American Whale Fishery from Its Earliest Inception to the Year 1876* (Waltham, MA: The Author, 1878), 145.

14. Peter Thiel, with Blake Masters, *Zero to One: Notes on Start Ups, or How to Build the Future* (New York: Crown Business, 2014), 85.

15. Eric Hilt, "Investment and Diversification in the American Whaling Industry," *Journal of Economic History* 67, no. 2 (2007): 292–314.

16. Raymond A. Rydell, *Cape Horn to the Pacific; the Rise and Decline of an Ocean Highway* (Berkeley: University of California Press, 1952), 68.

17. Rydell, *Cape Horn to the Pacific,* 66.

18. Kathryn Grover, *The Fugitive's Gibraltar: Escaping Slaves and Abolitionism in New Bedford, Massachusetts* (Amherst: University of Massachusetts Press, 2009), 58.

19. Davis, Gallman, and Gleiter, *In Pursuit of Leviathan,* 342–343.

20. A whale-oil barrel was not necessarily standard in measure. It could contain from thirty to thirty-five gallons. Hence, I report units in barrels or gallons, whichever is given in the source. For comparability purposes, however, I follow Davis, Gallman, and Gleiter, *In Pursuit of Leviathan,* and assume "a typical barrel of oil contained 31.5 gallons" (321).

21. David Moment, "The Business of Whaling in America in the 1850's," *Business History Review* 31, no. 3 (1957): 261–291, 263.

22. Eric J. Dolin, *Leviathan: The History of Whaling in America* (New York: W. W. Norton, 2008), 207.

23. Davis, Gallman, and Gleiter, *In Pursuit of Leviathan,* 427.

24. Starbuck, *History of the American Whale Fishery,* 603.

25. Grover, *The Fugitive's Gibraltar,* 99.

26. Starbuck, *History of the American Whale Fishery,* 149.

27. Stephen Currie, *Thar She Blows: American Whaling in the Nineteenth Century* (Minneapolis: Lerner Publications, 2001), 32. As explained later in the chapter, letters would be carried back to the home port by passing ships, or left for return on another ship when stopping at a port for provisioning.

28. Starbuck, *History of the American Whale Fishery,* 479.

29. Currie, *Thar She Blows,* 32.

30. Davis, Gallman, and Gleiter, *In Pursuit of Leviathan,* 17.

31. Davis, Gallman, and Gleiter, *In Pursuit of Leviathan,* 15.

32. Herman Melville, *Moby-Dick, or, the Whale* (New York: Harper & Brothers, 1851), 285.

33. Davis, Gallman, and Gleiter, *In Pursuit of Leviathan,* 417–418.

34. Wilson L. Heflin, *Herman Melville's Whaling Years,* ed. Mary K. B. Edwards and Thomas Farel Heffernan (Nashville: Vanderbilt University Press, 2004), 179.

35. Davis, Gallman, and Gleiter, *In Pursuit of Leviathan,* 196.

36. Elmo Paul Hohman, *The American Whaleman: A Study of Life and Labor in the Whaling Industry* (New York: Longmans, Green and Co., 1928), 316.

37. Lily Fang, Victoria Ivashina, and Josh Lerner, "The Disintermediation of Financial Markets: Direct Investing in Private Equity," *Journal of Financial Economics* 116, no. 1 (2015): 160–178.

38. Experimentation with the corporate form in the 1830s failed because diffuse ownership gave rise to incentive conflicts through the increased separation of ownership from control. Also see Eric Hilt, "Incentives in Corporations: Evidence from the American Whaling Industry," *Journal of Law and Economics* 49, no. 1 (2006): 197–227.

39. Davis, Gallman, and Gleiter, *In Pursuit of Leviathan*, 384.

40. Hohman, *The American Whaleman*, 323.

41. Hohman, *The American Whaleman*, 309.

42. Thomas Hellmann, Laura Lindsey, and Manju Puri, "Building Relationships Early: Banks in Venture Capital," *Review of Financial Studies* 21, no. 2 (2008): 513–541.

43. Michael C. Jensen and William H. Meckling, "Theory of the Firm: Managerial Behavior, Agency Costs and Ownership Structure," *Journal of Financial Economics* 3, no. 4 (1976): 305–360.

44. Oliver E. Williamson, *The Mechanisms of Governance* (Oxford: Oxford University Press, 1996), 182.

45. Naomi R. Lamoreaux, *Insider Lending: Banks, Personal Connections, and Economic Development in Industrial New England* (Cambridge: Cambridge University Press, 1994).

46. Howland Tripp, *In Whaling Days* (Boston: Little, Brown, 1909), 244.

47. Davis, Gallman, and Gleiter, *In Pursuit of Leviathan*, 106.

48. Hohman, *The American Whaleman*, 279.

49. Hohman, *The American Whaleman*, 279.

50. Davis, Gallman, and Gleiter, *In Pursuit of Leviathan*, 382–383.

51. Davis, Gallman, and Gleiter, *In Pursuit of Leviathan*, 397.

52. Kingston W. Heath, *The Patina of Place: The Cultural Weathering of a New England Industrial Landscape* (Knoxville: University of Tennessee Press, 2001), 39–40.

53. Davis, Gallman, and Gleiter, *In Pursuit of Leviathan*, 282–283.

54. Davis, Gallman, and Gleiter, *In Pursuit of Leviathan*, 396.

55. Davis, Gallman, and Gleiter, *In Pursuit of Leviathan*, 397.

56. Richard R. John, *Spreading the News: The American Postal System from Franklin to Morse* (Cambridge, MA: Harvard University Press, 1995); Lisa Norling, *Captain Ahab Had a Wife: New England Women and the Whalefishery, 1720–1870* (Chapel Hill: University of North Carolina Press, 2014), 150.

57. Davis, Gallman, and Gleiter, *In Pursuit of Leviathan*, 106.

58. Starbuck, *History of the American Whale Fishery*, 372–650.

59. Davis, Gallman, and Gleiter, *In Pursuit of Leviathan*, 107.

60. A wealth tax was levied on individuals, businesses, estates, trusts and other entities with at least $100 of taxable property.

61. Davis, Gallman, and Gleiter, *In Pursuit of Leviathan*, 413.

62. New Bedford Board of Trade et al., *New Bedford, Massachusetts: Its History, Industries, Institutions and Attractions* (New Bedford: Mercury Publishing Company, printers, 1889).

63. Davis, Gallman, and Gleiter, *In Pursuit of Leviathan*, 450–451.

64. William Goetzmann, Roger G. Ibbotson, and Liang Peng, "A New Historical Database for the NYSE 1815 to 1925: Performance and Predictability," *Journal of Financial Markets* 4, no. 1 (2001): 1–32. Their data set shows the total return on the NYSE with a "low dividends" assumption and the total return with a "high dividends" assumption. To avoid

extremes in the data I make the compound annual return calculation using the average of the two series.

65. Abner Forbes, *The Rich Men of Massachusetts: Containing a Statement of the Reputed Wealth of about Two Thousand Persons, with Brief Sketches of Nearly Fifteen Hundred Characters,* 2nd ed. (Boston: Redding & Company, 1852).

66. Arthur Korteweg and Morten Sorensen, "Skill and Luck in Private Equity Performance," *Journal of Financial Economics* 60, no. 3 (2017): 535–562.

67. Funds managed by highly capable VCs persistently outperformed the next VC fund for funds with vintage years in the 1980s and 1990s. See Steven N. Kaplan and Antoinette Schoar, "Private Equity Performance: Returns, Persistence, and Capital Flows," *Journal of Finance* 60, no. 4 (2005): 1791–1823.

68. Davis, Gallman, and Gleiter, *In Pursuit of Leviathan,* 450.

69. Hilt, "Incentives in Corporations," 215.

70. Davis, Gallman, and Gleiter, *In Pursuit of Leviathan,* 385–387.

71. See further Paul Gompers, Anna Kovner, Josh Lerner, and David Scharfstein, "Performance Persistence in Entrepreneurship," *Journal of Financial Economics* 96, no. 1 (2010): 18–32. They show in a large sample of entrepreneurs active between 1986 and 2000, that an entrepreneur who had successfully taken a venture-backed firm public had a 30 percent chance of succeeding in their next venture-backed firm, compared with a 22 percent chance for those who had previously failed and a 21 percent chance for first-time founders.

72. This professionalization role is also common in modern venture capital, where VCs nurture human capital inside the firm, including facilitating CEO transitions. See further, Thomas Hellmann and Manju Puri, "Venture Capital and the Professionalization of Start-up Firms: Empirical Evidence," *Journal of Finance* 57, no. 1 (2002): 169–197.

73. Baker Business Historical Collections, Business Manuscripts, Mss: 252, 1820–1865 M847 vol. 4, Baker Library, Harvard Business School.

74. Richard Ellis, *Men and Whales* (New York: Knopf, 1991; Guilford, CT: Globe Pequot Press, 1999), 174.

75. It is worth noting that in shore-based whaling fixed wage payments were made because under these circumstances geographic proximity made monitoring more feasible.

76. David Moment, "The Business of Whaling," 274.

77. Davis, Gallman, and Gleiter, *In Pursuit of Leviathan,* 161–167.

78. Lee A. Craig and Charles R. Knoeber, "Manager Shareholding, the Market for Managers, and the End-Period Problem: Evidence from the U.S. Whaling Industry," *Journal of Law, Economics, and Organization* 8, no. 3 (1992): 607–627, 609.

79. Davis, Gallman, and Gleiter, *In Pursuit of Leviathan,* 177.

80. That amount—$5.22 per month—would be equivalent to around $160 per month today. Fayette M. Ringgold, "A Consular Report on Whalers and the Whaling System (1858)," in Hohman, *The American Whaleman,* 312–313.

81. Robert E. Hall and Susan E. Woodward, "The Burden of the Nondiversifiable Risk of Entrepreneurship," *American Economic Review* 100, no. 3 (2010): 1163–1194.

82. David T. Robinson and Berk A. Sensoy, "Cyclicality, Performance Measurement, and Cash Flow Liquidity in Private Equity," *Journal of Financial Economics* 122, no. 3 (2016): 521–543.

83. Hilt, "Investment and Diversification."

84. Abhijit V. Banerjee, "A Simple Model of Herd Behavior," *Quarterly Journal of Economics* 107, no. 3 (1992): 797–817; David Scharfstein and Jeremy Stein, "Herd Behavior and Investment," *American Economic Review* 80, no. 3 (1990): 465–479.

85. Hilt, "Investment and Diversification," 293.

86. Hilt, "Investment and Diversification," 300.

2. The Early Development of Risk Capital

1. Eric J. Dolin, *Leviathan: The History of Whaling in America* (New York: W. W. Norton, 2008), 206; Hal Whitehead, "Estimates of the Current Global Population Size and Historical Trajectory for Sperm Whales," *Marine Ecology Progress Series* 242 (2002): 295–304, 301.

2. Lance E. Davis, Robert E. Gallman, and Karin Gleiter, *In Pursuit of Leviathan: Technology, Institutions, Productivity, and Profits in American Whaling, 1816–1906,* (Chicago: University of Chicago Press, 1997), 456.

3. Akira Osaki, "The Decline of the American Whaling Industry during the Industrial Revolution in the Latter Half of the 19th Century: New England's Evolution from Whaling Center to Hub of the Modern Cotton Industry," *Journal of Geography (Chigaku Zasshi)* 119, no. 4 (2010): 615–631, 622.

4. Sven Beckert, *Empire of Cotton: A Global History* (New York: Vintage Books, 2015).

5. Robert F. Dalzell, *Enterprising Elite: The Boston Associates and the World They Made,* Harvard Studies in Business History (Cambridge, MA: Harvard University Press, 1987).

6. Alfred D. Chandler, "Patterns of American Railroad Finance, 1830–1850," *Business History Review* 28, no. 3 (1954): 248–263.

7. Dave Donaldson and Richard Hornbeck, "Railroads and American Economic Growth: A 'Market Access' Approach," *Quarterly Journal of Economics* 131, no. 2 (2016): 799–858.

8. Richard Florida and Mark Samber, "Capital and Creative Destruction: Venture Capital and Regional Growth in US Industrialization," in *New Industrial Geography: Regions, Regulations and Institutions,* ed. Trevor J. Barnes and Meric S. Gertler (New York: Routledge, 1999); Naomi R. Lamoreaux, Margaret Levenstein, and Kenneth L. Sokoloff, "Financing Invention during the Second Industrial Revolution: Cleveland, Ohio, 1870–1920," NBER Working Paper No. 10923, National Bureau of Economic Research, November 2004.

9. W. W. Rostow, *The Stages of Economic Growth: A Non-Communist Manifesto* (Cambridge: Cambridge University Press, 1990).

10. Timothy Leunig, "A British Industrial Success: Productivity in the Lancashire and New England Cotton Spinning Industries a Century Ago," *Economic History Review* 56, no. 1 (2003): 90–117.

11. Gregory Clark, "The Condition of the Working Class in England, 1209–2004," *Journal of Political Economy* 113, no. 6 (2005): 1307–1340.

12. Robert C. Allen, *The British Industrial Revolution in Global Perspective* (Cambridge: Cambridge University Press, 2009).

13. Joel Mokyr, *The British Industrial Revolution: An Economic Perspective,* 2nd ed. (Boulder, CO: Westview Press, 1999).

14. Liam Brunt, "Rediscovering Risk: Country Banks as Venture Capital Firms in the First Industrial Revolution," *Journal of Economic History* 66, no. 1 (2006): 74–102.

15. Allen, *The British Industrial Revolution,* 96.

16. C. Aspin, *James Hargreaves and the Spinning Jenny* (Helmshore: Helmshore Local History Society, 1964), 48–49.

17. Rick Szostak, *The Role of Transportation in the Industrial Revolution: A Comparison of England and France* (Montreal: McGill Queen's University Press, 1991), 185.

18. Mokyr, *The British Industrial Revolution*, 15.

19. R. S. Fitton, *The Strutts and the Arkwrights, 1758–1830: A Study of the Early Factory System*, ed. Alfred P. Wadsworth (Manchester: Manchester University Press, 1958; Clifton, NJ: A. M. Kelley, 1973); R. S. Fitton, *The Arkwrights: Spinners of Fortune* (Manchester: Manchester University Press, 1989), 23–27.

20. Allen, *The British Industrial Revolution*, 919.

21. Fitton, *The Arkwrights*, 46.

22. Eric J. Evans, *The Forging of the Modern State: Early Industrial Britain, 1783–1870*, 3rd ed. (Abingdon: Taylor and Francis, 2001), 144.

23. Thomas K. McCraw, *The Founders and Finance: How Hamilton, Gallatin, and Other Immigrants Forged a New Economy* (Cambridge, MA: Belknap Press of Harvard University Press, 2012).

24. David J. Jeremy, *Transatlantic Industrial Revolution: The Diffusion of Textile Technologies between Britain and America, 1790–1830s* (Cambridge, MA: MIT Press, 1981).

25. Mary B. Rose, *Firms, Networks and Business Values: The British and American Cotton Industries since 1750* (Cambridge: Cambridge University Press, 2000), 41.

26. Robert D. Arbuckle, *Pennsylvania Speculator and Patriot: The Entrepreneurial John Nicholson, 1757–1800* (University Park: Pennsylvania State University Press, 1975), 110–111.

27. Peter J. Coleman, *The Transformation of Rhode Island, 1790–1860* (Providence, RI: Brown University Press, 1963; Westport, CT: Greenwood Press, 1985), 40–41.

28. James Blaine Hedges, *The Browns of Providence Plantations: The Nineteenth Century* (1952; Providence, RI: Brown University Press, 1968), 329–330.

29. Robert Sobel, *The Entrepreneurs: Explorations within the American Business Tradition* (New York: Weybright and Talley, 1974; BeardBooks, 2000), 14.

30. James L. Conrad, "Entrepreneurial Objectives, Organizational Design, Technology, and the Cotton Manufactory of Almy and Brown, 1789–1797," *Business and Economic History* 13 (1984): 7–19, 8.

31. Tom Nicholas and Matthew Guilford, "Samuel Slater & Francis Cabot Lowell: The Factory System in U.S. Cotton Manufacturing," HBS no. 814-065 (Boston: Harvard Business School Publishing, 2013), 7.

32. Steven N. Kaplan and Per Stromberg, "Financial Contracting Theory Meets the Real World: An Empirical Analysis of Venture Capital Contracts," *Review of Economic Studies* 70, no. 2 (2003): 281–315.

33. Noam Wasserman, *The Founder's Dilemmas: Anticipating and Avoiding the Pitfalls That Can Sink a Startup* (Princeton, NJ: Princeton University Press, 2012).

34. George S. White, *Memoir of Samuel Slater: The Father of American Manufactures* (Philadelphia: [s.n.], 1836), 188.

35. Jeffrey J. Hill, "Lives of the Workforce in the Industrial Revolution," in *The Industrial Revolution in America: Overview / Comparison*, ed. Kevin Hillstrom and Laurie Collier Hillstrom (Santa Barbara, CA: ABC-CLIO, 2007), 98.

36. Caroline F. Ware, *The Early New England Cotton Manufacture: A Study in Industrial Beginnings* (Boston: Houghton Mifflin, 1931), 138.

37. Ware, *Early New England Cotton Manufacture,* 138.

38. Dalzell, *Enterprising Elite,* 47.

39. Rose, *Firms, Networks and Business Values,* 84.

40. Charles W. Calomiris and Carlos D. Ramirez, "The Role of Financial Relationships in the History of American Corporate Finance," *Journal of Applied Corporate Finance* 9, no. 2 (1996): 52–73.

41. Dalzell, *Enterprising Elite,* 29.

42. Bernard Bailyn, *The New England Merchants in the Seventeenth Century* (Cambridge, MA: Harvard University Press, 1955), 78–81.

43. Herman Edward Krooss and Martin R. Blyn, *A History of Financial Intermediaries* (New York: Random House, 1971), 19–20.

44. Howard Bodenhorn, *A History of Banking in Antebellum America: Financial Markets and Economic Development in an Era of Nation-Building* (Cambridge: Cambridge University Press, 2000).

45. Chandler, "Patterns of American Railroad Finance," 248.

46. J. Bradford De Long, "Did J. P. Morgan's Men Add Value? A Historical Perspective on Financial Capitalism," NBER Working Paper No. 3426, National Bureau of Economic Research, August 1990.

47. Carola Frydman and Eric Hilt, "Investment Banks as Corporate Monitors in the Early Twentieth Century United States," *American Economic Review* 107, no. 7 (2017): 1938–1970.

48. Robert F. Bruner and Sean D. Carr, *The Panic of 1907: Lessons Learned from the Market's Perfect Storm* (Hoboken, NJ: Wiley, 2007), 12.

49. Elhanen Helpman, Introduction, in *General Purpose Technologies and Economic Growth,* ed. Elhanen Helpman (Cambridge, MA: MIT Press, 1998), 3.

50. Paul David, "The Dynamo and the Computer: An Historical Perspective on the Modern Productivity Paradox," *American Economic Review* 80, no. 2 (1990): 355–361.

51. Florida and Samber, "Capital and Creative Destruction," 265.

52. Lamoreaux, Levenstein, and Sokoloff, "Financing Invention."

53. H. G. Prout, *A Life of George Westinghouse* (New York: American Society of Mechanical Engineers, 1921), 274.

54. Lamoreaux, Levenstein, and Sokoloff, "Financing Invention," 20.

55. Ajay K. Agrawal, Iain M. Cockburn, Alberto Galasso, and Alexander Oettl, "Why Are Some Regions More Innovative Than Others? The Role of Firm Size Diversity," NBER Working Paper No. 17793, National Bureau of Economic Research, January 2012.

56. Florida and Samber, "Capital and Creative Destruction," 271.

57. David Cannadine, *Mellon: An American Life* (New York: A. A. Knopf, 2006), 163.

58. Cannadine, *Mellon,* 98.

59. Florida and Samber, "Capital and Creative Destruction," 285.

60. Mark Samber, "Networks of Capital: Creating and Maintaining a Regional Industrial Economy in Pittsburgh, 1865–1919" (Ph.D. diss., Carnegie Mellon University, 1995), 179–180.

61. Quentin R. Skrabec, *Henry Clay Frick: The Life of the Perfect Capitalist* (Jefferson, NC: McFarland, 2010), 175.

62. Cannadine, *Mellon,* 119–120.

63. Thomas Hellmann and Manju Puri, "Venture Capital and the Professionalization of Start-up Firms: Empirical Evidence," *Journal of Finance* 57, no. 1 (2002): 169–197.

64. John N. Ingham, *Biographical Dictionary of American Business Leaders* (Westport, CT: Greenwood Publishing Group, 1983), Vol. 1, 919.

65. Cannadine, *Mellon,* 167.

66. Samber, "Networks of Capital," 181.

67. Harvey O'Connor, *Mellon's Millions: The Biography of a Fortune; the Life and Times of Andrew W. Mellon* (New York: Blue Ribbon Books, 1933), xi.

68. O'Connor, *Mellon's Millions,* 400–401.

69. Emmanuel Saez and Gabriel Zucman, "Wealth Inequality in the United States since 1913: Evidence from Capitalized Income Tax Data," *Quarterly Journal of Economics* 131, no. 2 (2016): 519–578, 521.

3. The Rise of Private Capital Entities

1. Charles W. Calomiris and Carlos D. Ramirez, "Financing the American Corporation: The Changing Menu of Financial Relationships," in ed. Carl Kaysen, *The American Corporation Today* (Oxford: Oxford University Press, 2007): 128–186, 146.

2. Karl T. Compton, "George Eastman," *Science* 75, no. 1946 (1932): 402–405, 402.

3. Elizabeth Brayer, *George Eastman: A Biography* (Baltimore: Johns Hopkins University Press, 1996; Rochester, NY: University of Rochester Press, 2006), 45.

4. Lynne Warren, *Encyclopedia of Twentieth-Century Photography, 3-Volume Set* (Oxfordshire: Taylor and Francis, 2005), Vol. 1, 425.

5. M. Todd Henderson, "The Story of Dodge v. Ford Motor Company: Everything Old Is New Again," in J. Mark Ramseyer, ed., *Corporate Law Stories* (New York: Foundation Press, Thomson Reuters, 2009), 42.

6. Henderson, "The Story of Dodge v. Ford," 45.

7. Henderson, "The Story of Dodge v. Ford," 47.

8. Henderson, "The Story of Dodge v. Ford," 49; Alasdair G. M. Nairn, *Engines That Move Markets: Technology Investing from Railroads to the Internet and Beyond* (New York: Wiley, 2002), 210.

9. Robert J. Gordon, *The Rise and Fall of American Growth: The U.S. Standard of Living since the Civil War* (Princeton, NJ: Princeton University Press, 2017), 11.

10. Nathan Miller, *New World Coming: The 1920s and the Making of Modern America* (New York: Scribner, 2003), 179.

11. Edward L. Glaeser, *Triumph of the City: How Our Greatest Invention Makes Us Richer, Smarter, Greener, Healthier, and Happier* (New York: Penguin, 2011), 30.

12. Stephen B. Adams, "Arc of Empire: The Federal Telegraph Company, the U.S. Navy, and the Beginnings of Silicon Valley," *Business History Review* 91, no. 2 (2017): 329–359.

13. Geoffrey Maslen, "Magic Lamp of Radio," *New Scientist* 59, no. 861 (August 30, 1973): 495–497.

14. Glaeser, *Triumph of the City,* 31.

15. Timothy J. Sturgeon, "How Silicon Valley Came to Be," in *Understanding Silicon Valley: Anatomy of an Innovative Region,* ed. Martin Kenney (Stanford, CA: Stanford University Press, 2000), 46.

16. Thomas Ropp, "Philo Farnsworth: Forgotten Father of Television," *Media History Digest* 5, no. 2 (1985): 42–58.

17. Martin Kenney and Richard Florida, "Venture Capital in Silicon Valley: Fueling New Firm Formation," in *Understanding Silicon Valley: The Anatomy of an Entrepreneurial Region,* ed. Martin Kenney (Stanford, CA: Stanford University Press, 2000), 103.

18. W. Rupert Maclaurin, "Patents and Technical Progress: A Study of Television," *Journal of Political Economy* 58, no. 2 (1950): 142–157, 149.

19. Gordon, *The Rise and Fall of American Growth,* 409–413.

20. G. Wayne Miller, *Car Crazy: The Battle for Supremacy between Ford and Olds and the Dawn of the Automobile Age* (New York: PublicAffairs, 2015), 9.

21. Jonathan R. Hughes, *The Vital Few: The Entrepreneur and American Economic Progress,* expanded ed. (1966; New York: Oxford University Press, 1986), 288.

22. Kenney and Florida, "Venture Capital in Silicon Valley," 103.

23. Olav Sorenson and Toby Stuart, "Syndication Networks and the Spatial Distribution of Venture Capital Investments," *American Journal of Sociology* 106, no. 6 (2001): 1546–1588; Shai Bernstein, Xavier Giroud, and Richard R. Townsend, "The Impact of Venture Capital Monitoring," *Journal of Finance* 71, no. 4 (2016): 1591–1622.

24. Emmanuel Saez and Gabriel Zucman, "Wealth Inequality in the United States since 1913: Evidence from Capitalized Income Tax Data," *Quarterly Journal of Economics* 131, no. 2 (2016): 519–578.

25. Richard C. Sutch, "The Accumulation, Inheritance, and Concentration of Wealth During the Gilded Age: An Exception to Thomas Piketty's Analysis," (paper prepared for presentation, University of California at Riverside, January 25, 2016), 1, http://economics.ucr.edu /repec/ucr/wpaper/201601.pdf.

26. Richard R. Davis, *The Phipps Family and the Bessemer Companies* (Nashville: Turner Publishing, 2007), 36–38.

27. Davis, *The Phipps Family,* 112.

28. Davis, *The Phipps Family,* 46.

29. Davis, *The Phipps Family,* 75.

30. "Venture Capital: What Is It, Where Is It, How to Get It," *Business Management,* July 1964.

31. "Dynasties Unify," *BusinessWeek,* no. 876, June 15, 1946.

32. Alfred D. Chandler, "John D. Rockefeller: The Richest Man in the World," HBS no. 815-088 (Boston: Harvard Business School Publishing, 2014).

33. Ron Chernow, *Titan: The Life of John D. Rockefeller, Sr.* (New York: Random House, 1998; ebook Knopf Doubleday, 2007), 489.

34. John W. Wilson, *The New Venturers: Inside the High-Stakes World of Venture Capital* (Reading, MA: Addison-Wesley, 1985), 15.

35. John B. Rae, *Climb to Greatness: The American Aircraft Industry, 1920–1960* (Cambridge, MA: MIT Press, 1968), 242.

36. W. David Lewis, *Eddie Rickenbacker: An American Hero in the Twentieth Century* (Baltimore: Johns Hopkins University Press, 2005).

37. W. David Lewis, "Edward V. Rickenbacker's Reaction to the Civil Aviation Policy of the 1930s," in *Reconsidering a Century of Flight,* ed. Roger D. Launius and Janet R. Daly Bednarek (Chapel Hill: University of North Carolina Press, 2003), 118–131, 127.

38. Henry W. Berger, *St. Louis and Empire: 250 Years of Imperial Quest and Urban Crisis* (Carbondale: Southern Illinois University Press, 2015), 177.

39. "Space-Age Risk Capitalist," *Time* 74, no. 8, August 24, 1959.

40. Wilson, *The New Venturers,* 15.

41. Peter Crisp Papers, Baker Business Historical Collections, Business Manuscripts Mss: 784 1946–2008 C93, Box 1 Folder 30, Baker Library, Harvard Business School.

42. William A. Sahlman, "How to Write a Great Business Plan," *Harvard Business Review,* July-August 1997, 101.

43. Jonathan E. Lewis, *Spy Capitalism: ITEK and the CIA* (New Haven, CT: Yale University Press, 2008), 37–43.

44. Peter Crisp Papers, Box 1 Folder 4.

45. Laurance's investments are detailed in the Peter Crisp Papers, Box 1 Folder 4. I follow the public market equivalent calculation methodology in Steven N. Kaplan and Antoinette Schoar, "Private Equity Performance: Returns, Persistence, and Capital Flows," *Journal of Finance* 60, no. 4 (2005): 1791–1823.

46. "Venture Capital: What Is It, Where Is It, How to Get It."

47. Carl A. Dauten and Merle T. Welshans, "Investment Development Companies," *Journal of Finance* 6, no. 3 (1951): 276–290, 276–277.

48. "Venture Capital: What Is It, Where Is It, How to Get It."

49. Paul Gompers, "The Rise and Fall of Venture Capital," *Business and Economic History* 23, no. 2 (1994): 1–24, 19.

50. NVCA, "The National Venture Capital Association Yearbook 2011" (New York: Thomson Reuters, 2011), 9.

51. John Graham, Mark T. Leary, and Michael R. Roberts, "A Century of Capital Structure: The Leveraging of Corporate America," NBER Working Paper No. 19910, National Bureau of Economic Research, February 2014.

52. Peter Lyth, "Chosen Instruments: The Evolution of British Airways," in *Flying the Flag: European Commercial Air Transport since 1945,* ed. Hans-Liudger Dienel and Peter Lyth (Basingstoke: Palgrave Macmillan, 1999), 50–86, 62.

53. Dauten and Welshans, "Investment Development Companies," 282.

54. Dauten and Welshans, "Investment Development Companies," 282.

55. Wilson, *The New Venturers,* 17.

56. Wilson, *The New Venturers,* 18.

57. Edward B. Roberts and Charles E. Eesley, *Entrepreneurial Impact: The Role of MIT* (Hanover: Now Publishers, 2011), 60.

58. Briefing Session on the Small Business Investment Act of 1958, sponsored by the American Management Association, New York, December 1–2, 1958. Committee on Banking and Currency and Select Committee on Small Business. 117 (1959) (Testimony of Charles Wrede Petersmeyer).

59. "Risk Capital Plays It Safer," *BusinessWeek,* no. 1498, May 17, 1958.

60. Robert S. Harris, T. I. M. Jenkinson, and Steven N. Kaplan, "Private Equity Performance: What Do We Know?" *Journal of Finance* 69, no. 5 (2014): 1851–1882; Erik Stafford, "Rep-

licating Private Equity with Value Investing, Homemade Leverage, and Hold-to-Maturity Accounting" (Working Paper, Harvard Business School, 2015), https://www.hbs.edu/faculty/Pages/item.aspx?num=50433.

61. Ramana Nanda, Sampsa Samila, and Olav Sorenson, "The Persistent Effect of Initial Success: Evidence from Venture Capital," NBER Working Paper No. 24887, National Bureau of Economic Research, August 2018.

62. Martha L. Reiner, *The Transformation of Venture Capital: A History of Venture Capital Organizations in the United States* (Ph.D. diss., University of California, Berkeley, 1989), 144.

63. "Venture Capital: What Is It, Where Is It, How to Get It."

64. Henry Etzkowitz, *MIT and the Rise of Entrepreneurial Science* (London: Routledge, 2002), 90.

65. Kenney and Florida, "Venture Capital in Silicon Valley," 105.

66. Paul Wendt, "The Availability of Capital to Small Business in California," unpublished mimeo, University of California, Berkeley, 1947, 43–54, 139–142; Reiner, *The Transformation of Venture Capital*, 202–215.

67. Wendt, "The Availability of Capital," 86.

68. Wendt, "The Availability of Capital," 149.

69. Wilson, *The New Venturers*, 19.

4. The Market versus the Government

1. Robert Bleiberg, "New Kind of Company Finances Ventures," *Barron's National Business and Financial Weekly* 29, no. 8, February 21, 1949.

2. Spencer E. Ante, *Creative Capital: Georges Doriot and the Birth of Venture Capital* (Boston: Harvard Business Press, 2008); David H. Hsu and Martin Kenney, "Organizing Venture Capital: The Rise and Demise of American Research & Development Corporation, 1946–1973," *Industrial and Corporate Change* 14, no. 4 (2005): 579–616.

3. A closed-end fund consists of a pool of capital raised by issuing a fixed number of shares at an initial offering. The pool of capital in the closed-end fund is essentially permanent capital. When a share is sold it is transferred to the new investor at the market price rather than being redeemed from the pool of capital itself, as in an open-end fund. Shares in an open-end fund are not fixed and can only be purchased and sold directly from the fund at their net asset value.

4. Linda Weiss, *America Inc.?: Innovation and Enterprise in the National Security State* (Ithaca, NY: Cornell University Press, 2014), 58.

5. Josh Lerner, *Boulevard of Broken Dreams: Why Public Efforts to Boost Entrepreneurship and Venture Capital Have Failed—and What to Do about It* (Princeton, NJ: Princeton University Press, 2009).

6. Alan R. Earls and Nasrin Rohani, *Polaroid* (Charleston, SC: Arcadia, 2005), 7.

7. AnnaLee Saxenian, *Regional Advantage: Culture and Competition in Silicon Valley and Route 128* (Cambridge, MA: Harvard University Press, 1996), 20.

8. Charles D. Ellis, *Joe Wilson and the Creation of Xerox* (Hoboken, NJ: John Wiley and Sons, 2006), 39–50.

9. Donald Wilhelm, "How Small Business Competes for Funds," *Law and Contemporary Problems* 11, no. 2 (1945): 220–247.

10. William Stoddard, "Small Business Wants Capital," *Harvard Business Review* 18 (1940): 265–274, 269.

11. Martha L. Reiner, "The Transformation of Venture Capital: A History of Venture Capital Organizations in the United States" (Ph.D. diss., University of California, Berkeley, 1989), 1.

12. Alexander J. Field, "The Most Technologically Progressive Decade of the Century," *American Economic Review* 93, no. 4 (2003): 1399–1413.

13. Ralph C. Epstein and Florence M. Clark, *Industrial Profits in the United States* (New York: National Bureau of Economic Research, in cooperation with the Committee on Recent Economic Changes, 1934); W. A. Paton, *Corporate Profits as Shown by Audit Reports* (New York: National Bureau of Economic Research, 1935).

14. Ante, *Creative Capital*.

15. John W. Wilson, *The New Venturers: Inside the High-Stakes World of Venture Capital* (Reading, MA: Addison-Wesley, 1985), 20.

16. Daniel Yergin, *The Quest: Energy, Security, and the Remaking of the Modern World* (New York: Penguin, 2011), 560.

17. Lee Stout, "Women in Leadership: An Untold Story," *Directors and Boards* 36, no. 3 (2012): 38–43, 42.

18. Georges F. Doriot papers, 1921–1984, Baker Business, Historical Collections, Business Manuscripts Mss: 784 1921–1984 D698, volume 127, no. 1, Harvard Business School Club Buffalo: "Thoughts," January 26, 1967, Baker Library, Harvard Business School.

19. Status and Future of Small Business: Hearing before the Senate Committee on Small Business. Ninetieth Congress. 155 (1967) (Testimony of Georges Doriot).

20. Hoover Medal Board of Award, biography by J. W. Roe, "Ralph Edward Flanders, Seventh Hoover Medalist," Hoover Medal Board of Award, New York, 1944.

21. David M. Hart, *Forged Consensus: Science, Technology, and Economic Policy in the United States, 1921–1953* (Princeton, NJ: Princeton University Press, 1998), 158–172.

22. Henry Etzkowitz, *MIT and the Rise of Entrepreneurial Science* (London: Routledge, 2002), 83.

23. Ralph E. Flanders, *Senator from Vermont* (Boston: Little, Brown, 1961), 188.

24. Volume and Stability of Private Investment: Hearing before the Joint Committee on the Economic Report. Eighty First Congress. 453 (1949) (Testimony of Merrill Griswold).

25. Testimony of Merrill Griswold, 454.

26. Hart, *Forged Consensus*, 165–168; Hsu and Kenney, "Organizing Venture Capital," 586–587.

27. Testimony of Merrill Griswold, 447.

28. Testimony of Georges Doriot (1967), 156.

29. Volume and Stability of Private Investment: Hearing before the Joint Committee on the Economic Report. Eighty-first Congress. 481 (1949) (Testimony of Horace S. Ford).

30. Investment Trusts and Investment Companies: Hearing before a Subcommittee of the Committee on Banking and Currency. Seventy-sixth Congress. 949 (1949) (Testimony of David Schenker).

31. Reiner, "The Transformation of Venture Capital," 171–174.

32. Testimony of Merrill Griswold, 460.

33. Hsu and Kenney, "Organizing Venture Capital," 592.

34. Wilson, *The New Venturers*, 19; Reiner, "The Transformation of Venture Capital," 176.

35. Testimony of Horace S. Ford, 486.
36. Reiner, "The Transformation of Venture Capital," 177.
37. Ante, *Creative Capital*, 113.
38. See, for example, US patent 2,134,840 for a "Water Separator." Patented by Eidon K. Ralston, Cleveland, Ohio, assignor to Circo Products Company, Cleveland, Ohio, a corporation of Ohio. Filing date June 25, 1936.
39. Ante, *Creative Capital*, 114.
40. Jane Jacobs, *The Economy of Cities* (New York: Random House, 1969), 205–206.
41. Edward B. Roberts, *Entrepreneurs in High Technology: Lessons from MIT and Beyond* (New York: Oxford University Press, 1991), 135.
42. Testimony of Georges Doriot (1967), 158–159.
43. Roberts, *Entrepreneurs in High Technology*, 135.
44. Edward B. Roberts and Charles E. Eesley, *Entrepreneurial Impact: The Role of MIT* (Hanover, NH: Now Publishers, 2011), 53.
45. Testimony of Horace S. Ford, 476.
46. Hsu and Kenney, "Organizing Venture Capital," 593.
47. Hsu and Kenney, "Organizing Venture Capital," 598.
48. Testimony of Georges Doriot (1967), 156, 165.
49. Testimony of Georges Doriot (1967), 157.
50. Economic Concentration: Hearing before the Senate Committee on the Judiciary, Subcommittee on Antitrust and Monopoly. Eighty-eighth Congress. 2716 (1964) (Testimony of Georges Doriot).
51. Tom Nicholas, "The Origins of High-Tech Venture Investing in America," in *Financial Market History: Reflections on the Past for Investors Today*, ed. David Chambers and Elroy Dimson (Charlottesville, VA: CFA Institute, 2016), 229.
52. Patrick R. Liles, *Sustaining the Venture Capital Firm* (Cambridge, MA: Management Analysis Center, 1977), 86–87.
53. Liles, *Sustaining the Venture Capital Firm*, 46.
54. Liles, *Sustaining the Venture Capital Firm*, 40–41.
55. Hsu and Kenney, "Organizing Venture Capital," 607–608.
56. Testimony of Georges Doriot (1967), 165.
57. Hsu and Kenney, "Organizing Venture Capital," 610.
58. Liles, *Sustaining the Venture Capital Firm*, 62.
59. Liles, *Sustaining the Venture Capital Firm*, 67.
60. Georges F. Doriot papers, 1921–1984, vol. 114, no. 7, "Memorandum: Venture Capital," November 1953.
61. Liles, *Sustaining the Venture Capital Firm*, 71, 83.
62. Testimony of Georges Doriot (1967), 159.
63. Roberts, *Entrepreneurs in High Technology*, 135.
64. Testimony of Georges Doriot (1964), 2718–2719.
65. Kenneth H. Olsen, "Learning the Dangers of Success: The Education of an Entrepreneur," *New York Times*, July 19, 1987, F2.
66. Saxenian, *Regional Advantage*, 96.
67. Liles, *Sustaining the Venture Capital Firm*, 83. In its registration statement filed with the SEC in July 1968, Digital Equipment Corporation had 2,926,600 common shares outstanding.

ARD held 60 percent of these, Olsen 11 percent, and the management team 17 percent (ownership of the remaining 12 percent is not included in the SEC document). In the IPO ARD sold 215,000 of its shares for $26,385,394.

68. Clifford M. Baumback and Joseph R. Mancuso, *Entrepreneurship and Venture Management* (Englewood Cliffs, NJ: Prentice-Hall, 1975), 114.

69. Liles, *Sustaining the Venture Capital Firm,* 150.

70. Hsu and Kenney, "Organizing Venture Capital," 609.

71. Liles, *Sustaining the Venture Capital Firm,* 80.

72. Testimony of Georges Doriot (1964), 2724.

73. Elmus Wicker, *The Banking Panics of the Great Depression* (Cambridge: Cambridge University Press, 1996), 95.

74. Ernest M. Klemme, "Industrial Loan Operations of the Reconstruction Finance Corporation and the Federal Reserve Banks," *Journal of Business* 12, no. 4 (1939): 365–385.

75. R. L. Weissman, *Small Business and Venture Capital: An Economic Program* (New York: Harper and Brothers, 1945), 77.

76. Liles, *Sustaining the Venture Capital Firm,* 12–26.

77. Stoddard, "Small Business Wants Capital," 265.

78. Charles M. Noone and Stanley M. Rubel, *SBICs: Pioneers in Organized Venture Capital* (Chicago: Capital Pub. Co., 1970), 27–28.

79. Liles, *Sustaining the Venture Capital Firm,* 77.

80. *Federal Reserve Bulletin,* July 1957, 767.

81. Irving Schweiger, "Adequacy of Financing for Small Business since World War Two," *Journal of Finance* 13, no. 3 (1958): 323–347.

82. "Superfluous Crutch," *Barron's National Business and Financial Weekly* 38, no. 47, November 24, 1958.

83. Peter Henig, "The Old Guard," *Venture Capital Journal,* October 2002, 27.

84. Testimony of Georges Doriot (1967), 161.

85. Wilson, *The New Venturers,* 22.

86. Liles, *Sustaining the Venture Capital Firm,* 98–99.

87. Liles, *Sustaining the Venture Capital Firm,* 116–117.

88. Jeffrey L. Cruikshank, *Shaping the Waves: A History of Entrepreneurship at Harvard Business School* (Boston: Harvard Business School Press, 2005), 114.

89. Liles, *Sustaining the Venture Capital Firm,* 100.

90. William Rotch, "The Pattern of Success in Venture Capital Financing," *Financial Analysts Journal* 24, no. 5 (1968): 141–147, 146.

91. Rao Hayagreeva and Martin Kenney, "New Forms as Settlements," in *The Sage Handbook of Organizational Institutionalism,* ed. R. Greenwood et al. (Los Angeles: SAGE Publications, 2008), 360.

92. Small Business Investment Incentive Act Hearing before the Subcommittee on Consumer Protection and Finance of the Committee on Interstate and Foreign Commerce. Ninety-sixth Congress. 92 (1979) (Testimony of Frank Chambers).

93. Liles, *Sustaining the Venture Capital Firm,* 92.

94. Testimony of Georges Doriot (1967), 160.

95. Role of the Venture Capital Industry in the American Economy: Hearing before the Subcommittee on International Trade, Finance, and Security Economics of the Joint Economic

Committee. Ninety-seventh Congress. 32 (1982) (Testimony of National Association of Small Business Investment Companies).

96. Mark Suchman, "Dealmakers and Counselors: Law Firms as Intermediaries in the Development of Silicon Valley," in *Understanding Silicon Valley: The Anatomy of an Entrepreneurial Region,* ed. Martin Kenney (Stanford, CA: Stanford University Press, 2000), 71–97.

97. Cruikshank, *Shaping the Waves,* 123; William H. Draper, *The Startup Game: Inside the Partnership between Venture Capitalists and Entrepreneurs* (New York: Palgrave Macmillan, 2011), 36.

98. Arun Rao and Piero Scaruffi, *A History of Silicon Valley: The Greatest Creation of Wealth in the History of the Planet,* 2nd ed. (Omniware Group, 2013).

99. Henig, "The Old Guard," 27.

100. Ante, *Creative Capital,* 153; Reiner, "The Transformation of Venture Capital," 332.

101. Bruce R. Scott, *Capitalism: Its Origins and Evolution as a System of Governance* (New York: Springer, 2011).

102. New Enterprise Associates, "Business Opportunity in Venture Investing," internal memorandum, NEA archives, 1977.

5. The Limited Partnership Structure

1. Paul A. Gompers and Josh Lerner, "The Use of Covenants: An Empirical Analysis of Venture Partnership Agreements," *Journal of Law and Economics* 39, no. 2 (1996): 463–498, 468.

2. Leslie Berlin, "The First Venture Capital Firm in Silicon Valley: Draper, Gaither & Anderson," in *Making the American Century: Essays on the Political Culture of Twentieth Century America,* ed. Bruce J. Schulman (New York: Oxford University Press, 2014), 20.

3. Frederick Pollock, *Essays in Jurisprudence and Ethics* (London: Macmillan and Company, 1882), 100.

4. Eric Hilt and Katharine O'Banion, "The Limited Partnership in New York 1822–1858: Partnerships without Kinship," *Journal of Economic History* 69, no. 3 (2009): 615–645, 615.

5. Berlin, "The First Venture Capital Firm."

6. Paul A. Gompers and Josh Lerner, *The Venture Capital Cycle,* 2nd ed. (Cambridge, MA: MIT Press, 2004), 37.

7. Robert Premus, "Venture Capital and Innovation: A Study," prepared for Joint Economic Committee, US Congress, 98th Session, December 28, 1984 (Washington DC: US GPO, 1985), https://www.jec.senate.gov/reports/98th%20Congress/Venture%20Capital%20and%20Innovation%20(1316).pdf.

8. Amalia D. Kessler, *A Revolution in Commerce: The Parisian Merchant Court and the Rise of Commercial Society in Eighteenth-Century France* (New Haven, CT: Yale University Press, 2007), 172–174.

9. Francis M. Burdick, *The Law of Partnership, Including Limited Partnerships* (Boston: Little, Brown, 1899; Littleton, CO: F. B. Rothman, 1983), 360.

10. Clement Bates, *The Law of Limited Partnership* (Boston: Little, Brown, 1886), 24.

11. Naomi R. Lamoreaux and Jean-Laurent Rosenthal, "Legal Regime and Contractual Flexibility: A Comparison of Business's Organizational Choices in France and the United States during the Era of Industrialization," *American Law and Economics Review* 7, no. 1 (2005): 28–61.

12. William George, *Handbook of the Law of Partnership* (St. Paul, MN: West Pub. Co., 1897), 422.

13. Hilt and O'Banion, "The Limited Partnership in New York," 632–638.

14. Burdick, *The Law of Partnership*, 370.

15. Bates, *The Law of Limited Partnership*, 83.

16. New York Supreme Court, *New York Supplement* (St. Paul, MN: West Publishing Company, 1922), 296.

17. Leone Levi, *Manual of the Mercantile Law of Great Britain and Ireland* (London: Smith, 1854), 215.

18. "The Uniform Limited Partnership Act," *Columbia Law Review* 22, no. 7 (1922): 669–672, 670.

19. Stanley E. Howard, "The Limited Partnership in New Jersey," *Journal of Business of the University of Chicago* 7, no. 4 (1934): 296–317, 314–315.

20. Howard, "The Limited Partnership in New Jersey," 317.

21. "The Limited Partnership," *Yale Law Journal* 45, no. 5 (1936): 895–907, 904.

22. Josh Lerner, *The Architecture of Innovation: The Economics of Creative Organizations* (Boston: Harvard Business Review Press, 2012), 159.

23. Ronald M. Shapiro, "The Need for Limited Partnership Reform: A Revised Uniform Act," *Maryland Law Review* 37 (1977): 544–593, 546.

24. John T. Maginnis, "Financing Oil and Gas Development," *Business Lawyer* 15, no. 3 (1960): 693–712.

25. Gompers and Lerner, *The Venture Capital Cycle*, 24.

26. Leo J. Pircher, "Tax Sheltered Investments: What, Who, When and Which?" *Business Lawyer* 28, no. 3 (1973): 897–914, 907–908.

27. Charles O. Galvin, "The 'Ought' and 'Is' of Oil-and-Gas Taxation," *Harvard Law Review* 73, no. 8 (1960): 1441–1509, 1458–1461.

28. Robert N. Davies and Kelvyn H. Lawrence, *Choosing a Form of Business Organization* (Durham, NC: Duke University, 1963), 88.

29. "New Popularity for Limited Partnerships," *Business Week*, no. 2206, December 11, 1971, 88–90.

30. *Encyclopedia of Tax Shelter Practices*, (Englewood Cliffs, NJ: Prentice-Hall, 1963), 83–84.

31. *Encyclopedia of Tax Shelter Practices*, 83–84.

32. The main intuition behind participating preferred is to allow the holder to receive a specified liquidation multiple of their investment and to participate with the common stock holders in any remaining proceeds from a liquidation as if the holder had converted their preferred shares to common.

33. Steven N. Kaplan and Per Stromberg, "Financial Contracting Theory Meets the Real World: An Empirical Analysis of Venture Capital Contracts," *Review of Economic Studies* 70, no. 2 (2003): 281–315, 286.

34. Montgomery Rollins, *Convertible Securities* (London: G. Routledge & Sons, 1909); Fred L. Kurr, "Participating Preferred Stocks," *The Magazine of Wall Street and Business Analyst*, July 1922, 352.

35. The literature on the tax benefits associated with convertible securities is contentious. See further, Ronald J. Gilson and David M. Schizer, "Understanding Venture Capital Structure: A Tax Explanation for Convertible Preferred Stock," *Harvard Law Review* 116, no. 3 (2003): 874–916; Gregg D. Polsky and Brant J. Hellwig, "Examining the Tax Advantage of Founders' Stock," *Iowa Law Review* 97 (2012): 1085–1145.

36. Gompers and Lerner, *The Venture Capital Cycle*, 8.

37. William H. Draper, III, *The Startup Game: Inside the Partnership between Venture Capitalists and Entrepreneurs* (New York: Palgrave Macmillan, 2011); Berlin, "The First Venture Capital Firm."

38. Draper, *The Startup Game,* 23.

39. "Blue-Ribbon Venture Capital," *Business Week,* no. 1626, October 29, 1960, 64–69.

40. Berlin, "The First Venture Capital Firm," 8.

41. Morey Greenstein, interview by Carole Kolker, Menlo Park, CA, February 20, 2014.

42. Berlin, "The First Venture Capital Firm," 7.

43. "Investing with 'Tax Dollars,'" *Business Week,* no. 2107, January 17, 1970, 66–68.

44. Berlin, "The First Venture Capital Firm," 9. "Investing Firm Forms on Coast," *New York Herald Tribune,* August 13, 1959.

45. Berlin, "The First Venture Capital Firm," 9.

46. William Rotch, "The Pattern of Success in Venture Capital Financing," *Financial Analysts Journal* 24, no. 5 (1968): 141–147, 147.

47. Berlin, "The First Venture Capital Firm," 9.

48. Ted Caldwell, "Introduction: The Model for Superior Performance," in *Hedge Funds: Investment and Portfolio Strategies for the Institutional Investor,* ed. Jess Lederman and Robert A. Klein (Burr Ridge, IL: Irwin Professional Publishing, 1995).

49. Robert G. Hagstrom, *The Essential Buffett: Timeless Principles for the New Economy* (New York: Wiley, 2002), 25.

50. "Blue-Ribbon Venture Capital."

51. Berlin, "The First Venture Capital Firm," 11.

52. Lin Tso [Zuo], *The Sensible Investor's Guide to Growth Stocks* (New York: J. Messner, 1962), 169.

53. Michael S. Malone, *The Big Score: The Billion-Dollar Story of Silicon Valley* (Garden City, NY: Doubleday, 1985), 48.

54. Tso [Zuo], *The Sensible Investor's Guide to Growth Stocks,* 169.

55. Berlin, "The First Venture Capital Firm," 12.

56. "Smith Kline Agrees to Buy Corbin-Farnsworth for Stock," *Wall Street Journal,* March 23, 1964.

57. Michael E. Porter, *The Competitive Advantage of Nations,* with a new intro. (1990; New York: Free Press, 1998), 198.

58. Berlin, "The First Venture Capital Firm," 12.

59. Berlin, "The First Venture Capital Firm," 23.

60. Berlin, "The First Venture Capital Firm," 16.

61. William Elfers, *Greylock: An Adventure Capital Story* (Boston: Greylock Management Corporation, 1995), 113.

62. Elfers, *Greylock,* 114.

63. Elfers, *Greylock,* 158–159.

64. Elfers, *Greylock,* 16–18.

65. Elfers, *Greylock,* 42.

66. Briefing Session on the Small Business Investment Act of 1958, sponsored by the American Management Association, New York, December 1–2, 1958. Committee on Banking and Currency and Select Committee on Small Business. 113 (1959) (Testimony of William Elfers).

67. Elfers, *Greylock,* 49.

68. Elfers, *Greylock,* 155.

69. Elfers, *Greylock,* 43.

70. Elfers, *Greylock,* 23–24.

71. Elfers, *Greylock,* 41–42.

72. Elfers, *Greylock,* 160–161.

73. Elfers, *Greylock,* 42.

74. Elfers, *Greylock,* 43.

75. Elfers, *Greylock,* 161.

76. Elfers, *Greylock,* 52–53.

77. Peter Crisp Papers, Baker Business Historical Collections, Business Manuscripts Mss: 784 1946–2008 C93, Box 1 Folder 2-2, Baker Library, Harvard Business School.

78. Peter Crisp Papers, Box 2 Folder 4.

79. John W. Wilson, *The New Venturers: Inside the High-Stakes World of Venture Capital* (Reading, MA: Addison-Wesley, 1985), 99.

80. Peter Crisp Papers, Box 1 Folder 3.

81. Peter Crisp Papers, Box 1 Folder 5.

82. Wilson, *The New Venturers,* 92–93.

83. Peter Crisp Papers, Box 1 Folder 5.

84. Wilson, *The New Venturers,* 94.

85. Peter Crisp Papers, Box 1 Folder 3.

86. Apple Computer, Confidential Private Placement Memorandum, November 18, 1977. Provided courtesy of Bill Sahlman.

87. Wilson, *The New Venturers,* 96.

88. Gompers and Lerner, *The Venture Capital Cycle,* 37.

89. Pension Simplification and Investment Rules Joint Hearings before the Subcommittee on Private Pension Plans and Fringe Benefits of the Committee on Finance and the Select Committee on Small Business. Ninety-fifth Congress. 8 (1977) (Testimony of Nancy L. Ross).

90. Harvard College v Amory (1830) 26 Mass (9 Pick) 446.

91. Briefing Session on the Small Business Investment Act of 1958, sponsored by the American Management Association, New York, December 1–2, 1958. Committee on Banking and Currency and Select Committee on Small Business. 569 (1959) (Testimony of William Elfers).

92. Robert C. Pozen, "The Prudent Person Rule and ERISA: A Legal Perspective," *Financial Analysts Journal* 33, no. 2 (1977): 30–35.

93. Pension Simplification and Investment Rules Joint Hearings before the Subcommittee on Private Pension Plans and Fringe Benefits of the Committee on Finance and the Select Committee on Small Business. Ninety-fifth Congress. 112 (1977) (Testimony of Stewart Greenfield).

94. Pension Simplification and Investment Rules Joint Hearings before the Subcommittee on Private Pension Plans and Fringe Benefits of the Committee on Finance and the Select Committee on Small Business. Ninety-Fifth Congress (1977), Opening Statement by Lloyd Bentsen, 11–12.

95. Pension Simplification and Investment Rules Joint Hearings before the Subcommittee on Private Pension Plans and Fringe Benefits of the Committee on Finance and the Select Com-

mittee on Small Business. Ninety-fifth Congress. 94 (1977) (Testimony of David T. Morgenthaler).

96. Elizabeth Popp Berman, *Creating the Market University: How Academic Science Became an Economic Engine* (Princeton, NJ: Princeton University Press, 2012), 73.

97. Michael E. Murphy, "Pension Plans and the Prospects of Corporate Self-Regulation," *DePaul Business & Commercial Law Journal* 5 (2006): 503–578, 508.

98. Paul A. Gompers and Josh Lerner, "What Drives Venture Capital Fundraising?" *Brookings Papers on Economic Activity Microeconomics* 29 (1999): 149–204, 166.

99. Testimony of David T. Morgenthaler, 98.

100. Steven A. Bank, *Anglo-American Corporate Taxation: Tracing the Common Roots of Divergent Approaches* (Cambridge: Cambridge University Press, 2011), 101.

101. William J. Federer, *The Interesting History of Income Tax,* Amerisearch Incorporated, 2004, 148.

102. James M. Poterba, "Venture Capital and Capital Gains Taxation," *Tax Policy and the Economy* 3 (1989): 47–67, 49.

103. Capital Gains Tax Bills: Hearings before the Subcommittee on Taxation and Debt Management Generally of the Committee on Finance. Ninety-fifth Congress. 15 (1978) (Testimony of William A. Steiger).

104. Capital Gains Tax Bills: Hearings before the Subcommittee on Taxation and Debt Management Generally of the Committee on Finance. Ninety-fifth Congress. 271 (1978) (Testimony of Robert Noyce).

105. Capital Gains Tax Bills: Hearings before the Subcommittee on Taxation and Debt Management Generally of the Committee on Finance. Ninety-fifth Congress. 273 (1978) (Testimony of E. F. Heizer, Jr.).

106. Capital Gains Tax Bills: Hearings before the Subcommittee on Taxation and Debt Management Generally of the Committee on Finance. Ninety-fifth Congress. 275 (1978) (Testimony of B. Kipling Hagopian).

107. Premus, "Venture Capital and Innovation: A Study."

108. Premus, "Venture Capital and Innovation: A Study," xi.

109. Morey Greenstein, interview by Carole Kolker.

110. Poterba, "Venture Capital and Capital Gains Taxation."

111. See for example, Ufuk Akcigit, Salomé Baslandze, and Stefanie Stantcheva, "Taxation and the International Mobility of Inventors," *American Economic Review* 106, no. 10 (2016): 2930–2981.

6. Silicon Valley and the Emergence of Investment Styles

1. Pension Simplification and Investment Rules Joint Hearings before the Subcommittee on Private Pension Plans and Fringe Benefits of the Committee on Finance and the Select Committee on Small Business. Ninety-fifth Congress. 119 (1977) (Testimony of David T. Morgenthaler).

2. See for example, A. L. Saxenian, *Regional Advantage* (Cambridge, MA: Harvard University Press, 1996); Timothy J. Sturgeon, "How Silicon Valley Came to Be," in *Understanding Silicon Valley: Anatomy of an Innovative Region,* ed. Martin Kenney (Stanford, CA: Stanford University Press, 2000); Chrisophe Lécuyer, *Making Silicon Valley: Innovation and the Growth*

of High Tech, 1930–1970 (Cambridge, MA: MIT Press, 2006); Arun Rao and Pietro Scaruffi, *A History of Silicon Valley: The Greatest Creation of Wealth in the History of the Planet*, 2nd ed. (Omniware Group, 2013).

3. Edward L. Glaeser, *Triumph of the City: How Our Greatest Invention Makes Us Richer, Smarter, Greener, Healthier, and Happier* (New York: Penguin, 2011), 31.

4. Bruce Cumings, *Dominion from Sea to Sea: Pacific Ascendancy and American Power* (New Haven, CT: Yale University Press, 2009), 445.

5. See for example, patent 2,269,456 for an "Electron Beam Oscillator," patented by William W. Hansen and Russell H. Varian, Stanford University, California, assignors to Board of Trustees of Stanford University. Filing date January 22, 1938.

6. Saxenian, *Regional Advantage*, 177.

7. Saxenian, *Regional Advantage*, 23–24.

8. Lécuyer, *Making Silicon Valley*, 250.

9. Walter Isaacson, *Steve Jobs* (New York: Simon and Schuster, 2011), 61.

10. John W. Wilson, *The New Venturers: Inside the High-Stakes World of Venture Capital* (Reading, MA: Addison-Wesley, 1985), 98.

11. Arthur Rock, "Arthur Rock and Co.," in *Done Deals: Venture Capitalists Tell Their Stories*, ed. Udayan Gupta (Boston: Harvard Business School Press, 2000), 142.

12. Sturgeon, "How Silicon Valley Came to Be," 16.

13. Arnold Thackray, David C. Brock, and Rachel Jones, *Moore's Law: The Life of Gordon Moore, Silicon Valley Quiet Revolutionary* (New York: Basic Books), 75.

14. Nathan Newman, *Net Loss: Internet Prophets, Private Profits, and the Costs to Community* (University Park: Pennsylvania State University Press, 2010), 92.

15. Olav Sorenson and Toby E. Stuart, "Syndication Networks and the Spatial Distribution of Venture Capital Investments," *American Journal of Sociology* 106, no. 6 (2001): 1546–1588.

16. Sturgeon, "How Silicon Valley Came to Be," 21.

17. Paul Rhode, "The Impact of World War Two Spending on the California Economy," in *The Way We Really Were: The Golden State in the Second Great War*, ed. Roger W. Lotchin (Urbana: University of Illinois Press, 2000), 94.

18. Stuart W. Leslie, "The Biggest 'Angel' of Them All: The Military and the Making of Silicon Valley," in *Understanding Silicon Valley: The Anatomy of an Entrepreneurial Region*, ed. Martin Kenney (Stanford, CA: Stanford University Press, 2000), 55.

19. Lécuyer, *Making Silicon Valley*, 172.

20. Leslie, "The Biggest 'Angel' of Them All," 49.

21. John E. Tilton, *International Diffusion of Technology: The Case of Semiconductors* (Washington, DC: Brookings Institution Press, 1971), 90–91, 218.

22. Lécuyer, *Making Silicon Valley*, 101.

23. Lécuyer, *Making Silicon Valley*, 55, 293.

24. Lécuyer, *Making Silicon Valley*, 63.

25. Leslie, "The Biggest 'Angel' of Them All," 53.

26. Lécuyer, *Making Silicon Valley*, 92; Leslie, "The Biggest 'Angel' of Them All," 55–56.

27. Rhode, "The Impact of World War Two Spending on the California Economy," 100.

28. Lécuyer, *Making Silicon Valley*, 295.

29. Lécuyer, *Making Silicon Valley*, 6.

30. Saxenian, *Regional Advantage,* 117.

31. Lécuyer, *Making Silicon Valley,* 172.

32. Lécuyer, *Making Silicon Valley,* 46–47.

33. Lécuyer, *Making Silicon Valley,* 11, 192.

34. Saxenian, *Regional Advantage,* 70.

35. Saxenian, *Regional Advantage,* 14.

36. Saxenian, *Regional Advantage,* 38–39.

37. Climate for Entrepreneurship and Innovation in the United States: Hearings before the Joint Economic Committee. Ninety-eighth Congress. 10 (1985) (Testimony of Robert Noyce).

38. Lécuyer, *Making Silicon Valley,* 16–26.

39. Daron Acemoglu, Ufuk Akcigit, and Murat Alp Celik, "Young, Restless and Creative: Openness to Disruption and Creative Innovations," NBER Working Paper No. 19894, National Bureau of Economic Research, February 2014, rev. August 2015.

40. Testimony of Robert Noyce, 10.

41. Lécuyer, *Making Silicon Valley,* 98.

42. Saxenian, *Regional Advantage,* 50.

43. Lécuyer, *Making Silicon Valley,* 41, 82–85.

44. Carola Frydman, "Rising through the Ranks: The Evolution of the Market for Corporate Executives, 1936–2003," *Journal of Economic History* 66, no. 2 (2006): 516–517.

45. Maryann P. Feldman, Lauren Lanahan, and Jennifer M. Miller, "Inadvertent Infrastructure and Regional Entrepreneurship Policy," in *Handbook of Research on Entrepreneurship and Regional Development,* ed. Michael Fritsch and R. E. Riggio (Cheltenham: Edward Elgar, 2011), 217–218.

46. Ronald Gilson, "The Legal Infrastructure of High Technology Industrial Districts: Silicon Valley, Route 128, and Covenants Not to Compete,"*New York University Law Review* 74, no. 3 (1999): 575–629; Matt Marx and Lee Fleming, "Non-Compete Agreements: Barriers to Entry . . . and Exit?" *Innovation Policy and the Economy* 12, no. 1 (2012): 39–64.

47. Arthur Rock, interview by Tom Nicholas, San Francisco, September 21, 2012.

48. William Lazonick, *Sustainable Prosperity in the New Economy? Business Organization and High-Tech Employment in the United States* (Kalamazoo, MI: W. E. Upjohn Institute for Employment Research, 2009), 42.

49. Wilson, *The New Venturers,* 32.

50. David A. Kaplan, "Gordon Moore's Journey," *Fortune,* September 24, 2012, 3.

51. Wilson, *The New Venturers,* 33.

52. Leslie Berlin, *The Man Behind the Microchip: Robert Noyce and the Invention of Silicon Valley* (New York: Oxford University Press, 2006), 76; Lécuyer, *Making Silicon Valley,* 166.

53. Wilson, *The New Venturers,* 33.

54. Berlin, *The Man Behind the Microchip,* 159.

55. Ross Knox Bassett, *To the Digital Age: Research Labs, Start-up Companies, and the Rise of MOS Technology* (Baltimore: Johns Hopkins University Press, 2002), 171.

56. William Lazonick, ed., *American Corporate Economy: Critical Perspectives on Business and Management* (New York: Routledge, 2002), Vol. 4, 188–189.

57. Wilson, *The New Venturers,* 32.

58. Arthur Rock, "Strategy vs. Tactics from a Venture Capitalist," *Harvard Business Review* 65, no. 6 (1987): 63–67, 63.

59. Transcript of a video interview at his San Francisco office in March 2001. Interviewer: Amy Blitz, HBS Director of Media Development for Entrepreneurial Management, http://www .hbs.edu/xentrepreneurs/pdf/arthurrock.pdf.

60. Wilson, *The New Venturers,* 35.

61. Michael Moritz, "Arthur Rock: The Best Long-Ball Hitter Around," *Time* 123, no. 4, January 23, 1984, 55.

62. Wilson, *The New Venturers,* 37.

63. Peter Crisp Papers, Baker Business Historical Collections, Business Manuscripts Mss: 784 1946–2008 C93, Box 3 Folder 1, Baker Library, Harvard Business School.

64. Moritz, "Arthur Rock."

65. "Venture Capitalist with a Solid Intuition," *Businessweek,* no. 2126, May 30, 1970, 102–103.

66. John Markoff, "An Evening with Legendary Venture Capitalist Arthur Rock, in Conversation with John Markoff," Computer History Museum, Catalog Number 102658253, May 1, 2007.

67. Wilson, *The New Venturers,* 36.

68. Charles D. Ellis, *Joe Wilson and the Creation of Xerox* (2006; Hoboken, NJ: John Wiley and Sons, 2011), 342.

69. Details of this investment were gained through personal email correspondence with Arthur Rock, March 11, 2013.

70. Wilson, *The New Venturers,* 37; Jeffrey L. Cruikshank, *Shaping the Waves: A History of Entrepreneurship at Harvard Business School* (Boston: Harvard Business School Press, 2005), 122; Lécuyer, *Making Silicon Valley,* 167.

71. Bassett, *To the Digital Age,* 173.

72. Rob Walker, Interview with Arthur Rock, Silicon Genesis Oral History Project, Department of Special Collections, Stanford University Libraries, recorded in San Francisco, CA, on November 11, 2002, https://silicongenesis.stanford.edu/transcripts/rock.htm.

73. Rock, "Arthur Rock and Co.," 144.

74. Berlin, *The Man Behind the Microchip,* 158.

75. Berlin, *The Man Behind the Microchip,* 166.

76. Berlin, *The Man Behind the Microchip,* 167.

77. Wilson, *The New Venturers,* 38.

78. Michael Moritz, *Return to the Little Kingdom: Steve Jobs, the Creation of Apple, and How It Changed the World* (London: Gerald Duckworth & Company, 2010), 139.

79. Richard S. Tedlow, *Andy Grove: The Life and Times of an American Business Icon* (New York: Penguin, 2007).

80. Tedlow, *Andy Grove,* 133.

81. Felda Hardymon, Tom Nicholas, and Liz Kind, "Arthur Rock," HBS no. 813-138 (Boston: Harvard Business School Publishing, 2013).

82. Berlin, *The Man Behind the Microchip,* 255.

83. Moritz, "Arthur Rock."

84. "Venture Capitalist with a Solid Intuition."

85. Wilson, *The New Venturers,* 39.

86. Berlin, *The Man Behind the Microchip*, 250.

87. Apple Computer, Confidential Private Placement Memorandum, November 18, 1977, 9. Provided by Bill Sahlman.

88. Michael B. Becraft, *Steve Jobs: A Biography* (Westport: ABC-CLIO, 2014), 48.

89. Rock, "Arthur Rock and Co.," 145–146.

90. Wilson, *The New Venturers*, 40.

91. Arthur Rock, interview by Tom Nicholas.

92. Peter Henig, "The Old Guard," *Venture Capital Journal*, October 2002, 30.

93. Richard L. Stern, "Solid as a Rock?" *Forbes* 133, no. 5, February 27, 1984, 89.

94. Wilson, *The New Venturers*, 85.

95. Anthony Bianco, *The Big Lie: Spying, Scandal, and Ethical Collapse at Hewlett Packard* (New York: PublicAffairs, 2010), 17.

96. Bianco, *The Big Lie*, 31.

97. Bianco, *The Big Lie*, 22.

98. Bianco, *The Big Lie*, 21.

99. Bianco, *The Big Lie*, 21.

100. Wilson, *The New Venturers*, 74–75.

101. Wilson, *The New Venturers*, 77.

102. Martha L. Reiner, "The Transformation of Venture Capital: A History of Venture Capital Organizations in the United States" (Ph.D. diss., University of California, Berkeley, 1989), 229.

103. Thomas J. Perkins, *Valley Boy: The Education of Tom Perkins* (New York: Gotham Books, 2007), 102.

104. Wilson, *The New Venturers*, 69.

105. Kate Litvak, "Venture Capital Limited Partnership Agreements: Understanding Compensation Arrangements," *University of Chicago Law Review* 76, no. 1 (2009): 161–218.

106. Paul A. Gompers and Josh Lerner, *The Venture Capital Cycle*, 2nd ed. (Cambridge, MA: MIT Press, 2004), 23.

107. Wilson, *The New Venturers*, 77.

108. Paul Gompers, "The Rise and Fall of Venture Capital," *Business and Economic History* 23, no. 2 (1994): 1–24, 11.

109. Perkins, *Valley Boy*, 102.

110. Wilson, *The New Venturers*, 78.

111. Perkins, *Valley Boy*, 107.

112. "How Kleiner Perkins Flies So High," *BusinessWeek*, no. 2774, January 24, 1983, 66–68.

113. William D. Bygrave and Jeffry A. Timmons, *Venture Capital at the Crossroads* (Boston: Harvard Business School Press, 1992), 108.

114. Wilson, *The New Venturers*, 79.

115. "A Computer That Won't Shut Down," *BusinessWeek*, no. 2410, December 8, 1975, 81–82.

116. Perkins, *Valley Boy*, 118.

117. Wilson, *The New Venturers*, 70.

118. Perkins, *Valley Boy*, 139.

119. Roger Lewin, "Profile of a Genetic Engineer," *New Scientist*, September 28, 1978.

120. Iain Cockburn, "The Changing Structure of the Pharmaceutical Industry," *Health Affairs* 23, no. 1 (2004): 10–22.

121. Gary P. Pisano, *Science Business: The Promise, the Reality, and the Future of Biotech* (Boston: Harvard Business School Press, 2006).

122. Lewin, "Profile of a Genetic Engineer."

123. Sally Smith Hughes, *Genentech: The Beginnings of Biotech* (Chicago: University of Chicago Press, 2011), 1–19.

124. Bianco, *The Big Lie,* 50.

125. Wilson, *The New Venturers,* 80.

126. Bianco, *The Big Lie,* 50.

127. Hughes, *Genentech,* 41–42, 158.

128. Hughes, *Genentech,* 47.

129. Hughes, *Genentech,* 75.

130. Thomas J. Perkins, "Thomas J. Perkins, Kleiner Perkins, Venture Capital, and the Chairmanship of Genentech, 1976–1995," an oral history conducted in 2001 by Glenn E. Bugos for the Regional Oral History Office, The Bancroft Library, University of California, Berkeley, 2002.

131. Thomas J. Perkins, interview by Glenn E. Bugos, 2002.

132. Hughes, *Genentech,* 63.

133. Hughes, *Genentech,* 85–103.

134. Thomas J. Perkins, interview by Glenn E. Bugos, 2002.

135. Perkins, "Thomas J. Perkins, Kleiner Perkins," 9.

136. Wilson, *The New Venturers,* 81–82.

137. Cruikshank, *Shaping the Waves,* 139.

138. Email correspondence between Tom Perkins and Felda Hardymon, March 14, 2013. Provided by Felda Hardymon.

139. "Donald T. Valentine, Early Bay Area Venture Capitalists: Shaping the Economic and Business Landscape," interviewed by Sally Smith Hughes, 2009, transcript at Regional Oral History Office, The Bancroft Library, University of California, Berkeley, http://digitalassets.lib .berkeley.edu/roho/ucb/text/valentine_donald.pdf, p. 63.

140. Wilson, *The New Venturers,* 60.

141. Moritz, *Return to the Little Kingdom,* 107.

142. Rob Walker, "Interview with Don Valentine," Silicon Genesis Oral History Project, Department of Special Collections, Stanford University Libraries, recorded at Menlo Park, CA, on April 21, 2004.

143. "Peaks and Valleys," *Inc.,* May 1985.

144. Lécuyer, *Making Silicon Valley,* 270–271.

145. "Don Valentine," *Forbes,* October 1993, 135–137.

146. Wilson, *The New Venturers,* 61.

147. "Donald T. Valentine, Early Bay Area Venture Capitalists," 22.

148. Charles D. Ellis, *Capital: The Story of Long-Term Investment Excellence* (Hoboken, NJ: Wiley, 2005), 132.

149. Ellis, *Capital,* 132.

150. Don Valentine, "Sequoia Capital," in *Done Deals: Venture Capitalists Tell Their Stories,* ed. Udayan Gupta (Boston: Harvard Business School Press, 2000), 169.

151. Ellis, *Capital,* 137.
152. Ellis, *Capital,* 137.
153. Lily Fang, Victoria Ivashina, and Josh Lerner, "The Disintermediation of Financial Markets: Direct Investing in Private Equity," *Journal of Financial Economics* 116, no. 1 (2015): 160–178.
154. Ellis, *Capital,* 136n35.
155. Wilson, *The New Venturers,* 62–63.
156. Wilson, *The New Venturers,* 64.
157. Wilson, *The New Venturers,* 63–64.
158. Don Valentine, "Target Big Markets," speech, Stanford Graduate School of Business View from the Top Series, Palo Alto, CA, October 5, 2010, https://www.youtube.com/watch?v=nKN-abRJMEw&list=PL5C14B375A7F2FEA8&t=0s&index=84 (quote at 33:33).
159. Moritz, *Return to the Little Kingdom,* 108.
160. Wilson, *The New Venturers,* 65.
161. Wilson, *The New Venturers,* 63; "Peaks and Valleys."
162. Michael S. Malone, *The Big Score: The Billion-Dollar Story of Silicon Valley* (Garden City, NY: Doubleday, 1985), 29.
163. David Bunnell, with Adam Brate, *Making the Cisco Connection: The Story Behind the Real Internet Superpower* (New York: John Wiley and Sons, 2000), 8–10.
164. Shane M. Greenstein, *How the Internet Became Commercial: Innovation, Privatization, and the Birth of a New Network* (Princeton, NJ: Princeton University Press, 2015), 127.
165. Bunnell and Brate, *Making the Cisco Connection,* 11.
166. "Peaks and Valleys."
167. Jeffrey Zygmont, *The VC Way: Investment Secrets from the Wizards of Venture Capital* (New York: Basic Books, 2002), 27.
168. "Peaks and Valleys."

7. High-Tech, an Evolving Ecosystem, and Diversity during the 1980s

1. "Peaks and Valleys," *Inc.,* May 1985.
2. "Venture Capital," *Dun's Review,* February 1977.
3. Robert S. Harris, T. I. M. Jenkinson, and Steven N. Kaplan, "Private Equity Performance: What Do We Know?" *Journal of Finance* 69, no. 5 (2014): 1851–1882.
4. Paul Gompers, "The Rise and Fall of Venture Capital," *Business and Economic History* 23, no. 2 (1994): 1–24, 2.
5. Jerry Neumann, "Heat Death: Venture Capital in the 1980s," *Reaction Wheel* (blog), January 8, 2015, http://reactionwheel.net/2015/01/80s-vc.html.
6. Richard S. Tedlow, *Andy Grove: The Life and Times of an American Business Icon* (New York: Portfolio, 2006), 184.
7. Stephen Manes and Paul Andrews, *Gates: How Microsoft's Mogul Reinvented an Industry—and Made Himself the Richest Man in America* (New York: Simon and Schuster Touchstone, 1994), 176.
8. John W. Wilson, *The New Venturers: Inside the High-Stakes World of Venture Capital* (Reading, MA: Addison-Wesley, 1985), 197.
9. "Lotus," *PC Magazine,* June 25, 1985.

10. William H. Janeway, *Doing Capitalism in the Innovation Economy: Markets, Speculation and the State* (Cambridge: Cambridge University Press, 2012), 61–64; "Venture Capitalist Fred Adler Hunts Ideas That Pay Off Ten to One," *New York Magazine,* June 25, 1984.

11. "The Billion-Dollar Gamble," *Inc.,* September 1981.

12. "Stoking the Micro Fire: Venture Capitalists Affect What You Can Buy," *InfoWorld,* December 3, 1984.

13. Wilson, *The New Venturers,* 71.

14. William A. Sahlman and Howard H. Stevenson, "Capital Market Myopia," *Journal of Business Venturing* 1, no. 1 (1985): 7–30.

15. Wilson, *The New Venturers,* 195.

16. "Stoking the Micro Fire."

17. "Stoking the Micro Fire."

18. Wilson, *The New Venturers,* 196.

19. "Stoking the Micro Fire."

20. Paul A. Gompers, "Grandstanding in the Venture Capital Industry," *Journal of Financial Economics* 42, no. 1 (1996): 133–156.

21. "Stoking the Micro Fire."

22. Stanley E. Pratt, "Soothsayers Look at Venture Capital Industry," *Venture Capital Journal,* May 1984, 1–2.

23. "Tough Times Ahead for Venture Capitalists," *Boston Globe,* December 9, 1984.

24. William E. Wetzel, "The Informal Venture Capital Market: Aspects of Scale and Market Efficiency," *Journal of Business Venturing* 2, no. 4 (1987): 299–313.

25. Amar Bhide, *The Origin and Evolution of New Businesses* (Oxford: Oxford University Press, 2000).

26. Jay Ritter, "IPO Dataset," 2016, University of Florida, Warrington College of Business, https://site.warrington.ufl.edu/ritter/ipo-data/, accessed December 2016.

27. William A. Sahlman, "The Structure and Governance of Venture-Capital Organizations," *Journal of Financial Economics* 27, no. 2 (1990): 473–521, 478.

28. Paul A. Gompers and Josh Lerner, "The Determinants of Corporate Venture Capital Success: Organizational Structure, Incentives, and Complementarities," NBER Working Paper No. 6725, National Bureau of Economic Research, September 1998, 160–161.

29. "The Folks Who Brought You Apple," *Fortune,* January 12, 1981; Ritter, "IPO Dataset."

30. "Hambrecht & Quist Loses Its Edge," *New York Times,* March 31, 1985.

31. "Bleeding Edge of Technology: New-Issue Specialist Hambrecht & Quist Feels the Pain," *Barron's National Business and Financial Weekly,* April 23, 1984.

32. Ralph King, Jr., "The Money Corner," *Forbes,* March 5, 1990, 39.

33. Michael Moritz, *Return to the Little Kingdom: Steve Jobs, the Creation of Apple, and How It Changed the World* (London: Gerald Duckworth & Company, 2010), 177.

34. Wilson, *The New Venturers,* 121.

35. William J. Torpey and Jerry A. Viscione, "Mezzanine Money for Smaller Businesses," *Harvard Business Review* 65, no. 3 (1987): 116–119.

36. Ann Leamon and Felda Hardymon, "Silicon Valley Bank," HBS no. 800-332 (Boston: Harvard Business School Publishing, 2001).

37. Joyce Lane, "Banking on High Tech," *The California Executive,* October 1987.

38. "Silicon Valley's High-Tech Financier Lender Finds Success in a Field with Few Competitors," *American Banker,* December 1987.

39. Paul A. Gompers, "Xedia and Silicon Valley Bank (a)," HBS no. 298-119 (Boston: Harvard Business School Publishing, 2001), 9.

40. Gary Dushnitsky, "Corporate Venture Capital in the Twenty-First Century: An Integral Part of Firms' Innovation Toolkit," in *The Oxford Handbook of Venture Capital,* ed. Douglas Cumming (Oxford: Oxford University Press, 2012), 162.

41. William Copulsky, "New Venture Management," in *Successful Product and Business Development,* ed. N. Giragosian (New York: Taylor and Francis, 1978), 69.

42. Wilson, *The New Venturers,* 152.

43. Copulsky, "New Venture Management," 68.

44. Wilson, *The New Venturers,* 149.

45. Sally Smith Hughes, *Genentech: The Beginnings of Biotech* (Chicago: University of Chicago Press, 2011), 105.

46. Paul A. Gompers and Josh Lerner, *The Venture Capital Cycle,* 2nd ed. (Cambridge, MA: MIT Press, 2004), 135.

47. G. Felda Hardymon, Mark J. DeNino, and Malcolm S. Salter, "When Corporate Venture Capital Doesn't Work," *Harvard Business Review* 61, no. 3 (May / June 1983): 114–120.

48. George L. Hegg, "A Corporate View of Venture Capital," in *Managing R&D and Technology: Building the Necessary Bridges,* ed. James K. Brown and Susan Henriksen (New York: Conference Board, 1990).

49. Ian C. Yates and Edward B. Roberts, "Initiating Successful Corporate Venture Capital Investments," Working Paper #3308-91-BPS, Alfred P. Sloan School of Management, MIT, Cambridge, MA, June 1991, 29, https://dspace.mit.edu/bitstream/handle/1721.1/48257 /initiatingsucces00yate.pdf?s.

50. "Small, High Technology Firms and Innovation, Report." United States Congress, House, Committee on Science and Technology, Subcommittee on Investigations and Oversight of the Committee on Science and Technology. Ninety-sixth Congress (Washington, DC: G.P.O., 1980).

51. Elliott C. Kulakowski and Lynne U. Chronister, *Research Administration and Management* (Burlington, MA: Jones and Bartlett Learning, 2008), 866.

52. S. 881, the Small Business Innovation Research Act of 1981. Hearing before the Subcommittee on Innovation and Technology of the Committee on Small Business. Ninety-seventh Congress. 104 (1981) (Testimony of James L. Watts).

53. Charles W. Wessner, *SBIR Program Diversity and Assessment Challenges: Report of a Symposium* (Washington, DC: National Academies Press, 2004), 89.

54. Josh Lerner, "The Government as Venture Capitalist: The Long-Run Impact of the SBIR Program," *Journal of Business* 72, no. 3 (1999): 285–318.

55. Sabrina T. Howell, "Financing Innovation: Evidence from R&D Grants," *American Economic Review* 107, no. 4 (2017): 1136–1164.

56. Josh Lerner, "Arch Venture Partners: November 1995," HBS no. 295-105 (Boston: Harvard Business School Publishing, 1995).

57. Richard P. Shanley, *Financing Technology's Frontier: Decision-Making Models for Investors and Advisors,* 2nd ed. (Hoboken, NJ: Wiley, 2004), 45.

58. Chuck Newhall, email correspondence with Tom Nicholas, August 11, 2017.

59. Peter Crisp Papers, Baker Business Historical Collections, Business Manuscripts Mss: 784 1946–2008 C93, Box 3 Folders 6–7, Baker Library, Harvard Business School.

60. Robert Premus, "Venture Capital and Innovation: A Study," prepared for Joint Economic Committee, US Congress, 98th Session, December 28, 1984 (Washington DC: US GPO, 1985), https://www.jec.senate.gov/reports/98th%20Congress/Venture%20Capital%20and%20Innovation%20(1316).pdf.

61. Steven N. Kaplan and Josh Lerner, "Venture Capital Data: Opportunities and Challenges," NBER Working Paper No. 22500, National Bureau of Economic Research, August 2016.

62. "The Two-Tier Market for Venture Firms," *Institutional Investor,* September 1984.

63. "Insurers Become More Aggressive with Venture Capital—Some Major Firms Form Separate Units Where Managers Share Profits," *Wall Street Journal,* February 10, 1987.

64. Michelle R. Garfinkel, "The Causes and Consequences of Leveraged Buyouts," *Federal Reserve Bank of St. Louis Review* (1989), 23–34.

65. Gompers, "The Rise and Fall of Venture Capital," 17.

66. Harris, Jenkinson, and Kaplan, "Private Equity Performance," 1874.

67. Ralph King, Jr., "The Money Corner," *Forbes,* March 5, 1990, 39.

68. Charles Newhall, interview by Tom Nicholas, 2012.

69. New Enterprise Associates Annual Report, 1977, provided by Chuck Newhall.

70. Spencer E. Ante, *Creative Capital: Georges Doriot and the Birth of Venture Capital* (Boston: Harvard Business Press, 2008), 7.

71. Wilson, *The New Venturers,* 121.

72. C. Richard Kramlich, "Venture Capital Greats: A Conversation with C. Richard Kramlich," interviewed by Mauree Jane Perry on August 31, 2006, in San Francisco, California, National Venture Capital Association, Arlington, Virginia.

73. Michael Ewens and Matthew Rhodes-Kropf, "Is a VC Partnership Greater Than the Sum of Its Partners?" *Journal of Finance* 70, no. 3 (2015): 1081–1113.

74. Wilson, *The New Venturers,* 123.

75. Chuck Newhall, interview by Tom Nicholas, 2012.

76. Hegg, "A Corporate View of Venture Capital," 29.

77. Chuck Newhall, interview by Tom Nicholas, 2012.

78. Wilson, *The New Venturers,* 121.

79. Chuck Newhall, interview by Tom Nicholas, 2012.

80. Chuck Newhall, interview by Tom Nicholas, 2012.

81. Thomas Hellmann and Manju Puri, "Venture Capital and the Professionalization of Start-up Firms: Empirical Evidence," *Journal of Finance* 57, no. 1 (2002): 169–197.

82. Frank Bonsal, interview by Tom Nicholas, Lutherville, Maryland, December, 2012.

83. Chuck Newhall, interview by Tom Nicholas, 2012.

84. Wilson, *The New Venturers,* 123–124.

85. Kramlich, interview by Mauree Jane Perry, 2008.

86. Frank Bonsal, interview by Tom Nicholas, 2012.

87. Chuck Newhall, interview by Tom Nicholas, 2012.

88. Ewens and Rhodes-Kropf, "Is a VC Partnership Greater Than the Sum of Its Partners?"

89. Wilson, *The New Venturers,* 84.

90. "Symantex Tackles Artificial Intelligence," *InfoWorld,* May 6, 1985.
91. "Kleiner Perkins Names Entrepreneur, Vinod Khosla, Ninth General Partner," *Wall Street Journal,* January 18, 1988.
92. "How Kleiner Perkins Flies So High," *BusinessWeek,* no. 2774, January 24, 1983, 66–68.
93. "Two Top Venture Capitalists Trim Roles: Move by Rosen and Sevin Illustrates a Trend," *Wall Street Journal,* July 27, 1987.
94. "Donald T. Valentine, Early Bay Area Venture Capitalists: Shaping the Economic and Business Landscape," interviewed by Sally Smith Hughes, 2009, transcript at Regional Oral History Office, The Bancroft Library, University of California, Berkeley, 2010, http://digitalassets.lib .berkeley.edu/roho/ucb/text/valentine_donald.pdf.
95. "Two Top Venture Capitalists Trim Roles"; "The Networker," *New Yorker,* August 11, 1997.
96. "How Do Venture Firms Pick a Winner? Carefully," *Electronic Business,* December 10, 1988.
97. "The Networker."
98. Chuck Newhall, interview by Tom Nicholas, 2012.
99. Chuck Newhall, interview by Tom Nicholas, 2017.
100. Bruce D. Meyer, "Why Are There So Few Black Entrepreneurs?" NBER Working Paper No. 3537, National Bureau of Economic Research, December 1990.
101. Paul A. Gompers and Sophie Q. Wang, "Diversity in Innovation," NBER Working Paper No. 23082, National Bureau of Economic Research, January 2017.
102. "Ann L. Winblad, Early Bay Area Venture Capitalists: Shaping the Economic and Business Landscape," interviewed by Sally Smith Hughes, 2012, transcript at Regional Oral History Office, The Bancroft Library, University of California, Berkeley, 2012, http://digitalassets.lib .berkeley.edu/roho/ucb/text/winblad_ann.pdf, 7.
103. "Q&A: Ann Winblad," *InfoWorld,* June 11, 1984.
104. "Ann L. Winblad, Early Bay Area Venture Capitalists," 18–21.
105. "Stoking the Micro Fire."
106. Jeffrey L. Seglin, "Can Old Boys Change?" *Venture* 8, no. 7 (1986): 60–66, 62.
107. Peter Finch, "Cigar Chomping Venture Capitalist Named Francine," *Businessweek,* July 20, 1987.
108. Seglin, "Can Old Boys Change?" 62.
109. "This New York Woman's Work Is Done with Venture Capital," *Chicago Tribune,* October 28th, 1985.
110. Seglin, "Can Old Boys Change?" 62.
111. "Venture Capital—A Special Background Report on Trends in Industry and Finance," *Wall Street Journal,* May 2, 1985.
112. Seglin, "Can Old Boys Change?" 61.
113. Seglin, "Can Old Boys Change?" 60.
114. Gompers and Wang, "Diversity in Innovation," 45.
115. Marianne Bertrand, Claudia Goldin, and Lawrence F. Katz, "Dynamics of the Gender Gap for Young Professionals in the Financial and Corporate Sectors," *American Economic Journal: Applied Economics* 2, no. 3 (2010): 228–255.
116. Seglin, "Can Old Boys Change?" 66.
117. Seglin, "Can Old Boys Change?" 62.

118. "Women in STEM Occupations: 1970 to 2011," US Census Bureau, US Department of Commerce, Washington, DC, 2013, https://www.census.gov/content/dam/Census/newsroom/releases/2013/cb13-162_stem_female.pdf.

119. Andy White, "Harvard, 4 Other Schools, Make Up Most MBA at Private Equity & Venture Capital Firms," Pitchbook, Seattle, September 18, 2013, https://pitchbook.com/news/articles/harvard-4-other-schools-make-up-most-mbas-at-pe-vc-firms.

120. Waverly W. Ding, Fiona Murray, and Toby E. Stuart, "From Bench to Board: Gender Differences in University Scientists' Participation in Corporate Scientific Advisory Boards," *Academy of Management Journal* 56, no. 3 (2012): 1443–1464.

121. Udayan Gupta and Christopher J. Chipello, "Cash Pours Into Venture-Capital Funds, But Investors Are Increasingly Selective," *Wall Street Journal*, April 18, 1988, 9.

122. National Venture Capital Association, Address by Paul Bancroft III, May 8, 1987, provided by Felda Hardymon.

8. The Big Bubble

1. NVCA, "The National Venture Capital Assocation Yearbook 2011" (New York: Thomson Reuters, 2011), 20.

2. Preqin Venture Capital Database, accessed 2016.

3. Paul A. Gompers and Josh Lerner, *The Money of Invention: How Venture Capital Creates New Wealth* (Boston: Harvard Business School Press, 2001), 61–84.

4. Marc Andreessen, "Why Software Is Eating the World," *Wall Street Journal,* August 20, 2011.

5. Carlota Perez, *Technological Revolutions and Financial Capital* (Cheltenham: Edward Elgar Publishing, 2003), 118.

6. NVCA, "The National Venture Capital Assocation Yearbook 2011," 21.

7. William A. Sahlman, "Risk and Reward in Venture Capital," HBS no. 811-036 (Boston: Harvard Business School Publishing, 2010), 2.

8. William Shockley, *Electrons and Holes in Semiconductors: With Applications to Transistor Electronics* (New York: Van Nostrand, 1950; repr. Huntington, NY: Robert E. Krieger, 1976).

9. Michael Mandel, "The Triumph of the New Economy," *BusinessWeek,* December 30, 1996.

10. Samuel Kortum and Josh Lerner, "What Is Behind the Recent Surge in Patenting?" *Research Policy* 28, no. 1 (1999): 1–22.

11. Gary Dushnitsky, "Corporate Venture Capital in the Twenty-First Century: An Integral Part of Firms' Innovation Toolkit," in *The Oxford Handbook of Venture Capital*, ed. Douglas Cumming (Oxford: Oxford University Press, 2012), 163.

12. Shane M. Greenstein, *How the Internet Became Commercial: Innovation, Privatization, and the Birth of a New Network* (Princeton, NJ: Princeton University Press, 2015).

13. Steve Lohr, *Go To: The Story of the Math Majors, Bridge Players, Engineers, Chess Wizards, Maverick Scientists, and Iconoclasts* (New York: Basic Books, 2008), 59–61.

14. Pamela Samuelson and Hal Varian, "The 'New Economy' and Information Technology Policy," in ed. Jeffrey A. Frankel, Peter R. Orszag, *American Economic Policy in the 1990s* (Cambridge, MA: MIT Press, 2002), 361–412, 365.

15. Greenstein, *How the Internet Became Commercial,* 104.

16. Lohr, *Go To,* 204.

17. Greenstein, *How the Internet Became Commercial*, 296–297.

18. "Cascade Communications Data Transmission Switches," *Fortune*, July 8, 1996.

19. Stefan H. Thomke, *Experimentation Matters: Unlocking the Potential of New Technologies for Innovation* (Boston: Harvard Business School Press, 2003), 45.

20. Millennium Pharmaceuticals S1 filed with the Securities and Exchange Commission, EDGAR Online, May 1996, 42.

21. Gary P. Pisano, *Science Business: The Promise, the Reality, and the Future of Biotech* (Boston: Harvard Business School Press, 2006).

22. Jay Ritter, "IPO Dataset," University of Florida, Warrington College of Business, https://site.warrington.ufl.edu/ritter/ipo-data/, accessed December 2016.

23. Robert S. Harris, T. I. M. Jenkinson, and Steven N. Kaplan, "Private Equity Performance: What Do We Know?" *Journal of Finance* 69, no. 5 (2014): 1851–1882, 1864.

24. Josh Lerner and Jay Light, "Yale University Investments Office," HBS no. 296-040 (Boston: Harvard Business School Publishing,1995), 8.

25. Daniel P. Mosteller, "Venture Capital Brings Harvard Riches," *Harvard Crimson*, April 18, 2000.

26. Kate Litvak, "Venture Capital Limited Partnership Agreements: Understanding Compensation Arrangements," *University of Chicago Law Review* 76, no. 1 (2009): 161–218, 161.

27. Litvak, "Venture Capital Limited Partnership Agreements," 178.

28. Dan Primack, "The Big Squeeze Part II: How VC Firms Are Coping," *Venture Capital Journal*, May 1, 2002, 27, 29+, 29.

29. Reports of the United States Tax Court. Todd A. and Carolyn D. Dagres, Petitioners v. Commissioner of Internal Revenue, Respondent Docket no. 15523–08. Filed March 28, 2011.

30. Molly Knight Raskin, *No Better Time: The Brief, Remarkable Life of Danny Lewin, the Genius Who Transformed the Internet* (Boston: Da Capo Press, 2013), 107.

31. Scott Woolley, "Building the Infinite Internet," *Forbes* 179, no. 9, April 23, 2007.

32. "The Networker," *New Yorker*, August 11, 1997.

33. Yael V. Hochberg, Alexander Ljungqvist, and Yang Lu, "Whom You Know Matters: Venture Capital Networks and Investment Performance," *Journal of Finance* 62, no. 1 (2007): 251–301.

34. For a more detailed account of Netscape's origins see, Michael Lewis, *The New New Thing: A Silicon Valley Story* (New York: W. W. Norton, 1999).

35. Jim Clark, with Owen Edwards, *Netscape Time: The Making of the Billion-Dollar Start-up That Took on Microsoft* (New York: St. Martin's Press, 2000), 7.

36. Netscape S1 filed with the Securities and Exchange Commission, June 1995, 43.

37. Clark, *Netscape Time*, 8.

38. "The Networker."

39. Clark, *Netscape Time*, 125.

40. Clark, *Netscape Time*, 7, 25.

41. Clark, *Netscape Time*, 125.

42. Clark, *Netscape Time*, 76–77.

43. Andrew Metrick and Ayako Yasuda, *Venture Capital and the Finance of Innovation*, 2nd ed. (New York: John Wiley & Sons, 2010), 85.

44. Karen Angel, *Inside Yahoo!: Reinvention and the Road Ahead* (New York: John Wiley and Sons, 2002), 18–19.

45. Greenstein, *How the Internet Became Commercial*, 247.

46. "Way out There," *Forbes,* May 12, 2003.

47. David A. Vise and Mark Malseed, *The Google Story* (New York: Delta Trade Paperbacks, 2006), 63–65.

48. Sahlman, "Risk and Reward in Venture Capital," 3.

49. William R. Kerr, Ramana Nanda, and Matthew Rhodes-Kropf, "Entrepreneurship as Experimentation," *Journal of Economic Perspectives* 28, no. 3 (2014): 25–48, 26.

50. Greenstein, *How the Internet Became Commercial,* 11.

51. David F. Swensen, *Unconventional Success: A Fundamental Approach to Personal Investment* (New York: Free Press, 2005), 141.

52. Sahlman, "Risk and Reward in Venture Capital," 3.

53. Melanie Warner and Jane Hodges, "Inside the Silicon Valley Money Machine," *Fortune* 138, no. 8 (October 26, 1998): 128–140.

54. National Venture Capital Association Address by Paul Bancroft III, May 8, 1987, provided by Felda Hardymon.

55. NVCA, "The National Venture Capital Assocation Yearbook 2011," 17, 27.

56. Dushnitsky, "Corporate Venture Capital," 165.

57. Sahlman, "Risk and Reward in Venture Capital," 3.

58. Gary Rivlin and Lark Park, "Fallen VC Idols," *The Industry Standard,* May 21, 2001.

59. "Torrent of Venture Capital Financings in 1999 Outstrips '96, '97, '98 Totals Combined," *PR Newswire,* February 7, 2000.

60. "Torrent of Venture Capital Financings."

61. Rivlin and Park, "Fallen VC Idols."

62. Scott MacDonald, "The Devil's in the Details of the New U.S. Economy," *Electronic Engineering Times,* March 20, 2000.

63. Dan Primack, "The Big Squeeze Part I: After Expanding for Seven Years . . . ," *Venture Capital Journal,* May 1, 2002, 20–26, 20.

64. Malcolm Baker, "Essays in Financial Economics" (Ph.D. diss., Harvard University, 2000), 1.

65. Elizabeth A. Clancy and Andrew N. Rowan, "Companion Animal Demographics in the United States: A Historical Perspective," in *The State of the Animals II: 2003,* ed. Deborah J. Salem and Andrew N. Rowan (Washington, DC: Humane Society Press, 2003) 9–26, 10.

66. Thomas Eisenmann, "Petstore.Com," HBS no. 801044 (Boston: Harvard Business School Publishing, 2000), 9.

67. Josh Newman, interview by Tom Nicholas, Oakland, CA, April, 2009.

68. Pets.com S1 filed with the Securities and Exchange Commission, December 1999, 41, 45.

69. Josh Newman, interview by Tom Nicholas, 2009.

70. Pets.com S1 filed with the Securities and Exchange Commission, December 1999, 9.

71. John McDonough and Karen Egolf, *The Advertising Age Encyclopedia of Advertising* (Abingdon: Taylor & Francis, 2015), 515.

72. Jack Willoughby, "Burning Up," *Barron's,* March 20, 2000.

73. Matthew Zook, *The Geography of the Internet Industry: Venture Capital, Dot-Coms, and Local Knowledge* (Malden, MA: Blackwell, 2005), 78.

74. Melanie Warner, "Nice Work If You Can Get It," *Fortune* 140, no. 11, December 6, 1999.

75. Andreessen, "Why Software Is Eating the World."

76. Greenstein, *How the Internet Became Commercial,* 391.

77. Josh Newman, interview by Tom Nicholas, 2009.

78. Ethan Lieber and Chad Syverson, "Online versus Offline Competition," in *The Oxford Handbook of the Digital Economy*, ed. Martin Peitz and Joel Waldfogel (Oxford: Oxford University Press, 2012), 191.

79. Christiaan Hogendorn, "Excessive(?) Entry of National Telecom Networks, 1990–2001," *Telecommunications Policy* 35, no. 11 (2011): 920–932.

80. Ramana Nanda and Matthew Rhodes-Kropf, "Financing Risk and Innovation," *Management Science* 63:4 (April 2017), 901–918.

81. Steve Papa, comments at Silicon Valley Bank CEO Summit, New York, NY, April 27, 2012, https://www.youtube.com/watch?v=SiYOVChiDvA (at 3:49).

82. William H. Janeway, *Doing Capitalism in the Innovation Economy: Markets, Speculation and the State* (Cambridge: Cambridge University Press, 2012), 188.

83. Ryan Mac, "From Doghouse to Penthouse," *Forbes* 196, no. 4, September 8, 2015.

84. "Down in the Valley," *Financial Times*, May 27, 2002.

85. Kailash Sundaram, "Faulty Ratings: How Analysts Fueled the Internet Bubble," unpublished ms, July 31, 2017, https://projects.iq.harvard.edu/files/lead/files/faulty_ratings_-_how_analysts_fueled_the_internet_bubble.pdf.

86. Roger Lowenstein, *Origins of the Crash: The Great Bubble and Its Undoing* (New York: Penguin Press, 2004), 112; Randall Smith, *The Prince of Silicon Valley: Frank Quattrone and the Dot-Com Bubble* (New York: St. Martin's Press, 2010), 125.

87. Eli Ofek and Matthew Richardson, "Dotcom Mania: The Rise and Fall of Internet Stock Prices," *Journal of Finance* 58, no. 3 (2003): 1113–1137.

88. Zook, *The Geography of the Internet Industry*, 125–128.

89. Josh Newman, interview by Tom Nicholas, 2009.

90. Primack, "The Big Squeeze Part I," 23.

91. Primack, "The Big Squeeze Part I," 23.

92. Ann Grimes, "Venture Capitalists Get 'Clawed': Funds Brace for Demands by Investors for Payments under Partnership Provisos," *Wall Street Journal* (Europe Edition) December 11, 2002, M1.

93. "A Desert Wind Blows Down Sand Hill Road," *Financial Times*, October 3, 2001.

94. Peter Henig, "The Old Guard," *Venture Capital Journal*, October 2002, 26.

95. Rivlin and Park, "Fallen VC Idols."

96. Primack, "The Big Squeeze Part I," 21.

97. Andreessen, "Why Software Is Eating the World."

Epilogue

1. David F. Swensen, *Unconventional Success: A Fundamental Approach to Personal Investment* (New York: Free Press, 2005), 141.

2. Robert S. Harris, T. I. M. Jenkinson, and Steven N. Kaplan, "Private Equity Performance: What Do We Know?" *Journal of Finance* 69, no. 5 (2014): 1851–1882, 1864.

3. Note that this method is only a rough approximation. It will be distorted, for example, if the benchmark return is negative.

4. "Space-Age Risk Capitalist," *Time* 74, no. 8, August 24, 1959.

5. Arthur Korteweg and Morten Sorensen, "Skill and Luck in Private Equity Performance," *Journal of Financial Economics* 60, no. 3 (2017): 535–562; Yael V. Hochberg Alexander Ljungqvist, and Annette Vissing-Jørgensen, "Informational Holdup and Performance Persistence in Venture Capital," *Review of Financial Studies* 27, no. 1 (2014): 102–152; Paul Gompers, Anna Kovner, Josh Lerner, and David Scharfstein, "Performance Persistence in Entrepreneurship," *Journal of Financial Economics* 96, no. 1 (2010): 18–32.

6. Ramana Nanda, Sampsa Samila, and Olav Sorenson, "The Persistent Effect of Initial Success: Evidence from Venture Capital," NBER Working Paper No. 24887, National Bureau of Economic Research, August 2018.

7. Peter Henig, "The Old Guard," *Venture Capital Journal*, October 2002, 29.

8. John W. Wilson, *The New Venturers: Inside the High-Stakes World of Venture Capital* (Reading, MA: Addison-Wesley, 1985), 98.

9. Henig, "The Old Guard," 26.

10. Henig, "The Old Guard," 28.

11. Shikhar Ghosh and Ramana Nanda, "Venture Capital Investment in the Clean Energy Sector," Working Paper 11-020, Harvard Business School, August 1, 2010, https://www.hbs.edu/faculty/Publication%20Files/11-020_0a1b5d16-c966-4403-888f-96d03bbab461.pdf.

12. Alfred D. Chandler, *Strategy and Structure: Chapters in the History of the Industrial Enterprise* (Garden City, NY: Doubleday, 1962).

13. Michael Ewens and Matthew Rhodes-Kropf, "Is a VC Partnership Greater Than the Sum of Its Partners?" *Journal of Finance* 70, no. 3 (2015): 1081–1113.

14. Robert S. Harris, Tim Jenkinson, and Steven N. Kaplan, "Private Equity Performance: What Do We Know?" *Journal of Finance* 69, no. 5 (2014): 1851–1882, 1872.

15. Lance E. Davis, Robert E. Gallman, and Karin Gleiter, *In Pursuit of Leviathan: Technology, Institutions, Productivity, and Profits in American Whaling, 1816–1906* (Chicago: University of Chicago Press, 1997), 298.

16. "VC Mavericks," *San Francisco Chronicle*, February 4, 2001.

17. W. H. Janeway, *Doing Capitalism in the Innovation Economy: Markets, Speculation and the State* (Cambridge: Cambridge University Press, 2012), 96.

18. David T. Robinson and Berk A. Sensoy, "Do Private Equity Fund Managers Earn Their Fees? Compensation, Ownership, and Cash Flow Performance," *Review of Financial Studies* 26, no. 11 (2013): 2760–2797.

19. L. Gallagher, *The Airbnb Story: How Three Ordinary Guys Disrupted an Industry, Made Billions . . . and Created Plenty of Controversy* (Boston: Houghton Mifflin Harcourt, 2017), 25.

20. Yael V. Hochberg, "Accelerating Entrepreneurs and Ecosystems: The Seed Accelerator Model," *Innovation Policy and the Economy* 16 (2016): 25–51, 26.

21. "Venture Capital," *Dun's Review*, February 1977.

22. Jessica Livingston, *Founders at Work: Stories of Startups' Early Days* (Berkeley, CA: Apress, 2008), 451.

23. Josh Lerner, *Boulevard of Broken Dreams: Why Public Efforts to Boost Entrepreneurship and Venture Capital Have Failed—And What to Do about It* (Princeton, NJ: Princeton University Press, 2009).

24. David Autor, David Dorn, Lawrence F. Katz, Christina Patterson, and John Van Reenen, "The Fall of the Labor Share and the Rise of Superstar Firms," NBER Working Paper, no. 23396 (2017).

25. Jan De Loecker and Jan Eeckhout, "The Rise of Market Power and the Macroeconomic Implications," NBER Working Paper No. 23687, National Bureau of Economic Research, August 2017.

26. Chang-Tai Hsieh and Peter J. Klenow, "The Reallocation Myth," unpublished manuscript, March 31, 2018, https://www.kansascityfed.org/~/media/files/publicat/sympos/2017/hsieh -klenow-paper.pdf.

27. Ryan A. Decker, John Haltiwanger, Ron S. Jarmin, and Javier Miranda, "Declining Business Dynamism: What We Know and the Way Forward," *American Economic Review* 106, no. 5 (2016): 203–207.

28. James M. Poterba, "Venture Capital and Capital Gains Taxation," in ed. Lawrence H. Summers, *Tax Policy and the Economy* (Cambridge, MA: MIT Press, 2007), Vol. 3, 47–67, 61–62.

29. Ufuk Akcigit, Salomé Baslandze, and Stefanie Stantcheva, "Taxation and the International Mobility of Inventors," *American Economic Review* 106, no. 10 (2016): 2930–2981; Sari Pekkala Kerr, William Kerr, Özden Çağlar, and Christopher Parsons, "Global Talent Flows," *Journal of Economic Perspectives* 30, no. 4 (2016): 83–106.

30. William R. Kerr, "U.S. High-Skilled Immigration, Innovation, and Entrepreneurship: Empirical Approaches and Evidence," NBER Working Paper No. 19377, National Bureau of Economic Research, August 2013.

31. Stuart Anderson, "American Made 2.0: How Immigrant Entrepreneurs Continue to Contribute to the U.S. Economy," National Venture Capital Association, June 20, 2013, https:// nvca.org/wp-content/uploads/delightful-downloads/American-Made-2.0.pdf.

32. Sari Pekkala Kerr and William R. Kerr, "Immigrants Play a Disproportionate Role in American Entrepreneurship," *Harvard Business Review,* October 3, 2016.

33. Robert Premus, "Venture Capital and Innovation: A Study," prepared for Joint Economic Committee, US Congress, 98th Session, December 28, 1984 (Washington DC: US GPO, 1985), https://www.jec.senate.gov/reports/98th%20Congress/Venture%20Capital%20 and%20Innovation%20(1316).pdf.

34. Lerner, *Boulevard of Broken Dreams,* 10.

35. Sabrina T. Howell, "Financing Innovation: Evidence from R&D Grants," *American Economic Review* 107, no. 4 (2017): 1136–1164.

36. David Blum, "Exploring Gender Disparity in U.S. Based Venture Capital Firms," *Journal of Diversity Management* 10, no. 1 (2015): 33–42.

37. Paul A. Gompers and Sophie Q. Wang, "Diversity in Innovation," NBER Working Paper No. 23082, National Bureau of Economic Research, January 2017.

38. Leslie Berlin, *The Man behind the Microchip: Robert Noyce and the Invention of Silicon Valley* (Oxford: Oxford University Press, 2006), 200–202.

39. Chang-Tai Hsieh, Erik Hurst, Charles I. Jones, and Peter J. Klenow, "The Allocation of Talent and U.S. Economic Growth," unpublished manuscript, April 6, 2018, http://klenow.com /HHJK.pdf; Gompers and Wang, "Diversity in Innovation."

Acknowledgments

The research for this book was generously financed and supported by the Division of Research and Faculty Development at Harvard Business School.

I am very grateful to Laura Linard, senior director of Baker Library Special Collections at Harvard Business School, and her team for providing access to archives. I also thank the many venture capitalists and entrepreneurs who gave me archival material or engaged in conversation about their industry. Carole Kolker was excellent at interviewing key figures. Arthur Rock was extremely helpful. He always responded kindly to my queries about his career in VC. Stuart Janney, chairman of the board at Bessemer Trust Company, generously granted me access to the archives at Bessemer Trust. Chuck Newhall supplied an amazing array of documentary evidence from his own archive.

I owe an enormous debt of gratitude to Jonas Akins, David Chen, Matthew Guilford, Liz Kind, David Lane, and James Lee for helping to shape how I wrote this book. They did judicious research on everything from whaling to Silicon Valley and I coauthored a number of Harvard Business School cases with them. I thank the remarkable students who took my courses at Harvard Business School and made probing comments about the VC industry and America's economic development more generally. I also acknowledge my colleagues Tom Eisenmann, Walter Friedman, Paul Gompers, Shane Greenstein, Bill Kerr, Joe Lassiter, Mathew Rhodes-Kropf, Mike Roberts, and Bill Sahlman for thoughtful discussions over the years, helpful comments, and access to sources on entrepreneurship and the VC industry.

I owe special thanks to Mihir Desai, Geoff Jones, Josh Lerner, Ramana Nanda, and Toby Stuart. They gave me numerous ideas and offered critical guidance and encouragement. I am also indebted to Felda Hardymon, with whom I taught an elective course on the history of the venture capital industry at Harvard Business School in 2013 and 2014—it was there that the blueprint for this book emerged. Felda, as a long-time partner at Bessemer Venture Partners, taught me a lot about how the VC industry used to function, as well as its present-day opportunities and challenges. His countless insights were key to this book's development.

I thank Thomas LeBien, executive editor-at-large at Harvard University Press, for his guidance and Julia Kirby, senior editor at Harvard University Press, for improving my writing and for valuable additions to the book's arguments. The two anonymous readers solicited by Harvard University Press made excellent suggestions at an early stage on how to improve the content and structure of the book. I am truly grateful for their effort and contributions. Any errors or infelicities are my own responsibility.

Index

DATE DUE

DEC 30			
MAR 1 3 2020			
			PRINTED IN U.S.A.